The Rise & Fall of Nigeria's Second Republic: 1979-84

Toyin Falola
and
Julius Ihonvbere

The Rise & Fall of Nigeria's Second Republic: 1979-84

Toyin Falola
and
Julius Ihonvbere

Zed Books Ltd.

The Rise & Fall of Nigeria's Second Republic was first published
by Zed Books Ltd., 57 Caledonian Road, London N1 9BU in
1985.

Copyright © Toyin Falola and Julius Ihonvbere

Cover design by Magenta Designs

Printed by The Pitman Press, Bath

British Library Cataloguing in Publication Data

Falola, Toyin
   The rise and fall of Nigeria's second
   republic, 1979-1984.
   1. Nigeria — Politics and government
   — 1979-
   I. Title II. Ihonvbere, Julius
   966.9'05   DT515.8

   ISBN 0 86232 379 7
   ISBN 0 86232 380 0 Pbk

US Distributor:
Biblio Distribution Center, 81 Adams Drive,
Totowa, New Jersey 07512, USA

Contents

Tables

Acknowledgements

We have accumulated many debts in our attempt to understand contemporary Nigeria's political economy. In Nigeria, Claude Ake, Okwudiba Nnoli, Bade Onimode, Ralph Onwuka, Segun Osoba, Bala Usman and a few others have provided us with inspiration and challenges. Several Nigerian liberal scholars, in their views and criticisms of our works, have indirectly enabled us to clarify our viewpoints, strengthen our position, and re-examine our concepts, methodologies and arguments. We have also benefited from contacts with scholars in other countries.

For the greater part of 1983 we carried out extensive fieldwork in Nigeria. It is not possible to mention all our informants by name; but those in the Nigeria Labour Congress Lagos, Warri and Port Harcourt oil industries, the Kaduna refinery, the Ajaokuta Steel Company and the Cabinet Office in Lagos deserve our gratitude. Messrs Akinlaja and Okougbo of the National Union of Petroleum and Natural Gas Workers (NUPENG) Headquarters, and Isaac Aberare of NUPENG Warri Zone have also helped us immensely with information and materials.

We have also benefited from the libraries of the Universities of Ife, Lagos, Benin, Nsukka, Ibadan and Ahmadu Bello, and those of the Institute of International Affairs and the National Library, both in Lagos. We really appreciate the assistance of the members of staff in these places for their co-operation and understanding. We hope that many of them would have forgotten our impatience, incessant demands for materials and other lapses.

To our wives and children who showed forbearance, to the eight typists who typed the manuscript, and to those who showed us hospitality in all the numerous Nigerian towns and villages we visited, we say thank you.

Our gratitude goes to Miss Joke Ladipo, a part I law student at the University of Ife, who generously loaned us the money to produce the manuscript. Finally, we hope our views and conclusions would not disappoint the Nigerian masses who have provided the inspiration for this study.

Preface

Nigeria's second experiment with bourgeois democracy, this time an American presidential system, came to a predictable and inevitable end on 31 December 1983. The fourth successful coup in Nigeria's history was welcomed by the public and, though it was executed by the right wing in the army, it was a relief from a terrible, backward, useless and bankrupt government. Our motivation for writing on this defunct republic arose from four major reasons. First, before orthodox apologists for Western bourgeois democracy and subservience to international capitalism flood the market with descriptive and shallow materials lamenting the death of democracy and proferring peripheral reasons for the demise of the Second Republic, we felt it necessary to produce an analytical work. Our second reason was the need to go beyond existing theories of political and economic development, most of which focus on the superstructure at the expense of dynamics and contradictions within the substructure. Extant explanations of the causes of underdevelopment, corruption, political intolerance and instability, coups d'etat and mass poverty outside the Marxist genre have been escapist, diversionary and pro-status quo. Our work seeks to place the emphasis on the historical experience and specificity of the Nigerian formation, the nature of the state and social classes, the accumulative base of the dominant classes, inter- and intra-class contradictions and struggles, and Nigeria's historically determined location and role in the world capitalist system.

A third reason is to document in a correct (dialetical) manner, the dynamics and conditions of Nigeria's Second Republic.

We attempt to expose the bourgeois nature of the 1979 constitution, the poverty and shallowness of Nigerian social science as it is presently constituted, the nature of the six political parties, particularly the ruling NPN, and how they contributed to the crisis and eventual demise of the Second Republic. Finally, particularly in our last chapter, we attempt to raise some theoretical issues crucial to a clear and serious understanding of the fundamental roots of instability and coups in peripheral economies like Nigeria. In fact, there appears to be a basis for contending that civilian rule in Nigeria has only been an interregnum. The colonial period was an undemocratic military era, since the colonial state, with the active support of the metropolitan state, relied on violence in order to reproduce itself. The first attempt at so-called democratic rule after political independence, in October 1960 lasted for less than six years as it was overthrown in a military coup d'etat in January 1966. Thirteen years of military dictatorship followed. The second attempt, in spite of so-called constitutional changes, did not last as long as the first experiment; it was overthrown after four years. No one can predict for sure how long the current Buhari regime intends (or would be forced) to remain in power. It has made it clear that reviving the economy is its priority and that a return to 'democratic rule' is not yet on its agenda. One fact is, however, certain: in so far as the Buhari regime has not addressed the structural contradictions in society which have in fact been the roots of instability and the reproduction of underdevelopment, more military coups can be expected.

Our work is located within the emerging Marxist political economy *genre*. While this Marxist approach and methodology is still in its stage of achieving clarity and effectively addressing issues of relevance and practice, it focuses on class, state, class struggles, contradictions, self-reliance and the strategies and tactics for the eventual overthrow of capitalism.

There have not been many efforts at analysing the class structure of Nigeria. While we recognize that such efforts must necessarily be tentative at all times given the fact that the process of class formation, expansion, alliance, re-alliance and consolidation is still an ongoing one, theoretical and empirical moves must be made in this direction. In our work, we assume the following. First, that Nigeria is a class society and that there is an intense class struggle going on—a precipitate of the pattern of production and accumulation which concentrates wealth in the hands of a few and subjects the majority of workers and peasants to unbridled exploitation, dehumanization and degradation. Second, that though social classes exist in Nigeria, they do not approximate the classical Marxian bourgeoisie/proletariat division. Rather, there are fractions, factions, sub-fractions and sub-factions of these social classes. In addition, the linkages between these classes are important to a clear understanding of the content and context of class contradiction and struggles in contemporary Nigeria. For instance, an urban worker has numerous rural — peasant or semi-proletarianized — familial dependants. Third, we believe that, though the non-bourgeois classes are locked in an intense class struggle with dominant forces for power and survival, to succeed in liquidating underdevelopment, capitalism and imperialism, and establishing a proletarian state with popular institutions, workers and peasants must forge and strengthen alliances, develop concrete political programmes and struggle along class lines. Fourth, though non-bourgeois forces have traditionally employed overt forms of protest against the capitalist system — strikes, work-to-rule actions, riots, demonstrations, sabotage, etc., it is essential to understand and study *covert* forms of protest against the capitalist system. A lack of understanding of these leads to an inability to propose viable strategies and tactics of struggle (from the left) or understand the intensity and direction of class struggles (from the right).

Thus, in analysing the class structure of Nigeria, we suggest two approaches. The first is to establish the obvious fact that the international bourgeoisie represented by the transnational corporations, banking and foreign commercial institutions, foreign 'experts', etc., is the dominant class. Its specific interests are profits and control (hegemony) in the interests of the metropole. This makes its activities antithetical to the needs of the Nigerian masses — food, shelter, employment, social security and so on. This dominant international bourgeoisie determines the actual process of economic reproduction, through its control over the vital resource-producing sector and the import–export business. Below this international bourgeois class is the governing class of petty bourgeois elements working in the service of foreign capital and presiding over the *distribution* of the rents collected from oil exports and goods imported from the metropole. Below this, to put it broadly, are the working class, lumpen elements and the peasantry. Each of these classes has its factions, fractions, sub-factions and sub-fractions.

At a second level of analysis, we can begin by examining the dynamic of the *specific* mode of production and how the disarticulation within it conditions the process of class formation and struggle. When we take this approach, we shall discover that the governing class, the petty-bourgeoisie, is really the dominant class in Nigeria. This does not mean a departure from the fact that we are still discussing the same system — capitalism. This bourgeoisie — with its national, comprador, technocratic and bureaucratic fractions — determines the pattern of its relations to external forces, internal production, exchange and accumulation. It presides over the allocation of national resources and determines how state power is constituted, expanded and employed. It determines the strategies and tactics for domesticating and exploiting non-bourgeois forces. Finally, this class determines, autonomously, or in collaboration with the international bourgeoisie, how it manipulates 'civil society' — education, church, culture, world-view, propaganda, the mass-media, etc., to contribute to the reproduction of the system and thus consolidate or re-structure the social formation's location and role in the international division of labour. This mode of analysis reduces the power and impact of transnational forces to a secondary level by realizing that changes within the substructure can determine and condition the nature and role of transnational forces within the substructure. In fact, the factors and forces which affect the nature and power of the bourgeoisie are precipitates of the contradictions within the mode of production. Thus, transnational forces only come in to complement the internal nature of social arrangement.

Whichever approach is adopted, the following classes can be identified as existent in Nigeria: (i) the international bourgeoisie; (ii) the national bourgeoisie which is still tiny and weak and, in fact, frequently reduced to the role of compradors in the service of the international bourgeoisie; (iii) the comprador/bureaucratic bourgeoisie — which has interests opposed to the national bourgeoisie and is frequently in support of the international bourgeoisie from whom it receives 'commissions' as agents, advisers, contractors, shareholders, etc.; (iv) the working class which sells its labour power to survive, i.e. is dependent on wages and salaries, including the lower rungs of the bureaucracy, there is of course the aristocratic fraction of the working class which may move downwards or upwards; (v) the lumpenproletariat-*declassé* element — vagabonds, thieves, lunatics and those on the fringe of 'rational' existence, the partially employed or visibly underemployed. These are in reality, part of the proletariat. They live, interact and sometimes depend on the proletariat, and finally, (vi) there is the peasantry. A highly differentiated class of kulaks, semi-proletarianized elements, poor farmers and so on. They have strong links with urban residents and workers and are under heavy attack from the capitalist state and international finance capital.

In addition to the above, we think that a proper understanding of the nature of Nigeria's capitalism and peripheral state is crucial if we are to understand the sources of perpetual or persistent instability and poverty.

This work, therefore, is addressed first and foremost to liberal scholars whom we hope will shift their attention from useless theories and models long discarded in Latin America, not to mention Europe. It is also addressed to all Nigerian patriots and other progressive forces in Africa and the Third World at large in the hope that the analysis of *epochs* in the historical development of specific societies would constantly reveal not just the demise of regimes, personalities, orthodox prescriptions and projections but also the intensity of class struggles.

Toyin Falola
Julius Ihonvbere
Ile-Ife

1. Social Science and Nigeria's Political Economy

The postcolonial crisis of Nigeria's political economy is not clearly reflected in the country's academic tradition until the late seventies. Before then, most 'radical' works were largely nationalist and pan-African in nature. Unlike the orthodox body of literature by indigenous and expatriate contributors which dominated the scene, the nationalist works were quite critical of the peripheral capitalist nature of the economy and society. Unfortunately, the focus was largely superstructural and unable to capture and explain clearly the dynamics of class contradiction and social reproduction within the Nigerian formation. By and large, nationalist critics were operating with the models and methodologies of orthodox analysts and were thus incapable of distancing themselves from the *descriptive*, myopic and, in several instances, diversionary methods, analyses and prescriptions of orthodox traditions.[1]

The hallmark of the orthodox approach is, to put it blankly, to flatter regimes, and to overlook internal socio-economic and political contradictions, the tenuousness of state hegemony and the consequences of unequal exchange arrangements between local dominant forces and transnational interests. In addition, orthodox works overlook imperialist penetration, domination and exploitation of the Nigerian economy, the process of taste transfer, the fragility and instability of the state, the neocolonial content of the educational system and general contradictions arising from peripheral capitalist relations of production and accumulation.

On the contrary, Nigeria, a peripheral capitalist, distorted and backward economy, with a very low GNP per capita, literacy and life expectancy rates, was seen in the 1960s as 'the giant of Africa', the 'hope of the black race' and in the 1970s, it came to be regarded as 'a black power' and even a 'superpower'. The orthodox approaches, utilizing outmoded and already discarded bourgeois models and methodologies imported intact from advanced capitalist formations, failed to note the specificities of the Nigerian social formation. The question of involving the masses of the people whose lives were being planned in the process of development was out of the question – they were seen as too ignorant and lazy. Growth and GNP per capita and capital accumulation by a few were emphasized at the expense of *development*, – the meeting of basic human needs and justice and equality in the appropriation of social and collectively produced wealth. Negotiations and compromises with transnational interests, dependence on foreign aid, loans, food imports and technology as well as high- and middle-level manpower were emphasized at the expense of self-reliance, rapid development, mobilization and integration of local human and material resources, a rapid process of re-orienting the socio-economic base of the economy, vigorous control over transnational corporations and the elimination of all contradictions and distortions inherited from past colonialism.

While one can understand the fact that the treacherous divide-and-rule policies of the British colonial government and the manipulation of the politics of decolonization facilitated a 'programmed transition to neo-colonial dependence' and that the incorporating activities of transnational forces in the latter period severely domesticated local 'power elite' and assured its loyalty to the status quo, the activities of local and expatriate orthodox analysts promoted and facilitated the process. The petty-bourgeois nationalists – teachers, lawyers, licensed agents to Marketing Boards, interpreters, journalists and so on – who had bought shares in the foreign firms were determined and committed to the preservation and rationalization of foreign participation and domination of the Nigerian economy. This was clearly reflected in the hostility of the dominant classes who also occupied the major economic, political and academic positions after independence, to the question of nationalizing the commanding heights of the economy (not the whole economy and not its socialization!) In fact, when a tiny radical-nationalist fraction suggested this in the sixties, Dr M. I. Okpara, the Premier of the NCNC controlled eastern region, called them 'communists' and warned against any attempt to disrupt existing working arrangements with foreign capital.[2] The subservient nature and mentality of the Nigerian bourgeoisie, its tenuous relation to *production* as against importation and distribution, and its corruption, consolidated the patron-client relation between it and foreign capital with the latter dominating relations and the economy.

Though the 'junior' position of local forces in this arrangement was lucrative – as political and legal advisers, sole agents and distributors, shareholders, etc., – it nonetheless exposed state policies, the political, economic and social stability and future of Nigeria to foreign penetration and manipulation. This has, to a very large extent, been responsible for the decadence, corruption, planlessness, waste, arrogance and idiosyncracies of the various governments in Nigeria since 1960. This subservience, which orthodox scholars were content to ignore or address at a very superficial level, is evidenced for instance, in the statement by Allison A. Ayida, former secretary to the Federal Government, at the 1969 Conference on National Reconstruction and Development that:

> As a matter of historical interest, both the World Bank in Washington and the United States Agency for International Development through an appraisal mission led by the late Arnold Rivkin, were given the facilities and the confidential information which enabled them to finalize their assessment of the New National plan (1970–74) *before*

the data were made available to the public in Nigeria.[3]

And as another critic of the planning process has noted on the relation between non-dominant and dominant forces as well as between the latter and transnational forces:

> Neither the planning process nor the resultant plan shows evidence of any serious attempt to make the economic targets and policies represent national goals in more than the vaguest sense. For all practical purposes, the Federal Plan was drawn up by a limited number of ex-patriate economists working virtually in a vacuum so far as detailed direction of consultation with political leaders went, and with only peripheral advisory contact with Nigerian civil servant planners. The social and political preferences of the plan, as was inevitable given this method of preparation, represent what the planners preferred or felt Nigerians ought to prefer rather than any expressed Nigerian preferences.[4]

It is important to stress the content and context of the planning process in Nigeria because since 1945 when the colonial state introduced the so-called Ten Year Plan for the Development and Welfare of Nigeria, the planning process and the allocation of resources have been avenues for re-directing the flow of capital, investment and labour and using public funds to rationalize and subsidize private capital accumulation. It has also been an avenue, at both Federal and State levels, to 'punish' recalcitrant communities which refuse to support certain political figures or policies, creating and nurturing a contractor class and diverting public funds into private bank accounts usually in foreign lands.

Development plans are supposed to take cognizance of available human and material resources, the level of socio-economic development and popular mobilization, the existing pattern of production and exchange and through deliberate (planned) policies and programmes allocate resources in such a manner as to eliminate inequities, promote living standards, move society away from dependence towards self-reliance and guarantee justice, equality, opportunities for all and the survival of society through popular mobilization and education. In Nigeria since 1945 quite the opposite has happened.[5] It is completely unacceptable for Ojetunji Aboyade, who was the chief architect of the Second National Development Plan (1970–74) and has been one of the intellectuals behind revenue allocation in Nigeria, to have argued that 'it is the task of planners to plan according to the established political economic structure'.[6] Thus, in a neocolonial society such as Nigeria, dependent on food, technology, manpower and capital goods imports, dominated by foreign companies, where inefficiency, corruption and institutional decay are high, planners, according to Aboyade, must plan according to existing structures, institutions and dynamics. One obviously does not need a degree in economics to know that such an act will only deepen social contradictions, inequalities and reproduce the country's underdevelopment. The overall consequence of a complete refusal to break with neocolonialism and private capital accumulation with public patronage and subsidy would be the consolidation of Nigeria's peripheral location and role in the international divison of labour. Taken together, Bade Onimode's critique captures very well the disservice of orthodox foreign 'experts', advisers and their heavily indoctrinated indigenous allies:

> . . . the collective impact of elitist conception of planning with bureaucrats and bourgeois economists alone and the grossly unequal distribution of the gains of development have been the inability of Nigeria to mobilise a mass base for planning. In spite of vitriolic and suffocating propaganda about planning from the grassroots, the truth is that the masses of Nigerian peasants, workers, market women, artisans, youths and patriotic professionals have not been participating actively in our national planning at any level.[7]

The situation above is the direct outcome of four major factors. 1) The continued peripheralization of the Nigerian formation in the world capitalist system, a historical peripheralization, initiated in the colonial period and perfected after political independence, which dominant bourgeois forces have preferred to nurture rather than re-structure and overthrow. 2) The reproduction of this peripheralization internally with the confinement of local dominant forces in the commercial, transport, real estate and bureaucratic sectors of the economy with foreign capital effectively dominating and controlling the commanding heights of the economy. Even in those sectors to which foreign capital has relegated the Nigerian bourgeoisie the latter is still dependent on the former for supplies and survival.[8] 3) The overriding influence of orthodox and mainstream as well as some radical-nationalist intellectuals who have been unable, in spite of the numerous contradictions in society, to conceptualize the reality of the underdeveloped Nigerian formation in critical and popular perspectives. State policies are thus subsumed under foreign and bourgeois interests which are directly opposed to self-reliance, mobilization and national vigilance. 4) The ineptitude, corruption, 'drone character' and myopic perspectives of the Nigerian power elite who, in spite of past experiences, continue to reproduce past mistakes of injustice, discrimination, planlessness and 'kleptocracy' (government by thieves). The net result of this has been increasing inter- and intra-class contradictions and struggles, political instability, lack of consistency in policy output and regime changes.

Orthodox perspectives on political instability and regime changes in Nigeria since 1960 have continued to emphasize the virtues and myths of democracy and advocate the replication of institutions, forms and processes that operate in advanced capitalist societies. While these perspectives are essentially diversionary and reflective of efforts to provide ideological mystifications and/or rationalizations for the perpetuation of the status quo, a more worrying trend has recently emerged in Nigerian politics. Fed up with the repeated failure of 'democratically' elected regimes to ensure stability and 'good' government, there have been some calls for permanent or 'consolidated' military rule.

It is, however, important to expose the ideological role of the emphasis on the superstructural aspects and determinants or features of democracy in a peripheral social formation such as Nigeria. It is impossible to discuss the nature of democracy in any society without locating such a discussion within the historical experiences and specificities of the formation, the nature of the state and class forces, inter- and intra-class struggles, the power and interests of factions and fractions of social classes, the nature and historical origins and role of the armed forces and the social formation's role in the world system. The point thus remains that analyses which continue to focus on peripheral manifestations of class-based policies and programmes such as political party programmes, electioneering campaigns, the number of political parties, voting exercises, free and fair elections and so on, miss the crucial point that these are fundamentally influenced and, in fact, determined by the pattern and context of production and exchange as well as the total system of class reproduction.

The historical experience of the Nigerian formation, in so far as the precipitates of the experience have been preserved or only slightly modified since 1960, means that the nature and practice of democracy would be reflective of the contradictions and crises of the country's peripheral capitalism. In fact, the definition of democracy in any capitalist formation, has historically emphasized the importance of the electorate only in the brief period when campaigns are on and an audience is needed or during the act of voting, only to legitimize the figures which the ruling elite has already allotted to itself. The point is that the narrow definition of democracy attempts to 'fetishize' the concept when it speaks of a government of the people for the people and by the people without explaining several crucial points: 1) Who are these people? 2) What is the relation between the 'people' and their government? 3) What level or amount of control do the people have over the government once it is elected? 4) Can we divorce economic relations and programmes from the superstructural manifestations of democracy? 5) If democracy is an aspect of total politics, what is the nature and goal of politics in the specific society in question? 6) To what extent has the historical experience of the social formation defined the context and content of politics and democracy?

In a system where democracy is given an exclusively *political* definition, the point remains that such a definition or practice is ideological. In other words, it is in the interest of any dominant capitalist class to gloss over the fact that failure to meet the basic needs of the toiling majority is in itself a negation of democracy. Failure to provide food, shelter, security, clothing, health services, good roads, efficient transport and bureaucracy and of course pay workers' wages and salaries as and when due are direct negations of democracy. In a distorted, crisis-ridden and backward peripheral capitalist

5

society like Nigeria where it has been the tradition of the dominant class to 'Nigerianize' the unequal and exploitative relations of production and exchange, the state can hardly meet the basic needs of people. The intense intra-bourgeois class struggle to win access to the state and thus preside over the allocation of public funds prompts the manipulation of the means of coercion, politicization of the bureaucracy and armed forces and the use of ethnic, state and religious chauvinism. The dependent nature and outlook of the dominant class, the pre-hegemonic nature of the state and the peripheralization of the formation in the world capitalist system are all direct causes of political instability and crises. The net result of this is an inability even to mediate class contradictions and blunt, at a primary level, the edges of class struggles in society. Such conditions promote military intervention, or the unregulated use of coercion in order to perpetuate the status quo. (See Conclusion.)

In peripheral formations, as in Nigeria, the military is part and parcel of class dynamics in society. The officer corps is only the military wing of the bourgeoisie. In spite of its historical role — in which it brutalized the local communities on behalf of the imperialist powers — the army has constantly intervened in politics to stabilize the system without making structural changes. It has not been free from the problems of corruption, mediocrity, waste, inefficiency, misplaced priorities and subservience to international capitalism. To this extent, even where military intervention marks the end of 'democracy' at any time in the Third World, in so far as the relations of production and exchange remain intact, nothing can be said to have changed. Admittedly, under a 'democratic' system, it is possible for opposition forces to organize and constitute themselves into a counter-hegemonic bloc, a process which direct military rule blocks. This is however not a guarantee given the existence of several non-military fascist governments all over the Third World.

The point must therefore be made that a distorted peripheral capitalist society, with an unstable state and unproductive, corrupt and inept dominant class cannot practise democracy. Any attempt to copy the 'forms', i.e. superstructural manifestations of 'democracy' in other constitutions, titles, language etc., — would not only lead to waste but deepen political instability. What is more, a capitalist system cannot be democratic in so far as it gives democracy a political interpretation but permits the operation of an inhuman, exploitative and vicious pattern of production and accumulation. Military intervention in the political processes of the Third World is only a manifestation of structural contradiction and the crisis of hegemony which promotes all-round instability. 'Democracy', which obviously develops and reflects the overall maturity of contradictions and the development of production and exchange forces, cannot be extricated from the overall pattern of political conflicts in society and analysed in isolation. A system which does not have clear-cut ideological goals and institutions for popular mobilization, education and vigilance, and cannot involve the majority in policy initiation and implementation, cannot hope to build *democracy* which would mobilize and involve the masses as well as ensure personal and collective liberties, freedoms, rights and obligations.

It is in the light of the discussion so far and noting the reactionary, deceptive and shallow content and context of Nigerian social science that it becomes difficult not to accept Okwudiba Nnoli's contention that:

> . . .Nigerian social science has rendered a disservice to the cause of Nigerian development. In its present form it is incapable of providing intellectual leadership and an adequate theory for the revolutionary tasks required by that process. Therefore the necessary revolutionary transformation of Nigerian society must include the radicalisation of Nigerian social science.[9]

Though this 'radicalization' is now being *forced* on Nigerian social science and social scientists, thus compelling orthodox analysts to distance themselves some what from the discarded 'modernization', 'growth-pole', 'trickle-down', etc., bourgeois theories of political and economic development, class, state, contradiction and struggle still play a minor role in their conceptualization, analysis, prescriptions and projections. They have been scared to admit that it is no longer possible to explain away poverty, dependence, political and social violence on the majority, corruption, waste and so on, on the basis of ethnicity, low level of institutionalization, the absence of democracy and the need for more external aid. This is because in the past, all problems were seen in terms of regions (later states) versus the centre, Yoruba versus Igbo or some other ethnic groups, minorities versus majorities, military rule versus civilian rule and so on. The amorphous nature of categories such as 'elite', 'businessmen', 'rich and poor', rural and urban and so on, did not deter their being employed in policy papers and prescriptions. This inevitably means not only the neglect of the accumulative base of social classes, patterns and strategies of class reproduction, but also the nature and use of state power, the overt and covert forms of resistance by non-bourgeois forces and the *factions* and *fractions* of social classes. For, as Eddie Madunagu, one of the few and yet embryonic emerging materialist analysts, has noted:

> On the level of social formations, it is not even enough to know that there are three main classes in Nigeria: the capitalists, the peasantry and the working class. It is also necessary to know that there are differentiations (often politically crucial) within each class, that the boundaries between the classes are extremely fluid, unstable and in some areas almost indeterminate, that there are several (some of them strategic) intermediate social groups and stratas . . . in Nigeria − just as in several other parts of the world − class oppression often merges with ethnic oppression and conversely.[10]

This succinct realization is yet to make an impact on policy makers, the

7

academic environment or on the Nigerian state. There is still a strong adherence or often a last recourse to ethnic explanations (or sometimes religious considerations) in the allocation of resources, appointments, granting of concessions or the use of sanctions. There is a stubborn refusal to note the materialist and political dimensions of ethnic rivalries and manipulations and because this aids the intra-class struggles for the very limited contracts and political positions available, the bourgeoisie and its intellectual partners have been content to sell ethnicity to the public as the major problem. In spite of the increasing crystallization of class forces, the numerous covert and overt strategies and tactics for challenging the state and bourgeoisie and numerous indicators of class consciousness and action amongst the working classes, Henry Bienen, to take just one example, is able to point out recently that:

> It has been argued that political competition in Nigeria would shift from its former ethnic or communal base to a more class-oriented competition once the Nigerian Federal Republic was changed from regions into a system of 12 and then 19 states . . .
> . . . However, after a civilian regime returned to power in late 1979 revenue allocation between the Federal government and the states continued to be a major issue. A clear shift to class and sectoral terms of reference is neither taking place nor likely to take place in the future in Nigeria in any simple or straightforward fashion.
> . . . In objective terms Nigeria is forming a class structure, but most Nigerians do not perceive this.[11]

This ridiculous, wrong and escapist analysis by Bienen is shared by the majority of Nigerian intellectuals and policy makers. This shared position and perspective is largely informed by an inability (or a refusal) to study the historical development and nature of social classes and to locate class dynamics with the objective contradictions within the substructure and the country's peripheral location and role in the world capitalist system.

Bienen's statement above is obviously confused. On the one hand, 'revenue allocation' has continued to be the major issue, against a background of an unshifting 'ethnicity', and on the other hand, 'Nigeria is forming a class structure'. Two immediate points of criticism. First, Bienen, like most expatriate and indigenous mainstream analysts who are heavily committed to the survival of the orthodox approach, fail to see the class dimension of contradiction and competition between the bourgeoisies in the centre and in the states. The dominant forces who have temporarily and permanently located their interests at the centre strive, through their control over revenues, particularly from oil since the 1970s, to dominate the states and keep them in line. The state bourgeoisies on the other hand, where the resources are extracted, strive to retain or 'win back' a large part of the revenues under federal control. The interests of both the centre and the states are thus diametrically opposed. At the same time, among the states, there is a contradiction between the oil and non-oil states with the former emphasizing derivation and the negative consequences of oil production and the latter emphasizing need and equity and not derivation. The competition between and within the states, is thus an aspect of intra-class struggles in Nigeria with direct implications for inter-class struggle to the extent that revenues received by the centre and states are expended in the expanded domestication of non-bourgeois forces and the reproduction of the social system.

A second point of criticism is the extent to which Bienen can claim that though 'Nigeria is forming a class structure, — most Nigerians do not perceive this'. The basis of this claim cannot be substantiated. The fact that explanations, labels and actions do not approximate Western phraseology or terms does not mean that the oppressed and exploited in Nigeria cannot (and have not) differentiated between the capitalist and the worker. Phrases and songs abound in Nigeria which capture this class differentiation, e.g. 'poorman dey suffer, baboon dey chop': the poorman, known to the majority, is the worker, the 'baboon', who appropriates all the product of the worker, is the capitalist.

Finally, because the depth and extent of state power, the constant use of the police and army against workers, the numerous familial and work-place pressures on the worker and the numerous punitive labour laws of the state are neglected, the extent to which these largely compel workers to initiate covert means of protest and opposition are equally neglected by orthodox analysts. The extent to which increasing organization, consciousness and militancy amongst the working classes compel bourgeois forces at the state and federal levels to make concessions and initiate some popular measures are completely neglected by orthodox analysts. The concessions are praised but not the forces which necessitate their being made.

Thus, the crisis of the Nigerian state and economy continues to deepen. While the emergence of the tiny Marxist (socialist) School of Thought both indigenous and expatriate, has been a welcome development, the problems of clarity, specificity (peculiarities) and praxis (practice) continue to (and should for some time to come) dominate debates. The need to transcend *description* and peripheral prescriptions and projections becomes more crucial given intensifying class struggles and deepening crisis within the economy. This need refers to

> . . . a theoretical framework that focuses on conflict, that assumes there are systematic connections among production, power, stratification, and ideas, that asserts that outcomes are neither largely structurally determined nor largely the result of individual behaviour, that regards history as dialectical and contradictory, and that presumes that both the dialectic and the contradictions can be understood.[12]

Obviously, this would offer a more powerful vehicle for studying Nigerian society and economy and would transcend the cosmetic compartmentalization of disciplines into economics, political science and whatever.

The approach highlighted above will enable the identification and analysis of contradictions (often seen as 'problems' in orthodox literature) in the society. Correct identification of the source and nature of contradictions would contribute to correct analysis, policy prescriptions and projections. Thus it is possible to identify contradictions within social classes — the bourgeoisie — its commercial, bureaucratic, national and comprador fractions; the working class — its semi-proletarianized, proletarianized and aristocratic fractions; the peasantry — the kulaks or rich peasants and the real peasantry. It is also possible to identify contradictions within institutions and seats of power — oil and non-oil states, senior and junior army officers, top bureaucrats and junior civil servants and political leaders and their followers. The structural factors which have continued to contribute to the reproduction of Nigeria's underdevelopment, the obstacles to the emergence of a *productive* bourgeoisie, the inability of the state to impose a viable hegemonic force or effectively domesticate non-bourgeois forces, the attempts by the state and bourgeoisie to become paramount in civil society through the use of a national anthem, pledge, National Youth Service Corps, national honours, the infiltration of trade unions, and the manipulation of ethnic, religious and other sentiments, would be highlighted.

However, the crucial point is not in the highlighting of these contradictions but in the exposure of the sources. Contradictions, poverty, injustice, skewed development, corruption and so on are precipitates of more fundamental structural problems. These structural problems can only be identified if analysis is focused on (1) the historical experiences of the social formation, (2) the origins and nature of the state, (3) the accumulative base of the dominant forces and their relations with transnational interests, and (4) the content and intensity of class contradictions and struggles. It is these factors that determine not only the historical role of the formation in the international division of labour but issues such as revenue allocation, the need to employ ethnic and other sentiments in the struggle to expand and reproduce class interests, policy output and political stability. As Claude Ake has rightly noted:

> Our problems are rooted in our history and in the concrete economic and social structures which it has evolved. By the very nature of the problems they cannot be solved without, at the very least, breaking our exploitative dependence on the West, and doing away with the existing relations of production. . . the contradictions of the present system are creating the conditions that will change it.[13]

Eddie Madunagu has also noted the corrupt, inept, individualistic and ostentatious nature of the Nigerian bourgeoisie. Such a bourgeois class has never moved any society towards historical progress; and its failure to achieve any level of control over the Nigerian economy since 1960 is reflected in the continued domination of the economy by foreign capital, the country's technological backwardness and dependence on foreign countries:

The Nigerian bourgeoisie are . . . extremely irrational and under-developed. Their counterparts in Europe, North America and Japan have long realised that to ensure an exclusively comfortable life for themselves, they have to make some concessions to the masses. Thus a developed bourgeoisie would build good roads to their exclusive hotels, ensure good and efficient water and electricity supplies in the major industrial, commercial and administrative centres – facilities which the masses by default, will also enjoy. But what do we see in Nigeria? Colour television sets but an unreliable and inefficient electricity supply, luxurious cars but bad roads, ultra-modern airports but extremely backward and inefficient postal and telecommunications systems, ultra-modern residential areas which are surrounded by, and approached only through, filthy slums.[14]

It would be ridiculous, therefore, to expect such a seriously dominated and corrupt bourgeoisie to provide a distorted and disarticulated society with the correct political and moral leadership even if only to promote private capital accumulation, an accumulative process with a domestic dynamic which can lay a viable base for self-sustained growth and development. On the contrary, the efforts of the Nigerian bourgeoisie have been concentrated on winning access to political power and national resources, looting them and storing same in *foreign* bank accounts. The pressures and contradictions arising from this pattern of primitive accumulation have promoted instability and underdevelopment. Peter Evans, in a comparative study of Brazil and Nigeria, has debunked all the flattery showered on the crisis-ridden Nigerian economy by orthodox economists and analysts in relation to its rapid rate of industrialization and so on:

To call Nigeria the 'Brazil of Africa' underlines the difference between the two continents as much as it does the similarities between the two countries. In an African context the structure of the Nigerian economy may appear relatively advanced; in a Latin American context it would appear anachronistic . . . From the role of the state to the position of the multinationals, the structure of the Nigerian elite is in many ways more suggestive of the period of classic dependence than of the current period of dependent development in Brazil and Mexico.[15]

The peripheral state which was expected to control foreign capital and support the emergence of a dynamic and productive bourgeois class is neither hegemonic nor stable. Its control over national resources and the dependence of the bourgeoisie on state patronage and support for accumulation makes it the focus of class struggles and capital accumulation. This struggle, often intensified by the direct or indirect involvement of transnational corporations, contributes to the state's instability and constant regime changes. The most far-reaching efforts by the state were the indigenization decrees of the 1970s, which were practically abrogated by the civilian regime which came to power in 1979 and was overthrown in 1983:

> . . . the state itself has fathered a new capitalist class. In the indigeni-
> zation process . . . the state ordered banks to extend credit to Nigerians
> to purchase . . . shares. By mid-1979, the fortunate few — the importers,
> contractors, lawyers, businessmen and academics — who had obtained
> bank loans had acquired over 500 million shares in 1,858 companies
> valued (actually undervalued) at \$736 million. Dividends were high; the
> risk was negligible, the state served as the creator of large-scale domestic
> capital and as the intermediary between domestic and foreign private
> capital.[16]

Given the unstable nature of the Nigerian state, an instability made worse
by its near-total dependence on a foreign-dominated oil sector and on an oil
market over which it has no control, it meant that the fluctuations in the
fortunes of the state directly affected social classes dependent on it. In
addition, since these classes lacked a dynamic of survival on their own, the
financial fortunes of the state which was dependent on Western markets for
oil sales and transnational oil corporations, were inextricably linked to those
of the bourgeoisie. Even though the efforts at indigenization had initially
expanded the ranks of the petty-bourgeoisie and strengthened its economic
base, the definition of spheres of interest by the decrees did not challenge
foreign domination of the 'commanding heights' of the economy. On the
contrary, it rationalized and legitimized the presence, participation and
domination of foreign capital in the economy. And since the profit and hegemonic interests of transnationals override all other concerns, the Nigerian
state had achieved very little either in consolidating its hegemony, fathering
a dynamic and productive bourgeoisie or ensuring its own stability and
continuity:

> The sphere of foreign capital accumulation has not been greatly
> affected by the growth of the Nigerian bourgeoisie, by indigenization,
> or by the extension of the state sector — state intervention has greatly
> favoured large scale foreign enterprise, the indigenization exercise
> notwithstanding.[17]

The rentier nature of the Nigerian state since the 1973-74 OPEC oil price
increases which transformed the techno-economic autonomy of the oil sector
into the socio-economic autonomy of the state, deepened contradictions to
levels which bridged perceptions and analysis between orthodox and radical
works at the level of criticism. Though a few elements continued to see the
state as judiciously using oil wealth — over ₦52 billion in 25 years of oil
production — in the liquidation of underdevelopment, the general consensus
was that the state and bourgeoisie had mismanaged the oil wealth and
increased Nigeria's dependence on: (1) foreign oil companies, which in spite
of the creation of the NNPC in 1977 have continued to dominate down-

and upstream operations in terms of technology, capital supplies, high-level manpower, and information; (2) the western capitalist market, which consumes over 80% of monthly oil exports, thus linking Nigeria's future to developments in the contradiction-ridden capitalist economies; (3) international finance agencies, to the extent that increasing mismanagement of national finances has necessitated large-scale borrowing from the IMF, Saudi Arabia, the Euro-market, the World Bank and the USA. This debt problem has moderated Nigeria's 'international behaviour'; (4) food imports, which topped ₦2 billion in 1983, thus mortgaging the political stability of the urban and rural areas since there was a corresponding neglect of agriculture; (5) capital goods imports of over ₦1.2 billion monthly, which operated against the development of local initiative and continued to promote not only technological backwardness but also the dependence syndrome; and (6) the pursuit of a 'defensive radical' foreign policy which was to say the least extravagant and reckless. Nigeria's 'leadership role in Africa', was confined to rhetoric, empty boasts, speeches, declarations and financial contributions to all countries in the underdeveloped world, liberation movements and liberated territories.[18]

These contradictions and developments did not arise because the country was poor. If there was a country in Black Africa with enough human and material resources to promote viable and self-reliant development, it was probably Nigeria. But two decades of political independence have witnessed decay, planlessness, waste, the triumph of mediocrity, clannishness and the reproduction of poverty. This is because, in spite of a population of over 80 million, a fertile territory, huge oil reserves and revenues (until the present glut in the world market), the *structural* nature of the unstable state, the bourgeoisie and imperialist forces have drained resources, promoted wrong policies and facilitated the country's re-incorporation into world capitalism. The limited relative financial autonomy which the state enjoyed with the advent of the oil boom, to the extent that it was considered unqualified for US development assistance from 1974 (until 1981), was only to promote the influx of foreigners, and transnational corporations. At the local level it consolidated the belief among planners that Nigeria could 'import all importables', and in spite of beautiful speeches and declarations, the consequences of over-dependence on the oil sector were ignored:

> As the oil boom gathered momentum, the cities of Nigeria took on the character of gold rush towns. Foreigners flocked to cash in on the bonanza, Greek merchants and Arab doctors, Filipino nurses and Indian school teachers, Italian construction workers and German lorry salesmen, American bankers and British lecturers jostled one another on the streets all attempting to sell services of good, bad or indifferent quality. Firms reckoned to retrieve their initial investment in two to three years.[19]

The activities of these 'foreigners' received the open support and assistance of Nigerian comprador and bureaucratic elements. Thus, gradually, the government, in spite of increasing budgets — ₦82 billion in the Fourth National Plan 1981–1985 — neglected the rural areas and rural producers, food and cash crop production; the country became dependent on imports, and importation and distribution came to replace production. Four national development plans, huge oil rents and expanded state power hardly made any impact on the living standards of the majority of Nigerians; a fact which orthodox analysts found difficult to accept. However, even the International Labour Office (ILO), in its 1981 report on Nigeria, noted the problems of insecurity, agricultural stagnation, institutional inefficiency and decay and concluded that:

> There is little evidence that Nigeria's big expenditure has made much impact on the conditions of the majority of the population. The distortions experienced by the other oil exporters seem to have been repeated in Nigeria. The (past) plans ... attached far too much importance to economic growth *per se*. To meet the country's basic needs and achieve greater self-reliance would have required a very different, indeed the opposite of priorities.[20]

This succinct point, made by an organization which can hardly be described as left or radical, demonstrates the hypocrisy of orthodox views on Nigeria's political economy. As late as 1981 when the ILO's report was published, indigenous and expatriate economists and 'experts' were still claiming that the Nigerian economy was buoyant and that critics were being alarmist. In fact, Henry Bienen, in a 1981 book edited with Victor Diejomaoh who is now the Director-General of the country's Institute for Social and Economic Research, claimed that 'in general, Nigeria does not appear to have an unequivocally and rapidly worsening income distribution situation'.[21] Nothing could be farther from the truth. Inequalities, poverty, disease, unemployment, crime and hunger had by 1981 become common sights and experiences in Nigeria. In fact, the ILO, following its in-depth study, concluded that large numbers of Nigerians 'are worse off in numerous respects, especially in the rural areas but also in the big new slums of the cities'.[22]

It is obvious, therefore, that if Nigeria is to translate influence, which was dependent on its former oil wealth, into *power*, there is an urgent need to address structural problems which have promoted contradictions and instability. The Shagari administration could have performed an unbelievable feat if it had survived until 1987. It inherited a heavily mortgaged and disarticulated economy and an alienated society full of contradictions and conflicts. The opportunistic and comprador nature of the dominant forces within the political parties and the fact that the state, through its control over oil rents on which everything was dependent, became the focus of capital accumulation, prevented the initiation of far-reaching policies and programmes. As a precipitate of reliance on orthodox prescriptions, projections and flattery, the Second Republic overlooked developments within oil-consuming nations, neglected the majority of Nigerians and condoned corruption, the looting of public funds, waste and the fascist nature of the police force which attempted to terrorize the populace into docility. Its fall was therefore inevitable, for, right from the beginning, it lacked the zeal, courage and foresight of bourgeoisies that have historically made contributions to societal transformation.

There is no doubt that with the demise of a second so-called democratic experiment, the increasing militancy of workers, students, market women and peasants, increasing alliances among the non-bourgeois forces and challenges to the state, and the proletarianization of the upper-middle class, orthodox perspectives would be forced to move closer to examining contradictions (as against problems), conflict (as against compromises), and self-reliance (as against dependence and so-called interdependence). Radical perspectives, on the other hand, must continue to work harder on the problems of praxis, relevance and specificities which would enhance the liquidation of underdevelopment, a redefinition of the country's role in the international division of labour, and self-reliance.

Notes

1. Examples of orthodox works on Nigeria include, R.O. Ekundare, *An Economic History of Nigeria* (London: Methuen and Co. Ltd., 1973); W. Stopler, *Planning Without Facts* (Cambridge, Mass: Harvard University Press, 1966); H. Bienen and V.P. Diejomaoh (eds), *The Political Economy of Income Distribution in Nigeria* (New York: Africana, 1981); T.J. Biersteker, *Distortion or Development: Contending Perspectives on the Multinational Corporation* (Cambridge, Mass: MIT Press, 1978) and Anthony Kirk-Green and Douglas Rimmer, *Nigeria Since 1970: An Economic and Political Outline* (London: Hodder and Stoughton, 1981). Compare the approaches, models, prescriptions and projections with Eddie Madunagu, *Problems of Socialism: The Nigerian Challenge* (London: Zed Press, 1982); Okwudiba Nnoli (ed), *Path of Nigerian Development* (Dakar: Codesria, 1981); Gavin Williams (ed), *Nigeria: Economy and Society* (London: Rex Collins, 1976) and Bade Onimode, *Imperialism and Underdevelopment in Nigeria* (London: Zed Press, 1983).

2. For details and other examples which clearly demonstrate the subservient nature of the Nigerian bourgeoisie and its open acceptance of its junior role in the exchange and accumulation process see Segun Osoba, 'The Nigerian Power Elite, 1952–1965' in P.C.W. Gutkind and P. Waterman (eds), *African Social Studies: A Radical Reader* (New York: Monthly Review Press, 1977) and 'Ideology and Planning for National Economic Development, 1946–1972' in M. Tukur and T. Olagunju (eds), *Nigeria: In Search of a Viable Polity* (Zaria: ABU Press, 1972). In fact, the tendency to isolate and ridicule radical, particularly Marxist, analysts as well as trivialise their ideas and frustrate their persons is still very strong in virtually all departments in higher institutions of learning in Nigeria today.

3. Allison Ayida, cited in Nkenna Nzimiro, 'The Political and Social Implications of Multinational Corporations in Nigeria' in Carl Widstrand (ed), *Multinational Firms in Africa* (Uppsala: SIAS, 1975), p. 237 (emphasis added).

4. Ibid.

5. In cases where very noble objectives have been included in official documents, plan indiscipline and misplaced priorities ensured that such programmes were never implemented.

6. Ojetunji Aboyade in Ola Oni, 'A Critique of Development Planning in Nigeria', *Review of African Political Economy*, 4, November, 1975, p. 89. See also Bade Onimode, 'A Critique of Planning Concepts and Methodology in Nigeria', *Review of Black Political Economy*, 7, 3, Spring 1977.

7 Bade Onimode, ibid., p. 301.

8. The indigenization decrees of the early and late seventies have expanded indigenous participation through ownership but not control. However, after the civil war in 1970, the Central Bank revealed startling figures which showed the high level of foreign domination of the economy. For instance, of a total of 46 enterprises dealing in consumer non-durables, 32 were foreign and 14 Nigerian, of the 9 in consumer durables, 6 were foreign and 3 Nigerian, of the 12 in capital equipment 10 were foreign and 2 Nigerian, of the 14 in industrial supplies, 13 were foreign and 1 indigenous; the only one in goods for export was foreign and of the 41 in mixed·commodities, none was indigenous. See Central Bank of Nigeria, *Economic and Financial Review*, 8, 2, December, 1970, p. 20.

9. Okwudiba Nnoli, 'Development/Underdevelopment: Is Nigeria Developing', in his collection, *Path to Nigerian Development*, op. cit., p. 46.

10. Eddie Madunagu, *Problems of Socialism*, op. cit., p. 98.

11. Henry Bienen, 'The Political Economy of Income Distribution in Nigeria', in H. Bienen and V.P. Diejomaoh (eds), *The Political Economy of Income*, op. cit., pp. 4–5.

12. Joel Samoff, 'On Class, Paradigm and African Politics', *Africa Today*, 29, 2, second quarter, 1982, p. 49.

13. Claude Ake, 'Off to a Good Start but Dangers Await', *West Africa*, 3330, 25 May, 1981, p. 1163.

14. Eddie Madunagu, *Problems of Socialism*, p. 40.

15. Peter Evans, *Dependent Development: The Alliance of Multinationals, State and Local Capital in Brazil* (Princeton: Princeton University Press, 1979), p. 309.

16. Jon Kraus, 'Nigeria Under Shagari', *Current History*, 81, 473, March, 1982, p. 108.

17. Tom Forrest, 'Recent Developments in Nigerian Industrialisation', in Martin Fransman (ed), *Industry and Accumulation in Africa* (London: Heinemann, 1982), p. 337.

18. See Julius O. Ihonvbere and Timothy M. Shaw, 'The Political Economy of Nigeria's "Radical" Foreign Policy Under Military Rule, 1966–1979' (forthcoming), Stephen Wright, 'Limits of Nigeria's Power Overseas', *West Africa*, 3339, 27 July, 1981 and Hans-Otto Sano, *The Political Economy of Food in Nigeria, 1960-1982: A Discussion of Peasants, State and World Economy* (Uppsala: SIAS, Research Report No. 65, 1983).

19. Bill Freund, 'Oil Boom and Crisis in Contemporary Nigeria',

Review of African Political Economy, 13, May–August, 1978, p. 97.

20. International Labour Office (ILO), *First Things First: Meeting the Basic Needs of the People of Nigeria* (Addis Ababa: JASPA, 1981), pp. 5 and 10.

21. Henry Bienen, op. cit., p. 13.

22. ILO, op. cit., p. v.

2. The Military and the Programme of Transition to Civilian Rule, 1975-79

Nigerian politics is characterized by its instability, like other Third World countries with underdeveloped economic systems. At independence in 1960, optimists looked ahead to a 'great Nigeria', a great democracy (indeed the greatest in Africa) and a buoyant economy. These optimists simply reckoned with the country's resource potentials, both human and natural. One crucial, decisive and significant factor was ignored: the colonial inheritance. Sixty years of British rule had left the country with a fragile political system and a neocolonial economy.[1]

The First Republic (1960–65) quickly collapsed mainly because of this colonial inheritance and the aggressive rivalries among the foster elite which controlled power at the centre and the three, almost autonomous regions — North, East and West. The so-called federal system inherited in 1960 was such that the regions were more powerful than the centre. The bourgeoisie and political parties were all regionally based. The regions all had conflicting and competing development plans and distrusted one another generally. This distrust did not imply that there were no common interests and objectives shared by the regionally based bourgeoisies, but since the ability to compete autonomously for foreign aid and attract transnational corporations depended on their ability to manipulate politics and resource allocation within the various regions effectively, it became necessary to 'protect' such spheres of influence.

Until the first military coup in 1966, the politicians believed that there was no viable alternative to a civilian government and also to them. The traditional rulers were believed to be ignorant in the art of modern, democratic politics. The civil service, though enlightened, had inherited and accepted the philosophy of political neutrality of the British civil service. The army was also assumed to have a non-interventionist orientation beside the fact that it was weak and poor in numbers, equipment, strike force and training experience.

The assumptions about the traditional rulers and civil service are true. In addition, even if both had been enlightened and had an interventionist orientation, they lacked the forces of coercion, specifically in terms of control over the police and the army. The popular opinion that soldiers were non-achievers and had very low social ratings seems to have deceived the politicians into thinking that the army could not overthrow them. The army, though it had the problems highlighted above, nevertheless had one advantage which other groups in the society lacked: it possessed the force of coercion.

It was precisely this force which it put into use on 15 January 1966 when the First Republic was overthrown. This coup inaugurated a military regime which lasted for thirteen years.

Despite the fact that the first coup and the subsequent ones were reliefs from bad government, there seemed to be a feeling of unease about a permanent military regime. It seemed that the Nigerian public could tolerate a temporary and corrective military regime. The army, too, tended to believe that a permanent military rule was illegitimate. The army was not elected; it only seized power through the use of force. The use of force creates the impression of illegitimacy in a world which has come to believe in the so-called democratic process. This feeling of illegitimacy (and sometimes of unpopularity) plagues most military regimes. To secure peace and placate the citizen, a military regime pledges to hand over power to civilians and creates conditions necessary for the working of democracy. This pledge not only confers legitimacy on the regime and gives it a sense of direction but also enables peace to thrive.

But while all military regimes promise disengagement programmes, only a few actually succeed in transferring power to civilians. Among the factors for the failure to disengage are the love of power, greed, procrastination, the false belief that there could be no better alternative, and the difficulties encountered by disengaging officers. Finer and Dare[2] have grouped these reasons under eight broad headings, all of which share the well-known Machiavellian thesis that man finds it difficult to relinquish power: (a) the return of their opponents at some future time, thus jeopardizing their own personal security; (b) the reversal of the principle in the name of which they made the interventions; (c) further military intervention against themselves; (d) the fear that the privileges enjoyed by the military may not be maintained by the succeeding civilian group; (e) the fear that political chaos may follow the departure of the military; (f) an exaggerated self-image held by the armed forces as a result of which they reason that the disciplined forces are the best agencies for governing and other groups will not do as well; (g) political pressure from anti-disengagement forces and beneficiaries of military rule, who urge the military to stay in power; (h) mere lust for power and the attractiveness of the perquisites of political power.

All the Nigerian administrations believed that military rule must be temporary, being an aberration necessitated by political and social crises. Major Nzeogwu, who led the country's first coup, said the army had no intention to govern:

> Neither myself nor any of the other lads was in the least interested in governing the country. We are soldiers and not politicians . . .We are going to make civilians of proven honesty and efficiency who would be

thoroughly handpicked to do all the governing . . . We would stand behind them with our fingers on the trigger.[3]

General Aguiyi-Ironsi, the first military head of state, promised to govern for three years.[4] Ironsi was, however, overthrown on 29 July 1966. His successor, Lt Col (later General) Yakubu Gowon promised to rule for only six months[5] but the outbreak of the civil war in 1967 gave him the excuse to shelve his plan indefinitely. When the war came to an end in 1970, Gowon announced a nine-point disengagement programme in October of that same year, promising to hand over power in 1976. This pledge gave Gowon a great deal of legitimacy and credibility. The key functionaries in Gowon's administration repeated this pledge over and over again. For instance, Brigadier Esuene, Governor of the former South-Eastern State, said in September 1973 that:

> As men of honour, we the men of the Nigerian Armed Forces are bound to keep our words that we shall hand over power to the civilians in 1976. We are doing our utmost to ensure that the programme we have set for ourselves and which aims at facilitating a return to civilian rule is carried out expeditiously and completed on schedule.[6]

As Claude Welch concluded,

> It is notoriously easier for the armed forces to seize control than to give it up . . . Having tasted power, excitement and rewards of political life, officers may be personally reluctant to step aside. Second thoughts and procrastinations about handing over to civilians thus become common phenomena in the history of military dominated government.[7]

Welch is right. At the same time that Esuene was re-affirming the commitment to transition, another Governor, Brigadier Johnson of Lagos, was dropping the hint of a perpetual military government:

> If by 1976, the nine-point programme was not completed, and the Nigerian public wished the military administration to continue, members of the armed forces would accept it.[8]

As it turned out, Johnson was speaking for Gowon. A year later, Gowon announced in his independence day broadcast to the nation that 1976 was unrealistic: 'it would indeed amount to a betrayal of trust to adhere rigidly to that date'.[9] According to him, he was not sure that there were capable leaders: 'it was clear that those to lead the nation on the return to civilian rule have not learnt any lesson from past experiences'.[10] Consequently, it would 'be utterly irresponsible to leave the nation in the lurch by a precipitate withdrawal which will certainly throw the nation back into confusion'.[11]

Gowon, however, still pledged his commitment to disengagement, though he fixed no particular date. But given the new programmes which he planned to execute from 1974 onwards, Gowon showed that he had no intention of returning to the barracks for a long period. He associated a mature political culture with disengagement:

> We consider it our responsibility to lay the foundation of a self-sustaining political system which can stand the test of time in such a manner that a national political crisis does not become a threat to the nation's continued existence as a single entity and which will ensure a smooth and orderly transition from one government to another.[12]

Gowon's announcement only came as a surprise to optimists. To be sure, he was acting in line with the pattern of military behaviour. In fact, up till 1974, his administration had not taken a single step to implement the nine-point programme, especially those relating to the creation of stable democratic structures.

By reneging on his promise, Gowon had more than he bargained for. From 3 October 1974, opposition to his regime became very vocal. In several newspaper editorials, features and analyses, his administration was condemned and attacked. Indeed, abusive language was employed, particularly by the *Nigerian Tribune* which had become an opposition newspaper. Several 'Gowon Must Go' movements emerged among students, lecturers and articulate members of the public. These movements distributed several booklets and pamphlets exposing the bankruptcy of the Gowon administration.

Gowon became extremely repressive, employing all available coercive weapons to deal with his critics whom he treated as subversive agents. Unfortunately for Gowon, his coercive measures escalated political violence and intensified the crusade to get rid of him. Top military officers also openly criticized his administration. His end came on 29 July 1975 when he was overthrown in a bloodless coup led by Murtala Muhammed and Olusegun Obasanjo. It was a popular coup,[13] and Muhammed's firm administration and commitment to his programmes earned him the admiration of many Nigerians. Nevertheless, articulate members of the public still wanted a temporary military regime. In its editorial to welcome the new administration, the *Nigerian Tribune* attributed the fall of Gowon partly to his inability to disengage and allow civilians who are versed in the art of politics to govern:

> The tenth reason for the fall of Gowon's Federal Military Government is that it had over-stayed its welcome. A military regime should be a transitional government and its tenure of office should be short and effective. For, by their very training and temperament, soldiers do not possess the qualities of politicians. What Gowon has demonstrated is that it takes much more than money, civil servants, and economic plans to govern a country. The art of government is purely practical

politics. And it is best left for those who have the necessary training, public confidence, temperament, experience, ability and the stomach for it.[14]

The Muhammed/Obasanjo regime was, however, determined to disengage. It chose a constitutional–evolutionary model of military disengagement.[15] A five-stage programme of transition was announced in 1975.[16]

Stage One:		Settlement of the question of states. The state review panel to report by December 1975. The creation of states to be completed by April 1976.
Stage Two:	i.	Local Government re-organization;
	ii.	Elections at the Local Government level without party politics;
	iii.	Establishment of the Constituent Assembly, partly elected and partly nominated; All these were to be completed by October 1978.
Stage Three:		The lifting of the ban on politics and the abrogation of Emergency Decree.
Stage Four:		The elections to State and Federal Legislatures in 1979.
Stage Five:		Handover to a civilian government on 1 October 1979.

This programme combined the restructuring of the federal political system (e.g. creation of states, local government reforms) with demilitarization. The reason for this approach, as Muhammed explained,

is to forge a viable political system which will be stable and responsive enough to the needs and realities of this country. This is not an exercise that begins and ends in the mere drafting of a constitution.[17]

Despite the fact that this programme for transition was made with specific dates, some analysts doubted whether it was not a deliberate attempt to seek legitimacy and quieten opposition. Others believed that the military should be given the benefit of the doubt but urged it not to stay for four years, fearing that there could be problems within that period which could force the military to change its mind. There were a few others who, mainly because of the largesse which they received from the military, urged it to stay in power.

Muhammed, however, pursued the programme with vigour. When he died in the February 1976 attempted coup, his successor, Obasanjo, continued with similar determination. Obasanjo, in fact, seized every opportunity to re-affirm his commitment to disengagement. In his July 1978 broadcast to the nation, he criticized those who lacked faith in his administration's programme of transition and warned those urging him to remain in power:

But let me sound a note of warning. This administration is committed to bringing about an elected government in 1979 through a peaceful process of free and fair elections and we will not tolerate from anybody or group any act that is capable of diverting us from this goal.[18]

In September of the same year, he repeated his unbending commitment:

Fears and lack of faith have led to whisperings and unaltruistic campaigns in some quarters for the military to reconsider their political programme. As professional men, we believe that the greatest heritage we can leave behind apart from a united, stable and economically strong country, is an untarnished and respected Armed Forces ... As men of honour, we in this administration are bound by our words and pledge, and 1979 remains realistic. It is the duty of all Nigerians to make it happen peacefully and painlessly.[19]

The Muhammed/Obasanjo regime was committed to the transition for at least three reasons. First, it believed that the long military rule had created a myriad of problems for the army: politicization and dissension among the top officers; unnecessary political ambition; quest for political offices to make wealth; diversion from the primary goal of defending the country against external aggressions. Second, it believed that Gowon's bankrupt administration and indecision over disengagement had contributed immensely to discrediting the army. Third, transition could curb unnecessary ambition for counter-coups. Indeed, a coup would have been unpopular during the period since the public was already tired of military regimes. The February 1976 coup led by Dimka was not only crushed but met with instant general public disapproval.

From August 1975, several bodies and structures were established to implement the transition programme. The major ones which we shall examine here are the drafting of a new constitution, the setting up of new local government bodies, the movement to the barracks and the reactivation of the Federal Electoral Commission.

The Constitution Drafting Committee (CDC)

On 4 October 1978, the Federal Military Government announced the names of 51 members of the Constitution Drafting Committee with Chief F.R.A. Williams, the eminent legal practitioner, as Chairman. Chief Obafemi Awolowo refused to serve on the committee, thus reducing the number to 50. These '50 wise men', as the newspapers referred to them, were drawn from the bar, universities, private sector, local government areas and the states. The membership was supposed to reflect all shades of opinion:

members of this committee were selected, first on a basis of two per state, so as to obtain as wide geographical coverage as possible and, secondly, from our learned men in disciplines considered to have direct relevance to constitution-making, namely . . . History, Law, Economics and other Social Sciences especially Political Science. Eminent Nigerians with some experience in Constitution-making were brought in to complete the spectrum. It is enough to ensure that all the broad areas of interest and expertise are brought into the Committee, and I am satisfied that members of this Committee gathered here today represent a cross-section of opinion in this country that can be trusted to do a good job.[20]

While the credentials of these Nigerians are not in doubt, they, however, represent the middle and upper class and also the business, bureaucratic, administrative and intellectual bourgeoisie. This composition allowed the elite to design the constitution in its favour and to perpetuate the socio-political and economic status quo. A thorough reading of the report of the CDC reveals very clearly that debates on issues that were of interest to the elite were not heated while those that threatened it were vigorous. Several of the debates were very trivial, mundane and unserious when they dealt with issues that affect the common people.

Since the masses were not represented, the CDC members assumed that they knew all their problems and could talk on their behalf. Reactionary ideas were expressed about the basic needs of the poor who constituted the majority. Indeed, certain members of the CDC expressed the opinion that the intricacies of constitution-making were beyond the comprehension of the ordinary people.

Two of the members — Segun Osoba and Yusuf Bala Usman — spoke on the implications of this composition, even at a time when it was not too late to make amends:

The CDC, judged by the content and tone of its debates and by the draft constitution that the majority of its members have adopted, has failed to compose the draft of a constitution . . . that clearly maps out for our people a new political road that should take them away from the detours and blind alleys of the past towards independent, self-reliant, just and genuinely democratic national development. The CDC has failed to place on the national political agenda the constitutional blueprint for a fresh direction for the Nigerian society in which optimal conditions would be built for the development of the physical, mental and spiritual capabilities of every Nigerian citizen and in which no Nigerian human being, however great or powerful in his or her own estimation, will be able to prey on another human being.[21]

Though the military did not interfere in the activities of the CDC, the guidelines suggested in the inaugural address of General Muhammed seems to have guided its deliberations. The military informed the CDC of its thinking and position on the kind of the constitution it expected:

(i) a commitment to a Federal system of government and free, democratic and lawful system of government which guarantees fundamental human rights;

(ii) the creation of viable political institutions which will ensure maximum participation and consensus and orderly succession to political power;

(iii) the committee should look into means of eliminating 'cut-throat political competition based on a system of winner takes all';

(iv) the committee should examine ways to 'discourage institutionalised opposition to the government in power, and instead, develop consensus politics and government';

(v) to introduce a system which would recognize public accountability for an office holder, depoliticize the census, guarantee a free and fair electoral system and eliminate overcentralization of power in a few hands; and

(vi) to look into how genuine and truly national political parties could be formed or whether governments could be formed without out the involvement of political parties.[22]

The draft constitution incorporated virtually all the above suggestions, thus lending credence to the assumption that the military simply made use of civilians to impose its wishes. The presidential constitution that later emerged was, in fact, in reaction to the guideline of the military which had suggested the establishment of an executive presidential system, in which the president and the vice-president would be elected and granted clearly defined powers. It was also suggested that the method of their assumption of office should reflect 'the federal character of the country'.[23]

On 14 September 1976, the chairman of the CDC submitted the draft constitution to General Obasanjo.[24] The draft constitution made a complete retreat from the British Westminster system and created an American-type model. On 7 October 1976 the government threw the draft constitution open to debate and requested memoranda to be submitted to the Constituent Assembly which would produce a final constitution.[25]

The Constituent Assembly

The Constituent Assembly (CA) was charged with receiving and collating comments from the public on the draft constitution. The CA consisted of 203 elected members from different Local Governments. Each state had five members on the basis of equality and the balance was computed on the basis of population.[26] In addition to these elected members, the Chairman of all the sub-committees of the CDC and twenty others representing interests that were ignored by the election process (e.g. women, students) were appointed as members.

Like the CDC, most of the members of the CA were bourgeois, interested in the consolidation and perpetuation of the neocolonial socio-economic order in Nigeria. The CA made not even a single attempt to entrench the interests of the common man into the constitution. Bala Usman's comment on the elite interest of the CA admirably summarizes our own position:

> The way private property and its accumulation has been elaborately protected, even more than human life, show this. Entrenching this and absolute interest in land flagrantly rejects the principle of collective ownership of land and land-for-the-user, in even the Land Use Decree. Provision for private ownership of television and radio broadcasting buttress all this. The decision to allow holders of public office to maintain foreign bank accounts is perhaps the most cynical, but in a way honest decision, as most of them have such accounts or aspire to them. This fits in with the scarcely veiled contempt with which, even the wishey-washey, fundamental objectives and principles were treated. They showed, quite brazenly, that they had no interest in the objectives of government but only in the mechanics of getting power and wielding it. But I wonder how much all this is actually in their long-term interest. Naked elite interest rarely survives its aggressive assertion.[27]

The debates at the CA were not only poor but puerile. The issue that generated the most important and the hottest debate was over the Sharia Court system. It brought into the open the extent to which the elite could use religion to manipulate the common citizens. Other major issues of interest dealt with the creation of states and the proscription of corrupt public officers and politicians from public office. Rather than probe into serious issues, members used the CA to build their political fortunes and future by making allies and building a network of friends. The primary function of the CA became a forum for aspiring politicians to recruit supporters. A number of dubious political associations, disguised under various names such as the Progressives, Committee of Friends, Council for National Unity and Progress, National Union Council, Club 19, etc., came into existence. The majority of the members of the CA later featured in the activities of the five political parties and held prominent positions in the Second Republic.

The CA completed its assignment in August 1978. Its document was not much different from the earlier one by the CDC. The Supreme Military Council made seventeen amendments to reflect its own view of the Nigerian society. General Obasanjo rationalized the need for these amendments thus:

> ... the overriding concern of the Supreme Military Council has been the need to ensure good government, orderly progress and harmony of the nation. Conscious of this responsibility to the nation, it became

imperative for the Supreme Military Council, as the highest institution of administration, to amend certain provisions which, in its opinion, will either hinder or prolong the attainment of these objectives.[28]

The Supreme Military Council added three widely spoken languages – Hausa, Igbo and Yoruba – to section 42 while still retaining English which the CA had recommended as the only official language. Certain decrees relating to the National Youth Service Corps, National Security Organisation, Public Complaints Commission and the Land Use Decree were also integrated into the constitution. Section 256 was amended to make removal of judicial officers possible. Finally, in order to make the composition of certain public organs manageable, the maximum number of members was fixed at ten for the Public Service Commission and sixteen for Supreme Court Judges.

On 21 September 1978, the head of state signed Decree No. 25 which promulgated the Constitution of the Federal Republic of Nigeria into law with effect from 1 October 1979.

Local Government Reforms

The Muhammed/Obasanjo regime also tied up military disengagement with the creation of states and local government reforms. Seven new states were created on 3 February 1976, bringing the number of states to 19.[29] The FMG was equally interested in reforming local government which it regarded as the pivot of its political programme. General Shehu Musa Yar'Adua, Chief of Staff Supreme Headquarters, put the government's intention in the following words:

> The reform of our system of local government is not only important and desirable in itself, but it is a crucial element in the political programme of the Federal Military Government. Indeed, having disposed of the question of the creation of new states, the local government reforms are the next important exercise in the process of building a sound foundation for the return of this country's administration to civil rule.[30]

The FMG consulted state governments, traditional rulers and some scholars in working out appropriate reforms. On the basis of these consultations, the government came to the conclusion that what was required was a one-tier local government system throughout the country. It went on to establish guidelines for action by the states. The new reforms spelt out the functions of local governments, sources of finance, relationship with the state, etc.[31]

Deployment of Military Governors

A major aspect of the transition programme was to redeploy officers who

27

were performing political and administrative functions into the army. This has always been the most difficult aspect of disengagement given the fact that the soldier-cum-politician has tasted power, has used and abused it, has enjoyed its perquisites — car, siren, lavishly furnished government house, etc. More importantly, the soldier-politician would have been exposed to limitless opportunities for making money, investing it and distributing largesse.

Gowon for instance found it difficult to replace his governors, despite the fact that most of them had been discredited. Obasanjo, however, showed a great deal of boldness and political maturity in this respect. The decision to redeploy top military officers was announced to the nation on 14 July 1978.[32] The government not only believed that military officers in political roles must disengage psychologically before the final military withdrawal but that the act alone would convince all doubting Thomases of the sincerity of the military government's intention to leave the stage.

The officers were given two options: to remain in office and retire from the armed forces; or return to active military careers with effect from 24 July. The civilians in the administration — centre and states — who had political ambitions were also told to resign immediately. Obasanjo and his lieutenants, Yar'Adua and Danjuma, decided to retire, while all the 19 governors and four Federal Commissioners were redeployed. To fill the vacuum, military officers commanding garrisons and brigades, naval and air force officers of equivalent rank were charged with the responsibility of maintaining law and order in the states. These new administrators became tutelary heads of state civilian executive councils. Besides this redeployment, Obasanjo promised that:

> The military will be less visible in non-military functions and activities as we move towards the final stages of our political programme. The role of the armed forces in complementing the police and in maintaining law and order will continue to be most crucial.[33]

The General kept his promise. The redeployment exercise further reinforced the sincerity of the military to leave the stage.

The Federal Electoral Commission (Fedeco)

The Federal Electoral Commission was charged with the responsibility of organizing elections and regulating certain activities of political parties. Fedeco was brought into existence by Decree No. 73 of 1977. Its first Chairman was Chief Michael Ani, a retired civil servant. The Decree spelt out its functions as conducting elections, accepting nomination papers from candidates and political parties, registering parties and organizing actual balloting. A new Decree was passed on 29 December 1977 to amend the earlier one.[34] The new amendments were to facilitate election administration, enable Fedeco to discharge its responsibility more effectively in matters relating to registration of political parties, sponsorship and eligibility of candidates to contest elections and to reflect the relevant provision of the 1979 constitution. The Decree gave wide power to the Commission. It also gave it legal immunity in some of its decisions. For instance, the Commission's decision on the registration of political parties was final as no court of law could hear or determine any question pertaining to it.[35]

Having established certain structures and approved the constitution, the military lifted the ban on politics on 21 September 1978.

In all the programmes of disengagement, the military never considered it of importance to re-structure the economy, especially in terms of the control of the means of production and of reducing dependence. The military in fact favoured the economic status quo as was reflected in the constitution. This inability to consider the economic along with political changes was later to spell the doom for the Second Republic.

Nevertheless, the point should be made that even if the 1979 constitution made some concessions to the poor these were quickly eroded when it came to putting the document into practice. The bourgeois character of the constitution is not in doubt. From the beginning, issues and debates were weighted in favour of the dominant classes. Provisions in the section on the formation of political parties were aimed at checking clannishness, but it was evident that only the propertied class could meet the requirements for registration. Worse still, the masses had no constitutional right to recall 'representatives' who were seen as inefficient, ineffective or corrupt. The corrupt and often irresponsible activities of the bourgeoisie made it unable to separate the responsibility of public office from that of personal gains.

The unwritten alliance, in the three arms of government, between fractions of the bourgeoisie to operate irrespective of constitutional provisions coupled with the desire to manipulate the coercive instruments of state power to promote private accumulation, gradually moved the country toward anarchy. State governors engaged one another in political and personal duels; the assemblies, where they were dominated by opposing parties, busied themselves with the task of impeaching governors, the President himself flouted Supreme Court decisions, and ministers neglected their functions and responsibilities to concentrate on the importation of rice and tyres. As the economy decayed and oil revenues declined, corruption and competition within the ranks of the bourgeoisie deepened and the constitution became almost irrelevant. In fact, in August 1983, the Nigerian police force itself was operating outside the law of the land.

To be sure, the constitution also tried to enhance the integration of the Nigerian bourgeoisie. For instance, it stipulated that the appointment of ministers had to reflect the national character. This meant that the ruling fraction of the bourgeoisie was required to draw its members from states and ethnic groups other than those at the centre. But again, despite this *positive* provision, the subservient and corrupt nature of the dominant class prevented them from being able to exploit such constitutional provisions.

29

The above points are intended to identify the contradictions within the bourgeois class. It is not enough to have a constitution geared to promoting class unity. The structures and institutions of society, as well as the orientation of the ruling class must be viable and positive, even nationalist enough to exploit such constitutional provisions. In the case of Nigeria, the bourgeoisie, perhaps outside the Chambers of Commerce, have never really understood the importance of class unity. At the CDC, bitter quarrels ensued over the choice of a national language, pattern of revenue allocation, the distribution of powers to the three arms of government and so on. These quarrels, it must be pointed out, did not prevent the CDC and CA from relegating to the non-judicial part of the constitution, the provision on fundamental objects and directive principles of state policy.

Finally, since the constitution did not make binding (assuming it could have done so) on the ruling class the need to restructure internal socio-economic and power relations, as well as the need genuinely to transfer power to the masses, it meant that the document was superimposed on existing corrupt, distorted and dependent relations of production and exchange. This simple fact explains why the document was by-passed by the bourgeoisie in the bitter struggles to gain access to the state oil revenues and the criminal manipulation and use of the coercive instruments of state power to terrorize the masses. These conditions directly prevented the masses from even capitalizing on the few concessions which the constitution had made to them.

Notes

1. J. Ihonvbere and Toyin Falola, 'The Re-cycling of Oil Rents and Nigeria's Incorporation into World Capitalism'. Unpublished manuscript, University of Ife, 1984.

2. S.E. Finer, 'Military Disengagement From Politics' in *The Politics of Demilitarisation* (London University Institute of Commonwealth Studies Conference, April–May 1966), p. 2 and Leo Dare, 'Military Withdrawal From Politics in Nigeria', *International Political Science Review*, 2, 3, 1981, p. 352. See also his 'Dilemma of Military Disengagement: The Nigerian Case', *Nigerian Journal of Economic and Social Studies*, 16, 2, July 1974, pp. 297–309.

3. *The Nigerian Tribune*, 2 July 1967.

4. *Daily Times*, 15 February 1966, p. 4.

5. Ibid., 8 August 1966, p. 8.

6. Ibid., 8 September 1973.

7. C. Welch, *Soldier and State in Africa* (Evanston: Northwestern University Press, 1970), p. 50.

8. *Daily Times*, 5 July 1973. The nine-point programme to transfer power to civilians was announced in 1970 and repeated in 1974; it read: (a) The reorganisation of the Armed Forces; (b) The implementation of the National Development Plan and the repair of the damage and neglect of the war; (c) The eradication of corruption in our national life; (d) The settlement

of the question of the creation of more states; (e) The preparation and adoption of a new constitution; (f) The introduction of a new Revenue Allocation Formula; (g) Conducting a national population census; (h) The organisation of genuine political parties; (i) The organisation of elections and installation of popularly elected governments in the states and the centre.

9. Text of a Broadcast to the Nation, 1 October 1974.

10. Ibid.

11. Ibid.

12. Ibid.

13. See for instance the editorial of *Daily Times*, 2 August 1975.

14. *The Nigerian Tribune*, 1 August 1975, p. 1.

15. For different types of military disengagement, See J. Adekson, 'Dilemma of Military of Disengagement' in O. Oyediran (ed), *Nigerian Government and Politics Under Military Rule* (London: Macmillan, 1979).

16. *Daily Times*, 1 October 1975.

17. Ibid.

18. General Olusegun Obasanjo, Text of a Broadcast to the Nation, 14 July 1978.

19. General Olusegun Obasanjo, Text of a Broadcast to the Nation, 21 September 1978.

20. *Report of the Constitution Drafting Committee Containing the Draft Constitution* (Lagos: Government Printer, 1976), Vol. 1, p. xliii; address by General Mohammed.

21. O. Osoba and Y.B. Usman, *A General Report on the Work of the Constitution Drafting Committee: A Minority Submission*, August 1976, pp. 3 and 4. We are grateful to the authors for giving us a copy of this document.

22. *Report of the Constitution Drafting Committee*, op. cit., p. xli et seq.

23. Ibid.

24. J.O. Ojiako, *13 Years of Military Rule, 1966-79* (Lagos: Daily Times of Nigeria Ltd., 1979), p. 178. See also *West Africa*, 8 October 1976.

25. *Daily Times*, 8 October 1976.

26. Membership by State was as follows: Anambra 11, Bauchi 10, Bendel 10, Benue 10, Borno 11, Cross River 12, Gongola 10, Imo 13, Plateau 9, Kaduna 13, Kano 16, Kwara 8, Lagos 8, Niger 7, Ogun 8, Ondo 10, Oyo 15, Rivers 8, and Sokoto 14.

27. Y.B. Usman, *For the Liberation of Nigeria* (London: New Beacon Books, 1979), p. 131.

28. General Olusegun Obasanjo, Text of a Broadcast to the Nation, 21 September 1978.

29. General Murtala Muhammed, Text of a Broadcast to the Nation, 3 February 1976.

30. Federal Government of Nigeria, *Guidelines For Local Government* (Kaduna: Government Printer, 1976).

31. See ibid for details.

32. General Olusegun Obasanjo, Text of a Broadcast to the Nation, 14 July 1978.

33. Ibid.

34. See *New Nigerian*, 31 December 1977.

35. Ibid.

3. The Presidential Constitution

This chapter is divided into two parts: the first describes the main features of the 1979 constitution and the second undertakes a critique of it within the framework of political economy.

Main Features

The 1979 constitution, like the earlier ones, is federal, with the aim of recognizing the diverse and heterogeneous nature of the country. Federalism involves the distribution of power between a centre and the regions and 'the frustration of the will of the majority on issues deemed to be of special importance to regionally grouped minorities'. Federalism implies willingness to hasten slowly by means of compromises and bargains, legalistic solutions to governmental problems, political pluralism and decentralized administration and policy decisions.[1] Though his view has been queried and revised, K.C. Wheare states that federalism exists when the powers of government for a community are divided substantially according to the principle that there is a single independent authority for the whole area in respect of some matters and that there are independent regional authorities for other matters, each set of authorities being co-ordinate with and not subordinate to the others within its own prescribed sphere.[2]

The 1979 constitution provides for a presidential system of government, unlike the parliamentary system of the First Republic. The president is independent of the legislature and is not a member of the National Assembly. He is both the head of state and the head of government. A Nigerian by birth who has attained the age of 35 years is qualified for election to the office of president. His constituency is the whole country: to win, a candidate must secure a majority of the votes, and in addition secure not less than one-quarter of the votes cast at the election in each of at least two-thirds of all the states in the federation.[3]

Each state is headed by a governor, who must be a citizen of Nigeria by birth and have attained the age of 35 years. To be elected he must win not only a majority of votes cast but also not less than one-quarter of the votes cast at the election in at least two-thirds of all the local government areas in the state.[4]

These provisions about the distribution of the votes are designed to ensure that whoever is elected president or governor has the broadly based support of the people.

While the centre has a bicameral legislature, the states are unicameral. The National Assembly consists of a Senate and a House of Representatives. The House of Representatives is made up of 450 members spread over the country on a population basis while the Senate is made up of 5 Senators from each state, making a total of 95.[5]

Senators and Representatives must be citizens of Nigeria, the minimum age for Senators being 30 and for Representatives 21.[6] In an attempt to prevent the 'carpet-crossing' so prevalent in the First Republic, the constitution provides that Senators and Representatives who leave the party on whose ticket they are elected and join another party forfeit their seats. And to ensure that members attend sessions and that sessions are regularly held, again in the light of the experience of the First Republic, the constitution lays down that the National Assembly shall meet for 181 days a year and that members absenting themselves for a total of one-third of the meetings will lose their seats. Membership of the Assembly is incompatible with tenure of an executive post.[7] Similar rules apply to members of state Houses of Assembly.[8]

The constitution enshrines the principle of the separation of powers, both at the centre and in the states. The relative powers of the National Assembly and the state Houses of Assembly are prescribed in an Exclusive Legislative List, laying down those areas reserved to the centre, and a Concurrent Legislative List, listing areas on which both centre and states can legislate, with laws passed by the National Assembly prevailing in the event of conflict.[9]

Other legislative provisions outlaw the making of any retrospective laws in criminal matters and subordinate the exercise of legislative powers to the jurisdiction of the judiciary.[10] The president must, within 30 days, indicate whether he assents to a bill passed by both Houses or not; if his assent is withheld, and the bill is again passed by each House, by a two-thirds majority, it automatically becomes law.[11] Analogous provisions apply in the states.[12]

Judicial powers are vested in different courts – the Supreme Court, Federal Court of Appeal, Federal High Court, High Court of a state, Sharia Court of Appeal of a state, Customary Court of Appeal of a state,[13] all of which are courts of first instance and of appeal. The judicial powers of the courts 'extend . . . to all inherent powers and sanctions of a court of law', 'to all matters between persons, or between government or authority and any person in Nigeria, and to all actions and proceedings relating thereto, for the determination of any question as to the civil rights and obligations of that person'. The powers do not extend to 'questions as to whether any act or omission by any authority or person . . . is in conformity with the Fundamental Objectives and Directive Principles of State Policy' (discussed below) nor do they 'extend to any action or proceedings relating to any existing law made on or after 15 January 1966 for determining any issue or question as to the competence of any authority or person to make any such law'.[14]

The chief justice of the federation is appointed by the president subject to confirmation by a simple majority of the Senate. Other judges of the court are appointed by the president on the advice of the Federal Judicial Service Commission. 'A person shall not be qualified to hold the office of chief justice or of a justice of the Supreme Court unless he is qualified to practise as a legal practitioner and has been so qualified for a period of not less than 15 years'. The Chief Justice may 'be removed by the President acting on an address supported by a two-thirds majority of the Senate', while other judges may be removed on the recommendation of the Judicial Service Commission for stated cause.[15] State Judicial Service Commissions exercise similar powers over state judiciaries.

The whole of Chapter II of the constitution is devoted to the 'Fundamental Objectives and Directive Principles of State Policy', which attempts to lay down the democratic principles on which Nigeria is to be governed. It is however non-justiciable. Sovereignty rests with the people, whose security and welfare are laid down as the primary purpose of government. Section 14(3) lays down that

> The composition of the Government of the Federation or any of its agencies and the conduct of its affairs shall be carried out in such a manner as to reflect the federal character of Nigeria and the need to promote national unity, and also to command national loyalty thereby ensuring that there shall be no predominance of persons from a few States of from a few ethnic or other sectional groups in that government or any of its agencies.

The following sections make analogous provisions for the states.

There follows a long list of political, economic, social, educational and foreign policy objectives. The political objectives include promoting national integration and eliminating all forms of discrimination. To this end, free mobility of people, goods and services is to be encouraged, the right of Nigerians to reside anywhere in the federation to be secured, intermarriage among different religions, ethnic and linguistic groups to be encouraged, associations formed across ethnic, linguistic and sectional lines to be promoted, and 'a feeling of belonging and involvement' to be fostered.

The economic objectives include the goals of welfare, freedom and happiness of all citizens; they provide for the state to 'manage and operate major sectors'[16] of the economy, as well as others, but also preserve the rights of individuals to participate in those same areas. State policy is to be directed at promoting 'a planned and balanced economic development'; while 'concentration of wealth or the means of production and exchange in the hands of a few individuals or of a group' is to be avoided.

The social objectives enjoin equality among all citizens, the sanctity of the person, the independence of the courts and access thereto, and that the good of the community alone shall be the sole reason for the exploitation of human and natural resources. To these ends, policy is to be directed towards ensuring the elimination of discrimination so that all have the opportunity to secure a livelihood, fair working conditions and adequate leisure, adequate medical services, equal pay for equal work and the protection of children.

There are three educational objectives. First, 'government shall direct its policy towards ensuring that there are equal and adequate educational opportunities at all levels.' Second, 'government shall promote science and technology'. And third, 'government shall strive to eradicate illiteracy; and to this end government shall as and when practicable provide (a) free, compulsory and universal primary education; (b) free secondary education; (c) free university education; and (d) free adult literacy programme'.

Finally, the State is enjoined to uphold 'Nigerian culture', and the National ethic shall be 'Discipline, Self-reliance and Patriotism'.[16]

On foreign policy,

> The State shall promote African Unity, as well as total political, economic, social and cultural liberation of Africa and all other forms of international co-operation conducive to the consolidation of universal peace and mutual respect and friendship among all peoples and States, and shall combat racial discrimination in all its manifestations.

Chapter IV of the constitution contains the fundamental rights of the citizen. It contains provisions to ensure the right to live, the right to dignity for the human person, the right to a fair hearing, the right to privacy and family life, including the privacy of 'citizens, their homes, correspondence, telephone conversations and telegraphic communications', the right to freedom of thought, conscience and religion, freedom of expression and the press, the right to free assembly (although secret societies are outlawed) and freedom of movement.

Any person who believes that his fundamental rights have been tampered with may apply to a High Court in his state for redress. Nevertheless, restriction on and derogation from fundamental rights can be justified by any law made 'in the interest of defence, public safety, public order, public morality or public health; or for the purpose of protecting the rights and freedom of other persons'.

The Political Economy of the Constitution[17]

A constitution grows out of several historical experiences, and is also more or less a set of legal statements on the distribution of power among classes in a society as well as on the balance of social forces and interest groups. As long as there is no crisis of power within a society, the constitution tends to remain. The ruling elite tries to defend and uphold the constitution that works in its favour. A faction of the ruling elite may attempt to tinker with the constitution if there is a crisis of hegemony within the state. But the changes which the faction or fraction of a dominant ruling class can make depend on the interests which it wants to consolidate. There is usually a major, far-reaching constitutional change (or revolution) when a ruling class is supplanted together with its mode of production, world view, moral values and judicial system.

In the case of Nigeria, the 1979 constitution was not a by-product of any revolution. Rather, it emanated from the struggles between the factions and fractions of the ruling elites. The ruling class that drew up the 1979 constitution was only interested in modifying the 1963 parliamentary constitution which it believed was poor in political procedures and in the allocation of functions and powers. The ruling class also believed that modifications were necessary to regulate the excesses of political actors and parties and to take care of the federal character of the country. The final product thus took care of the prevailing socio-economic structure and only provided political modifications. Those who drew up the constitution deliberately ignored the most dominant aspects of Nigerian history and the causes of political instability during the First Republic.

The most acute analysis of the constitution was made by Yusufu Bala Usman in various speeches and writings brought together in his book, *For the Liberation of Nigeria*, and in the so-called '*Minority Report*' on the draft constitution which he prepared with Sigun Osoba. Usman identifies five aspects of this history, as follows:[18]

1. The existence of an economic system which permanently generates instability and gross inequalities of (a) standards of living between the majority of the people and those who control public institutions and business; and (b) economic development between various villages, districts, provinces, states and sections of the country and sectors of the economy.

2. The great amount of material benefit which accrues to those holding public offices due to the very high level of official and unofficial remuneration, arising out of the failure to clearly and sharply separate the holding of public office from the private accumulation of wealth in all the major public institutions. This failure intensified the competition for office and control of access to it along the lines in 3 below.

3. The conduct of public affairs on the basis of the belief widely propagated that political activity is about the competition for material resources and public status between areas, tribes, clans, families and individuals.

4. The absence of any systematic and effective means by which the common people can on a regular basis understand, guide and discipline those who are supposed to represent and serve them. The substitution of this by the 'market-place' view of political activity and

the myth of power through the ballot box. The key institutions of political representation and public service — the political parties and civil service, overawed and confused the common people and refused to be genuinely subjected to a coherent and permanent system of public accountability.

5. The manipulation of political activity by foreign interests through the supply of funds and ideas. The funds came directly from abroad and through businesses operating in this country to intensify competition between and within various political organisations. The ideas came directly and through personnel and institutions here to rationalise the superiority or inferiority of various tribes and the inevitability of conflict between them.

Rather than recognize the above, particularly the implications of a neo-colonial economy, most members of the CDC and CA subscribed to the view expressed by Alhaji Shehu Malami, a member of the CDC, to the effect that capitalism has been the driving force of Nigerian history and should be entrenched:[19]

> If we may briefly look at the history of our Constitution-making efforts, we may see that about the same Ideology informed the Constitutions of 1951, 1957, 1960 and 1963. The unspoken ideology then called for the minimum control of a man's personal freedom to embrace whatever religion he wanted, form any political association he chose, engage in any economic pursuit, save in a few utilities owned by government, and to own any amount of property and in any form as he could acquire. This philosophy showed in the Development Plans of the period in which government contented itself with providing infrastructure and left the productive sector to private investment ... I would, gentlemen, conclude by urging that we grapple seriously with this issue of a national ideology suited to our history and traditions and our developmental needs. A suitable ideology should, therefore, allow for a good measure of individual freedom in religious and political matters and for a mixed economy such as I have described. We really should ensure that the limited human resources we have of people with good technical and managerial training, men with the spirit of enterprise, and all those willing to work, are sufficiently motivated by the national ideology, by the mobilising efforts of the government, by the attraction of better remuneration and profit.

Several other members of the CDC and the CA subscribed to Malami's view. And given this pro-capitalist view by the Nigerian dominant class, it should therefore be understood why it chose the first out of the three options which Usman suggests may be the outline of any constitution:

(a) to provide the framework for the consolidation of the existing socio-economic structure by codifying an existing political system with or without some modifications of detail;

(b) to provide the framework for the transformation of the existing economic and social structure and political system to become like others which have existed at some time in the past. This past system being exactly duplicated or allowing for some differences in form; or

(c) to provide the framework for the transformation of the existing economic and social structures and political systems into essentially new structures and systems. These may be envisaged clearly or may be only broadly defined.[20]

Since the constitution was designed to satisfy the ruling class, it could not, at the same time, serve the interests of the masses. Consequently, the constitution fails to:[21]

(a) make provisions to create the right social and political atmosphere for the workings of democracy;

(b) avoid the concentration of powers in a clique and parasitic cabal;

(c) deal with the destabilising issue of winner-take-all style of politics and make provisions for the establishment of viable consensus politics based on a general commitment to the needs, interests and aspirations of the common people;

(d) provide for a genuinely just and egalitarian society;

(e) avoid the elite-generated problem of ethnic, sectional and religious rivalry and suspicions;

(f) provide excellent guidelines for determining which political parties will be regarded as genuinely national; and

(g) deal with the problem of how to free the people and the resources of the country from all forms of imperialist domination and exploitation.

At one level it would have been an expression of class suicide for the constitution to have made the provisions above given that it was drafted and ratified by members of the dominant class, and was thus a reflection of the then on-going inter- and intra-class contradictions and struggles as well as the aspirations of this class to entrench capitalism and hegemony. However, every effort was made to present these aspirations in such a way as to make them acceptable to a population more concerned with the real politicking or working of the constitution, than with its provisions. It is obvious, from the various failings of the document, that it did not strive to (a) mobilize the populace, (b) promote awareness, education and vigilance, (c) attack the capitalist mode of production and exchange, (d) attack imperialist domination of the country's economy and society and (e) create a society with popular access to the means of production and socially produced wealth. Essentially, it sought to consolidate Nigeria's peripheral capitalist role in the international division of labour. The ability of socialist-oriented (but not necessarily socialist) parties to take advantage of the provisions of a constitution such as this would be dependent on the extent to which it is not seen as a threat to the established order. In any case, the ballot-box road to *socialism* in practice as against in theory or propaganda holds inherent risks given the nature of forces that such a party has to content with – the army, dominant classes whose factions/fractions become united in the face of opposition, transnational interests and an 'uneducated' and often unmobilized populace. At best, progressive organizations can take advantage of 'liberal' constitutional provisions to raise critical issues for debate in society. If the Jamaican, Tanzanian and Chilean failures are anything to learn from, it becomes crucial not just to focus on the 'open' spaces available for radical transformation within bourgeois constitutions but also on the concrete obstacles within the system and external to it, which are interested in the reproduction of the system.

Given the provisions of the 1979 constitution, a socialist party stands no chance of being registered or raising critical issues for debate in the society. A well organized and acceptable socialist party would have to play the game by the rules set down by those interested in reproducing the status quo and in this quest, was bound to loose its socialist orientation.

The constitution, however, sets out several welfarist provisions under the fundamental objectives of state policy. The execution of this policy is based on a preposterous belief that politicians are humanitarians who will loot the treasury and remember to bribe the populace with education, food, water and electricity. It has, however, been argued that a socialist-oriented party could make use of the provisions to transform the society. This is hardly plausible, given several other provisions in the constitution which definitely cripple the emergence of a mass-oriented political party.

The welfarist provisions in the constitution are fake and illusory; they are more like promises which political parties are not obliged to keep. None of the provisions is justiciable, no citizen can challenge the state in any court of law for its refusal to implement any of the provisions. He could not even monitor the performance of the government in line with the constitution on his rights and privileges. Even if he does, the constitution effectively shields key holders of government offices from the rigours of law. How then could democracy be genuine, when it is optional to carry out the objectives of state policy and when key functionaries have legal immunities? For democracy to be genuine, it should be upheld uniformly, both by the governors and the governed. To achieve this, the masses have to be convinced that politicians primarily pursue goals not for their own narrow, selfish interests but for the welfare and advancement of the majority. The constitution fails to do this; rather it makes sure that the poor and the rich cannot enjoy similar status and privileges.

Being pro-elitist and anti-masses, the constitution can be condemned as also anti-society; it is supposed to cater for the majority and not the minority. It lacks an adequate framework to transform the Nigerian society, and protect its human and natural resources from all forms of exploitation, especially external. No serious attempt is made even to liberate the economy from foreign domination. The major attempt, as contained in section 15 (3a and b), is simply backward:

> A body shall be set up by an Act of the National Assembly which shall have power (a) to review from time to time the ownership and control of business enterprises operating in Nigeria and make recommendations to the President on the same; and (b) to administer any law for the regulation of the ownership and control of such enterprises.

The provision does not in any way suggest nationalization or even state control and ownership of the leading heights of the economy. By 1979, it should have been clear to perceptive analysts that anything short of total state control and ownership of the key economic sectors can only entrench foreign domination, intensify exploitation by neocolonial collaborators and deepen economic underdevelopment.

The same attitude to objectives of state policy is also reflected in the fundamental human rights provisions. It is wrong to talk of rights without duties, especially to defend the nation, the constitution, to engage in productive labour and to oppose crime, assist all persons in distress and need and support the law:[22]

> [t]his is because rights are not conferred on a people simply because a few egg-heads have committed such rights into writing in a constitution. On the contrary, a people as a whole has to fight and work very hard to create rights for itself and be able to defend such rights against all the forces that may threaten their effective operation.[23]

Secondly, the rights on full participation in politics by the masses are so circumscribed that they are left with virtually nothing. Thirdly, there are several provisos which a reactionary government, like the Shagari administration which operated the constitution, could use to deny citizens their rights. For instance, socio-economic rights ignore the threats posed by Euro-American monopoly capital and its agents, the Nigerian bourgeoisie of commission agents who work against the interests of the toiling masses. Other necessary rights to education and employment are only to be fulfilled 'as and when practicable'. But rights which serve the interests of the bourgeoisie, especially the right to private property, are so detailed and neatly defined that they could not be easily denied.

The rights of the masses to courts of law could be denied with impunity because the judiciary is supposed to serve the interests of the hegemonic class. In spite of provisions to the contrary, the judiciary and the executive are mutual co-travellers — governors rubbed shoulders with judges. The constitution entrenches a colonial-oriented American-type system which is glaringly unintelligible and irrelevant to the norms, values, principles and procedures of the majority. Of course, the bourgeois elite understands it, and thinks that this is what is important and vital if it is to trample the masses under its feet. More importantly, the judiciary has been rigged in favour of the hegemonic class since the courts do not make laws but only interpret them, and most often conservatively and with little regard to the interest of the majority.

The common people are also edited out of the provisions on consensus politics and divisions of power. We recognize that it is necessary to avoid the concentration of excessive powers in a few hands, in the hands of an individual, a small cabal or even an institution. To be sure, such a concentration would inevitably undermine the basis of democracy, create oppressive tin gods, promote suspicion in the people towards their leaders and threaten the ability of the political elite in mobilizing the people to achieve a meaningful programme. But the constitution's understanding of division of power is merely legalistic, superficial and formal. It is only between central government and local government authorities, between the centre and the states and between the three arms of government. Nowhere in the constitution is the division (or balance) of power between the people who wield sovereignty and the governments stated; except of course that the people are to vote every four years and thereafter fold their arms and take all measures, policies, insults and mismanagement. When the constitution was put into practice, the people easily discovered that they had no power, even in the exercise of electing their leaders since ballot papers were not counted. The leadership elite continually gained in power to such an extent that it had acquired the power over life and death by 1983. And in any case, what power could the majority have in an economic system skewed in favour of the minority? Indeed, we could generalize that there will be inequalities in power distribution in any capitalist, free enterprise economy. All laws to regulate equality, social justice, equity, etc., will only operate at the level of rhetoric and excellent slogans which the hegemonic class can tirelessly evoke.

Still on power distribution, the constitution prides itself on the creation of powerful executives — the president and the governors. In fact, those who have faith in the constitution repeatedly emphasized the position of the executive president. His wide power is believed to be sufficient to initiate changes (reforms?) to transform the society. But the faithful ignore the simple fact that the presidency is just an office within the political system. Its effectiveness and role depend, as Usman says,

> on the nature of the whole system and the economic and social structure. If the dominant political forces operate through the maintenance of sectional conflict and bargaining, for the private accumulation of wealth, then the executive presidency will dither and dance, according to their squabbles. Its 'leadership' and 'strength' will only be expressed in popular and nationalist forces. What to examine is not the novelty of an office however central but the whole system. In our own case

even the cut-throat ambitions of the candidates point to the nature of this system and the type of dominant political forces it produces. ... If on the other hand the dominant political forces are the common people — the peasants, petty craftsmen, traders and wage-earners — whose interests can only be satisfied by a decisive resolution of the problems of poverty, uneven development and dependence, then the presidency and other organs of government will be decisive and strong.[24]

Osoba and Usman made a prophetic analysis of the implications of these wide powers even at a time when the constitution was being debated:

... The most dangerous implication of the amount of authority vested in the President and the Governor at their respective levels of government is the dangerous concentration of powers in the hands of these so-called chief executives.

In such situation of excessive concentration of powers, including the virtually unlimited initiative of the President or the Governor to appoint and fire his ministers or commissioners, the ideal conditions would have been created for the emergence of the chief executive as a monstrously powerful and authoritarian political figure. Correspondingly, the other major political actors and aspirants among our grasping bourgeoisie who would want to share in the chief executive's powers as ministers, commissioners or members of various statutory commissions and corporations, are likely to be reduced to sycophants and lackeys vis-a-vis the chief executive at whose pleasure alone they can fulfil their personal ambitions of power. Such a situation could also result in enhanced political instability as the chief executive's power might become an object of considerable envy among his actual and potential rivals who might be tempted to resort to extra-constitutional and violent methods disruptive of national unity to push him out of office in the bid to create room for themselves at the top.[25]

To compound the above problems, the constitution encourages a winner-take-all politics, despite the provisions to the contrary. The attempt to base consensus politics on 'national unity' is crudely fraudulent since the primary motive is to distribute power and wealth to the ruling elite, either in the states or in the centre. In fact, between 1979 and 1983, 'national unity' really assumed its role — that of frantic bargaining among ethnic notables, self-appointed heavyweights and leaders for political offices which would enable them to loot the treasuries. And to protect the leadership elite from the people's wrath, the constitution does not make public functionaries accountable to those who elected them but to themselves and their colleagues. The public referred to in the constitutional provisions on public accountability is not the Nigerian public (or citizens) but powerful political groups — rich people cannot account to the poor just as a landlord does not account to his tenant. Public accountability can only be effective in a just and democratic socio-economic system.

'National unity' can only operate at the level of slogan and as a means to acquire power and wealth given the framework provided for it by the constitution. Unfortunately, national cohesion is so important in all modern states, especailly in order to build a viable socio-economic and political structure. Without national cohesion, bankrupt politicians will find it easy to manipulate ethnicity and religion to achieve their goals, and attribute their failures and lapses to the fragility of national unity. Whilst the constitution talks of measures to promote integration, it at the same time contains measures that could lead to disintegration. It emphasises statism;

> 'belong to' or its grammatical expression when used with reference to a person in a State refers to a person either of whose parents or any of whose grandparents was a member of a community indigenous to that State.[26]

This ignores what constitutes a community indigenous to a state, the wish of a person to settle permanently in any state of his choice, the heterogeneous character of most urban centres, and ancient and recent migrations of people from one area to another. In other words, the only qualification for state citizenship is biological and whether a person has resided for so long or was even born in a state is immaterial if the parents or grandparents are not indigenes. This definition cannot but deepen ethnicity, since indigenes of a state can always discriminate against non-indigenes, especially in the allocation of scarce resources and in the distribution of social, health and educational amenities. There are several instances between 1979 and 1983 of discrimination in employments and admission into post-primary institutions. By November 1983, Bendel State had begun to contemplate issuing identity cards to indigenes while Oyo had hinted that it would dismiss non-indigenes in its civil service. These acts of discrimination are nothing short of war against the poor who lack the resources to adjust.

The military government was satisfied with a final constitution.[27] But others agreed with Usman:

> . . . if the constitution is adopted, far from moving towards national cohesion Nigeria will become torn with ethnic and religious disunity and sectionalism. Far from providing a basis and framework for the development of national cohesion and democracy, there will be an intensification of the present grossly uneven pattern of under-development, greater capitalist and bureaucratic greed, individualism and chaos. When that happens the Nigerian peoples will be accused of being too immature and irresponsible for democracy and preparations will be made for consolidating the status quo and ensuring 'law and order' through repression and terror. From the individualism, greed, chaos and thuggery of capitalist bureaucrats and politicians we shall move to the indiscipline, chaos, individualism, greed and repression of capitalist

bureaucrats and soldiers. And all of this would be done in the name of national unity and national cohesion which, however, every attempt has been made to block and prevent.[28]

And these have truly come to pass!

Notes

1. See for instance, De Smith, *New Commonwealth and its Constitutions* (London: Steven and Sons, 1964).
2. K.C. Wheare, *Federal Government* (London: Oxford University Press, 4th ed., 1963).
3. *The Constitution of the Federal Republic of Nigeria, 1979* (Lagos: Federal Ministry of Information, 1979), sections 123, 125, 126(1a) and 126(2a).
4. Ibid., sections 125(b), 126(1b), 126(2b), 163 and 164(6 & 7).
5. Ibid., sections 44 and 45.
6. Ibid., section 61(b).
7. Ibid., sections 64(1) (a-e) and 37(b).
8. Ibid., sections 37(b), 86, 100 and 103.
9. Ibid., section 4(5) (c).
10. Ibid., section 4(8 and 9).
11. Ibid., sections 54 and 55.
12. Ibid., section 94.
13. See ibid., for details on these courts, sections 212, 213, 214, 217, 218, 219, 235, 236, 240, 241, 242, 245, 246 and 247.
14. Ibid., section 6(1-4).
15. Ibid., section 256.
16. Ibid., section 16(4) defines the key words in this provision thus: (a) the reference to the "major sectors of the economy" shall be construed as a reference to such economic activities as may from time to time be declared by a resolution of each House of the National Assembly to be managed and operated exclusively by the Government of the Federation; and until a resolution to the contrary is made by the National Assembly economic activities being operated exclusively by the Government of the Federation on the date immediately preceding the day when this section comes into force, whether directly or through the agencies of a statutory or other corporation or company, shall be deemed to be major sectors of the economy; (b) "economic activities" includes activities directly concerned with the production, distribution and exchange of wealth or of goods and services; and (c) "participate" includes the rendering of services and supplying of goods.
17. We have been privileged to participate in several lectures, conferences and symposia on the constitution. This has enabled us to be exposed to several comments. We wish to acknowledge in particular the contributions of Segun Osoba, Yusufu Bala Usman, Bade Onimode, Ola Oni, Tai Solarin, Pius Okigbo and Claude Ake, to our understanding of the 1979 constitution.
18. Y. B. Usman, *For the Liberation of Nigeria*, op. cit., pp. 100-1.

19. Quoted in Usman, op. cit., p. 99.

20. Ibid., pp. 97–8.

21. We have drawn heavily from pages 3–5 of the *General Report on The Work of The Constitution Drafting Committee: A Minority Submission*, op. cit.

22. *Minority Constitution*, op. cit., p. 11.

23. *Minority General Report*, op. cit., p. 9.

24. Usman, *For The Liberation*, op. cit., p. 132.

25. *Minority General Report*, p. 18.

26. *Nigerian Constitution*, op. cit., section 277.

27. General Obasanjo, text of a broadcast to the nation. He said, *inter alia*:

> ... what we have tried to achieve ... is an arrangement that would promote the best interest of the whole country. It is quite conceivable that certain people would not be happy with the outcome of this exercise wholly or in part, because it does not conform with their own conception of the best political arrangement for this country. Such people must realise that in a nation as big and complex as ours it is inconceivable to make everybody happy on every point at every stage. However, they should take consolation in the fact that their alternative view had helped to stimulate the debate for more reliable and acceptable constitutional arrangement for this country and had made significant contribution to the final outcome.

28. Usman, *For the Liberation*, op. cit., p. 127.

4. Political Parties, the 1979 Elections and Politics in the Second Republic

By 21 September 1978 the military had satisfied itself on its execution of the programme of transition and lifted the ban on politics. The news did not catch the politicians unawares since there had been underground moves to form political parties. By this date also, the rules guiding the formation and organization of political parties had been approved as part of the constitution. An understanding of these rules is important if the activities of political parties during the Second Republic is to be properly understood and appreciated.

The Constitution and Political Parties: Theory and Practice

Political parties occupied the most crucial place in the politics of the Second Republic. 'No association other than a political party [was allowed to] canvass for votes for any candidate at any election or contribute to the funds of any political party or to the election expenses of any candidate at an election'.[1] There were restrictions on the formation of political parties; and no association was allowed to function as a political party unless:

(a) the names and addresses of its national officers are registered with the Federal Electoral Commission;

(b) the membership of the association is open to every citizen of Nigeria irrespective of his place of origin, sex, religion or ethnic grouping;

(c) a copy of its constitution is registered in the principal office of the Commission in such form as may be prescribed by the Commission;

(d) any alteration in its registered constitution is also registered in the principal office of the Commission within 30 days of the making of such alteration;

(e) the name of the association, its emblem or motto does not contain any ethnic or religious connotation or give the appearance that the activities of the association are confined to a part only of the geographical area of Nigeria; and

(f) the headquarters of the association is situated in the Capital of the Federation.[2]

The constitution of every political party must provide

> (a) for the periodical election on a democratic basis of the principal officers and members of the executive committee or other governing body of the political party; and (b) ensure that the members of the executive committee or other governing body of the political party reflect the federal character of Nigeria.[3]

The constitution allows the parties to formulate their objectives in a manner they like and only enjoins them to recognize fundamental human rights and objectives of state. Whilst the provision on aims is poor, that on the finances of political parties is set out with rigour. Section 205 states as follows:

> (1) Every political party shall, at such times and in such manner as the Federal Electoral Commission may require, submit to the Federal Electoral Commission and publish a statement of its assets and liabilities.
>
> (2) Every political party shall submit to the Commission a detailed annual statement and analysis of its sources of funds and other assets together with a similar statement of its expenditure in such form as the Commission may require.
>
> (3) No political party shall hold or possess any funds or other assets outside Nigeria nor shall it be entitled to retain any funds or assets remitted or sent to it from outside Nigeria, and any such funds or other assets remitted or sent to a political party from outside Nigeria shall be paid over or transferred to the Commission within 21 days of its receipt with such information as the Commission may require.
>
> (4) The Commission shall have power to give directions to political parties regarding the books or records of financial transactions which they shall keep and to examine all such books and records.
>
> (5) The powers conferred on the Commission under subsection (4) of this section may be exercised by it through any member of its staff or any person who is an auditor by profession, and who is not a member of a political party.

The Constitution also insists on an annual report on finances. The Fedeco must prepare an annual account and balance sheet of every political party which must be submitted to the National Assembly. It was also

> the duty of the Commission, in preparing its report, to carry out such investigations as will enable it to form an opinion as to whether proper books of accounts and proper records have been kept by a political party; and if the Commission is of the opinion that proper books of accounts have not been kept by a political party, the Commission shall so report . . . Every member of the Commission or its duly authorised

agent also shall have a right of access at all times to the books and accounts and vouchers of all political parties and shall be entitled to require from the officers of the party such information and explanation as he thinks necessary for the performance of his duties under the Constitution. [If the Commission] fails or is unable to obtain all the information and explanation which to the best of [its] knowledge and belief are necessary for the purposes of the investigations, it shall state the fact in its report.

Quasi-military organisations were prohibited. Section 207 states that

no association shall retain, organise, train or equip any person or group of persons for the purpose of enabling them to be employed for the use or display of physical force or coercion in promoting any political objective or interest or in such manner as to arouse reasonable apprehension that they are organised and trained or equipped for that purpose.

Finally, the National Assembly could exercise five powers on political parties:

(a) for the punishment of any person involved in the management or control of any political party found after due inquiry to have contravened the provisions dealing [with quasi-military organisations, finances of political parties and political activities of certain association] [4];
(b) for the disqualification of any person from holding public office on the ground that he knowingly aids or abets a political party in contravening [the provision of finances of political parties];
(c) for an annual grant to the Federal Electoral Commission for disbursement to political parties on a fair and equitable basis to assist them in the discharge of their functions; and
(d) for the conferment on the Commission of other powers as may appear to the National Assembly to be necessary or desirable for the purpose of enabling the Commission more effectively to ensure that political parties observe the provisions [of the Constitution].

The above provisions were intended to achieve two major things; to create a national party and check external control of political parties. But the provisions are utterly inadequate on both counts, and also on the objectives of political parties. The majority of the Nigerian population was excluded from the 'national party' since what mattered were several offices in different locations and officers drawn from several states. As it later turned out, that is in even keeping to the letters and spirit of the constitution, political parties were nothing more than unstable coalitions of ethnic notables who united together for the primary purpose of winning (rigging) elections and sharing offices. Each of the notables assumed an overdeveloped sense of self-importance and became, to employ the 1983 political jargon, a 'factor' in an area. To win/rig an election, obtain contracts and import licences, one must consult or take into consideration, one 'factor' or the other. The 'factors' were not equal in strength; while they all regarded themselves as heavy-weights, the *primus inter pares* among them employed such other additional names as king, timber, jaugernaut, caterpillar, etc.

Just as a caterpillar need not bother about the complaints of debris nor did these ethnic notables who were allowed by the constitution to operate without any regard whatsoever to the wishes of the masses. In effect, the constitution failed to create genuine national parties which would pursue programmes for the maximum well-being of the majority.

The constitution also took care of the interests of the financially and politically ambitious fraction of the Nigerian bourgeoisie by allowing it to sponsor, to the maximum of its financial capabilities, any party of its choice. The constitution also pretended that there is no link between this fraction and foreign business interests, even when it is generally recognized that it derives its wealth essentially as agents of foreign capitalist interests. And indeed, foreign business interests funded parties and party notables, and were thus able to manipulate them, influence policies and monitor major events. All the Nigerian politicians attached importance to money since it was a major instrument of political manipulation and made no attempt at all at mobilizing the people. Rather than do this they paid the people poor sums of money to attend their rallies and also to secure their votes. The most wealthy of them became the most influential. And to convince their colleagues of their enormous wealth, they had to throw scandalous parties, buy jets, donate to party funds, etc. For instance in 1982, at a time of hardship for the majority, less than ten NPN members donated the staggering sum of ₦5 million at a fund-raising ceremony in Lagos. Those among them who held political offices diverted government money to the party's purse. The commitment of these politicians was, therefore, first and foremost, to money. Whether as a legislator in the National Assembly and House of Assembly or as a member of the executive in the centre or states, the politicians represented nobody but themselves—they did not identify with the wishes and aspirations of those who appointed them and could not be questioned, disciplined or removed by those whom they were supposed to serve. Political representation became nothing short of a passport to accumulation:

> A representative is simply any indigene of an area who perpetuates the illusion that the various parts of the country are engaged in a competition for the allocation of scarce resources and he is a champion of one part. His representativeness begins and ends with ethnicity and the appropriation of the 'scarce resources', into his pockets.[5]

Political Parties and the Masses

Six legal political parties existed during the Second Republic: the National Party of Nigeria (NPN), Unity Party of Nigeria (UPN), People's Redemption

Party (PRP), Great Nigeria People's Party (GNPP), Nigeria People's Party (NPP) and the Nigeria Advance Party (NAP), which was the last to be registered but not until after the 1979 elections.

The National Party of Nigeria

The NPN emerged as a reincarnation of the old NPC (Northern People's Congress).[6] The party set out to pursue six aims based on social justice and social welfare, equality of opportunity for all the citizens, personal liberty and fundamental rights and freedom of the citizens, supremacy of the will of the people democratically expressed, self-respect and self-reliance and the unity of Nigeria. These aims were elegantly stated as follows:

> to maintain and protect the unity and sovereignty of Nigeria as one indivisible political entity; to promote unity, solidarity, harmonious co-existence amongst all Nigerians irrespective of their religious, tribal and other differences; to uphold federalism as a form of government for Nigeria; to ensure the practice and maintenance of democracy, the rule of law and social justice in the Federal Republic of Nigeria; to promote mutual respect for the understanding of the religions, cultures, traditions and heritage of all the various communities of Nigeria; to preserve, promote and safeguard Nigerian cultural heritage; to eradicate illiteracy and promote learning, science and culture; to achieve and consolidate real political and economic independence and self respect of Nigeria; to build and sustain a strong, modern economy under the control of Nigerians; to promote the principal of equal opportunity and treatment for every citizen of Nigeria; to co-operate with progressive African and other Nationalist movements and organizations working for the eradication of colonialism, imperialism, neocolonialism and racism from the African Continent; to co-operate with all members of the OAU and UNO and any regional groupings that shall be in the best interest of Nigeria; and help to find just and peaceful settlements of international problems

and finally to undertake other activities which in the opinion of the party are conducive to the attainment of the aims and objectives of the party.[7]

Of all these programmes, the NPN emphasized three as the most urgent and crucial: provision of shelter, of food and of qualitative education. It promised to transform the country in five years, especially in respect of the three programmes.

The party believed very strongly in capitalism. It seems to have recognized the problems posed by the revolutionary demands of the masses, and this partly explains its programmes and proposals highlighted above. The programmes, however, were nothing more than an attempt to arrest a crisis situation posed by the genuine demands made by the masses. As such, they were reformists, with the sole intent of preventing a revolution and encouraging instead gradual changes in line with the constitution and the ruling class-oriented economic arrangement. The NPN's reformist manifesto was crudely bourgeois since it was deliberately intended to perpetuate the supremacy of a ruling, wealthy class and the relations of power between the oppressed and the oppressors. The NPN advocated a *laissez-faire* capitalism, and strongly maintained that capitalism could work in the country if the state could get less and less involved in the economy. This was why prominent members of the party were strongly opposed to state control, management and ownership of companies such as the Airways, the Railways, National Electric Power Authority, Shipping, etc. They indeed succeeded in putting pressure on the government to sell some of these enterprises to private citizens. But they were not opposed to a mixed economy: the state should be able to allocate funds to productive sectors, especially the financial institutions which would then provide liberal loans to enterprising individuals, provide subsidized services and take other measures to lay a solid foundation for private capitalism. The state should participate in certain unprofitable institutions (e.g. running schools, universities, hospitals) but these should be forced to organize profit-making projects to obtain funds to supplement government resources. To avert the shortage of capital and transfer capital, the NPN's liberal reformist programme warned against indigenization, except of small-scale enterprises, and maintained an open-door policy to foreign investment.

The NPN's reformism also had its political dimension to strengthen the economic philosophy. Freedom and democracy must be restricted in order to create a political climate conducive to the appropriation of capital and reforms to promote and stabilize dictatorship. The centre should be for all ethnic notables a forum for sharing wealth and resources whilst the states should be for those who could not get to the centre. Political stability was considered necessary to legitimize the regime and cling to power. Indeed, the NPN regarded stability as the hall mark of its achievements.[8]

To understand the NPN's view, it is important to know that the party was a coalition of buccaneer capitalists and feudal elements 'bent on boosting their declining influence by economic power and the feudalization of modern institutions'.[9] All the members believed in primitive accumulation, making wealth not from productive activities but from politics. Its leading members were contractors, businessmen (some without any tangible business or even offices) discredited citizens, etc. The members' loyalty was not to the people but to their pockets. Given the propensity of its members to loot and their commitment to reckless spending, the party could not even undertake the minimum of positive changes; contrary to its promises, there were neither food, shelter nor qualitative education. And as pointed out in chapters 5, 6 and 7, the NPN which controlled the federal government throughout the Second Republic gave the country neither economic nor political development but huge debts, intensified dependence on foreign powers, inflation, hunger, misery and unemployment.

The NPN's vaunted success of establishing national unity and creating the most national party deserves more comments since it brings into focus the strategy of the party for controlling wealth and power. The ideology of the party is clear enough: a nation should first be forged before creating conditions for justice, fair play and equality. In other words, the country must undergo first a 'horizontal integration' before 'vertical levelling'.[10] There is no evidence to suggest that the members of the party had no knowledge of the differences between national integration and social democratization. It, however, deliberately rejected this dichotomy since it accords with the liberal socio-political theory of national integration of first integrating the rich and the powerful in different communities and not the poor and the powerless who should be manipulated for specific ends. If 'social levelling' is to succeed integration, it stands to reason that only the powerful and the wealthy were to be involved as leaders, opinion-moulders, vanguards and representatives of their communities. Thus, the party's slogan of 'One Nation, One Destiny, One God' was only for the notables and not for everybody.

The main instrument of this integration was through zoning, which the party's constitution vaguely defined as a 'convention in recognition of the need for adequate geographical spread'. The country was zoned into four: (a) the north, (b) the west, (c) the east and (d) the minorities. The following offices at the national level were to be zoned: chairman of the party, president, vice-president, president and deputy president of the senate, speaker and deputy speaker of the House of Representatives, Senate leader and the majority leader in the House of Representatives. In the states, the offices to be zoned were those of chairman, governor, deputy governor, state secretary, speaker, deputy speaker and majority or minority leader in the assembly.

The party believed that zoning had two advantages. First, it would make it possible for each zone to present a candidate for the presidency. Second, every zone would participate at the highest level of decision-making. In keeping with the zoning arrangement, the presidency went to the north, the vice-presidency to the east, the national chairmanship to the west and the presidency of the senate to the minority areas.

In spite of this arrangement, the party could still not integrate successfully all the notables within its rank. It drew more notables (the propertied class) than all the other five parties. But the aim of these notables, as pointed out earlier, was not to forge any unity but to have access to power and wealth. Those among them who wanted strategic offices and big contracts had to engage in protracted and bitter struggles, conflicts and competition which clearly demonstrated their primary intention. The major dispute from 1979 to 1983 centred on which fraction of the party (a fraction or faction was regarded by the party as a zone, each representing an ethnic grouping) obtained specific contracts, posts and the highest office—the presidency. As each faction or fraction defended its interests, it at the same time exposed the corruption, the weaknesses and the strength of the others.

But the specific role of each zone was not even made clear to all members. To most people outside of the party, and even to some within it, zoning was a grandiose strategy of the conservative faction from the north to retain political dominance. It was mainly for this reason that Chief M.K.O. Abiola, the president of ITT in Africa and the proprietor of the influential Concord group of newspapers opted out of the party late in 1982. Before then he was a vice-chairman of the party and the leading member in Ogun state. Abiola later revealed that major decisions in the party were taken by the Hausa-Fulani oligarchy which, in addition, regarded the party as a company and itself as the board of directors.[11] The pronouncements of the hegemonic faction from the north (zone A) tended to have confirmed Abiola's view. Both Dan Musa, the speaker of the Kaduna State House of Assembly and Umaru Dikko, the ubiquitous minister and Shagari's right-hand man, said on several occasions that the zone B faction (that is, the Yoruba) could not produce a presidential candidate since it could not deliver votes for the party in 1979.[12] Analysts have in fact suggested that the massive rigging in Oyo and Ondo states during the 1983 elections was to create the impression of the party's strong base in zone B and the ability to deliver votes. The hegemonic fractions in zones C and D (the Igbo and the minorities in Bendel, Rivers and Cross River) also made claims to the presidency and warned their counterparts in zone B that the struggle for the post was not a simple matter of alphabetical rotation from A to B and later to C and D. The ethnic notables in zones C and D, notably Alex Ekwueme, the Vice-President, and Joseph Waya, the Senate President, were equally ambitious. While the rankling animosities continued between the southern representatives, those in the north also gave hints that nothing in the party's constitution excluded them from any office, that zoining was meant only for the 1979 elections, and that it was better to present a candidate who had a strong base instead of talking of rotation. In November 1982, Alhaji Takuma, the party's chief scribe, openly announced the renunciation of the zoning principle as contained in Article 21 of the party's constitution.

These contests and wranglings, or what the editor of the *Nigerian Democratic Review* calls ideological spasms,[13] clearly demonstrated that the party's 'historic mission' of creating a one Nigeria was merely a slogan to deceive and obscure the real intention of using ethnicity to corner fat contracts and secure sinecure positions.

The Nigeria People's Party
The NPP was a faction of an earlier NPP which broke up when Ibrahim Waziri pulled out to form the GNPP. Its predecessor was the NCNC (National Council of Nigerian Citizens) and its base was in Igbo-speaking areas, to allow the Igbo ruling class to bargain with its colleagues in other parts for its share of the national wealth. The party promised to modernize the country by effecting programmes which would:

(a) Fight relentlessly against poverty, disease, ignorance, intolerance, indiscipline, feudalism, racism, neo-colonialism and unjust exploitation of man by man;
(b) achieve full employment of the country's manpower and natural resources in order to build a self-reliant economy;

(c) mobilize the rural population for effective participation in the development process and the incorporation of the urban working class more and more in the management process, and

(d) enshrine democracy, freedom and equality and respect for human dignity.[14]

The above programmes attempted to combine radical slogans (anti-feudalism, anti-exploitation, anti-racism and anti-colonialism) with humanist rhetoric (anti-poverty, anti-disease, anti-ignorance). But it is difficult to take the NPP seriously, mainly because of its commitment to welfarism as a strategy of development. Its definition of welfarism was not different from that of the NPN described above. The party accepted the economic status quo and believed that it should be made more efficient, which should simply be interpreted to mean that the ruling class should be very clever in its exploitation. Welfarism in Nigeria has always encouraged nepotism and unjust socio-economic relations. The party's promise of effective participation in development and incorporation into the management process did not in any way threaten capitalism since what it intended was that the workers would be co-opted into running enterprises. But the profits will go to the foreign and indigenous entrepreneurs.

The party's commitment to this backward socio-economic base was due to the fact that its members throve on 'commerce, contracts and political access'. As Ake rightly observed, it was a party of the lower bourgeoisie:

> a sub-class foot-loose in search of opportunity, the NPP is not noted for strong passions or ideological purity, and its loyalty is fitful. The NPP wants a share of federal power somehow because political power is a critical part of the economic base of its leaders. Also because the NPP fears that it would be quickly dissipated as a political force if it remains out of office.[15]

The party controlled three states — Anambra, Imo and Plateau — from 1979 to 1983, though it lost Anambra to the NPN in the shoddy elections of 1983. All three states were badly governed — the party could not combat ignorance, eradicate inequality and disease. The *Socialist Forum* of July, 1983 pointed out five aspects of NPP's failure:

(a) International capitalist companies dominated the economy of the NPP states, just like all other states in Nigeria. There was no movement towards workers' participation in capitalism;

(b) NPP-controlled governments were basically anti-working class. The attempts by the Plateau state government to impose an unpopular union on Plateau Water Board workers are well known. The Plateau state government condoned the retrenchment of workers in the mining companies. The Nigerian Cement Factory, Anambra and the Mercedes assembly plant in Anambra, in which the Anambra State Government has shares, were involved in the retrenchment wave. So was Niger Steel, Enugu;

(c) In education, neither the Anambra nor the Imo State Government provided decent education at the lower levels, yet each government established a prestigious state university. The biggest assault on Nigerian teachers was dealt by Governor Mbakwe in June 1982 when he sacked all 45,000 teachers who had gone on strike over salaries and other demands. While the NPP programme promised self-reliance, both the Imo and Anambra state governments expressed eagerness to hand back to private ownership schools previously owned by religious organizations and private individuals. NPP-ruled states were first among states which borrowed directly from outside.

(d) In foreign policy, the NPP was pro-zionist and operated within the assumption that Nigeria is a 'natural' ally of the capitalist powers. This is as it should be, given the capitalist domination of Nigeria.[16]

On the basis of the above, the *Socialist Forum* concluded, *inter alia*:

Our suspicion is that the NPP has no strong commitment to particular reformist programmes and that what policy the party will pursue at any given time will depend upon the calculations by its leaders of the most profitable course — most profitable for the class that controls the party.[17]

The Great Nigeria People's Party

The GNPP, anchoring its campaign on a rather impressionistic slogan of 'politics without bitterness' promised to promote national unity, build a dynamic economy, and to ensure better living standards for all Nigerians irrespective of age, religion or ethnic group. It also promised a dynamic foreign policy and the involvement of the masses in all aspects of national development.[18]

The GNPP achieved none of these objectives in the two states (Borno and Gongola) which it controlled for four years. Indeed, the party grounded education to a halt in the two states, provided poor medical services and sacked several workers. The GNPP could not have performed better; it was essentially like the NPN except in name. In fact, a major reason for its establishment was conflicts between the Kanuri and Fulani/Hausa ruling aristocracies. The party could not articulate its ideology of mixed economy. Rather, it preached a gospel of 'politics without bitterness' to the point of boredom. Alhaji Waziri Ibrahim, the party leader, equated politics with business — the profit was too important to be lost by bitter rivalries and enmity. He even said that he was qualified to rule the country because he was the first Nigerian to be a UAC manager and was able to control ten white subordinates. He in fact treated the party as a business venture in which he was the sole entrepreneur, hiring and firing his workers (i.e. other politicians) and distributing his largesse to his favourites. He tolerated no opposition and often confused honest suggestions to which he was opposed as evidence of rudeness and indiscipline. His dictatorial tendencies boomeranged as most of his followers, including legislators and the two Governors, later abandoned him to join either the NPP, UPN or NPN.

The Nigeria Advance Party

The NAP was never at any time a serious party, in spite of its manifesto — which was heavily loaded with socialist jargon and populist rhetoric — such as 'freedom from exploitation', 'eradication of unemployment', 'agricultural revolution', 'scientific and technological revolution', 'revolutionary education', etc. The party was launched on Thursday, 28 September 1978 and it lost its credibility that same week because it saw the eradication of mosquitoes as one of its urgent priorities, at a time when the other parties were exploiting the masses' demand for food and education. It was not registered for the 1979 elections. Its leader, Tunji Braithwaite, the wealthy Lagos contractor and businessman, continued to struggle for recognition until it was registered for the 1983 elections. Its registration had the strong backing of the NPN which believed it could constitute a nuisance to the UPN in the Yoruba states. The NAP, however, constituted only a nuisance to itself: it evolved no definite character, lacked any vision and failed to mobilize the youths which it thought it could easily appeal to by its rhetoric, fine symbol and the cowboy dressing habits of its leader. The party failed woefully to articulate its views, and its representatives even found it extremely difficult to define its brand of socialism. To deal with multinationals, mobilize the working class and provide essential services the party would convert the country into a secular-cum-religious state: 'take the nation back to God programme is the answer to national paralysis, spiritual decay, callousness and bloodshed'. In other words, the party believed that the country had problems because it ignored God. The 1983 elections in which the party did not win a single seat throughout the federation should have convinced it that God has nothing to do with Nigerian politics, despite its flirtations with Him.

The two other parties — the UPN and the PRP — were the loudest in shouting socialism, change and revolution. It is necessary to consider both parties separately because of the mistake of confusing both as the same and thus misunderstanding what they both stood for and the interests they protected.

The Unity Party of Nigeria

The UPN emerged from the ashes of the old Action Group of Western Nigeria, and drew its support essentially from the Yoruba-speaking areas and the Bendel State. From its inception to the end, the UPN represented the interests of the Yoruba faction of the Nigerian bourgeoisie. Several prominent Yoruba teachers, lecturers, professionals, land speculators, businessmen, contractors, agents of multinational companies and many others of dubious character but with substantial wealth and connections belonged to the party. Its leader, Chief Obafemi Awolowo, was himself a distinguished lawyer, a businessman, estate agent, dealer, etc. He is a millionaire but always pretends that money is not important to him though he has a network of business ventures, and has never ceased to accumulate more since the 1950s. His political philosophy deliberately ignores the relationship between extensive accumulation and meaningful social change.

The UPN was officially launched on 22 September 1978 in Lagos. Its manifesto[19] contained four cardinal programmes:

(a) Free education at all levels for all, with effect from October 1, 1979;
(b) Integrated rural development which is aimed at boosting food production and feeding 60 million hungry citizens of this country;
(c) The provision of free health facilities for all citizens of Nigeria, and
(d) Full employment.

The manifesto which contained other programmes as well is a very poor analysis of Nigeria's political economy. The party stressed the ideology of modernisation:

> The real bane of the underdeveloped countries of the world and the source of most of all their political and social instability are to be found essentially in the failure of their governments to deliver the economic and social goods that fulfill the promises of independence. We of the Unity Party of Nigeria, therefore, have decided to reorder and modernise the economy.[20]

The party talked or re-ordering and not of revolutionizing the economy. For this re-ordering, the party planned to adopt socialism, but its leader quickly hinted in 1978 that this was not an immediate goal:

> no one nation ever attains a worthwhile goal designed for the benefit of the entire people in one fell swoop without courting irreparable or prolonged disaster for the people concerned. Indeed any attempt to attain the goal of socialism in one frantic leap is bound to generate widespread alarm, social upheaval and distress and attendant violence.[21]

It was impossible for the UPN to plan any revolution or take immediate steps towards socialism because its membership was dominated by a bourgeoisie with a firm base in industry and commerce. Its bourgeoisie was, however, more enlightened and more efficient than that of the NPN. In addition, unlike the others, it understood the need for defensive radicalism, especially radical sloganeering, productive capitalism, discipline and efficiency. But these strong points made it a much more dangerous party than the others, since it was deeply entrenched in capitalist production (like the others) but more efficient and adroit in the defence of capitalism (unlike the others).

A critique of its manifesto and its performance in the five states which it governed would serve to advance the above argument. The party emphasized education but it seems to have believed that this meant the creation of more schools and universities to absorb more and more students. The party ignored the content and quality. of education, and the conditions of study and learning. In Lagos, Oyo, Ogun, Bendel and Ondo states which the party controlled, education deteriorated rapidly as teachers were not regularly paid (especially in Ondo and Bendel) and as facilities for learning became poor or non-existent. Most primary schools had insufficient chairs and desks, most secondary schools had no laboratories and most university students were denied their bursary allowances. Subsidized hostels, boarding-houses and catering were cancelled. In the bid to search for money to run the schools, the UPN ignored other essential services and indirectly transferred the cost of education to parents and teachers. By cancelling subsidized catering, the parents had to provide more money; by not paying the teachers, they had to bear with poor conditions of living; and by providing poor education, the potentials of youths were underdeveloped or distorted.

Its execution of its free health programme was worse than that of education, worse to such an extent that party leaders had to ignore local hospitals and go to Britain for medical care. Hospitals were always short of drugs and equipment and simple things such as benches. The hospitals became so congested that patients needed about eight hours to see a doctor and receive their drugs if they were at all available.

The programme on full employment remained on paper. Rather than fulfil this, the UPN-controlled states were involved in the retrenchment of workers and defaulted on the payment of salaries. For instance, in 1982 the Ogun State government cancelled most of the fringe benefits and attempted to reduce the salaries of workers by 50%. The Governor even went to the extent of saying that his workers were very comfortable and earned more than they thought because of the several free services which they enjoyed. Unfortunately, 1982 was a most difficult year for the working class because of inflation and scarcity of goods. In Bendel and Ondo, workers generally had a three-month salary arrears. Only a few lucky workers were able to secure vehicle loans while car and motor-bicycle allowances and leave bonuses were not paid.

All the other 'modernization programmes' were poorly implemented and badly conceived. The party noted, like the others, that the country's agriculture is archaic and the industries are backward. To solve these two problems, the party hoped to embark on a programme of 'integrated rural development' and 'Nigerian industrial revolution'. On the first, the party and its representatives found it difficult to explain what they meant, and simply left it in the books. On the second, the party believed that technology transfer would be an effective answer.

The party, however, assigned very little role to the people in its modernization programme, except, of course, that the economy would be controlled by a few indigenous entrepreneurs and international capital:

> We wholeheartedly support the objectives of the indigenization of the national economy. We shall evolve policies that will aid Nigerian entrepreneurs to feel more confident about investing their resources and energies in the area of industrialization. But we will also actively encourage foreign capital investment in those areas of industrialization which immediately require the more sophisticated production processes, and managerial and technical skills.[22]

The above position was not peculiar to the UPN but was that of all political parties in most African states which believe that their bourgeoisie should play a subservient role in the international division of labour and the system of international capitalism

On the whole, the UPN was a backward, liberal reformist party with bourgeois ideas, narrow vision and ideals. Like all reformist parties, it had too much concern for resolving the contradictions among the ruling classes, especially in creating a good atmosphere for the power-sharing arrangement and also in taking care of the interests of the contractors, businessmen and other big capitalists. But the party also believed in resolving the contradictions between the working class and the ruling class. It considered the programmes of the other parties as inadequate in solving the problems of the poverty of the masses, and unless more concessions were granted to the people, the political economy would be unstable. But the UPN wanted this stability in order to retain the neocolonial status quo and *laissez-faire* capitalism. The UPN tended to have reached the conclusion that inadequate provision of educational and social services would constitute a major obstacle to the development of efficient capitalism in Nigeria. Consequently, the gap between the rich and the poor should be bridged to some extent or prevented from widening. The UPN believed that its four cardinal programmes would redress the imbalance between the poor and the rich. It was primarily on the basis of this belief that the ideologists of the party argued that the UPN was a socialist, anti-capitalist party. As we pointed out above, in theoretical perspective and practice, there was nothing to suggest that the party was anti-capitalism or in fact different from the other reformist parties. The theoretical underpinnings of the party's programme are contained in Chief Obafemi Awolowo's three books — *The People's Republic, The Strategy and Tactics of the People's Republic* and *Thoughts on Nigerian Constitution,*[23] — all of which are radically apologetic and extremely bourgeois in perspective. The Chief intelligently applied capitalist economics, taking note of its defects as propounded by Keynes, and British constitutional law to the Nigerian situation. He also attempted to integrate Christian ethics into his thoughts. The Chief extremely underplayed the impact of imperialism, neocolonialism and the comprador nature of the Nigerian bourgeoisie. While he recognized different classes, he failed to build this into his political model; rather, he believed in a federal integration of ethnic groups, and like the

NPN, of their notables.

His disciples were more noise-makers than scholars. While the Chief could be very painstaking in his analysis, thorough in his presentation and honest in his articulation, most of his disciples were very much unversed in political and economic thought and usually resorted to abuse in their defence of socialism. Perhaps, the most formidable book to emanate from his disciples is *Awoism* [24] written by Chief Akin Omoboriowo, the Deputy Governor of Ondo State, who found it too easy to defect to the NPN when he lost the bid to contest for the governorship election on the platform of the UPN. According to Omoboriowo, Awoism rejects Marxism, class struggle, dialectical materialism and atheism. Awoism does not believe in violence and bloodshed to establish a new socialist order; rather it believes in peaceful, gradual processes. These are the revisionist views of pro-capitalists rather than of the left, even of the most confused. Awoism has very little to do with socialism but much with welfare reformism.

It was precisely the intellectualism enunciated in *Awoism* that influenced the practice of the UPN governments. Like the NPN states, the UPN-controlled states relied on the centre for funds and adopted similar techniques of resource mobilization, modes of implementing projects, contract system, manipulation of taxes and simple restructuring of expenditure to implement priority projects. The UPN never knew how to mobilize the people for collective production, made not a single attempt to tap the reservoir of under-employed labour of the masses, and also failed to eliminate capitalist bourgeois relations.

Whether in theory or in practice, the UPN's claim to socialism can, therefore, be flawed. The party only fulfilled the historical role of such liberal parties — that of spreading mere palliatives to the masses in order to halt a revolutionary alternative.

The People's Redemption Party
The PRP was an off-shoot of NEPU (Nigerian Elements Progressive Union) founded during the colonial period as a rival party to the NPC and primarily to struggle against the feudal oligarchy of the Northern Region. The Sawaba Declaration of 8 August 1950 by NEPU was perhaps the most ideological document of that era. NEPU was optimistic about a mass-oriented party which it advocated:

> ... at present the Machinery of Government, including the armed forces of the nation exist only to conserve the privilege of this selfish minority group [that is, the ruling elite], The Talakawa [that is, the poor] must organize consciously and politically for the conquest of the powers of Government — both nationally and locally — in order that this machinery of Government, including these forces, may be converted from an instrument of oppression into the agent of emancipation, and the overthrow of bureaucracy and autocratic privilege. [25]

NEPU was later to lose its character but its message had deep roots among the poor intelligentsia and workers, especially in the north. In 1978, the ideals of NEPU were revived by the new PRP. The PRP was the only one to do a thorough historical analysis of the country's problems.

It concluded that the country was moving rapidly towards a society in which individualism, greed for materialism, maximization of profits at all costs, personal acquisition and protection of private property were the goals of public and private activities. These activities, concluded Balarabe Musa, the first PRP governor of Kaduna state and the only one to be impeached during the Second Republic, were

> dominated by a tiny majority of rich and powerful Nigerians with a strong vested interest in maintaining subjugation of the people and resources of our country to the business and strategic interests of the Western capitalist system. This direction our country is heading, is towards the entrenching of what is known as neo-colonialism or dependent capitalism.[26]

On the basis of its analysis on the direction in which the country was moving, the PRP arrived at certain principles, two of which related to the need to struggle to achieve true independence and to re-allocate power relations in favour of the 'common people'. The party believed that:

> if politics is to work out to the good of the people, political power has to be in the hands of the people themselves. For us, peoples [sic] power is not a propaganda gimmick. It is a cardinal concept in political organisation. It proceeds logically from our view that, in the last analysis, the people are the motive power of history . . . . Peoples [sic] political power has to be organised effectively. It requires a set of institutions appropriate to it. It simply cannot make use of the existing state apparatus created by erstwhile ruling elites. Hence peoples power needs a new State — the organs of power (civil service, military, police, judiciary, executive, legislature) have to be so organised as to reflect the will of the people at all levels and at all times.[27]

On national independence, the party held that:

> the enemy of our national independence has been, and remains, western imperialism which now takes the form of neo-colonialism . . . In order to build an independent, balanced, self-sustained and people-oriented national economy, there is the need to . . . get rid of production relations based on exploitation; there is the need to vest control of the commanding heights of the national economy in the State while preserving and encouraging bona fide Nigerian private enterprise; there is the need to guarantee a living income to every citizen.

The party advocated the creation of a People's Democratic State which would vest power in the hands of the people. In the peoples' state envisaged by the PRP, five major principles among others which would govern production stand out:

(a) public ownership of minerals, forest, water and energy;
(b) public ownership and operation of key sectors of the economy, specifically finance and banking, insurance, oil, import/export, capital goods industries;
(c) right to trade unionism, including the right to strike;
(d) worker participation in the management of public enterprises; and
(e) guaranteed maximum 40 hour week, 5-day week, and minimum 3 weeks holidays per annum with full pay.[28]

The PRP also had policies and programmes on health, education, agriculture and other essential services. Radical opinions were expressed on all these. Take agriculture for instance: while the other parties were emphasizing the importation of food and fertilizers, the PRP believed that there would be no 'green revolution' unless the peasant-farmer was made the centre-piece of the agricultural programme. It called for changes in economic and socio-political relations which would make it possible for the peasantry to have:

(a) security that he and his family will benefit fully from the products of his farm and these are not extorted away;
(b) security of tenure of the land of his farm;
(c) guaranteed access to agricultural inputs at fair prices, in good time and without any debt burden;
(d) guaranteed prices for his products against price fluctuations caused by hoarding and other forms of profiteering;
(e) guaranteed access to seasonal, and longer-term credit at low interest rates and not involving any additional social and political burdens;
(f) mass literacy and numeracy for himself and all the adults in the household to enable them to improve their knowledge of farming, commerce, finance and know-how to defend his rights and those of others.

None of the other parties had principles as radical as those of the PRP.

The party tried to establish an infrastructure for a new social order in the two states — Kano and Kaduna — which it controlled. Its policies on land, taxation and local government reforms struck blows at power relations and ownership of property. Four of these policies can be examined here as illustrations.

The PRP showed some commitment to democracy by ensuring that as many people as possible participated in the running of government. There were, however, the constraints imposed by the constitution; and the party only had to take those steps considered legal within its framework.

The party provided details of information about its policies. More importantly, it reformed the local government system by dissolving emirate councils and transferring chieftaincy and customary matters to the council of chiefs. New smaller village and city-ward councils were established with officials who were to be democratically elected. The belief was that smaller councils would enable more people to participate in government. Attempts were also made to review and simplify criminal and civil laws and the criminal procedure code in such a way that every literate person would understand them.

The PRP abolished the payment of poll-tax, cattle-tax and income rate for poorly paid workers. It believed that these taxes were oppressive. The party did not, however, call for the total abolition of taxation, since it raised more revenue from those with the ability to pay.

On land, it was regarded as a gift of God and private ownership was rejected. Its policy was to treat land as the property of the people who live and work on it.

Finally, the party attempted to establish an industry in every local government area. This was a departure from the previous practice of concentrating industries in urban areas. These industries were intended to make use of locally available raw materials and to produce goods for an internal, domestic market. In addition, private individuals were not allowed to control the industries, but only the state government, local governments and workers' co-operatives.

The PRP could not, however, implement its policies for two main reasons, while its manifesto also had serious theoretical and ideological limitations. The first had to do with the powers of its opponents, reactionary elements in the two states and in the other parties, especially the NPN. To the northern aristocracy (emirs, chiefs and others who, though wealthy, rely largely on tradition and 'history' to reproduce their power and accumulative base), the PRP was a threat. Its manifesto and policies in the first two years hit very hard at the interests of the northern bourgeoisie (which includes some members of the aristocracy but also the intelligentsia, the so-called 'Kaduna Mafia', the younger businessmen and top bureaucrats) especially in chieftaincy matters, land and contracts. The aristocracy quickly resisted and decided to liquidate the party in its infancy. The PRP's leadership was infiltrated, and it was too easy to convert men such as S.G. Ikoku, the Secretary, into the NPN, to render Malam Aminu Kano, the party leader, impotent in his hold over the party, and in criticizing the federal government and to impeach Balarabe Musa, the more fanatical and ideologically committed of the two governors.

The second reason is a corollary of the first — the emergence of various factions within the party eroded its credibility and it also lost its direction. The party was perhaps the most unstable of all the parties throughout the Second Republic. By early 1983, it had at least four factions, each struggling for hegemony. The first was the most radical group which aimed at executing the party's programmes as spelt out in 1979. It saw the party as 'the vanguard of the broad masses of the people under the leadership of peasants and workers' and articulated four non-negotiable principles:

(a) the need for a proletarian state in Nigeria free from all forms of oppression and exploitation;
(b) the existence of private enterprise as a temporary necessity to be phased out after a reasonable transitional period;
(c) the liberation of women; and
(d) the liberation and unity of Africa, an anti-colonial, anti-apartheid and anti-zionist foreign policy

While this first group had ideas, it lacked finance, especially when Balarabe Musa, one of its chief spokesmen, had lost power. And without finance, it lacked the capability to organize, recruit more members and deal with its opponents. Indeed, it could not participate in the 1983 elections since its faction was not recognized by the FEDECO.

A second group, led by S.G. Ikoku, preferred conservative policies and favoured an alliance with the NPN. The group believed that the time was not ripe for socialism and that what any party should aim at was to create an efficient capitalism. S.G. Ikoku had in fact maintained this position long before the establishment of the PRP. For instance in 1975, he wrote that:

> While not denying the existence of classes in African society (some nascent, others moribund and yet others adolescent), I nonetheless doubt the relevance of bourgeois/proletariat class war in African politics. It can directly involve only a small section of the people; and it runs counter to African psychology and social organisation.[29]

Ikoku did not recognize class conflicts and the contradiction between the bourgeoisie and the oppressed. And since that contradiction is absent, he regarded a socialist struggle as irrelevant. The PRP radical group, on the other hand, anchored its principles on class struggle:

> Two great forces face each other, and are locked in a grim struggle for survival and ascendancy. On the one side, the forces of privilege. These are the conservatives, because their political stand is to protect, retain and sustain the existing social order. On the other side, the forces of the people are determined to replace the existing social order that harbours so much hardship and frustration for them, with a new social order in which there will be equality, liberty, freedom from want and justice. These are the progressives.[30]

Ikoku only recognized the struggle between the Nigerian people and neo-colonialism:

The African reality is very different from Western European society in the mid or late 19th century. The motive force of African politics is the conflict between neo-colonialism and the people in the grips of revolution in expectation.[31]

From Ikoku's exposition, the conclusion that can be drawn is that the country is still at the stage of a national bourgeois revolution where the primary task is to build a nation-state and liberate the people from imperialism. Since this task does not need any class war, it can be done within the existing administrative and electoral arrangements. Acting on this belief, Ikoku found it easy to identify with any political party, since all of them talked of self-reliance, and it was not difficult for him to quickly forget all his ideological jargon to join the thoroughly discredited NPN before the 1983 elections. Thereafter, he became one of the principal agents used to blackmail his former colleagues.

The third group was led by the late Aminu Kano. It advocated a government of national unity based on a political compromise among all political parties. This suggestion was never taken seriously by any of the rival parties.

The last group was led by Abubakar Rimi, the governor of Kano state who was not radical enough to join the first group, and both anti-NPN and anti-Aminu.

The ideological limitations of the PRP, especially in its early years when it had not been plagued with factionalism, had to do with its commitment to social democratic reformism which is based on the belief that existing legal and constitutional systems could be used to effect radical changes and, if possible, re-organize the structure of power. Contrary to the party's rhetoric, it was not well prepared for any socialist struggle. For instance, the party never had a mass base, and this made it easy for its opponents to attack it in its attempt to open up class struggle for structural changes. The faith of the party in the state and consititution was also misplaced since it underrated the power of the established bourgeoisie and ignored the fact that it is difficult to liberate a people from oppression, feudalism and imperialism by a gradual, constitutional peaceful process.

The foregoing review of the country's political parties has shown that the parties had much more in common, including their objectives. Most of the parties were re-incarnations of those of the first Republic. The actors were also the same. The politicians were too committed to making money to the detriment of the nation and the masses, and to sharing power, to the detriment of stability, democracy and progress. We are in complete agreement with Usman's view that:

> To be frank, it is difficult to see how some of these dumb robots who defend vested interests almost by reflex, can play any 'politics' beyond the usual back room intrigue, horsetrading and public posturing in pompous dress. But then they would probably say, that is 'politics'.[32]

The 1979 Elections and the Struggle for Power

The schedule of elections was as follows: (a) 7 July 1979 – Senate; (b) 14 July 1979 – House of Representatives; (c) 21 July 1979 – State Houses of Assembly; (d) 28 July 1979 – election of governors; (e) 4 August 1979 – run-off for gubernatorial elections, if any became necessary; and (f) 11 August 1979 – presidential election.

All the five parties campaigned vigorously for these elections. Four features characterized these campaigns. First, promises were not limited to what were contained in the manifestos; but to everything which the parties believed the people wanted to hear. Consequently, the parties said almost the same thing, and failed to assume distinct characters on the basis of their programmes. Second, ethnicity and religion were manipulated to seek support, such that the parties were quickly identified with certain regions – UPN with the Yoruba, NPP with the Igbo, NPN with the Hausa and Fulani, GNPP with the Kanuri and PRP with the Hausa. Third, the parties tried to bribe the electorate with money. People were paid to attend rallies, shout party slogans and even to vote. Finally, there was sporadic violence in the attempt to win voters. The military, however, prevented the outbreak of any serious crisis. There was a Public Order Decree to regulate public assemblies and procession. In addition General Obasanjo held a meeting with the presidential candidates and requested their support in organizing peaceful elections while he also threatened to deal ruthlessly with anybody who disturbed public peace.

The first election to the Senate was not, however, free of protests, allegations, counter-allegations and charges. Among the major complaints were that: several centres were short of ballot papers; Fedeco officials favoured a certain political party, denied many centres ballot boxes, allowed multiple voting, and failed to seal boxes in the presence of all party representatives. Other problems of the elections were either attributed to Fedeco's incompetence or partiality towards the NPN.

The NPN led the Senate elections with 36 seats, followed by UPN's 28. Others were: NPP 16, GNPP 8 and PRP 7 (see Table 4.1). This pattern did not change in the results of the elections to the House of Representatives as the NPN still led, having won 168 seats to UPN 111, NPP 78, GNPP 43 and PRP 49 (see Table 4.2).

These first two results showed that none of the parties had an absolute majority in the National Assembly and also gave the hint that the presidential election could be inconclusive, thus warning that there would be an electoral college to make a final choice. This pattern of election results intensified the struggle for power. The NPN became a threat to the other parties. While the NPN's strategy was to evolve the means to secure additional votes, the other parties tried to stop it from winning the presidency. Chief Awolowo and Alhaji Waziri formed the nucleus of a 'progressive alliance' to fight 'the forces of reaction'. Late in July, they called a press conference in which they alleged that the NPN owed its lead to election malpractices in collaboration with

Table 4.1:
Election Results for Senate

States	GNPP	UPN	NPN	PRP	NPP
Anambra	12,832	10,932	210,101	19,574	699,157
Bauchi	188,819	28,959	323,392	127,279	39,868
Bendel	38,332	316,511	650,194	2,055	80,639
Benue	46,452	14,769	832,967	–	75,523
Borno	278,352	22,145	184,633	31,508	–
Cross River	161,353	77,479	310,071	–	68,203
Gongola	223,121	124,707	203,226	30,708	17,830
Imo	101,184	7,553	145,507	8,609	750,518
Kaduna	33,824	85,094	410,883	278,305	61,807
Kano	35,430	13,831	233,985	683,367	–
Kwara	32,383	126,065	54,282	328	1,020
Lagos	14,480	428,573	35,730	2,556	52,738
Niger	71,498	13,860	175,597	8,139	207
Ogun	1,018	230,411	31,953	–	119
Ondo	4,905	501,522	49,612	–	6,417
Oyo	9,472	758,696	200,372	2,497	4,397
Plateau	41,287	20,024	154,792	19,017	220,278
Rivers	46,985	20,106	153,454	30	86,138
Sokoto	910,310	34,145	571,562	98,305	–
Total seats	8	28	36	7	16
%	8.4%	29.5%	37.9%	7.3%	16.9%

Fedeco officials.[33] To forestall the NPN, the 'progressives' called for the collaboration of the other parties, and suggested that they should all close ranks and support Awolowo as the only candidate. The alliance met with an instant failure, as both the NPP and PRP presidential candidates denied being a party to it. Both Azikiwe and Kano still had a grudge against Awolowo who had supported Fedeco in the attempt to disqualify them on the grounds that they were tax defaulters.[34] Both, however, challenged Fedeco's decision in the courts and won the cases. All the registered candidates intensified their campaigns and worked out further strategies to win. While no more steps were taken to realize the objectives of the alliance, the members still nursed the hope that the presidential elections would not produce any successful candidate, and they would then vote for Awolowo, whose party was second to the NPN in performance, at the electoral college. But Chief Awolowo still reckoned that it would be in his best interest to work with the other parties and pretend as if their coldness towards the idea of an alliance was not a sufficient obstacle. On 24 July, the UPN issued directives to its state branches on a new formula for the gubernatorial election. The UPN supporters in Kano and Kaduna states were directed to

Table 4.2
Election Results for House of Representatives

States	Registered voters	Total votes cast	Per cent	GNPP	UPN	NPN	PRP	NPP
Anambra	2,606,663	1,108,771	43	33,944	18,535	253,979	14,954	787,359
Bauchi	2,096,162	807,210	39	196,967	27,049	481,581	68,531	33,082
Bendel	2,400,174	780,163	33	30,420	371,033	303,882	2,167	72,661
Benue	1,636,371	513,359	31	59,538	13,728	353,551	6,971	79,571
Borno	2,945,925	736,327	25	390,365	31,558	260,762	46,202	7,440
Cross River	2,464,184	729,667	30	157,975	94,443	388,354	3,066	85,829
Gongola	2,308,355	668,381	29	237,548	142,326	231,126	29,973	27,408
Imo	3,490,484	1,162,689	33	103,993	16,585	223,456	14,128	804,254
Kabuna	3,455,047	1,256,780	36	253,536	87,947	497,931	362,001	55,365
Kano	5,226,598	1,045,154	20	26,378	10,804	235,489	772,483	–
Kwara	1,108,029	340,692	31	33,024	138,359	167,737	841	731
Lagos	1,829,369	595,149	33	5,703	528,629	56,559	3,186	1,072
Niger	1,051,160	299,712	29	60,597	13,003	212,944	9,900	3,268
Ogun	1,663,608	612,454	37	1,841	557,316	53,297	–	–
Ondo	2,573,960	824,759	32	2,569	755,696	55,688	1,008	9,798
Oyo	4,534,779	1,011,233	22	10,579	790,580	199,972	3,090	7,012
Plateau	1,748,868	584,167	33	53,329	22,693	190,562	18,447	299,136
Rivers	1,675,934	491,264	29	56,480	25,542	287,575	4,374	117,293
Sokoto	3,818,094	1,250,647	33	455,268	25,727	748,262	21,390	–
Total	48,633,782	14,818,578	30	2,170,054	3,671,553	5,202,707	1,382,712	2,391,279

vote for the PRP; those in Anambra, Imo and Plateau for the NPP, those in Bauchi, Borno, Cross River, Gongola, Niger, Rivers and Sokoto for the GNPP, while those in Ogun, Lagos, Oyo, Kwara, Benue and Bendel were to vote for the UPN.[35] The GNPP reciprocated the second day by instructing its gubernatorial candidates to withdraw from the race in Lagos, Plateau, Kano, Kwara, Oyo, Bendel, Ondo, Ogun, Imo and Anambra states. Fedeco, however, did not support these withdrawals on the ground that they should have been made four days before the election. And except in Kaduna state where the PRP won, contrary to expectation, the voting pattern did not change. It has also been suggested that the withdrawal would make it possible for the GNPP to win in Gongola. While this is controversial, the alliance between the UPN and the GNPP made it possible for the State Assembly made up largely of both parties to work together, and also strengthened the relationship between Awolowo and Waziri between 1979 and 1982.

The military found this new development unsettling, and tended to view the alliance with suspicion. It could not proscribe the alliance since it would give credence to the widespread rumour that it wanted to impose the NPN which it believed would continue with its programmes. At the same time, it feared that to allow the alliance to function, and especially for it to wield influence at the electoral college, could lead to disorder and the suspension of the return to civilian rule.

Rather than resolve the crisis, the military abandoned its neutrality and became interested in the presidential elections, and especially in making it possible for a winner to emerge. But earlier in 1978, Obasanjo had given the pledge that the military would remain neutral:

> We all, as members of this administration have no particular or special interest in who succeeds us. We are not interested in partisan politics and we have absolute confidence in the sense of judgement of our people. We will therefore, not tolerate anybody or any group of people using the name or office of any of us to canvass for political support or patronage.[36]

This pledge was only as good as the piece of paper on which it was written. The military did not want a hostile successor or a radical party. The NPN would be an ideal successor since it had its base in the north, comprised notables, was extremely conservative and was also in support of the military's approach to politics and economy.[37]

Fedeco as well lost its partiality; it began to work more closely with the military administration, especially in the interpretation of section 162 (2a and 2b) which is discussed below. Party representatives were kept away from a number of polling stations, and UPN observers who were sent to oversee elections in the northern states where the party suspected that there would be mass rigging were arrested and detained. It was widely believed that the military ordered these arrests and detention.[38]

It was during this period of suspicion, distrust and little faith in the electoral system that the remaining two most crucial elections were held. The results of the gubernatorial elections gave 7 states to the NPN, 5 to the UPN, 3 to the NPP, 2 to the PRP and 2 to the GNPP.[39]

The general expectation before the presidential elections on 11 August was that no party would be able to satisfy section 126, 2(a) and (b) of the constitution which can be repeated here:

A candidate for an election to the office of President shall be deemed to have been duly elected where, there being more than 2 candidates for the election [if]
(a) he has the highest number of votes cast at the election; and
(b) he has not less than one-quarter of the votes cast at the election in each of at least two-thirds of all the States of the Federation.

The results of the elections are shown in Table 4.3. While Shagari satisfied the first requirement by scoring the largest number of votes cast, he failed to fulfil the second. Before 11 August both Fedeco and the military had regarded 13 as the two-thirds of 19; but after the elections, controversy was raised over the meaning of 'one-quarter of the votes cast in each of at least two-thirds of all the States in the Federation'. The military, in collaboration with Fedeco, decided to appoint Shagari as the president, by re-interpreting the meaning of one-quarter of two-thirds of nineteen. The hint of this was dropped to the nation by Chief Richard Akinjide, NPN's legal adviser and later the country's Attorney-General, when he said on 15 August that two-thirds of nineteen states was $12\frac{2}{3}$, and not 13. Fedeco's controversial announcement, made unexpectedly in the afternoon of 15 August by an obscure civil servant, agreed with Akinjide's interpretation:

The Federal Electoral Commission considers that in the absence of any legal explanation or guidance in the electoral decree, it has no alternative than to give the phrase 'at least two-thirds of all the States in the Federation' in section 34a subsection 1(c) (iii) of the electoral decree the ordinary meaning which applies to it. In the circumstances, the candidate who scores at least one-quarter of the votes cast in 12 states and one-quarter of two thirds, that is, at least one sixth of the votes cast in the 13th state satisfies the requirement of the sub-section. Accordingly, Alhaji Shehu Shagari is hereby declared President of the Federal Republic of Nigeria.[40]

This announcement caught non-NPN voters by surprise and all the other political parties were dismayed. The NPP rejected Fedeco's decision, calling it a fraud and also gave the hint that it would 'take whatever constitutional steps it considered right to protect the integrity of this nation and democracy'.[41] The PRP described it as 'outrageous and showed clearly that Shagari was the favoured baby'.[42] The UPN also rejected the result and urged the Federal Military Government to dissociate itself from it.[43]

Table 4.3
Results of the Presidential Election

States	Total votes cast	Waziri Ibrahim GNPP votes	%	O. Awolowo UPN votes	%	S. Shagari NPN votes	%	Aminu Kano PRP votes	%	N. Azikiwe NPP votes	%
Anambra	1,209,039	20,228	1.67	9,063	0.73	163,164	13.50	14,560	1.20	100,083	82.83
Bauchi	998,683	154,215	15.44	29,960	3.00	623,989	62.45	143,202	14.34	47,314	4.72
Bendel	669,511	8,242	1.23	356,381	53.23	242,320	36.19	4,939	0.73	57,629	5.60
Benue	538,879	42,993	7.89	13,864	2.57	411,648	76.37	7,277	1.35	63,077	11.71
Cross River	661,103	100,105	15.14	77,775	11.76	425,815	64.40	6,737	1.01	50,671	7.66
Gongola	639,138	217,914	34.09	138,561	21.67	227,057	35.52	27,750	4.31	27,556	4.35
Borno	710,968	384,278	54.04	23,885	3.35	246,778	34.71	46,385	6.52	9,842	1.35
Imo	1,153,355	34,616	3.00	7,335	0.64	101,516	8.80	10,252	0.89	999,636	86.69
Kaduna	1,382,712	190,936	13.80	92,382	6.68	596,302	43.12	437,771	31.66	65,321	4.71
Kano	1,220,763	18,482	1.54	14,973	1.23	242,423	19.94	932,803	76.41	11,082	0.91
Kwara	354,605	20,251	5.71	140,006	39.48	190,142	53.62	2,376	0.67	1,830	0.52
Lagos	828,414	3,943	0.48	781,762	82.30	59,515	7.18	3,874	0.47	79,320	9.57
Niger	383,347	63,278	11.50	14,155	3.69	287,072	72.88	4,555	3.79	4,282	1.11
Ogun	744,668	3,974	0.53	689,655	92.61	46,358	6.23	2,338	0.31	21,343	0.32
Ondo	1,369,849	3,561	0.26	1,294,666	94.50	57,361	4.19	2,509	0.5	11,752	0.86
Oyo	1,396,547	8,029	0.57	1,197,983	85.78	177,999	12.75	4,804	0.32	7,732	0.55
Plateau	548,405	37,400	6.82	29,029	5.29	190,458	34.73	21,852	3.98	269,666	49.17
Rivers	687,951	15,025	2.18	71,114	10.33	499,846	72.65	3,212	0.46	89,754	2.35
Sokoto	1,348,697	359,021	26.61	34,102	2.52	98,094	66.58	44,977	3.33	12,503	0.92
Total	16,846,633	1,686,489	10.0	4,916,651	29.2	5,688,587	33.8	1,732,113	10.3	2,822,523	16.7

Of all the other presidential candidates, Chief Awolowo was the most bitter. He had tried to head the government of the First Republic but he believed he was robbed of victory. In addition, he was convicted for treasonable felony in 1963 and sentenced to a ten-year imprisonment. This imprisonment, more than anything else, boosted his political image and fortune, and also made him the unquestioned leader of the Yoruba faction of the Nigerian bourgeoisie. He was released from prison by Gowon in 1966 and later appointed Commissioner for Finance and Vice-President of the Federal Executive Council, the highest civilian position in the military administration. After the civil war in 1970 and calculating that the military would soon hand over power, Awolowo resigned from the Gowon cabinet to prepare his strategy for politics. From 1970 to 1979, he was a thorn in the flesh of the military, exposing its misrule in most uncompromising language. In 1975, he was appointed a member of the Constitution Drafting Committee but he refused to participate, on the poor excuse that he was not a constitutional lawyer when in actual fact he had written articles and books on the Nigerian constitution. His refusal to participate in the CDC and in the Constituent Assembly robbed him of the chance to impose his mark on the constitution and to make political allies, especially from the north. He, however, found it necessary to teleguide members of the Constituent Assembly, though about 230 members were later to deny this.[44]

When the ban on politics was lifted, he was the first to launch a political party the following day. His party had several initial advantages: a manifesto had been worked out; a party organization had been established; Awolowo's candidacy for the presidency had been announced and governorship candidates in the nineteen states were also known. While the other parties were engaged in struggles for power, Awolowo embarked on a nation-wide campaign. The programmes of his party were also couched in phrases simple enough for the electorate to understand. He made free education a major campaign issue and was able to force other parties either to agree or argue that it was impossible at the moment. He also had strong credibility to back up the party's manifesto – as the former premier of the Western Region, he had acquired the reputation of not reneging on his promises.

Awolowo had put everything he had into the 1979 elections, and he could not quickly reconcile himself to Shagari's so-called victory as he was later to do in 1983 when even under a situation of massive rigging, he decided to keep silent. He immediately protested against Fedeco's decision to the Election Tribunal. He contended that Alhaji Shagari was not duly elected by a majority of lawful votes because he had not satisfied section 34A subsection (i) (c) (ii) of Electoral Decree 1977 and Section 7 of the Electoral (Amendment) Decree 1978. He claimed that the election of Shagari was invalid by reason of non-compliance with the provisions of the decree since he had less than one-quarter of the votes cast at the election in each of at least two-thirds of all the states in the federation. He prayed the tribunal to declare that Shagari was not duly elected or returned and that his election was void. Awolowo also wanted the tribunal to order Fedeco to arrange for an election to be held in accordance with the provision of section 34A (3) of the Electoral (Amendment) Decree 1978.[45]

Awolowo lost and appealed to the Supreme Court. On 25 September 1979, the Supreme Court presided over by Chief Fatai Williams upheld Fedeco's interpretation in a five to two split decision.

The court, rather than the ballot box, became the last decisive factor in the election of Shagari. This recourse to the judiciary generated public interest and the military's direct interference in the process did a lot to discredit it. It was during the crisis that Fatai Williams was appointed as the new Chief Justice. While Obasanjo had on several occasions denied that he was influenced by the impending case, political analysts and Shagari's opponents asserted that the federal military government was very well aware that the petitions over the presidential election would reach the Supreme Court, and it appointed a pro-NPN Chief Justice in order to secure a favourable decision. For instance, Chief Awolowo believed that:

> The decision to appoint a new Chief Justice was hurriedly taken between last August 19 and 21 (1979). First, Alhaji Shagari was consulted all the way in the appointment . . . and it was he who expressed preference for the incumbent from a number of candidates. Secondly, it is now well-known that the only important issues of law which could have, and which had in fact arisen, then were raised in my election petition concerning the interpretation of 'each of at least two-thirds of the states in the Federation . . .'[46]

Awolowo went on to pose the following questions:

> Whether the Chief Justice knew the reasons for his appointment and acquiesced in them. Whether the incumbent knew that he was Alhaji Shehu Shagari's own choice from a list of candidates. Whether Alhaji Shehu Shagari ever talked to the present Chief Justice in order to ascertain his wishes in the matter before he (Shagari) made his preference known to the then military head of State, and finally will the Chief Justice have presided over my appeal and played such decisive role as it was his duty to play, if he had known previously that he was the choice of the respondent, who, at the time of his appointment had no constitutional rights whatsoever to take part in it?[47]

All these grave charges were never offically denied, but both Obasanjo and Fatai Williams had had cause to reply in language that reveals their deep-seated hatred for Awolowo.[48]

Three days prior to its handing over power, the military provided yet another drama by amending the constitution on the provisions for an electoral college which were deleted in preference for a second election if the first produced no clear winner. Several people had advocated this but the military ignored the suggestion until Shagari had been confirmed the president-elect. This amendment further served to strengthen the speculation that the military was not at all neutral, since it gave the impression that it deliberately aided the NPN by preventing the use of an electoral college. The military, however, had the future in mind, too, by trying to provide a better alternative to the electoral college.

A few other factors worked in favour of the NPN besides the indirect support of Fedeco and the military. The political base of the other parties was excessively restricted to particular ethnic groups. For instance, the UPN was dominant among the Yoruba where it won four of their five states. Awolowo was unable to widen this base except the few gains made in Gongola. He even chose Philip Umeadi of Anambra State, an unknown figure even in Igbo politics, as his running mate, thus totally excluding the north. And as it turned out, Umeadi fetched the party no votes. Even the areas traditionally regarded as pro-Awo (Cross River, Rivers, Kwara and Bendel) turned against the UPN in preference for the NPN. One reason for this change had to do with the creation of states under the military. Awolowo's popularity in these areas was not unconnected with his support, during the First Republic, for the creation of states in these areas. Since this issue had been resolved, there was little or no need for the minorities to cast protest votes against the majority. Among the Igbo, Chief Awolowo was very much disliked for his anti-Biafra activities during and immediately after the war. All attempts by the UPN to convince the Igbo to the contrary were futile.[49] In Niger state, Awolowo's opponents used his opposition to the establishment of Abuja as a new federal capital against him.

The other parties had the similar problem of not having a nation-wide acceptance. The NPP received its support mainly from Imo, Anambra and Plateau States. The encroachment on Plateau had much to do with the people's frustration with the Fulani/Hausa oligarchy and the ambition of the younger bourgeois elite to control power. In the case of the PRP and GNPP, while they were not dominantly ethnic parties, they nevertheless had a very localized base. The GNPP had its greatest support in Borno State, the home state of Waziri Ibrahim; and the PRP also had a most substantial following in Kano, the home base of Aminu Kano.

Though the NPN essentially belonged to the Fulani/Hausa aristocracy it was able to widen its base to the minority states, to win a total of seven states in the gubernatorial election. In the presidential election, Shagari was able to obtain one-quarter of the total votes cast in twelve states while his closest rival, Awolowo, obtained one-quarter of the votes cast in six states. Assuming that the elections were free and fair, the electoral college would have, if asked to decide, acted against the popular verdict if it chose Awolowo instead of Shagari. The NPN did better than the other parties in the three other elections. It won seats in the National Assembly from 16 states and had at least one representative in 17 state assemblies. The PRP had seats in 5 state assemblies. The UPN won seats to the National Assembly from 8 states and had seats in 10 state assemblies while the NPP had seats in the National Assembly from 9 states and seats in 10 state assemblies. As for the GNPP, it had seats in the National Assembly from 7 states and seats in 13 state assemblies.

Unlike the other parties, the NPN was able to attract more capitalist notables from all over the country. In the east and west, men who regarded themselves as competent politicians and leaders in their own right chose to join the NPN rather than the UPN or the NPP which they believed could limit their freedom of action and access to power because of the towering personalities of Azikiwe and Awolowo. The notables in the minority states preferred an amorphous party like the NPN where they could negotiate for positions. In addition, to the southern politicians, the northern factor in Nigerian politics was considered crucial. Some of them held that the NPN, with its strong base in the north, stood more chance to control the centre than any party.

To attract and retain the notables, the NPN came up with its ingenious but fraudulent zoning system, the limitations of which have been discussed above.

Politics in the Second Republic

The doubts and the problems of legitimacy which surrounded the appointment of Shagari influenced the course of political activities from 1 October 1979, when he assumed office. In his first press conference on 16 August, he asked all the other contestants to join him in the formation of a national government.[50] He said he would utilize all available talents to promote the welfare of the people. No party took his call with any seriousness. He repeated the call again on his first day in office. His first major task was to placate his rivals in view of the bitter struggle for power, the moves of his rivals to forge an alliance and the fact that his party had no majority in the National Assembly. In extending his hand of fellowship, Alhaji Shagari emphasized the distribution of offices rather than the implementation of concrete programmes. This was acting in accordance with the interests of the Nigerian politicians.

Both the GNPP and the UPN refused to have anything to do with the NPN. The UPN promised co-operation on one condition: if the NPN could execute its four cardinal programmes. The UPN rightly pointed out that the sharing of posts should not be regarded as crucial but the minimum programmes of economic and political objectives which the government must pursue. Chief Awolowo said that a coalition government would be 'a haven for abuse and misuse of power and for unabated corruption on the part of ministers'. The PRP favoured the formation of a national government based on a compromise manifesto of all political parties. Only the NPP honoured the invitation, and did so mainly to secure key appointments at the federal level for its members and money for development in the three states which it controlled.

In the terms of the NPN–NPP accord, both agreed to establish a special development agency to ensure the development of backward states and those that had suffered from natural disasters, poor geographical location and war. A Review Committee would also be set up to amend aspects of the constitution likely to promote political instability, examine the creation of additional states, problems of local government and the Land Use Decree, and the payment of adequate compensation to those whose property had been compulsorily acquired. Both parties also agreed to abide by the constitution, especially the provisions in sections 10, 35 and 39 which prohibit a state religion and guarantee the right to freedoms of thought, conscience and religion and from discrimination.

The accord was only meant to serve the interests of the bourgeoisie in both parties since it dealt only with those issues which could strengthen their accumulative base. Specific social and economic welfare issues were ignored.

With this accord, Shagari thought he could now count on the support of 52 out of 95 senators and 244 out of 449 members of the House of Representatives. Unfortunately for him, things did not work out in his favour, as the NPP legislators refused to vote en bloc or toe their party line. Nevertheless, the accord made it difficult for all the legislators to gang up against the president and this helped him to get his policies (though these were very few) through, have enough time to make friends among the legislators and win some of them over to his party.

The NPN–NPP accord was not based on any solid or genuine foundation. Its primary aim was no more than the sharing of ministerial positions. They did not make a single attempt at discussing or reconciling their manifestos, and also had no regular forum where they could exchange ideas. The best moment in the history of the accord was during the ratification of the ministerial appointments by the Senate. In other issues at the National Assembly, the NPP refused to support the NPN, and its members were as hostile as those of the other parties. As early as November 1979, members of the NPP had to be persuaded to support the confirmation of Richard Akinjide of the NPN as Attorney-General and Paul Unongo of the NPP as Minister for Steel Development.

In February 1981, the problems of the accord were brought into the open when Chief Njile Okereke, a top NPN member, accused the NPP of behaving like Oliver Twist in asking for more posts and contracts. Dr Alexander Fom, the Secretary-General of the NPP, quickly replied that his party regretted joining the accord and accused the NPN leaders as businessmen and contractors whose primary concern was to secure contracts.[51] In the same month, all the four NPP nominees for ambassadorial appointments were rejected by the Senate, partly because the NPN members withdrew their co-operation. Chief Nnamdi Azikiwe swiftly reacted, accusing the NPN-controlled federal government of encroaching on the residual powers of the states in housing, local government, health, agriculture, commerce and industries. He also criticized the centre for imposing Presidential Liaison Officers (PLOs)[52] and the NPN-controlled Kaduna State Assembly for refusing on four separate occasions to confirm the governor's list of nominees for commissionerships.

By mid-1981, the NPP was already worried about the NPN's move to swallow it up. On 6 July 1981, the NPP gave six month's notice to terminate the accord. The NPN decided to be firm, if only for once, by not only accepting the notice but deciding that it should be with immediate effect. All NPP-sponsored ministers were ordered to resign, and the president only decided to reject the letters of those who had either decamped to his party or who gave the indication of doing so.

The accord could not have survived for long. The two parties had conflicting interests. While the NPN wanted the accord to prevent opposition in the National Assembly, the NPP wanted a cheap avenue to power and resources with which it intended to develop its 'underdeveloped states'. President Shehu Shagari was later to comment on this divergent interest:

> The NPP leaders thought that an accord was basically an arrangement for sharing the booty, so to speak, but we did not regard it as such. Our own understanding of the accord was that it provided for co-operation between two parties in order to help stabilize government and get things moving. We found that the NPP was rather more interested in what it could get out of the accord than really working fot the government and the nation. They kept on demanding all sorts of favours and privileges from us . . . We found to our astonishment that these people were only interested in what they could get out of us and the government.[53]

But this was not the whole truth. The president's party was too reckless in wooing NPP members over to it, failed to consult the NPP on major decisions and regarded it as a subordinate partner without any veto power.

The three other parties quickly cashed in on the collapse of the accord by persuading the NPP to join the progressive alliance. It was not difficult to secure the membership of the NPP since it had no working relationship with any other party and had to avoid being isolated, and also because of the shabby and shameful way it was dismissed by the NPN.

The progressive alliance began in July 1979, when the NPP, UPN and GNPP allied to prevent Shagari's victory. After the elections, the UPN and the GNPP did not break the alliance. Regular meetings of the seven progressive governors were held to discuss common issues and plan the strategy for the future. The two PRP governors joined in 1980, following the NPN's imposition of Presidential Liaison Officers on the states. When the NPP joined in 1981, the alliance became a formidable force with the primary goal of combating the NPN and dislodging it from power in 1983.

But the progressives had two main problems. First, except for the UPN and NPP (for most of the time), the other parties lost their cohesion and became fractionalized because of this alliance. The GNPP broke into two factions, one led by Waziri and the other by Nduka Eze, the party secretary, who accused Waziri of forming a secret alliance with Awolowo. The Eze faction preferred to team up with the NPN. Eze had to be expelled from the party, but this was no solution to the party's internal crisis. In the case of the PRP, the Aminu Kano faction was opposed to the alliance, seeing it as the UPN's effort to destroy it and pave an easy way for Awolowo in the 1983 elections.

The second problem was the inability of the alliance to transform itself into a party or agree on a list of common candidates. This failure, surprisingly, was not owing to any serious NPN countermoves but rather to the unwillingness of the federating partners to surrender their autonomy. There was mutual distrust and the fear of possible domination by the UPN. The parties could not even resolve their conflicting policy positions while the two giants in the alliance — Awolowo and Azikiwe — were unwilling to step down for one another in the presidential race.

Yet, there were several moments of optimism. On 11 December 1981, Awolowo told the press in Lagos that is was in the best interest of the four parties to unite.[54] On 17 January 1982, Awolowo and Azikiwe agreed to work together, and on the following day, the four parties in the alliance decided on principle to field Awolowo as the sole presidential candidate.[55] On 12 March 1982, the summit meeting of the leaders of the four parties held in Maiduguri agreed to form an alliance called the Progressive Parties Alliance (PPA) and the idea was mooted by some that it could be registered as a political party. At this stage, the NPN became frightened. While it embarked on underground activities to destroy the PPA, it pretended not to be bothered. Shagari called the PPA 'an alliance of three hyenas' which would kill one another or unite to kill their common goal. A.M.A. Akinloye, NPN's party leader, saw it as a big joke, an illusion.[56]

Akinloye was proved right. The parties could not work together. In April, Waziri gave the hint of a new party, the Progressive Peoples Party, thus confirming the speculation that his relationship with Awolowo was no longer smooth. The PPP was proposed as a merger of a faction of the NPP and the GNPP. On 6 May, Waziri withdrew from the PPA on the grounds that it was incapable of working, and of transforming the country's economy.[57] Unfortunately for Waziri, Fedeco did not register the PPP. The PPA, on the other hand, could not resolve its leadership crisis. Consequently, the three leaders contested in 1983 as they had in 1979.

The PPA failed because of the conflicting aspirations of its members, its failure to evolve a unanimous programme of action, its ideological bankruptcy and the infiltration of the NPN into its rank and file.

The accord and alliances were partly symptomatic of the problems of political instability and the inability of the national bourgeoisie to create a viable hegemony (this is discussed fully in the last chapter). These problems were also reflected in state–federal relations, the inability of the president to command general acceptance and the tendency towards fascism and political repression.

The 1979 constitution focussed political conflicts on the federal–state nexus. Because different political parties dominated the states and Shagari was never a popular ruler, the interactions between the centre and the states operated essentially at the level of politics. Early in the life of the Second Republic, Shagari's lieutenants always threatened the states with funds, reminding them that they would go cap in hand to Lagos for money. State governors and functionaries replied that the money belonged to all and Shagari had no right to deny any state its share. There was also the trivial controversy over whether or not to hang Shagari's portrait in public offices. The most serious controversy was over the appointment of Presidential Liaison Officers. While Shagari saw it as an administrative innovation to promote co-operation between the states and the centre, other parties rejected it. Sam Mbakwe of Imo called the PLOs 'organising secretaries of the NPN in disguise'. The GNPP, UPN and NPP governors warned their workers not to deal with the PLO.

Shagari was treated with contempt by most of the non-NPN governors. His party and person were ridiculed daily in different media. As if the people did not know, Shagari had to remind them on several occasions that he was president of the country and not of the NPN. In 1980, following a personal confrontation he had with Governor Ambrose Alli of Bendel State during a state visit, Shagari criticized some governors for regarding themselves 'as politicians instead of administrators by throwing brickbats and talking as if they were on the soapbox'.

The relationship between the centre and the states and the different parties did not improve throughout the Second Republic. Members of minority parties were victimized in different states. The parties accused each other of political victimization and intimidation. For instance in 1980, the Kano branch of the NPN established a legal defence bureau for the constitutional defence of its members who were being oppressed and harassed by members of the ruling PRP.[58] The GNPP appealed to Shagari to curb 'organised acts of violence and lawlessness' and also alleged that the NPN had 'started to unleash systematically its sinister Grand Plan to rule even in the state where they are not in control of the government'.[59]

The NPN received more condemnation than any other party because it controlled the centre. Indeed, the Shagari administration exhibited its repressive tendencies very early. In January 1980, it arrested and deported to Chad the GNPP majority leader in the Borno State Assembly, Alhaji Shugaba Abdurrahman. On the unverified allegation that Shugaba was not a Nigerian, Lagos ordered his deportation on the night of 24 January. This incident popularly known as 'the Shugaba Affair', gave the NPN more trouble than it bargained for. Other political parties used the incident to further cement their alliance, and the UPN in particular was able to win more friends in Borno because it threw its weight behind Shugaba's legal steps to assert his freedom and prove his Nigerian nationality.

There was another celebrated case of attempted deportation, not of a politician but of a lecturer, Dr Patrick Wilmot of the Department of Sociology, Ahmadu Bello University, Zaria. But for the protests by students and university teachers, Wilmot would not have been left alone.

Other attempts to assert power resulted in widespread killing. The most notable example was at Bakolori in Sokoto State where several peasants were murdered in an attempt to deny them their land.[60]

And as the 1983 elections drew near, the federal government unleashed all its forces of coercion to subdue opposition, and build fear in the minds of people. Sunday Adewusi, the Inspector-General of Police, became so powerful that many newspaper columnists nicknamed him the 'president'.[61] He helped the federal government to create a police state. It was nonetheless obvious that the trials and tribulations of the presidency, the contradictions resulting from the over-extension and misuse of state power and the mediocre nature of the majority of Nigerian politicians would significantly affect the nature and outcome of the 1983 general elections.

Notes

1. 1979 Constitution, op. cit., section 20.
2. Ibid., section 202.
3. Two provisos are added to this: (a) the election of the officers or members of the executive committee of a political party shall be deemed to be periodical only if it is made at regular intervals not exceeding four years; and (b) the members of the executive committee or other governing body of the political party shall be deemed to reflect the federal character of Nigeria only if the members thereof belong to different States not being less in number than two-thirds of all the States comprising the Federation.
4. An 'association' means any body of persons corporate or unincorporate who agree to act together for any common purpose, and includes an association formed for any ethnic, social, cultural, occupational or religious purpose. (Section 209).
5. Y.B. Usman, *For the Liberation of Nigeria*, op. cit., p. 49.
6. For more information on this, see B.J. Dudley, *Parties and Politics in Northern Nigeria* (London: Frank Cass, 1968), chapter iv.
7. *NPN Manifesto* (Lagos: NPN Secretariat, 1979).
8. See Chuba Okadigbo, *The Mission of NPN* (Lagos, 1981).
9. Claude Ake, 'The State of the Nation', keynote address to Political Science Association of Nigeria, 1982.
10. Okadigbo, *The Mission of NPN*, op. cit.
11. *National Concord*, 19 January 1983.
12. See for instance *Nigerian Herald*, 4 March 1983.
13. *Nigerian Democratic Review*, Vol. I, No. 1, March 1983, p. 3.
14. *Our Manifesto* (Lagos: NPP Secretariat, n.d.).
15. Ake, 'The State of the Nation', op. cit.
16. *Socialist Forum; A Marxist Journal for Social Change*, July 1983, pp. 45–6.
17. Ibid., p. 46.
18. *Our Stand* (Ibadan: GNPP Secretariat, 1979).
19. *Manifesto of the Unity Party of Nigeria* (Lagos: UPN Secretariat, 1979).
20. Ibid., p. 2. The party saw the restructuring of the economy as

central to its plan: 'the most carefully thought out constitutional arrangements have no chance of succeeding in a nation bounded by economic frus-
trations and unfulfilled economic hopes and promises' *Nigerian Year Book,
1980* (Times Press Ltd.), p. 28.

21. *Daily Times*, 22 September 1978.

22. Ibid., p. 4.

23. See the bibliography for detailed citations.

24. A. Omoboriowo, *Awoism: Select Themes On the Complex Ideology Of Chief Obafemi Awolowo* (Ibadan, Nigeria: Evans Bros., 1982).

25. For details, see *The Struggle for a New Social Order in Kaduna
State: The Policies and Programmes of the PRP Government, 1979–1981*
(Kaduna: Government Printer, 1981).

26. Balarabe Musa, 'The meaning and purpose of our struggle for a
new Social Order in Nigeria', a speech delivered at the National Institute for
policy and strategic studies, Kuru, near Jos, 1982.

27. *General Programme of the PRP.*

28. The details of this are provided in *Myths and Realities, Documents
from the NEPU Days to the PRP*, Vol. I (Zaria: Gashiya Printing Press, n.d.).

29. S.G. Ikoku, 'How African Socialism can Succeed', *Daily Times*,
13 July 1975.

30. *Myths and Realities*, op. cit., pp. 130–1.

31. Ikoku, 'How African Socialism can Succeed', op. cit.

32. Usman, *For the Liberation*, op. cit., p. 132.

33. J.O. Ojiako, *Nigeria; Yesterday, Today and . . .* (Onitsha: Africana
Educational Publishers, 1981), pp. 289–90.

34. *Daily Times*, 25 April 1979.

35. *The Nigerian Tribune*, 25 July 1979.

36. General Obasanjo, Text of a Broadcast to the Nation, 14 July 1978.

37. Certain members of the military believed that a northern candidate
for the presidency would be ideal since Obasanjo was from the south and also
a Christian, and because of the northern factor in Nigerian politics.

38. *Sunday Times*, 12 December 1979.

39.

State	Party	Governor
Anambra	NPP	Jim Nwobodo
Bauchi	NPN	Tatari Ali
Bendel	UPN	Prof Ambrose Alli
Borno	GNPP	Mohammed Goni
Benue	NPN	Aper Aku
Cross River	NPN	Dr Clement Isong
Gongola	GNPP	A. Barde
Imo	NPP	Samuel Mbakwe
Kaduna	PRP	Balarabe Musa
Kano	PRP	Abubakar Rimi
Kwara	NPN	Adamu Atta
Lagos	UPN	Lafeef Jakande
Niger	NPN	Awwal Ibrahim
Ogun	UPN	Bisi Onabanjo
Ondo	UPN	Michael Ajasin
Oyo	UPN	Bola Ige
Plateau	NPP	Solomon Lar
Rivers	NPN	Melford Okilo
Sokoto	NPN	Muhammed Kangiwa

40. *Daily Times*, 18 August 1979.
41. *Daily Times*, 19 August 1979.
42. Ibid.
43. Ibid.
44. *Daily Times*, 16 March 1978.
45. Ibid., 20 August 1979.
46. Ibid., 14 December 1979.
47. Ibid.
48. See for instance, *New Nigerian*, 18 December 1979 and Fatai William's *Faces, Cases and Places*.
49. See for instance, *Does Awo Hate the Ibos?* (Lagos: Unity Party of Nigeria, Bureau of Publicity, 1980).
50. *Daily Times*, 17 August, p. 1.
51. *Daily Sketch*, 2 February 1981.
52. Presidential Liaison Officers (PLOs) were appointed by Alhaji Shehu Shagari and were directly accountable to him. They were not only to co-ordinate and 'project' Federal Government interests in all the states but also to serve as links between the centre and the states. Their appointment generated a heated debate, not only because there were no specific constitutional provisions for the existence of the office, but because of the political implications of their presence in non-NPN controlled states. In these states they were perceived as 'alternative governors' or spies, or party organizers. The states, therefore, vowed not to deal with PLOs. Their position was somewhat strengthened by the fact that all the states have traditionally maintained well-staffed liaison officers in Lagos. Thus, other than the desire to pay off political debts, and interfere in the affairs of non-NPN states, the appointment of the PLOs reflected, at one level, the relative insecurity of the NPN.
53. *Africa Now*, November 1982, p. 48.
54. *The Tribune*, 12 December 1981.
55. Ibid., 18 January 1982.
56. *Nigerian Year Book, 1983* (Lagos: Daily Times Publication), p. 135.
57. *Daily Times*, 7 May 1982.
58. *Times International*, 14 January 1980.
59. *New Nigerian*, 22 January 1980.
60. See for instance A. Essien-Ibok, *Political Repression and Assassination* (Kano: Research Unit, Governor's Office, 1983).
61. *The Guardian* (Lagos), 15 January 1984, p. 1.

5. The Economy

The Inheritance: Economic Changes and Underdevelopment

Conventional indices such as per capita income, GDP etc., will reveal a lot of economic changes in the pre-1979 military era. The industrial sector, which includes mining, construction and manufacturing expanded remarkably and had an impact on the sectoral distribution of the overall growth of the GDP. The mining and services subsector witnessed the most impressive growth rates. Exports recorded a moderate growth and imports grew tremendously from ₦1,737.3 million in 1974 to ₦8,368.7 million in 1978. The revenue collected by the federal government increased from ₦5,177.1 million in 1974 to ₦8,359 million in 1977/78 and declined to ₦7,033.9 million in 1978/79 due to the oil glut.[1] The real Gross Domestic Product nearly doubled from ₦9,443 million in 1970/71 to ₦18,740 million in 1979/80. This represented an average annual growth rate of 9.8% throughout the decade. The industrial sector accounted for the growth rate of the GDP in the 1970s. Domestic capital formation showed a remarkable improvement as the growth in the industrial sector affected the liquidity of the economy and the activities of the banking sector.

But the above only represents change and not economic development. By 1979 when the military left, the economy was backward, underdeveloped, disarticulated and dependent. Poverty was the common bond among Nigerians. The country had all the features of Plato's degenerate state and of Machiavelli's corrupt society characterized by poverty, dishonesty, disunity, lawlessness, violence, disorderly ambition, inequalities of wealth, etc.

Rather than emphasize indicators of economic change, as bourgeois academics and government officials do in order to show the country's progress and deceive the undiscerning citizens, it is better to dwell on underdevelopment. Indeed, any approach that ignores underdevelopment is deliberately dishonest and diversionary. And to understand underdevelopment one must take into cognizance the impact of colonialism, the nature of the neocolonial rentier state and the character of the Nigerian national proto-bourgeoisie.

Over five decades of British colonial rule and exploitation left Nigeria in 1960 a spatially distorted, underdeveloped and peripheral capitalist country in the international division of labour. It is difficult to identify a sector of the economy which experienced positive development as a result of deliberate colonial policy.[2]   Imperialist agents and institutions met their objectives to a large extent by structurally disarticulating, peripheralizing and incorporating the Nigerian social formation into the world capitalist system. At independence in 1960, the country was backward in all respects. As a primary producer for the world market, the country's cash crop exports and imports were concentrated on Western (particularly EEC) markets. The production of these cash crops was exclusively in the hands of peasants who were exploited by the state-owned Marketing Boards and their licensed agents. The colonial state had ensured that the oil, banking, import–export and the limited manufacturing sectors were all dominated by transnational corporations such as Shell–BP, Barclays Bank (now Union Bank), UAC, Leventis, etc.

The colonial state, through deliberate administrative manipulation and discrimination, underdeveloped indigenous entrepreneurship and relegated it to a compradoral role in the economy.[3] Since then, it has continued to serve as agents, distributors, junior partners, legal and political advisers, all of which are lucrative but unproductive positions in the production and exchange processes of the economy. The dominant class has also been fully committed to the preservation of Nigeria's peripheral location and role in the international division of labour. The dependence on foreign aid was reflected in the fact that even the so-called first post-colonial development plan of 1962–1968 was over 50 per cent dependent on foreign aid.

The dependence on the export of cash crops and the volatile prices of raw materials in the world capitalist exchange processes meant that at the internal level, resources with which to keep development projects afloat and mediate class contradictions always fluctuated with changes in the world market. The extent to which the country's trade was locked into dependence on the west is reflected in Tables 5.1 and 5.2.

From the mid-1960s, the country progressively shifted from cash crops to oil, and by 1973, oil had become the major foreign exchange earner (see Table 5.3). Three reasons, at least, are responsible for this shift.

One, Nigeria has historically lacked a bourgeoisie which has an accumulative base in agriculture. The second reason has to do with the nature of the state and the bourgeoisie. The state, being weak and unable to exercise hegemony over the totality of the Nigerian formation, was incapable of controlling transnational interests and using its power to support the emergence of a powerful and productive national bourgeois class. Thus, the triumph of transnational oil interests and the food-hawking transnational corporations was facilitated by the triumph of the comprador fraction of the dominant class. In the light of this, when the Middle-East crisis led to the tremendous increase in oil prices in 1973, the Nigerian state was easily manipulated to shift its area of interest from the rural areas and agriculture to the oil sector. Finally, given the 'drone'. character of the Nigerian bourgeoisie, it was unable to react positively to increasing returns from oil exports;

Table 5.1
Destination of Nigeria's Exports[a] by Regional Groupings, 1960-72 (fob)

Year	Eastern Europe	EEC	Japan	United Kingdom	USA	West Africa	Others	Total
Value (₦Million)								
1960	1.3	102.8	5.1	161.4	31.8	2.2	34.8	339.4
1961	1.2	115.9	6.6	153.1	38.2	2.9	29.5	347.4
1962	3.4	113.3	3.0	138.4	36.2	9.2	33.7	337.2
1963	2.9	138.6	4.7	147.6	34.8	11.2	38.8	378.6
1964	10.1	153.2	5.1	161.4	28.6	14.9	56.1	429.4
1965	177.5	186.4	6.3	203.0	52.4	10.6	60.2	536.4
1966	14.2	201.0	8.5	211.7	45.2	11.1	76.1	567.8
1967	14.3	197.4	12.4	144.2	37.9	7.2	70.2	483.6
1968	19.1	150.8	7.4	121.9	35.0	12.7	75.3	422.2
1969	22.7	226.0	6.0	175.6	80.2	9.3	116.6	636.4
1970	31.7	327.6	6.8	250.4	101.6	7.2	160.1	885.4
1971	44.3	499.8	18.6	278.8	223.5	26.8	201.4	1,293.0
1972	25.6	539.0	55.2	300.9	299.6	29.8	183.9	1,434.0
Percentages								
1960	0.4	30.2	1.5	47.6	9.4	0.6	10.3	100.00
1961	0.3	33.4	1.9	44.1	11.0	0.8	8.5	100.00
1962	1.0	33.6	0.9	41.0	10.7	2.7	10.0	100.00
1963	0.8	36.6	1.2	39.0	9.2	3.0	10.2	100.00
1964	2.4	35.7	1.2	37.6	6.7	3.5	13.1	100.00
1965	3.3	34.8	1.2	37.8	9.8	2.0	11.2	100.00
1966	2.5	35.4	1.5	37.3	8.0	2.0	13.4	100.00
1967	3.0	40.8	2.6	29.8	7.8	1.5	14.5	100.00
1968	4.5	35.7	1.8	28.9	8.3	3.0	17.8	100.00
1969	3.6	35.0	0.9	27.6	12.6	1.5	18.3	100.00
1970	3.6	37.0	0.8	28.3	11.5	0.8	18.1	100.00
1971	3.4	38.6	1.4	21.6	17.3	2.1	15.6	100.00
1972	1.8	37.6	3.8	21.0	20.9	2.1	12.8	100.00

a: Include re-exports

Note: This pattern of trade has not changed since 1973 with the increase in oil prices, Nigeria now exports mainly oil. Percentages (rounded) of estimated total exports in 1980 (₦14,077.0 million = 100): Eastern Europe 0.1; Western Europe 38.9; Japan 0.1; USA 43.0; Africa 2.8; Others 15.1.

Sources: (1) Central Bank of Nigeria, *Economic and Financial Review*, December 1973; (2) Central Bank of Nigeria, *Annual Reports*, 1980; (3) Federal Office of Statistics, *Review of External Trade*, 1972.

Table 5.2
Sources of Nigeria's Imports by Regional Groupings, 1960–72 (cif)

Year	Eastern Europe	EEC	Japan	United Kingdom	USA	West Africa	Others	Total
Value (₦Million)								
1960	8.6	84.3	55.6	182.8	23.2	1.3	76.0	*431.8*
1961	10.9	88.7	61.6	170.6	23.8	1.5	87.9	*445.0*
1962	12.1	78.5	49.7	147.7	29.9	0.8	87.3	*406.0*
1963	14.0	90.0	53.8	141.6	35.8	1.2	78.8	*415.2*
1964	15.1	117.6	61.6	157.4	57.8	2.2	95.7	*507.4*
1965	14.6	136.5	51.2	170.1	66.2	1.6	110.4	*550.6*
1966	14.2	135.6	28.6	152.5	83.0	2.4	96.3	*512.6*
1967	16.7	115.0	37.5	129.2	55.7	2.5	90.6	*447.2*
1968	19.1	106.6	14.3	119.7	44.6	3.8	77.1	*385.2*
1969	19.1	125.4	18.9	172.7	58.5	2.8	100.0	*497.4*
1970	34.2	202.8	44.4	232.0	109.6	3.3	127.1	*156.4*
1971	43.6	271.6	89.7	344.1	151.4	3.1	175.5	*1,079.0*
1972	25.4	299.0	98.2	291.9	103.1	3.1	169.8	*990.6*
Percentages								
1960	2.0	19.5	12.9	42.9	5.4	0.3	17.6	*100.00*
1961	2.4	19.9	13.8	38.3	5.3	0.3	19.8	*100.00*
1962	3.0	19.3	12.2	36.4	7.4	0.2	21.5	*100.00*
1963	3.4	21.7	13.0	34.1	8.5	0.3	19.0	*100.00*
1964	3.0	23.1	12.0	31.0	11.3	0.4	18.9	*100.00*
1965	2.7	24.7	9.3	30.9	12.0	0.3	20.1	*100.00*
1966	2.8	26.4	5.6	29.7	16.2	0.5	18.8	*100.00*
1967	3.7	25.6	8.3	28.7	12.5	0.6	20.3	*100.00*
1968	4.8	27.6	3.7	31.0	11.5	1.0	20.0	*100.00*
1969	3.8	25.2	3.8	34.7	11.8	0.6	20.1	*100.00*
1970	4.0	26.7	6.3	30.7	14.5	0.4	16.9	*100.00*
1971	4.3	25.2	8.4	31.9	14.0	0.3	16.2	*100.00*
1972	2.6	30.2	9.9	29.5	10.4	0.3	17.2	*100.00*

Source: Central Bank of Nigeria, *Economic and Financial Review*, December 1973; Federal Office of Statistics, *Review of External Trade*, 1972.

Note: Percentages (rounded) of estimated total non-oil imports in 1980 (₦9441.9 million = 100): Eastern Europe 2.2; Western Europe 65.9; Japan 10.8; USA 11.0; Africa 1.2; Others 8.9. See Central Bank of Nigeria, *Annual Report, 1980*, p. 2.

Table 5.3
Oil Revenues Since 1958/59

Year	Receipts (Million Naira)	
1958/59	0.2	
1959/60	3.4	
1960/61	2.4	
1961/62	17.0	
1962/63	17.0	
1963/64	10.0	
1964/65	16.0	
1965/66	29.2	
1966/67	45.0	
1967/68	41.0	
1968/69	29.6	
1969/70	75.4	
1970/71	176.4	
1971/72	603.0	
1972	1,403.3	
1974	5,365.9	
1975	4,190.4	
1976	5,224.2	
1977	6.4	billion
1978	5.2	billion
1979	10.4	billion
1980	13.123	billion
1981	$10.4	billion
1982	$14.3	billion
1983	$ 9.6	billion

Sources: NNPC, *Monthly Information*, Various Years; *OPEC Annual Statistical Bulletin, 1980*; and Shehu Shagari, Twenty-Second and Twenty-Third National Day Addresses, 1982 and 1983.

it merely sat back, joined OPEC in 1971 and initiated policies to increase state participation in terms of ownership but not control in the oil industry. Thus, all the state had to do was to hope that conditions in the world oil market would continue to improve, allow foreign oil companies to take the major risks and it would collect oil rents.

Unfortunately, oil revenues were recycled to deepen dependence, underdevelopment and contradictions. The process of recycling OPEC oil rents involved the oil-producing countries, transnational corporations, particularly oil corporations, international finance institutions and the oil-consuming economies. The oil economies exercised control over the land and oil deposits.

The transnational oil corporations helped with exploration, exploitation, refining and marketing activites while other transnational interests were involved in the supply of technology, high-level manpower and other requirements in both up- and down-stream operations. International finance institutions assisted with balance of payments, money transfers and other payments, and the home governments of the oil companies as well as the energy-consuming economies were involved in areas of influencing policies, prices and politics within the oil-producing economies. They also assisted their transnationals through various bilateral and multilateral talks and agreements with other governments so as to generate markets for their home products.[4] Thus, Nigeria as a dependent peripheral capitalist economy was involved in the recycling of oil rents at the level of (1) exporting oil to consuming countries and collecting rents for same; (2) higher payments in real terms for imports from developed economies; (3) investments in other economies, facilitated by oil rents already collected; (4) holding of reserves in Western banks and financial institutions, (5) massive food imports and (6) imports to meet defence requirements.

These aspects of recycling were heavily influenced not only by the nature and accumulative base of the dominant social forces but also by the nature of specific alignment and re-alignments of class forces and the nature of the state. In the Nigerian situation, we have already established the fact that the postcolonial state is weak; the hegemony of the bourgeoisie over non-bourgeois forces is largely tenuous, the economy is dominated by transnational interests and the society is full of contradictions. With the collection of huge oil rents, the Nigerian state became relatively autonomous from other internal social forces. The state became the focus of class competition and struggles in the effort to win access to and control the state and thus preside over the allocation of oil rents. Given the neglect of agriculture and the rural areas, the food problem which followed the oil boom in the 1970s highlights an aspect of Nigeria's efforts to recycle its petro-naira.

Oil production increased tremendously in the 1970s. Nigeria joined OPEC in 1971 and by 1973 moved to replace some Middle-East producers in the US market during the oil embargo. Thus, production moved from 2.1 million bpd in 1970 to 2.3 million bpd in 1973 and 1974 and reached its peak of 2.4 million bpd in 1979. In 1981, with the glut in the world oil market, production averaged 2.2 million bpd. At the same time, revenues which accrued to the state increased substantially from ₦1,403.3 million in 1973, to ₦6.4 billion in 1977 and about ₦10 billion in 1979. In relation to the collection and recycling of oil rents it is essential to note the heavy dependence on the Western market which takes almost all the oil exported by Nigeria. Within this, the United States alone takes between 42 and 50% of Nigeria's oil exports in any particular month. Since oil came to replace cash crop exports, the Nigerian state embarked on a massive food-import policy from the Western world. The bulk of the imported food — rice, meat, cereals, sugar and wheat — were hitherto produced in the country prior to the oil boom. By 1977, food imports alone began to take up to 15% of the country's budget. By mid-1978, Lagos port alone was doing 97% of its business as imports and only 3% in exports while the airports received more goods.[5] Food imports increased from ₦88 million in 1971 to ₦783.4 million in 1977, reached ₦1.56 billion in 1980 and by 1982, crossed the ₦2 billion mark. Thus, at a time when Earl Butz, the former American Secretary of Agriculture, was declaring food as a major instrument of American foreign policy,[6] Nigeria was employing its oil rents in locking itself into a dependent food policy with the West. In 1976, fish imports into Nigeria were ₦30 million; this increased to ₦77 million in 1977 and by 1978 had reached ₦101 million. Sugar imports went from ₦76.6 million in 1976 to ₦129 million in 1977. In 1975, Nigeria imported 15 million kg of rice, this tripled to 45 million kg in 1976 and by the end of 1977 the import level was well over 300 million kg. In fact, in September 1983 alone, Nigeria imported 49,291 tonnes of rice from Thailand at a cost of ₦10.1 million. In August 1983, Nigeria spent ₦11.4 million on Thai rice alone while between January and September, a total of ₦66.8 million was spent on rice imports from Thailand.

This is just an aspect of imports but it does not take into account the huge quantity that was frequently smuggled into the country. Lawrence Amu, the former Managing Director of the state-owned NNPC, noted that the bulk of Nigeria's

> oil revenue is spent on the importation of various consumer goods, capital goods, rice and other agricultural produce which could be cultivated in Nigeria. Thus we earned our oil revenue only to use it to keep foreign industries going.[7]

In an interview at the Federal Ministry of Agriculture, a Senior Official also noted:

> Whether Nigerians eat today or not is heavily dependent on foreign countries and their companies. If our oil dries up, then we are in trouble. There is no doubt that the oil boom contributed to this. The way the money was thrown about by the rich in the urban centres attracted people off the land. The contractors also attracted people to their building sites off the land. But policy makers must take the blame. They often hate the real truth, but it is obvious that not only have we mis-managed our oil money, we have given it to unreliable farmers to provide us with food whenever they wish.[8]

The country's import bill continued to rise in the oil boom era. As officials in government often put it, the country began to 'import all importables'. The import bill increased from ₦1,737 million in 1974 to ₦5,140 million in 1976 and by mid-1978 it reached ₦8,760 million.

The process of recycling Nigeria's oil rents also involved transnational corporations either in the area of executing contracts for the government or in terms of the huge profits they made in their participation in the oil boom economy. The indigenization decrees passed by the military which were completely abrogated by the Shagari administration did not in any way affect control, transnational interests or the level of profit. Tom Forrest has noted quite correctly that 'the sphere of foreign capital accumulation has not been greatly affected by the growth of the Nigerian bourgeoisie, by indigenisation, or by the extension of the state sector'.[9] With the Middle-East crisis of 1973, foreigners flocked to Nigeria from all corners of the globe to cash in on the boom, 'all attempting to sell services of good, bad or indifferent quality'.[10] For instance, the inflow of foreign private investments into Nigeria increased from ₦351.40 million in 1970 to ₦744.19 million in 1971, and ₦878.26 million in 1973. In any case, most of the transnational interests relied on internal sourcing from the foreign banks which were incorporated in Nigeria. The huge profits declared by various businesses is also a pointer to the extent to which they cashed in on the oil boom. The declared profits did not indicate the usually inflated cost of raw materials, spare parts, expert salaries, technical fees and other numerous methods through which surpluses were transferred abroad. Even in 1983 when the economy was bad, the profits declared by different companies (see Table 5.4) show how lucrative the Nigerian market was to established companies.

In the area of contracting, practically all major contracts in the country went to foreign agencies. Where local contractors benefitted from what became known as 'contractmania', they were known to have re-awarded same to foreign contractors. The inflated nature of most of these contracts, the poor quality of others and the extent to which they were dependent on the importation of materials also served to contribute to the recycling of Nigeria's petro-naira in favour of the developed countries. In 1977, Dumez, a French company, won a ₦107 million contract for the Okene-Kaduna road and ₦96 million for the Shagamu-Benin road. In 1975, G. Prono, an Italian firm, won an ₦18.5 million contract to build an annex to the Federal Palace Hotel in Lagos. Over 90% of the NNPC's oil pipelines and depots systems which cost the country over ₦5,000 million went to foreign firms, mainly Japanese and American. Recently, Saipen, an Italian firm, was awarded a ₦154 million contract by the NNPC to construct a 274-kilometre gas pipeline from Warri to Egbin in Bendel and Lagos States respectively. Since Nigeria hardly produced construction materials, and lacks both intermediate and skilled labour, not only did these companies import their own skilled labour but practically all their other requirements, which were paid for in foreign exchange.

The country also recycled its oil revenues in the name of a 'dynamic foreign policy' through soft loans, joint ventures, donations and grants on all sorts of proejcts. These did not include wasteful expenditure on white elephant projects and jamborees at home — the 1977 World Festival of Arts and Culture (FESTAC), the International Scout Jamboree, All Africa Games, etc. While they served particular purposes and interests, all contributed to the recycling of oil rents either through food imports or one form of pay-

Table 5.4
Profits Declared by Selected Companies, 1980 to 1983

Company	Turnover (Naira '000)				Profit (Pre-tax) (Naira '000)			
	1980	1981	1982	1983	1980	1981	1982	1983
Guiness (Nig.) Ltd	151,896	184,919	179,861	240,347	21,434	36,186	35,782	54,724
African Petroleum	168,076	217,511	282,889	—	20,515	26,591	29,470	—
Cappa and D'Alberto	25,889	26,972	40,555	43,691	0.654	2,042	3,724	3,189
SCOA	298,601	361,540	439,848	—	10,332	11,610	10,441	—
Union Bank	138,942	201,817	284,838	—	35,121	60,197	64,970	65,000
Vono	13,281	15,736	15,444	10,328	.549	1,203	.725	.723
Total*	224,127	—	173,362	169,541	23,807	—	16,600	15,500
UTC	230,165	346,544	396,396	311,520	18,756	36,358	39,664	22,233
Blackwood Hodge	32,652	35,354	18,627	—	3,112	2,178	4,853	—
R.T. Briscoe	176,408	208,290	277,794	145,462	23,747	33,182	24,286	14,865
Mobil†	—	—	148,615	149,382	—	—	17,281	18,207
John Holt	—	—	301,046	138,809	—	—	15,976	8,883
Golden Guinea Breweries	12,098	24,766	42,972	—	1,812	6,176	13,663	—
Texaco†	—	163,765	180,499	—	—	23,784	23,603	—
UAC†	—	—	437,925	387,983	—	—	30,207	15,307
Agip	—	122,142	127,148	—	—	11,937	10,214	—

* Half Year reports, except for 1980
† Half Year reports

Source: Compiled from respective Company Annual Reports and Accounts
Note: — = not available

ment or the other.

It is true that the security problems within the continent, particularly the support which 'Biafra' received from some Francophone States in the West African sub-region, Tanzania, Zambia, Rhodesia, South Africa, France and Portugal, the initial refusal of the United Kingdom to support the federal government and the so-called 'neutrality' of the United States, both of which were influenced by their huge investments in oil in the old Eastern Region, taught the post-civil war military government the need to diversify sources of external support, to mount an intensive diplomacy and propaganda against the minority regimes and colonizers in Southern Africa and to break the isolationist and reactionary pro-Western foreign policy which British colonizers bequeathed to Nigeria and the Balewa regime had tried to keep alive. The intensification of Nigeria's role in the OAU, the United Nations, the non-aligned movement, the group of 77, and the increased propaganda activity against racial discrimination and colonialism, increased material and diplomatic support for liberation movements and the creation of the Economic Community of West African States (ECOWAS) are evidences of the desire to break the inherited isolationist policies, win assured friends within the OAU and emerge as Africa's spokescountry. In the process, the country recycled its oil wealth. For instance, Nigeria constructed a highway linking Idi-Iroko to Porto Novo in the Republic of Benin at a cost of ₦1.8 million; a ₦2 million 25-year interest free loan was granted to Benin; and Nigeria agreed to invest ₦7.2 million in a joint cement project and ₦20 million in a sugar project also in Benin. The government of Benin also received printing machines worth over ₦42,000, ₦20,000 for cultural development and ₦55,000 for a Horticultural and Nutritional Centre. On a visit to an irrigation scheme in 1972 the Nigerian Head of State offered to finance the project. In a 1972 visit to Guinea, Nigeria donated ₦50,000 to their ruling party, agreed to invest ₦65,000 in an iron ore project and seconded 30 teachers to the country in 1973. Two lawyers were seconded to the Gambia in 1973, five tax officers to Swaziland in 1974, three lawyers and a bandmaster were seconded to Botswana in 1972 and two Hausa-teachers were seconded to Algeria in 1973. The government also gave ₦2 million grant to Sahelian countries in 1973. Ethiopia received ₦200,000 drought relief from Nigeria in 1974, Somalia received ₦250,000 in 1973 and another ₦657,895 in 1975. In 1974, ₦400,000 went to the Sudan 'for various purposes', ₦400,000, two lorries and six landrovers were donated to Sierra Leone. The Nigerian government even offered to pay the salary of Grenadian civil servants in 1975 while it spent ₦89,000 on the printing of Niger's official calendar in the same year. At a time when Nigeria was suffering from severe electricity supply problems, and while industries reported a 30% decline in productive capacity as a result of constant power cuts, Nigeria signed a 20-year agreement to supply Niger with electricity from its Kainji Dam at a maximum rate of 30,000 kilowatts and this was to cost ₦9.6 million.[11]

The Nigerian government was equally generous to liberation movements and liberated territories. In June 1972, the Nigerian government increased its contribution to the OAU Liberation Committee to £126,000 and in January 1973 it contributed $180,000. The MPLA received £10 million in 1977, ₦2.5 million went into the South Africa Relief Fund in July 1976, ₦250,000 was donated to Mozambique for the support of Zimbabwean freedom fighters while another ₦1 million was offered to 'help offset economic losses caused by the closing of its border with Rhodesia'. In 1975, Angola received $20 million while the ANC of South Africa got $32,000. These are just a few instances of Nigeria's 'generosity' which followed in the wake of the oil boom. These expenses were hardly popular with the public given the level of poverty and general alienation in society. We are in complete agreement with the following view expressed by an official of the Nigerian Labour Congress:

> The point is not that we are not patriotic or Pan-African in outlook. But the point remains that foreign policy is supposed to be a reflection of domestic policy. The level of unemployment, poverty, alienation, corruption and general inequalities in Nigeria today, hardly justifies the extravagance of the government. It is generous to foreign governments but selfish to Nigerians. I think the government ought to pay attention to the problems at home first before pursuing an extravagant foreign policy. No matter the amount spent to win friends abroad, if the population is alienated, security can hardly be guaranteed.[12]

Corruption and waste, particularly over-inflated contracts, increased food and capital goods imports all contributed to constantly depleting the country's foreign exchange earnings thus necessitating internal and external borrowing. In his 1976-77 budget speech, General Obasanjo noted that

> while government revenue for the 1975–76 fiscal year was ₦3.9 billion, recurrent and capital expenditures totalled ₦4.7. Thus a deficit of ₦0.8 billion was recorded in the first nine months of the fiscal year.

In the same fiscal year, the country spent all its foreign exchange receipts, 'dipped into accumulated reserves' and recorded a ₦125 million trade deficit.[13] By the time he delivered his 1977–78 budget speech, he noted that the previous fiscal year had experienced

> rapidly accelerating price inflation, economically crippling congestion of our ports, wide-spread shortages of essential commodities, a deficit in Federal Government's finances and . . . deterioration in our balance of payments position.[14]

In 1976, while total exports (mainly oil) increased by 36%– from ₦4,900 in 1975 to ₦6,700 million in 1976, total imports increased by 38 per cent – from ₦3,700 million in 1975 to ₦5,100 million in 1976. The balance of goods and services for 1976 recorded a deficit of ₦130.5 million.[15] The dependent process of recycling the country's oil rents did not provide 'exit options' for the state to rectify the problems identified by Obasanjo. Hence when Shehu Shagari came to power, he observed that:

> large increases in government revenue from petroleum have facilitated a sharp rise in the level of government investment and expenditure especially since 1975 . . . which in turn brought about rapid increases in domestic prices and the level of imports. Consequently, public spending has consistently outstripped revenue since 1975, resulting in overall budget deficits . . . As at 30th September 1979 . . . the overall financial position of the Federal Government showed a deficit of ₦1.4 billion . . . The State governments were in the same predicament and were likewise unable to meet their contractual obligations.[16]

According to the World Bank, the current account balance for Nigeria before interest payments on external public debts in 1970 was $348 million; this increased to ₦3,696 million in 1978. Interest payments on external public debt in 1970 were $20 million while in 1978, they were ₦78 million. This fluctuating financial position is largely a precipitate of the unviable base on which the country has recycled its oil wealth since 1973.

Shagari and the Crisis of a Rentier State, 1970-83

Shagari made no serious attempt to improve or diversify the economy and reduce dependence. Instead, he intensified all the economic problems and crises of the country. The problems and contradictions of a rentier state are, more than ever before, brought into the open under the Shagari administration. It is necessary to understand the nature of the rentier state in order to comprehend the implications of oil wealth for an economy which relies on revenues from a sector over which it has limited control and which is not integrated with other sectors in the economy.

The rentier state is a different state-type from the typical postcolonial state. The debate on the postcolonial state has generated some controversy in the efforts to conceptualize the historical peculiarities and specificities of the state-type which replaced the colonial state following political independence. Unfortunately, the debate on the nature of the state has been largely influenced by a mechanistic perception of social classes and political power which approximates conditions of advanced capitalism. Thus, the postcolonial state has been described as 'central', 'overdeveloped' and 'relatively autonomous'. Considering the weakness of the state structure of the underdeveloped social formations, relative to those of other social forces (students, peasants, the unemployed and organized labour) it is essential to locate the discussion of the power of the postcolonial state within the objective content of specific societies. More important perhaps is the crisis of hegemony from which the postcolonial state suffers. The inability to constitute a powerful hegemonic force has been largely responsible for the frequent use of violence and other extra-legal measures in the mediation of social contradictions and conflicts. In addition, the poverty of the post-colonial state, its domination by foreign capital, and the disarticulation of the social formation over which it presides all go to demand a reconceptualization of the peculiarity of the state-type which it represents.[17]

The postcolonial rentier state is a different state-type. The oil economy arises out of the conditions of the rentier state, i.e. an economy which receives substantial amounts of external rents on a regular basis, paid by foreign governments, institutions and agencies. The rents collected by the rentier state usually have very little to do with the production processes of the domestic economy, i.e. the inputs other than location are very insignificant. Thus, the rentier state benefits from differential and monopolistic rents that arise from the structure and nature of accumulation in the sectors concerned. In the case of oil, the benefits reaped by the rentier state arise not only from the monopolistic control of oil production and refining processes by oil companies but also from the price-fixing activities of these companies.

The rents received by the rentier state automatically make it the focus of capital accumulation and class struggles by various factions and fractions of dominant social forces as they compete to take control of the state and preside over the dispensing of the oil wealth. In a rentier state where the social class in control of the state is predominantly comprador or petty-bourgeois, the status of rent collector translates into a temporary boom in commercial activities, massive state expenditure, expansion of state institutions and an increasing alliance between international finance capital and the internal dominant class.

The ability of the rentier state to undertake gigantic expenditures internally leads to spectacular growth in certain sectors of the economy — an increase in GDP and sometimes GNP per capita — but often unaccompanied by fundamental structural changes in the society at large. Huge rents from oil also enable the state to finance some dependent form of industrialization while the resultant alliance between the state, dominant classes and international capital promotes the emergence of the rentier state as a regional or continental sub-imperial power. The simple fact that the state receives and disburses the oil revenues collected from participation in the world capitalist market transforms the techno-economic autonomy of the oil sector into the socio-economic autonomy of the state. The oil rents put the rentier state above other social classes at the internal level while at the international level it becomes less dependent on foreign aid and foreign donor countries.

While the control over oil rent can put the rentier state above other social forces internally, a development which has a direct effect on the form and substance of internal class structures, an underdeveloped rentier state perpetually remains at the mercy of two major forces, one internal and the other external. The internal countervailing force are the oil workers. Though few in number, the dependence of the state on their activities elevates them to a strategic location in the political economy. The state in alliance with the oil companies is then forced to adopt specific strategies and tactics for domesticating the oil workers in order to create conditions for the reproduction of the system. The external force the rentier state must contend with is the oil companies. Their control over oil technology and information on internal reserves as well as their vertically integrated mode of operation at the international level superimposes their power over that of the state. The power of the oil companies in the world oil market and the realization that the post-colonial rentier state is heavily dependent on the oil sector for revenues all combine to underline the fact that with a little pressure, manipulation or threat, transnational oil corporations can determine or condition the ability of the state to accumulate and spend funds and therefore its ability to rationalize the systemic contradictions and mediate conflicts among social classes.

Finally, where the rentier state is controlled by a commercial capitalist class, the tendency is not to use oil wealth in the creation of a viable foundation for industrialization or agriculture. Rather, the rentier economy becomes an import economy, exporting oil and using the rent collected to import manufactures, food, luxury items, expatriate labour and armaments. This open import policy creates a contradiction between the interests of the techno-comprador class and those of the weak nascent national bourgeoisie. However extravagant the rentier state might be, it takes a fundamental crisis for it to experience serious financial problems. Since a lack of savings or shortage of foreign exchange may not constitute constraints on the 'development' pattern of the rentier state, the nature of class alliances, the use of state power, the level of mass mobilization or popular participation and the concrete efforts made to redefine the structured location of the political economy in the international division of labour will in the final analysis determine the ways and manner in which oil wealth is used and the definition given to 'development'.[18]

In what follows in this and the next two chapters, attempts are made to highlight aspects of the numerous contradictions and distortions which oil wealth introduced into the economy, the level of dependence on oil wealth, the impact this dependence and wealth had on state power and internal politics, the impact of oil wealth on agriculture and, consequently, rural–urban relations, food import policy and urban poverty.

It is important to demonstrate the near-total dependence of the Nigerian state on revenues from the oil sector in order to make three major points. First, that the state is dependent on a sector that is non-renewable, dominated by foreign capital and involves only 6% of the total number of workers in the modern sector. The second point is that, if at independence in 1960 Nigeria was an exporter of primary products, and by 1982, oil had become the main source of foreign exchange earnings, it means that agriculture has been totally neglected due to the discovery of an alternative source of capital accumulation. Finally, the third reason relates to the consequences of such a dependence on the use of state power, the 'arrogance of power' which follows the perception of the state as the source of patronage and capital, and the possible over-extension of political responsibilities in the sub-region, region or continent.

In a 1982 speech delivered to a selected audience from the Armed Forces and senior public servants in Lagos, the then Managing Director of the Nigerian National Petroleum Corporation noted that Nigeria had

> totally become dependent on crude oil sales, this is a worrying develop-
> ment and the frightening aspect of this development is that it is likely
> to be a permanent feature and there is little hope for recovery in sight.[19]

The production of high quality, low sulphur oil and the relative proximity to the European market have combined to give Nigerian oil some advantages in the world oil market. The huge revenues that the state collected had had a major impact on development planning in the country. By 1980 when the fourth national development plan was launched, the total budget of $175 billion was to be financed from internal sources. With increasing budgetary allocations, the two sectors that experienced substantial expansion were services and commerce. The intensification of internal political competition, class alliances and re-alignments were precipitates of the struggle to take control of state power and preside over the sharing of 'the national cake' as Nigerians often put it. The tremendous increase in defence expenditure, often justified in the name of defending the country against a possible invasion from South Africa, has more to do with extending and consolidating state power as well as imposing state hegemony over the social formation than with defence against external aggressors.

The distortions created by oil wealth are however mostly pronounced in the impact it has had on agriculture and rural–urban relations. The dramatic decline in the contribution of agriculture to national revenue is highlighted in the next chapter. This decline is in the first instance the product of de-clining budgetary allocations to the rural areas by the Federal and state governments. It is equally the precipitate of efforts by the Nigerian state in alliance with the World Bank to introduce capitalist agriculture into the countryside through the use of complex, capital-intensive mechanisms. The neocolonial content of the Nigerian educational system has also contri-buted to the massive drift from the rural to the urban centres, discouraging the educated and young from engaging in agriculture and consequently the continued concentration of social services in selected sectors of the urban centres. The net effect of these developments is the continued inability to create a linkage between agriculture, which is now abandoned to the old and 'illiterate' in the rural areas and the foreign-capital sponsored industrial-ization in the urban centres.

With the oil revenues, the comprador state and commercial capitalists initiated a massive construction boom which directly contributed to dis-placing peasants from the peri-urban centres and further attracted skilled, semi-skilled and unskilled labour from the rural areas and agriculture. Though the construction boom was able to provide jobs for migrants, the nature of the jobs was seasonal. Even then, the construction boom could not provide employment for up to 30% of the total number of migrants. The unemployed, who could not find decent housing or receive adequate medical attention, not only increased the urban crime rate but also put pressure on employed relatives thus increasing the contradictions between the employed and the unemployed. This fact is one of the underlying causes of the increasing discontent of urban workers as they faced not only the 'squandermania' of the oil rich state but more importantly the demands put on them by their dependants in the rural and urban areas.

The director of the Nigerian National Petroleum Company in a speech cited earlier observed that 'the oil industry has generated vast revenues but these have been so managed as to generate rapid inflation and the aspects of the industry that could actually transform the economy have been neglected'. The food import policy initiated by the government to deal with the problem of declining food production was unable to meet the demands of the growing urban population. The elitist and urban-biased planning methodology continued to concentrate services and power in selected areas of the urban centres. The government had involved itself in numerous prestige projects in and outside the country. As an emerging sub-imperial power in the West African sub-region its involvement in the creation of the Economic Community of West African States (ECOWAS) had cost the country a lot of money and the protocols adopted had served to increase the inflow of foreigners 'in the spirit of ECOWAS'. This inflow meant an inability to plan effectively for urban residents, pressure on social services, increase in the crime rate and rising unemployment among indigenes. The populist educational system introduced under the military turned out its products into the saturated job market and because it had not emphasized vocational or technical training, the job seekers concentrated on the service sector which was already saturated. The 'contractmania' which had come to characterize oil-rich Nigeria, a situation in which virtually all services are contracted out, led to uncontrolled inflation and corruption while at the same time putting serious strains on the nation's finances.

A process of de-industrialization gradually set in as emphasis shifted from production to importation 'of all importables'. By 1983, every 80k out of ₦1 of the federal government revenue was spent on imports. Smuggling became a national problem and the cost of living index rose considerably in all urban centres. To bribe the workers who were hard hit by these increases, the government allowed wage increases which were not aimed at reducing the gap between the rich and the poor but at putting more money into circulation. The net result was a spiralling inflation. In the light of the general crisis caused by mismanagement of oil wealth and misplacement of national priorities, as the Nigerian President observed in his 1980 budget proposals to the National Assembly, oil wealth had resulted in rapid increases in domestic prices and the level of imports.[20] In the same speech, the Nigerian President declared that the country's unfunded external loans rose from ₦354 million in 1975/76 to ₦1,598.3 million in October 1979, an increase of 35%. This gloomy picture did not dictate caution in the pattern of state expenditure. The increasing discontent among the urban poor generated conflicts between workers and the state. The response of the state was to use its control over the means of coercion to suppress the workers, initiate numerous punitive labour laws, attempt to indigenize the peripheral capitalist economy without altering the relations of production, shift the blame for the economic crisis to the 'lazy and unproductive farmers' and workers and perpetuate the neocolonial educational system. In addition, where direct bribery of workers through periodic wage increases failed, ethnicity, religion and other extra-legal mechanisms were employed to stem the rising militancy of the workers and the increasing incidents of co-ordinated struggles by the rural and urban people.

In spite of these developments, the dominant social classes could not conceal their unproductive and wasteful location in the social formation. The gross inefficiency which came to characterize oil-rich Nigeria reached such a high level that the national airline was handed over to KLM Royal Dutch Airlines, the national railways were handed to the Indians to operate, the problem of smuggling was handed to a Swiss firm, while the cement factory at Nkalagu was handed over to another Swiss firm until it makes some profit. The massive level of corruption in high places and the luxurious life-style of state officials all served to alienate the average Nigerian from the institutions and goals of the power elite. These conditions combined with others to lay the foundation for the May 1981 General Strike in Nigeria (see Chapter 7).

If the masses were discontented, the rich were not. In recycling the oil naira under Shagari, the state focused attention on useless viability studies, on contracts, especially those associated with Abuja, the new Federal capital, on the importation of goods, especially fertilizers, on excessive expenditure on legislators whom the executives thought should be bribed in order to reduce intra-class rivalries and on corruption, which Shagari used to stabilize his regime. It is important to understand these forms of recycling in order to comprehend how the Shagari administration plundered the treasury and put the country into the most serious financial mess in its history.

Yet, the administration started with optimism. On 8 January 1980, after his first one hundred days in office, Shagari told a World Press Conference that:

> We have, during the last 100 days, witnessed a tremendous improvement in our economic situation. When I assumed office on 1st of October 1979 the daily cash balance of the Federal Government with the Central Bank was in the red to the tune of ₦521,748,00. On that date the country's reserve stood at ₦2,376,824,653. Within three months of our coming to office we have been able to reverse this unhealthy financial trend which had plagued the Federal Government since July 1976. Today I am happy to say that our financial position both internally and externally is improving steadily which is a good sign of hope for a prosperous future.[21]

The Ministry of Finance gave the reasons for this improvement in the middle of 1980:

> In the area of fiscal and monetary measures, the Ministry can look back with satisfaction on the various measures which made it possible for the financial position of the Federal Government to move from a deficit of ₦1,403,621,928 on the eve of the assumption of office by Mr. President to a surplus of ₦2,368,968,176 by July this year. Improved tax collection contributed to the healthy financial position. The total collection by the Department of Inland Revenue for the period 1st October 1979 to 30th June 1980, stood at ₦6,819,719,580 as against ₦3,111,611,623 for the previous corresponding period ended 30th June 1979. Apart from the vast improvement in Petroleum Profit Tax as a result of the increase in prices of crude oil which accounts for a substantial part of the difference, the improved tax collection efforts, and the renewed dedication of the nation's tax officers, also played a significant role in achieving this impressive record ... Equally encouraging has been the country's balance of payments and foreign reserve positions. In October 1979, foreign reserves stood at ₦3.4 billion; at the end of July this year, the reserves had achieved an all-time record of ₦4.7 billion – an increase of about 42%.[22]

Throughout 1980, the President and his ministers made numerous and vague promises to improve the economy. Indeed, the administration promised to make the country self-reliant in food production by 1984 and that by 1986, the problems of shelter would be no more. These vague promises were in fact made throughout the duration of the Second Republic. In March 1981, the federal government published the Fourth National Development Plan which was to be the economic blueprint for 1981–85. The plan contained elegantly worded promises on agricultural production, qualitative education, housing, industries and economic infrastructure. The plan also aimed at diversification of the economy from over-dependence on petroleum to a widened base for public revenue and export savings. The GDP was estimated to grow from a level of ₦36.078 billion in 1980 to ₦51.071 billion in 1985, representing about 7.2% growth rate for the 5-year period. Gross fixed capital formation was expected to grow from ₦13.112 billion in 1981 to ₦82 billion in 1985 and national savings from ₦14.162 billion in 1981 to ₦17.741 billion in 1985. Exports were expected to grow at 6.7% and foreign reserves from ₦5.357 billion in 1980 to a peak of ₦9.148 billion in 1983 before falling to ₦7.507 billion in 1985 (see Tables 5.5 and 5.6).

The Fourth Plan, 1981–85, had envisaged oil production averaging 2.19 million barrels per day and a selling price of US $55 by the end of the plan period. Thus, the total budget of ₦82 billion, the largest in the country's history, was to be largely financed from 'internal sources'. The oil sector was to be the major source of revenues for the financing of the huge projects of the plan. However, these were extremely optimistic projections.

Table 5.5
Balance of Payments (Naira million)

Item	1980	1981	1982	1983*	1984*	1985*
Merchandise:						
Exports	14,640	15,672	16,578	17,894	19,079	20,306
Imports	11,818	13,263	14,884	16,601	18,485	20,548
Trade Balance	2,822	2,409	1,874	1,293	594	242
Current Account Balance	1,589	1,150	544	200	1,160	2,380
Reserve Level	5,337	7,209	8,504	9,148	8,902	7,507

Source: *Federal Government Budget In Brief*, 1982, Annexure V

* Estimated

Table 5.6
GDP at 1977 Factor Cost: 1980–85 (Naira million)

Sector	1980	1981	1982	1983*	1984*	1985
Agriculture	4,372	4,547	4,729	4,918	5,115	5,319
Livestock, Forestry and Fishing	3,135	3,260	3,391	3,526	3,668	3,814
Mining and Quarrying	8,473	8,642	8,815	8,992	9,171	9,355
Manufacturing	2,657	3,056	3,514	4,014	4,647	5,344
Utilities	119	137	157	181	208	239
Construction	3,785	3,974	4,173	4,382	4,601	4,831
Transport	1,277	1,430	1,602	1,794	2,009	2,251
Communications	97	112	1,128	148	170	195
Wholesale and Retail Trade	7,215	7,937	8,730	9,603	10,563	11,620
Housing	1,490	1,609	1,738	1,877	2,027	2,189
Producer of Government Services	2,268	2,540	2,845	3,186	3,569	3,997
Other Services	1,190	1,309	1,440	1,584	1,742	1,917
Total	*36,078*	*38,533*	*41,262*	*44,232*	*47,490*	*51,071*

Source: *Federal Government Budget in Brief*, 1982, Annexure 1

* Estimated

Production declined to 700,000, occasionally rising to 1.1 million, barrels per day. Nigeria, in its search for revenues, was forced to break OPEC ranks and unilaterally reduced its oil price to match North Sea oil prices of US $34–35. This caused the immediate crisis of the Fourth Plan.

In launching the Fourth Plan, President Shagari declared that projects would be 'geared towards strengthening the foundations already laid by the earlier plans ... (and) towards removing known constraints to the growth and modernisation of our nation and national economy'.[23] The specific objectives of the Fourth Plan include

> i) the achievement of increased real income for all Nigerians, ii) a more even and equitable distribution of income, iii) increase in the supply of skilled manpower, iv) priority to agricultural production and processing, v) provision of food for the large and growing population, vi) production of adequate raw materials for industries, vii) national self-reliance, viii) priority status to housing, education and manpower development, and ix) priority status to power generation and supply, water supply and telecommunication, health care, industrial development, transportation — rail, land and water.

From the list above, it would appear that the post-military administration was going to accord 'priority status' to all sectors of the economy.

Of the total investment expenditure of ₦82 billion, ₦70.5 billion was to be accounted for by the various governments and their agencies. The private sector was to be responsible for the ₦11.5 billion balance. The governments involved were expected to generate budget surpluses totalling about ₦53.6 billion over the plan period. Federal Government planned investments were expected to generate an overall growth rate of 7% per annum in real terms and this was expected to contribute to a 'significant increase in the standard of living'.

The planned expenditures were to be made possible by increased oil production and exportation. The President made this clear in his launching address to the National Assembly:

> The Fourth Plan is being launched at a time when the country's production of crude oil, which is the main source of government revenue and foreign exchange earning, has virtually stabilised. A basic strategy of the Fourth Plan would therefore be the promotion of optional utilization of resources. Oil is a wasting asset. The resources generated from this sector must therefore be used to promote all-round expansion in the productuve capacity of the economy so as to ensure self-sustaining growth in the shortest time possible.[24]

As developments in the oil industry have shown, this expectation was completely misplaced. In fact, if one examines closely the specifics of allocations as well as the pattern of plan initiation and implementation, two facts can be easily discerned. The first is that comprehensive as the objectives look, they are clearly biased against aspects which involve the poor majority. Even where there appears to be some attention to aspects involving non-bourgeois forces, loopholes are created to rationalize the participation of transnational corporation and other capitalist interests.

Agriculture was expected to grow at an annual rate of 4% and it received 13% of the total capital investment of all governments. The emphasis was to be on food production and direct assistance to small farmers through the provision of farm inputs. At the same time, the state hoped to go into direct production, to encourage 'foreign partners' and Nigerians to invest in agriculture in partnership with foreign interests. The consequence has been the use of state resources and political power to support and rationalize capitalist penetration of the rural areas. The net result has been increased displacement of rural producers and migration to urban centres. The failure of food production policies as in the 'Green Revolution Programme' is clearly evidenced in the rising food import bill.

Manufacturing and industry were expected to grow at an annual rate of 15% over the plan period. Major programmes to be executed included the development of iron and steel, liquified natural gas, integrated sugar, cement, nitrogenous fertilizer, petrochemicals, and pulp and paper projects. Education was to receive ₦2.0 billion and seven new universities of technology have been established. An open university system is being introduced and existing Federal Colleges of Education are to be expanded. These two aspects of the plan have in no way addressed critical issues of developing indigenous capacities and thus generating a capacity for self-sustained *growth* and *development*. The emphasis is on *growth*, irrespective of the social costs. At a time when major capital projects were being set up, the state was dismantling the indigenization decrees passed by the military which in any case had emphasized ownership but not control. The educational system is still largely neocolonial in content and is hardly related to the objective problems of the society.

A second fact that can be easily seen in the biases of the plan is its adherence to the 'top down' or 'trickle down' methodology of plan initiation and implementation. While the Joint Planning Board (consisting of Permanent Secretaries of Ministries of Economic Development in all the 19 states, and the Ministers and State Commissioners responsible for Economic Planning), the National Economic Council chaired by the Vice-President, the Nigerian Association of Chambers of Commerce, Industry, Mines and Agriculture, and the Manufacturers Association of Nigeria were all involved in the initiation and formulation of the Fourth Plan, 90% of the working people of Nigeria were effectively barred from making inputs.[25] The Nigeria Labour Congress which consists of 45 industrial unions, professional and other associations, peasant organizations and co-operatives and student union organizations were not consulted. Thus, the established elitist and bourgeois content of the planning process remained intact. While education received only ₦2.0 billion and housing only ₦2.5 billion, the Federal Capital Territory alone received ₦2.5 billion. The relative concern for projects that would directly satisfy the tastes and political aspirations of the bourgeoisie influenced the pattern of budgetary allocation as well as the determination of plan priorities.[26]

Since the Fourth Plan was launched, the state and the plan have moved in opposite directions. As an official in the Central Planning Office reflected,

> it is an unfortunate development. The economy lacked the base to sustain the projects even if the oil market had performed as expected. But, it is clear that only a drastic and downward revision of the plan can redress the problems that are currently being generated in the economy.[27]

Perhaps the most critical report on the plan and the state of the economy was the ILO's referred to earlier.[28] Among other things, the report criticized the misplacement of priorities, over-dependence on the oil sector and food imports and wastage of national resources. It highlighted the rapidly deteriorating conditions of the rural and urban areas, agricultural stagnation, urban dislocation, social insecurity and institutional decay in the country. On the Fourth and other plans before it in the oil boom period, the ILO noted that 'there is little evidence that Nigeria's expenditure has made much impact on the conditions of the majority of the population,' and recommended that 'to meet the country's basic needs and achieve greater self-reliance would require a very different, indeed opposite set of priorities',[29] than those currently in operation. S.A. Madujibeya has equally criticized the Fourth Plan as consisting of nothing but 'massive expenditure programmes not related to domestic capacity' which would ultimately generate 'inflation, wasteful expenditures and severe balance of payments difficulties'.[30] Furthermore:

> Given that oil is now the main source of revenues and foreign exchange for Nigeria, it means that the more ambitious the expenditure programme adopted, the larger is the volume of oil that needs to be produced and sold to finance it. Such a strategy tends to tie the country more tightly to the fortunes of an uncertain international oil market and forms the basis of periodical cash-flow problems. Given the uncertainty in the world oil markets, the prospects of selling larger and larger quantities of crude oil as postulated by our increasingly ambitious expenditure programmes are becoming ever more dubious.[31]

The perceptive diagnosis above was made in 1981 at the beginning of the plan period and has come to pass. It is not the case that the state is unaware of the problems identified but there are fundamental structural inhibitions militating against the policies aimed at encouraging the dominant classes to 'look inwards and invest in production as against distribution' or policies aimed at by-passing the compradors and bureaucrats and promoting a form of state capitalism. Part of these structural problems have to do with the already entrenched power of the compradors and their transnational allies, the tenuous hegemony of the state and widespread corruption. The unproductive accumulative base of the bourgeoisie directly promotes corruption and waste and, therefore, an inability to diversify the sources of revenue. The fragility of state power and bureaucratic corruption and inefficiency also militate against efforts at popular mobilization and the involvement of non-bourgeois forces in plan initiation and implementation. The weak nature of the state equally prevents it from being able to control the compradors, bureaucrats and transnational interests.

Under the Fourth Plan, and with the precipitous decline in oil revenues on which the execution of major and secondary projects was hinged, the economy has deteriorated to the pre-oil boom situation. It is even possible to argue, that it is in its worst state in the country's history given the depth of contradictions evidenced in rising unemployment, particularly of university and polytechnic graduates,[32] social violence, armed robbery and inter- and intra-class struggles which have combined with the arrogance of power, drift and carelessness of the ruling class to disrupt efforts to rationalize and subsidize private capital accumulation with public funds. As at present, the hopes nurtured by members of the ruling class that with the oil boom and projects under the Fourth Plan, Nigeria could emerge as one of Newly Industrializing Countries have been dashed.

In his first year, 1979–1980, Shagari tried to continue with the economic programmes of the military but modifying them to reflect his so-called commitment to self-reliance. Monetary and credit policies were directed at stimulating domestic production and stabilizing prices through increased supply of goods and services. No impressive result was, however, achieved. Fiscal measures were based on the assumption that the import restriction measures of 1978–79 might have achieved their results of improving the balance of payments. However, restrictive measures led to smuggling and the dampening of productive capacity. The Shagari administration thought that it could solve the problems of smuggling and low productivity by abolishing import duties on certain items (e.g. fishing vessels), and lowering tariffs on raw materials to encourage local manufacturing and check inflation and regulating exchange controls. All these policies brought disastrous consequences because they made it possible for the wealthy and fraudulent politicians to transfer massive sums of money abroad, and to import all sorts of goods on a large scale.

The Shagari administration also attempted to bribe the working class and pretended to be benevolent by its 1980 income policy which increased the minimum wage from ₦720 to ₦1,200 p.a.[33]

By the end of 1980, the financial mismanagement and reckless importation of goods had begun to have an impact on the Nigerian society. The 1981 budget was christened the 'Budget of Caution', but in spite of all promises, 1981 did not witness any improvement. Indeed, austerity measures were introduced in that year, the employment market became saturated, foreign reserves declined and the balance of payments showed a deficit. But imports increased from ₦722 million in 1979 to ₦1.2 billion in 1981 while the estimated foreign exchange disbursement was ₦14 billion based on the monthly import rate of ₦1.204 billion.

The federal government ignored all the signs which showed clearly the poor state of the economy. President Shagari, in fact, deceived the public in his 1982 budget proposal when he said:

> The enumerated setbacks in our economy (in 1981) notwithstanding, our GDP has shown a slight improvement . . . available indicators show an encouraging growth of 15% in the manufacturing sector. There is a 3% rate of growth in the agricultural sector. Furthermore, there are increases in investments. These are, without doubt, expressions of confidence which investors have in the resilience of Nigeria's economy. This confidence has remained unshaken, despite the prophesies of gloom and doom, who are ignorant of the difference between resilience and buoyancy.[34]

But 1982 was worse for the nation than 1981. There was a slow down in the level of economic activities. The GDP in real terms dropped from ₦30.5 billion in 1981 to ₦29.8 billion in 1982 as a result of the 16% decrease in the contribution from the petroleum sector. While exports were only ₦10 billion, imports amounted to ₦11.4 billion, showing a deficit of ₦1.4 billion. The external reserves declined from ₦2.6 billion in 1981 to ₦1.1 billion in 1982. There was a budgetary deficit of ₦3.2 billion which had to be covered by external and internal loans. In April 1982, Shagari had to seek the special permission of the National Assembly to introduce stabilization measures; this was granted and his government planned to reduce the level of imports and conserve scarce foreign exchange, encourage and protect local industries and ensure strict adherence to government priorities. The government believed that these three measures would lead to the mobilization of domestic savings, investments and reduction in inflation rate. In addition, the government resorted to foreign borrowing to replenish its foreign reserves.

Being ill-conceived and poorly implemented, the measures to revamp the economy ended in disaster. By 1983, it had become too clear that the Shagari administration had no answer to the country's economic problems and mismanagement which it had created. The newspapers for 1983 carried tales of economic woes, inflation, unemployment, hunger and starvation.[35] In its editorial of 24 December 1983, captioned 'Sober Christmas', the *Guardian* reflected on the country's economic crisis:

> This year, all is quiet and sober. Economic hardship increasing almost daily in ugly dimensions, has taken all calculations to shreds, leaving pockets empty, markets deserted . . . This is the legacy of the economic crisis and the Nigerian twins: government mismanagement and corruption.[36]

To save face, the government blamed the global economic recession for the woes, urged citizens to tighten their belts, if possible to the point of suffocation, and repeatedly promised that food would soon flood the market.

The life-style of the politicians did not, however, reflect any austere mood. Throughout the 1983 campaign period, NPN politicians urged others to join them if they wanted to look as rosy and robust as they are. This reflected the truth that the Shagari administration spent a large part of the nation's resources on building the cheeks and bodies of a tiny ruling elite. First, most politicians became contractors, and they received huge contracts which were either poorly executed or not executed at all. There were stories of contractors who received money to supply furniture to houses which had not been built, to clear bush in obscure places, to supply fertilizers to ghost farmers, etc. Several of these received money and bolted, like the 1982 ₦50 million contract awarded by the Ministry of Housing and Environment to ghost contractors. It is not possible to estimate how much money was lost in this process.[37] Even in the case of a genuine contract (to refer to one that was executed) the cost was often so high that the end product never justified it. President Shehu Shagari himself knew that over-inflation of contracts was one of the several sources of leakage:

> We have observed that since the era of the so-called 'oil boom' in this country there has been the misguided impression that money was no problem to the Government. Against this background, project costs were often inflated. Designs were produced not primarily to suit our needs of society but to satisfy the taste of designers and engineers handling them. Invariably, the designs were over-costed, equipment and machinery for the projects over-priced. It was this genuine concern that led me to set up a panel which examined the problem and came to a conclusion that contracts in this country were often awarded at exorbitant costs. The recommendations of the committee which have been carefully studied and accepted by the Government will be used in costing projects in our Fourth National Development Plan. I intend to set up a Cost Monitoring Unit consisting of experts from relevant disciplines for this purpose.[38]

The President took no positive step; indeed, his regime was the most guilty, the most reckless and the most unserious in the over-inflation of contracts. For instance, ₦550 was the minimum spent on clearing 10,000 square metres (the size of a football field) whereas a peasant working with a simple cutlass would take a maximum of ₦10.

The President also promised in January 1981, when launching the Fourth Plan, to avoid white elephant projects:

> For the avoidance of doubt, there will be no room in the Plan for grandiose or prestige projects such as we have witnessed in our recent past. Rather, emphasis will be placed on simple, functional designs especially with respect to standard amenities such as schools, hospitals and residential buildings.

Again, this was another piece of rhetoric — Abuja, the so-called federal housing units and the steel-mill became grandiose projects, veritable gold mines for contractors and conduit pipes to make millions of money. Chinua Achebe captures the reality most effectively when he remarks:

> A few years ago a new cultural facility was opened in London by Queen Elizabeth II. It was called the Barbican Centre and it cost the British tax-payer £150 million, which is roughly equivalent to ₦180 million. It was such a magnificent structure that one account described it as the Eighth Wonder of the World.
>
> We know that Nigeria in the last decade has built many structures worth more (or rather that cost more) than ₦180 million. But show me one wonder among them, unless it be the wonder of discrepancy between cost and value!
>
> The reason for this is quite simple. A structure that costs us, say ₦200 million carries a huge hidden element of kickbacks and commissions to Nigerian middlemen and, increasingly, middlewomen; it carries inflated prices of materials caused largely by corruption; theft and inefficiency on the site fostered by more corruption; contract variations corruptly arranged midstream in execution, an inflated margin (or, more aptly, corridor) of profit. When all these factors are added to others which our corrupt ingenuity constantly invents, you will be lucky if on completion (assuming such a happy event occurs) your structure is worth as much as ₦80 million.[39]

Corruption was not, however, limited to contract inflation. The Second Republic was notorious for fraud: payment of huge sums of money to ghost workers; importation of fake products (e.g. mud and sand) in order to obtain foreign exchange; outright stealing of government property; illegal transfer of money to private accounts, etc. Those involved tried as much as possible to be clever but when they thought they could be caught, they resorted to large-scale destruction of official files and papers and arson. The NET building, Africa's tallest building, the Ministry of External Affairs and the Accounts section of the Federal Capital Development Authority, Abuja were all burnt following widespread allegations of fraud in these places. The Shagari government at first denied corruption, but later admitted it and set up a whole ministry late in 1983 to combat it. The government also tried to toy with the idea of an 'ethical revolution', urging the people, and not the fraudulent politicians, to re-orientate their lives. It was the corruption and this deceit on ethical revolution which partly spurred Wole Soyinka, Nigeria's well known playwright, to wax a popular record, whose wordings are quoted in full in appendix 5.1.

Nor was this all. All arms of government were involved in reckless spending. The governors and the president obtained large sums of money as security votes. The president obtained a contingency vote of ₦150 million annually except in 1983 when he obtained ₦300 million for reasons best known to

Table 5.7
Salaries and Allowances of Members of the National Assembly in 1980 (9 months)

Item	Approved Expenditure (in Naira)
Salaries	
President of Senate	12,750
Speaker	12,750
Deputy President	11,250
Leader of Senate	12,890
Leader of House	12,890
Party Leaders	103,090
Senators and Members	6,053,370
Other Charges:	
Salaries and allowances for legislative aid	15,825,350
Rent for offices in constituencies	5,112,300
Office equipment in constituencies	1,904,860
Local transport and travelling	1,200,000
Consolidated allowances	1,804,000
Office accommodation	5,000,000
Senators and representatives allowances	6,200,000
Visitors: travelling and entertainment	175,000
Legislative duty allowances	875,000
Entertainment allowances	32,550
Total:	*44,309,300*

Source: *Federal Government Budget*, 1980 Approved Estimates

himself and his associates. Legislators refused to be beaten in the game. They, too, bought several cars, furniture, etc.

All politicians also received fantastic salaries and fringe benefits, and justified this by repeatedly saying that 'the presidential system is expensive'. In 9 months in 1980, the members of the National Assembly (545 in all) obtained as salaries and allowances an astronomical sum of ₦44,309,300 (see Tables 5.7 and 5.8). This amount increased the year after. The salary and allowances of the president and his vice amounted to about ₦71,000 per annum. It is difficult to know the actual total of salaries and allowances paid to all functionaries since they were too many and the number was never fixed. There was a myriad of political advisers, presidential liaison officers, board members, chairmen of parastatals, ministers, etc. All these functions were also duplicated in the nineteen states where the legislature and the executive fixed the salaries and allowances they wanted. But the politicians forgot that the people they were supposed to represent are poor, so poor that only a few had any access to the minimum ₦1,200 per annum wage

Table 5.8
Annual Expenditure on the National Assembly, FEDECO, and the Presidency

HEAD 00180000000: NATIONAL ASSEMBLY

Personnel Costs

	Naira
Office of the President of Senate	210,570
Office of the Deputy President of Senate	62,120
Leader of the Senate	77,020
Party Leaders (Senate)	193,410
Senators	1,459,200
Senators' Staff	2,083,960
Office of the Clerk of the Senate	607,080
Office of the Clerk of the House of Representatives	1,031,840
Office of the Speaker of House of Representatives	173,310
Deputy Speaker of House of Representatives	61,540
Leader of House of Representatives	77,020
Office of the Party Leader (House of Representatives)	193,410
Honourable Members	6,077,170
Members' Staff	5,132,700
Office of the Clerk of the National Assembly	187,120
National Secretariat of Nigerian Legislators	166,620
Protocol and International Relations	289,940

Total deductions from National Assembly Personnel Costs   *18,084,030*

Sub-head 008100200094: National Assembly

Overhead Costs: Grants, Contributions and Subventions	*Naira*
Parliamentary Association and other international organizations	180,000
Public relations services including publications	300,000
Remunerations and allowances for members staff	13,216,770

Subhead – Miscellaneous Expenses

Welfare and special assistance	400,000
Legislative duty allowance	650,000
Overtime (Staff) development of legislative and parliamentary terminology	100,000

Subhead – Maintenance of Motor Vehicles and Other Capital Assets

Residential flats of members	4,500,000
Tafawa Balewa Square parking expenses	200,000
Maintenance of standby-generator, air-conditioning of National Assembly Hall, Senate Building and Members' residential quarters	700,000

Members' and Senators' office equipment	800,000
Staff residential accommodation hire	1,000,000
Maintenance of staff quarters	800,000
Motor vehicle guarantee scheme	800,000
Maintenance of motor vehicles and running costs	1,000,000
Vehicle advances	1,000,000

Total deductions from National Assembly, Overhead Costs   *25,646,770*

Summary — National Assembly:

	Naira
Personnel Costs	18,084,030
Overhead Costs	25,646,770
Total:	*43,730,800*

HEAD 005200000006: FEDERAL ELECTORAL COMMISSION

Overhead Costs:

Grants, Contributions and Subventions	*Naira*
Grants to Political Parties	5,162,360
Sub-head 005200200211: Operational Costs	40,000,000
Total deduction from Overhead Costs, FEDECO:	*45,162,360*

General Assembly	*Naira*
National Assembly	42,730,800
FEDECO	45,162,360
Total deductions:	*88,893,160*

HEAD 002100000009: PRESIDENCY

Office of the Special Advisers to the President:

Personnel Costs	*Naira*
7 Special Advisers	112,000
3 Special Assistants	33,150
Allowances	7,000
Total:	*152,150*

HEAD 002108200076: OVERHEAD COSTS

	Naira
Maintenance of vehicles and capital	159,188

Table 5.8 (continued)

HEAD 002108200124: MISCELLANEOUS EXPENSES

	Naira
Centre for Presidential Studies (CPS)	10,000
Total:	*169,188*

Summary:	
Personnel Costs	152,150
Overhead Costs	169,188
Total:	*321,338*

HEAD 005300000006: CONSOLIDATED REVENUE FUND CHARGES

Presidency:

Personnel Costs	*Naira*
President of the Federal Republic of Nigeria	30,000
Vice-President of the Federal Republic of Nigeria	21,000
Total:	*51,000*

Overhead Costs	
Allowances for President and Vice-President	88,870
Total:	*88,870*

Summary:	*Naira*
Personnel Costs	51,000
Overhead Costs	88,870
Total:	*139,870*

HEAD 00531300000009: FEDERAL ELECTORAL COMMISSION

Personnel Costs:	*Naira*
Chairman	14,270
Commissioners	293,560
Total:	*307,830*

Overhead Costs	
Rent Allowance	36,220
Transport Allowance	7,200
Consolidated Allowance for Commissioners	57,600
Total:	*101,020*

Summary	
Personnel Costs	307,830
Overhead Costs	101,020
Total FEDECO:	*408,850*

005318000009: NATIONAL POPULATION COMMISSION

Personnel Costs:	*Naira*
Chairman	15,000
Commissioners	285,000
Total:	*300,000*

005318100004: OVERHEAD COSTS

	Naira
Consolidated Allowances for Chairman and Commissioners	84,000
Total:	*84,000*

Summary	
Personnel Costs	300,000
Overhead Costs	84,000
Total National Population Commission	*384,000*

General Summary	*Naira*
Presidency	139,870
Federal Electoral Commission	408,850
National Population Commission	384,000
Total:	*932,720*

Source: *Sunday Sketch*, 22 January 1984, p. 5.

which Shagari emphasized as one of his major achievements, and that their own salaries and allowances were completely unrelated to the country's socio-economic realities.

There is hardly any economy which could absorb such large-scale fraud, mismanagement and reckless spending. By 1981, the treasury had become virtually empty, and the Shagari government had to beg all over the world for loans. Shagari needed the loans not for development but to mediate intra-class rivalries, remain in power, pay political debts and avert total economic disaster. All the nineteen state governments incurred heavy external debts, totalling about $8 billion by March 1983. The federal government itself negotiated for a ₦2.5 billion from the IMF, signed a ₦1.5 billion loan agreement with a consortium of 25 European, American and Middle East banks in July 1983, and it was also reported in November that the United States granted it credit loans totalling $180 million. These debts mortgaged the country's ability to take several autonomous decisions or policies at home or externally, and also demonstrated the dire need for foreign exchange and revenues to subsidise the country's dependent participation in the world capitalist system.[40] In fact, by April 1983, the former Minister for Finance blithely announced that the country's external debt was only ₦10.2 billion and that this was nothing to worry about. During the December 1983 Sixth Annual Congress of the UPN in Abeokuta, Chief Awolowo, who is highly respected for his accuracy with figures, announced that 'Nigeria has become a bankrupt nation which cannot pay its foreign indebtedness which now stands at between $16 billion and $20 billion'.[41] Even if the debts were nothing near those of Mexico and Brazil, they consolidated Nigeria's subservient role in the world capitalist system and reflected clearly the extent to which the economy had been looted and mismanaged.[42]

The Oil Glut, Economic Contraction and Contradictions, 1981-3

The glut in the world oil market should have sent the right signals to the custodians of state power. Shagari himself knew as far back as 1981 that it was dangerous to be over-dependent on oil and that there could be a glut:

> The estimated Federally collected revenue for 1981 is ₦14.745 billion out of which ₦14.033 billion will go to the Federation Account. The revenue expectations for 1981 are bedevilled by the somewhat unstable and unpredictable nature of the crude oil market. As you are aware, this commodity alone accounts for over 80 per cent of the total federally collected revenue. Moreover, the developed countries, who are major consumers of crude oil, have been stockpiling oil. For this and other reasons, the oil producing countries may be compelled to cut back production in response to the market trends.[43]

A year later, he repeated this same point and admitted, though inadvertently, that his government was yet to use the oil money to transform the economy:

> Despite Nigeria's oil prosperity there are the familiar problems of inadequate capital for investment in industrial ventures and social overheads such as electricity, water, port facilities, housing and telecommunications. There are also problems of migration from rural to urban areas, unemployment, inflation, inadequate resources and shortage of managerial and technical manpower . . . Increasing petroleum revenues to any developing country like Nigeria . . . cannot automatically mean such country is a rich one.[44]

The impact of dependence on the oil sector is many-sided. At the internal level, as we have mentioned, in spite of increasing state participation, government control is still very weak. The domination of technology, information, high-level manpower and other capital requirements as well as the experience the companies have acquired over the years since 1938, means that the state is a junior and weak participant in the industry which can be easily manipulated. More important is the fact that unless the oil wealth is employed to redress the inequalities, distortions and poverty in society, the consequences for continued political stability would be immense. Oil is a wasting asset. Unless derivable rents are expended on the development of a viable socio-economic base in order to generate a strong absorptive capacity, a precipitous decline in oil production, exports and revenues can throw an oil-dependent society into a major crisis. If not carefully managed, the net result of concentration would be increasing indebtedness, inflation and restlessness within non-bourgeois forces. It is equally essential in an attempt to comprehend the pattern of oil exploitation and exportation, to take cognizance of developments within oil-consuming economies. After 1973, the advanced capitalist economies not only initiated moves to destabilize OPEC but also to ensure 'enough' peace in the Middle East in order to prevent future price increases. The increase in the level of military cooperation between Saudi Arabia, Egypt and the USW, the isolation of Libya, the instigation of the war between Iran and Iraq and the Camp David Agreement are a few moves in this direction. The developed economies also initiated a two-pronged effort (1) to ensure the intensification of research into alternative sources of energy and ways to conserve energy and (2) through their global connections and interests to see that in the recycling of oil rents paid to OPEC member states substantial parts come back either directly or indirectly. For oil-producing economies which neglected these developments, when production and exports declined in 1978 and 1981, the crises which were generated within such economies are yet to be fully worked out. However, it is in the process of spending (recycling) the oil rents that Nigeria's full incorporation into world capitalism becomes evident.

The 1981 glut only drove home the reality which had existed at the level of theory up to January of that year. The Managing Director of the NNPC had noted that

> it is hazardous for a country to rely on one single commodity to this extent because any reversal in the fortunes of this commodity will automatically adversely affect the country's development programme. Besides, a country that depends on a single product is also highly susceptible to political blackmail.[45]

This was exactly what happened in February 1981 with the glut in the world oil market. Oil production declined from the 2.09 million bpd in January 1981 to 1.86 million bpd in March, 1.16 million bpd in May and 0.64 million bpd in August 1981. In order to avert the crisis, OPEC limited Nigeria's world market quota to 1.3 million bpd. This did not improve Nigeria's position as 'traditional customers walked away from their contracts in the effort to blackmail Nigeria into reducing the price of its high quality low sulphur oil';[46] thus, production declined to 500,000 barrels per day in early 1982. The Fourth Plan had envisaged a daily production level of 2.19 million

115

and an average price of $55 per barrel.

These precipitous declines in production, exports and revenues meant a serious crisis for the Plan and economy which were both extremely dependent on the oil market and the recycling of oil rents. But Nigeria had broken OPEC ranks and unilaterally reduced the price of its oil to $34 per barrel. This reduction did not help the level of revenues. Foreign reserves which stood at $10 billion in January 1981 declined to $1.7 billion by March 1982. By July 1983, the country's external reserves stood at barely ₦844.9 million and by August, there was a slight increase to ₦902.9 million.[47] The glut in the world oil market created a serious cash-flow problem for the state resulting in an inability to import sufficient food to feed the teeming urban population, pay workers in some states for up to six months, keep development projects afloat and mediate class contradictions through contracts, donations, bribery and so on. The severe inflationary trend which accompanied the shortage of goods, particularly food items, heightened contradictions and threatened the social order. The government was forced to borrow money from the Euro-market, a move which significantly contributed to the further integration of Nigeria into the world capitalist system. The erosion of the hitherto relative financial autonomy of the state, the contradictions within the economy and popular pressures from the working class forced the state to initiate two panicky measures.

The first was 'scapegoatism', which involved the expulsion of 'aliens' from Nigeria. Irrespective of the act, it was related to the economy and the inability of the state to deal effectively with the current of instability and disorder that was threatening it. In addition, the policy was aimed at diverting public attention from the mismanagement of the oil economy and the display of affluence by a few. The expulsion of 'aliens' made a deep dent on Nigeria's image in the sub-region and threatened commitment to the Economic Community of West African States (ECOWAS).

The second policy was the Economic Stabilisation Act alias 'Austerity Measures'. The Act imposed wide-ranging restrictions on economic activities, primarily imports and the disbursement of foreign exchange. Internally, commodities became scarce as industries could not import raw materials and spare parts and there was a temporary ban on new appointments which fuelled the problem of unemployment. It is interesting to note that, given the depth of contradictions generated by the decline in oil revenues, the various political parties, irrespective of their differences, closed ranks to pass the Economic Stabilisation Act. The Act did not solve the structural problems of the dependent economy. The Managing Director of the NNPC even referred to the Act as 'crash programmes calculated to bring about a balance between the inflow and outflow of our foreign reserves and prevent a state of national bankruptcy'.[48] J.K. Randle described the effect of the measures thus:

> The result was that local industries were severely crippled as more and more of them found themselves confronted with shortages of raw materials, spare parts and just about everything else. Many more re-

trenched staff thus adding to the pool of the desperate and unemployed, thereby further exacerbating our social problems. The economic and fiscal measures imposed by the government became the catalysts that would fuel inflation while providing a spiralling boom for the smugglers and foreign exchange racketeers.[49]

The Act resulted in the intensification of contradictions in both rural and urban areas. Most of those interviewed (including middle class persons) agreed that their standard of living experienced a sharp decline.[50]

To be sure, there were efforts by bourgeois scholars to mystify the crisis of the economy. Rather than raise debates on the exact nature and roots of the crisis, attempts were made to divert attention through debates on whether Nigeria should remain in OPEC or not. While politicians like Dele Adu of the UPN suggested that 'Nigerian crude oil should be bartered for goods and services, to conserve foreign exchange and flood the markets with essential commodities', the Shagari administration took no steps to curb corruption and waste. Huge sums of money voted for the importation of essential commodities vanished into thin air. Rather, the NPN leadership attempted to divert attention to the oil glut and the need to fear and respect God. For instance, at a time when Nigerians were particularly fed up with the system and political speeches, Shagari declared in December 1983:

> I intend to revamp the economy and continue to pilot our nation on the path to political stability as well as provide increased development in order to improve the quality of life and security of the individual. I will need the guidance of God in order to achieve these objectives.[51]

In this same speech, Shagari was able to promise housing and accommodation, qualitative and functional education and self-sufficiency in food production. An oil worker interviewed immediately after the speech was made reacted thus:

> I think say di man don dey craze for head. Na only foolishman naim go believe anything wey NPN talk. Since four-year ago, we never see anything. The man no dey even fear, na becos people no dey stone am. Wey people no see food to chop or money to pay rent, naim e day say God go help him? Na God get hand for all de bad thing them dey do since dem come enter pawer?

Translation:

> I think the man is now insane. Only a foolish person will take seriously any promise from the NPN. We are yet to see any visible achievement since 1979. The man (the president) appears to keep on the same deceitful track because he has not really faced the wrath of the public. At a time when workers cannot pay rents or find enough food to eat,

he (the president) is asking for God's help. Was God responsible for all the crimes committed since the NPN came to power (in 1979)?

The problems generated within the family contributed to alienating the working class and 'the fact that since 1982 no improvement can be identified in the economy and prices have continued to skyrocket demonstrates the futility of the measures'.[52] Lawrence Amu also contends that in spite of the measures, it is important to pay particular attention to

> the structural weaknesses and the nature of (the) economy, and the need to sort out major priorities for the Nigerian economy for appropriate medium term and long term planning.[53]

President Shagari also reflected on the crisis generated by dependence on oil, the declining revenues and inextricably, the unequal externally oriented process of recycling the oil rents in his last, twenty-third Independence Anniversary Broadcast to the Nation:

> Our oil export earnings, which reached a peak of 22.4 billion dollars in 1980, declined to an estimated 9.6 billion dollars in 1983 . . . With the fall in oil revenues, the country is now faced with a growing shortage of foreign exchange. At the same time our manufacturing sector which is unhappily import-oriented, continues to weaken . . . To revive and stabilize the economy on a long-term basis, it is imperative that the country now begins the structural re-adjustment process required for renewed economic buoyancy.[54]

In fact, the Minister for Employment, Labour and Productivity announced in 1983 that the country's 'industrial production level (had) fallen sharply due to lack of foreign exchange with which to import raw materials'.[55] The realization, even if not too late, had to put into account the specific and broad interests of factions and fractions of the bourgeois class; the nature, both short-term and long-term, of linkages with transnational interests; the extent to which the state was willing to exploit alternative and viable sources of revenues; the power of transnational corporations in the economy and the problems of corruption, ethnic and religious manipulation and the decay in the public sector. Shagari only talked of 'structural re-adjustment' without taking any positive measures to improve the vicious, unjust, confusing and chaotic economy. His failure brought alienation, increasing poverty, unprecedented corruption and abuse of power. By October 1983, the level of popular disaffection had reached a level where members of non-bourgeois classes were being forced to sing the praises of the military. The view of a Warri-based oil worker, interviewed before the 1983 coup, was representative of several others:

> When the civilians were not in power, things were not bad but much

better than today. I was secure in my job. I paid school fees, and my
children had teachers. My salary was regular and I did not have the
feeling that those ruling the country were foolish people who receive
huge pay-packets and allowances for doing almost nothing. Look at me
today. I have been retrenched. My children have no teachers. The
savings I made over the last eleven years have gone for food and exorbitant rents. I have no doubt that life is 100 per cent more difficult
under the civilians for me and my co-workers. Perhaps, it will be unwise
of us to expect a solution from those who caused our problems.[56]

Notes

1. Central Bank of Nigeria (CBN), *Annual Reports and Statement
of Accounts, 1979.*
2. For details, see Toyin Falola (ed.), *The Political Economy of
Colonialism in Nigeria* (London: Zed, forthcoming).
3. For details, see E.O. Akeredolu-Ale, *The Underdevelopment of
Indigenous Entrepreneurship in Nigeria* (Ibadan: Ibadan University Press,
1975).
4. See Fred Halliday, *Arabia Without Sultans* (Harmondsworth:
Penguin, 1974).
5. See Bill Freund, 'Oil Boom and Crisis in Contemporary Nigeria',
Review of African Political Economy, 13, May–August 1978.
6. Okelo Oculi, 'Dependent Food Policy in Nigeria, 1975-79', *Review
of African Political Economy*, 15-16, May–December 1979.
7. Lawrence Amu, 'A Review of Nigeria's Oil Industry', Lecture
delivered to a carefully selected audience in Lagos, 2 August 1982.
8. Field interview, Federal Ministry of Agriculture, Lagos, 16 August
1983.
9. Tom Forrest, 'Recent Developments in Nigerian Industrialisation'
in Martin Fransman (ed.), *Industry And Accumulation in Africa* (London:
Heinemann, 1982), p. 339.
10. Bill Freund, 'Oil Boom', op. cit., p. 97. See also features and editorials in *The Guardian*, 1 and 2 February 1984 and *The Concord*, 26 January
1984.
11. Details are from the Ministry of External Affairs (African Department) 'Technical Assistance to African Countries', CY, vol. V, 1978, 'Assistance to African Countries by the Federal Military Government', CY, vol.
VI, n.d.; *Africa Diary*, 1-7 April 1972, p. 5906.
12. Field interview, NLC, 19 August 1983.
13. General Olusegun Obasanjo, 1976/77 Budget speech Broadcast
to the Nation, 31 March 1976 (Lagos: Federal Ministry of Information).
14. General Olusegun Obasanjo, 1977/78 Budget speech Broadcast
to the Nation.
15. Ibid.
16. Alhaji Shehu Shagari, 1980 Budget Proposals to the National
Assembly.
17. For more on the post colonial state see Hamza Alavi, 'The State

in Post-Colonial Societies: Pakistan and Bangladesh', *New Left Review*, 74, July–August 1972; Jose Spalding, 'State Power and Its Limits: Corporatism in Mexico', *Comparative Political Studies*, 14, 2, July 1981; Paul Nursey-Bray, 'Class Formation and Post-colonial State Theory in Africa', *Africa Quarterly*, XX, 3–4, 1981; John S. Saul, 'The State in Post-Colonial Societies: Tanzania' in J. Saville and R. Milliband (eds.), *Socialist Register, 1974*; Michela von Freyhold, 'The Post-Colonial State and Its Tanzanian Version', *Review of African Political Economy*, 5, January–April 1977 and Colin Leys, 'The Overdeveloped Post-Colonial State: A Re-evaluation', *Review of African Political Economy*, 5, January–April 1976.

18. This is important because of the inherent confusion in the existing literature on development which more often than not fails to specify the 'development' being discussed — socialist or capitalist. While both are supposed to be characterized by increasing and sustained structural change and capital accumulation, the concentration of wealth, the circulation of social capital and class struggles, the use of state power, the level of popular participation and mass mobilization and the content of development planning are very different. While capitalist development might promote increasing capital accumulation, not only is wealth concentrated in the hands of the few but the basic needs of the majority are essentially secondary to the ability of the capitalist class to extract surpluses and reproduce the system.

19. 'NNPC Boss Warns on Oil', *News Review* (Nigeria High Commission, Ottawa, Canada), 31 August 1982, p. 2.

20. Alhaji Shehu Shagari, 'Historic Budget Proposals', *Nigeria Trade Journal*, 27, 2, March–April 1980, p. 10.

21. *Daily Times*, 9 January 1980.

22. *Progress Report*, Ministry of Finance, Lagos, 1980, p. 3.

23. Alhaji Shehu Shagari, Address to the National Assembly Introducing the Fourth National Development Plan, 1981–1985, 12 January 1981 (Lagos: Executive Office of the President, 1981).

24. Ibid.

25. Ibid. This was also confirmed in data collected from research in Nigeria, May–November 1983.

26. The use of budgetary allocation and control of transnational investments, especially their locational patterns to balance spatial inequalities, was ignored by the Fourth Plan like previous ones.

27. Field interview, Central Planning Office, Lagos, July 1983.

28. See International Labour Office, *First things First: Meeting the Basic Needs of the People of Nigeria* (Addis Ababa: Jobs and Skills Programme for Africa, 1981).

29. Ibid., p. 10.

30. S.A. Madujibeya, 'Slippery Position', *West Africa*, 28 September 1981, pp. 2244–2245.

31. Ibid.

32. On this, see *The Guardian*, 24 December 1983, p. 9.

33. For the highlights of the income policy see CBN, *Annual Reports and Statement of Accounts*, 1980, p. 8.

34. 1982 Budget Speech of President Shagari.

35. See for instance, *The Guardian*, 29 December 1983; *Sunday Sketch*, 25 December 1983; *Concord*, 21 December and 25 December 1983.

36. *The Guardian*, 24 December 1983.

37. See revelations of corruption in the country's daily newspapers for January and February 1984.

38. Shehu Shagari, Budget Speech to the National Assembly, January 1981.

39. C. Achebe, *The Trouble With Nigeria* (Enugu: Fourth Dimension 1983), p. 41.

40. See for instance, D. Efuwape, 'Foreign Debt and its Implications', *Daily Times*, 16 July 1983, p. 8; 'U.S. Grants ₦180m Loan to Nigeria', *Daily Times*, 8 November 1983, p. 11; '₦1.8b Loan Talks Concluded', *Daily Times*, 17 September 1983, p. 5.

41. 'Nigeria Owes $16 billion', *Nigerian Tribune*, 16 December 1983, p. 1.

42. See R. Umesi, 'External Reserve Declines', *Daily Times*, 22 December 1983, p. 1; 'Production Level Falls', *Daily Times*, 26 December 1983, p. 2; Jide Kutelu and Abiodun Adesola, 'Thunders of Recession: Dry Stands at Trade Fair '83', *The Punch*, 14 December 1983, pp. 8–9; 'Tales of Woe in Daily Struggle', *National Concord*, 27 October 1983, p. 1; 'Robbers are Right . . . But must go for Ikoyi Millionaires Legislator', *The Punch*, 13 December 1983, p. 1 and 'Economy Needs Re-adjustment', *Daily Times*, 11 November 1983, p. 2.

43. Shehu Shagari, Budget Speech to the National Assembly, January 1981.

44. *South*, February 1982, p. 72 and Lawrence Amu, 'Oil Glut And The Nigerian Economy', Lecture delivered at the Administrative Staff College of Nigeria, October 1982.

45. Ibid.

46. Ibid.

47. Central Bank of Nigeria, *Statement of Assets And Liabilities for August 1983*.

48. Amu, 'Oil Glut', op. cit.

49. J.K. Randle, 'Nigeria's Economy: A Desperate Disease', *National Concord*, 11 July 1983, p. 7.

50. 'Barter Oil For Goods', *Daily Times*, 13 December 1983, p. 11.

51. 'Revamping the Ailing Economy — Shagari Assures the Nation', *Daily Times*, 24 December 1983, p. 1.

52. Interview at the Lagos Headquarters of the National Union of Petroleum and Natural Gas Workers (NUPENG), 16 August 1983.

53. Lawrence Amu, 'Oil Glut', op. cit. The interesting thing about Mr Amu is that by status, training and income he is unquestionably a member of the dominant class; but his views on the economy, state policies and society are often frank and down-to-earth.

54. Alhaji Shehu Shagari, Twenty-Third Independence and Inauguration Address to the Nation, 1 October 1983.

55. 'Production Level Falls', *Daily Times*, 11 November 1983, p. 2.

56. Field interviews with an oil worker, Warri Zonal Office and NUPENG, 29 June 1983.

6. Agriculture and the Food Crisis

Two major points must be made in relation to the crisis of agriculture, and food production in particular, in Nigeria's Second Republic. First the Shagari administration inherited a terribly decaying agricultural system characterized by huge food import bills, migration from rural areas, bias against farmers, exploitation of rural producers by state agencies, limited or no provision of social amenities to rural areas and a general decline in budgetary allocations to agriculture. In addition, the regime inherited an economy in which food-hawking transnational corporations, assisted by indigenous politicians, bureaucrats and commercial capitalists, had developed far-reaching strategies to discourage local initiative and promote, as an alternative, dependence on food imports. The last military government of Murtala/Obasanjo relied on propaganda and rhetoric and refused to address the structural problems responsible for declining agricultural (cash and food crops) production. In spite of the constant cry over the fact that the contribution of agriculture was being overtaken by dependence on oil exports and revenues, very little was done to reverse the situation. As General Obasanjo himself put it:

> ... the present relative prosperity appears to be based rather pre-cariously on the performance of a single volatile sector dominated by petroleum production for export. Agriculture which constituted the main engine of growth of our economy up to early 1960s, is now vir-tually stagnant, if not declining. The agricultural surpluses of the 1950s and early 1960s, have all but disappeared, and we are having to import food to feed ourselves.[1]

The second point is that while it is quite tempting to attribute the crisis of food and cash crop production to the oil boom, it must be borne in mind that the 'boom' only intensified the crisis situation. Had the oil boom not taken place, the crisis of peripheral capitalist accumulation, corruption, institutional inefficiency, elitist planning methods and misplaced priorities would still have generated similar contradictions. Thus, the advent of the oil boom would appear to have deepened the crisis, as it exposed the unpro-ductive and undynamic accumulative base of the dominant forces, given the ease with which they came to rely on oil revenues to import food, keep development projects afloat and attempt to mediate class contradictions.

The nature of political alignment and re-alignment, in spite of the populist rhetoric of some of the political parties, particularly the People's Redemption Party and the Unity Party of Nigeria, were such that right from its inception, the fact that agriculture would be given priority only on paper, speeches and press statements was very clear. Those who had come to dominate the political parties and policy-initiating and -implementing institutions were not agriculture-based. In other words, unlike say in Taiwan, the Ivory Coast or Kenya, the accumulative base of the Nigerian bourgeoisie has never been historically linked with investments in agriculture. While it is true that a few ex-army Generals and other prominent politicians have moved into agriculture it is obvious that these 'farmers' do not strive to establish an integrated network which links agriculture with industry. In addition, most of them are actually politicians who have acquired the hundreds of acres of land through political influence. The crops on the farms are actually 'holding the land' for other major real-estate projects pending the expansion of the cities or other favourable developments.

This accumulative base of the Nigerian bourgeoisie must be conceptualized in its historical dimension. The colonial state was primarily after raw materials to feed metropolitan industries, markets to dump surplus products, and territories over which to exercise political control. It did not need to destroy the existing peasant mode of agricultural production in order to extract surpluses from the rural areas. Thus, other than a few state-owned or -controlled farms, the colonial state left the production of cash crops (it did not encourage food crop production) in the hands of peasants. Through occasional price incentives (constantly far below world market prices), force, administrative and political manipulation, the use of Marketing Boards and local licensed agents, the colonial state extracted enough agricultural surpluses to meet its needs. The emerging petty-bourgeois elements were incorporated by the bureaucracy, educational institutions, the commercial sector and transnational corporations. Thus, the basis of their power, following political independence, came to rely on the manipulation of the prices of imported products in the commercial sector or the effective use of state power to exploit peasants in order to obtain enough foreign exchange to subsidize developments in the urban centres.[2]

In spite of the dependence on the rural producers, there was a bias in the provision of social amenities, the provision of agricultural inputs and support services and resource allocation to the agricultural sector. While the advanced capitalist formations, which the Nigerian power elites wish so much to copy, were busy wiping out the peasant mode of production in the agricultural sector, international organizations, expatriates and indigenous bourgeois economists and 'experts' were romanticizing the life and importance of the peasant in Nigeria. The contradictions inherent in the outmoded, fragmented, small, unscientific, back-breaking and tedious mode of peasant production were romanticized. Where they were identified as objective obstacles to the use of scientific agricultural equipment, the expansion of landholdings, diversification of products and the formation of linkages with other sectors, the state, up till today, made two crucial mistakes. First, that it was possible to do these through the assistance of international capitalist institutions such as the World Bank and other aid agencies from the Western capitalist economies. The second was that, given objective linkages between the rural and urban sectors, the level of rural awareness and consciousness, it was possible to carry out a form of modern primitive accumulation which would benefit a few capitalists at the expense of the peasants. Thus, huge tractors, 'experts' and the police were often used to 'acquire' peasant land-holdings, they (peasants) were often displaced, unsettled or re-settled on harsh locations with no amenities, compensation was often small and paid late and the expectation was that the now unemployed peasants would take up wage employment on the 'farm centres', 'projects' or by whatever fancy name it went.

In addition to the erroneous hopes above, the Nigerian state since 1960 has failed to eliminate deliberately the traditional bias against farming, farmers and the rural areas. This neocolonial perception and perspective is still heavily entrenched in the country's educational system. Rural producers are seen as illiterate, lazy and dirty. The rural areas are places to retire to and to show off wealth acquired in urban centres on festive occasions.

Secondly, the efforts at self-sufficiency in food production have never been pursued with zeal. The belief was always that a decline in local production could always be met through food imports. The oil boom worsened the situation as bourgeois elements shifted their attention to competition to win access to the state and its huge oil rents. Agriculture was relegated to a far background.

Finally, where some initiatives have been made, these were either out of tune with the objective level of social and political education and mobilization or were so hypocritical in conception and execution that no one took them seriously. The lack of initiative within the dominant classes, except in the areas of commerce, real estate, contracts and so on, their corruption and disposition towards importation as against production, inhibited the successful implementation of policy or the equitable allocation of national resources. This was the fate of the operation Feed the Nation (OFN) which was initiated and executed on television and bill-boards by well-dressed and rosy-cheeked army generals and top bureaucrats. The public quickly nicknamed the programme Obasanjo Finish Naira (OFN) or Operation Finish Naira (OFN). The 'Green Revolution' has not fared better. It has promoted a 'fertilizer class', a 'rice bourgeoisie', and encouraged accumulation in the rural areas, thus removing some pressure from the centre and its successes have been exclusively on television, government-paid advertisements and official speeches.

In 1960, the essential institutions and exploitative mechanisms of the colonial period were 'Nigerianized' and preserved intact. The inequalities in resource allocation and power relations between the rural and urban sectors were preserved; the educational system which traditionally looked down on agriculture and on farmers was not restructured. Rural people were not involved in plan initiation or implementation since they were seen as 'ignorant and illiterate', in spite of the fact that the sector in which they operated was then the mainstay of the economy in terms both of food supplies to urban markets and of foreign exchange earnings. Prior to the 1973 Middle-East crisis and oil price increases, agriculture was contributing an average of 60% to GDP. The export of agricultural commodities accounted for 80% of the total value of exports and by the time the Second National Plan was launched after the war in 1970, the agricultural sector provided employment for over 70% of the total population. The total value of food imports in 1960 was £23.9 million. This declined to £14.2 million during the civil war in 1968 but rose to £28.8 million in 1970 after the war. In spite of the biases against the agricultural sector and the contradictions of individualistic peasant production methods, the country, until 1973, was relatively self-sufficient in food production.

The oil boom changed all this. Oil, which had contributed only 0.7% of GDP in 1958–59, became the dominant sector of the economy. Between 1970 and 1975, the contribution of the oil sector to GDP averaged 41.28% with agriculture in a distant second place, contributing an average of 28.8%. Its contribution to total government revenues moved up to 95%, with non-oil sources, including agriculture, contributing only 5%. By 1974, the export of agricultural commodities had declined to 6% as oil became the country's sole export (see Table 6.1).

By the time the Shagari administration came into office on 1 October 1979, oil had become 'the main source of government revenue and foreign exchange earnings' and 'the fortunes of the economy' had become 'closely linked with developments in the oil industry',[3] not agriculture. In presenting his 1982 budget to the National Assembly, and in spite of all the rhetoric on self-sufficiency and the Green Revolution, former president Shagari noted:

> As you all know Nigeria's economy for many years has been heavily dependent on a single commodity, namely oil.[4]

The neglect of the agricultural sector and in fact a recognition of some of the problems which have consistently promoted food deficits, rural decay and agricultural stagnation were equally addressed by a former Minister for Agriculture, Alhaji Ibrahim Gusau in 1981:

> With each passing year, farming became progressively unattractive and unproductive and remains characterised by inadequate capital, lack of suitable technology, inadequate supply of farm inputs, including credit and scarcity of farm labour which has worsened in recent years by the migration of young men and women from rural areas to the cities. With the advent of mineral oil, agriculture suffered an even greater neglect and was relegated to the background . . .[5]

The realizations above demonstrate, on the one hand, that state officials were

Table 6.1
Share of Agricultural and Petroleum in Nigeria's Exports, 1960-80*

Year	Agricultural Exports			Petroleum Exports		
	Quantity (tonnes)	Value	Share of Exports	Quantity (barrels)	Value	Share of Exports
1960	1,218.0	251.0	75.8	5.2	8.8	2.7
1965	1,506.0	289.0	54.9	81.3	136.2	25.9
1970	799.1	253.4	28.6	324.5	510.0	57.6
1971	785.4	232.8	18.0	451.7	953.0	73.7
1972	629.6	155.0	10.8	541.7	1,176.2	82.0
1973	718.5	224.5	9.9	594.1	1,893.5	83.1
1974	494.7	254.1	4.4	607.3	5,365.7	92.6
1975	417.7	216.1	4.4	538.7	4,563.1	92.7
1976	529.8	261.0	3.9	604.2	6,321.7	93.7
1977	391.2	364.9	4.8	741.4	7,072.8	92.7
1978	285.8	408.4	6.7	604.0	5,401.6	89.1
1979(b)	305.5	459.8	4.2	803.4	10,166.8	93.8
1980(c)	240.1	337.7	2.4	729.5	13,523.0	96.1

* Quantity in 1,000 tonnes barrels in millions;
Value in ₦ million
Percentage share of total exports.

(a) Including cocoa, cotton, groundnut and groundnut oil, palm oil and kernels, and rubber.
(b) and (c) 1979 revised figures and 1980 provisional.

Source: The World Bank, *Nigeria: Options for Long-Term Development. Report of a Mission sent to Nigeria* (Baltimore: The Johns Hopkins University Press, 1974), pp. 213-14 and Central Bank of Nigeria, *Annual Reports* 1970-80.

conscious of the dangers of export concentration on the oil sector alone and, on the other, that measures would be taken to rectify the crisis within the rural areas. Criticisms from official and non-official circles equally cautioned against a dependent food policy, dependence on oil and the neglect of the rural areas. Though the Third National Plan, 1975-80, itself admits that the rural areas have, since 1960, received a bad deal from the state:

> The rural areas in general would also require a new deal in the provision of social services. In almost every state, sizeable communities still exist without basic amenities, like clean water supply, hospital and health services, schools and electricity. The absence of such services obviously contributes to the low level of rural productivity and strengthens the pull exerted on rural dwellers by higher urban incomes.[6]

Little was done to rectify these conditions. As V.P. Diejomaoh rightly observed, it is possible to conclude on the basis of seasoned observation that the benefits of government expenditures

> are concentrated almost exclusively in urban areas. In sum, substantially less than 40 per cent of total government expenditure is designed for the benefit of rural communities who make up more than 70 per cent of the population.[7]

State Policies and the Food Situation, 1979–83

After 1979, the comprador nature of the Nigerian bourgeoisie triumphed over any attempt to pay serious, integrated and consistent attention to food production. In spite of the crisis of food supplies to both rural and urban areas and the problems of rural decay in general, the Nigerian ruling class continued to flatter itself that food was neither in short supply nor was there any reason for alarm. The Green Revolution, in spite of its bureaucratization and the corruption which plagued it right from its inception, was constantly referred to as a huge success. The role of international capitalist institutions, particularly the World Bank, was no less different. Its policies, which were designed to promote the elimination of peasant production and encourage the emergence of a rural capitalist class, contributed to rural disintegration, political clashes, waste, declining food production, corruption and above all the incorporation of the agricultural sector into international capitalism in a distorted fashion.[8] Reflective of the Tanzanian situation where

> under the label of ujamaa the World Bank extended schemes of supervised production of tobacco and tea so as to meet the requirements of capitalist companies rather than to ensure the best return to the farmer for his labour,[9]

the twelve World Bank projects in Nigeria have promoted crisis, decay and incorporation:

> Contrary to the World Bank's hypocritical rhetoric about concentrating resources on small farmers and aiding the rural poor, their projects are designed to subsidize rich farmers and have created a class of absentee 'overnight' farmers to take advantage to their assistance. Small farmers are specifically discriminated against in the allocation of resources or are unable to meet the cash costs of participation.[10]

Thus, though the alliance between the state and international capital has encouraged displacement and alienation of peasants from the land, thereby contributing to migration to the urban centres, the state has consistently presented a different picture of the situation.

The Nigerian state in the Second Republic consistently employed the mass media in its desire to convince Nigerians that huge strides were being made in agriculture and food production in particular. The president, while acknowledging occasionally that there was a food crisis, often re-assured Nigerians that the solution — a food glut — was just around the corner. When it was convenient to admit failure, the masses were assured that imported food was soon to be off-loaded at the ports, though questions of hoarding, skewed distribution and price inflation were deliberately overlooked. As a precipitate of the heavy propaganda, which was in reality never matched with actions, beyond the allocation of huge sums of money which comprador elements and bureaucrats usually siphoned to private bank accounts in foreign lands, the President and his team were content to have 'Green Revolution' as a 'household word' in the country.

In presenting his 1982 budget speech to the National Assembly, Alhaji Shehu Shagari was pleased to note that 'the green revolution programme ... today, in this country, has become almost a household word'.[11] He did not of course care to know the negative connotations which the phrase held for the common man, neither was he informed by his advisers, that as a precipitate of the failure of his green revolution programme, the unchecked activities of hoarders and middlemen and high food prices in the market, workers had converted Shagari to 'share-the-garri'[12] and his green revolution to 'Greed Revolution'. Nonetheless, the former president proceeded to rehash the claims which practically all administrations had made in the past, but existed permanently on paper:

> We have multiplied assistance to farmers in the form of agricultural inputs such as tractors and implements, fertilisers and improved seeds, rice, threshers and irrigation pumps. We have launched a special nationwide programme in 12 states of the Federation aimed at boosting rice production. We have given a similar boost to fish farming, construction of fishing terminals and acceleration of livestock and forestry projects.[13]

In a similar vein, in presenting his 1983 appropriation bill to the National Assembly, Alhaji Shagari reiterated his administration's commitment to agricultural development and the 'determination to make Nigeria self-sufficient in food production':

> We have to this end significantly increased the supply of agricultural inputs, such as fertilisers, improved seeds, insecticides, herbicides and equipment to farmers. These inputs are making the desired impact on specific programmes for boosting the production of rice, maize, cassava, guinea corn etc. Also the efforts of the River Basin Authorities in bringing thousands of hectares of hitherto uncultivated land under productive use, are yielding positive results. ...[14]

At one level it would appear that the President was recounting developments in another country and at another, nowhere in his speeches or in those of his aides does one find references to actual structural problems and the need to revamp the socio-economic, political and cultural obstacles to agricultural development in Nigeria. Even, as a beginning, if the items and programmes in the two statements above had been implemented, the food crisis that plagued the later part of the Second Republic which has been inherited by the armed forces would have been less severe.

The state also initiated more specific policies. Alhaji Shehu Shagari was convinced that Nigeria had 'abundant fertile land, water and generally favourable weather. Above all, we have fairly adequate manpower and a very hardworking population'.[15] He also knew that though the nation *'should* be self-sufficient in food production', it was not. Hence, the Green Revolution was expected to

> boost agricultural production (and) to ensure rural development through the establishment of agro-based industries, the construction of feeder roads, the provision of housing, educational facilities and water and electricity in the rural areas.[16]

The National Council on the Green Revolution, which was inaugurated on 14 April 1980 under the chairmanship of the President and charged with directing the implementation of the programme, involved the Ministries of Agriculture, Commerce, Finance, Industry, National Planning, Science and Technology and Water Resources. Among other things, the council had responsibility for monitoring and co-ordinating the programmes of the respective Ministries in the areas of agricultural planning, research, production, processing and marketing. In fact, in January 1980, the Shagari administration implemented a set of short-term measures at a cost of ₦18.3 million aimed at promoting food production. These measures included:

1. the purchase of 200 tractors to be distributed to the 19 States and the granting of ₦2.3 million to each state to facilitate the clearing of much larger areas to promote cultivation of food crops;
2. the spending of ₦900,000 on the importation of vaccine and drugs for the control of animal diseases;
3. the distribution of 500,000 tonnes of fertilizers, 500 tonnes of improved maize and rice, 500 maize shellers, 500 rice threshers and 500 irrigation pumps to farmers all over the country;
4. the importation of 45 medium-size fishing trawlers for distribution to fishing co-operatives;
5. the importation of 10,000 breeding cattle, 10,000 tonnes of cotton cake and 5,000 tonnes of cotton seed for sale to cattle rearers and
6. the intensification of efforts to develop inland fisheries.

In addition to the above, the Federal Ministry of Agriculture claimed in

October 1980 to have already purchased about 200 tractors, 50 ten-tonne lorries, 250 mobile ridge threshers, 250 small irrigation pumps, 44 publicity vans, 250 sorghum and millet threshers and 1,800 maize shellers for distribution to farmers all over the country. The Ministry even placed orders for some helicopters to strengthen its efforts at promoting agriculture.[17] The federal government reviewed the Credit Guarantee Scheme in order to maximize the use of agricultural loans, created the Ministries of Water Resources and Science and Technology, reorganized the Grains Boards in order to promote their efficiency and responsibilities and promised to combat drought and soil erosion.

The Nigerian state, as part of its programme for wiping out peasant relations of production, moved in to take the place of peasants. The first strategy in this direction was to go into direct production. Thus, while launching the Fourth National Plan, 1981-85, Alhaji Shagari noted that in the agricultural sector, 'Federal and State governments made their presence felt in the areas of direct production . . . No less than 147 farm centres were established by the various governments'. In his first independence anniversary speech in office on 1 October 1980, the President announced that the federal government had, through the Nigerian Grains Board, acquired 97,000 hectares of land for grain production all over the country. A second strategy was to encourage members of the bourgeois class to go into partnerships with the state and foreign investors and invest in capital-intensive large scale agriculture. As part of this, transnational corporations were also encouraged to go into farming. Texaco, a major oil company, and Coca-Cola have responded to this. Among other things, the latter has planned to establish an agricultural complex of 10,000 hectares to produce maize and other crops. The final strategy here was to form a strong alliance with the World Bank in the establishment of agricultural development projects which were often financed with foreign loans, dominated by foreign technical 'experts', capital-intensive in nature, pro-bureaucrat and absentee farmer as well as local rich farmers, and very exploitative. The agricultural Development Projects involving the World Bank were located in Funtua (Kaduna State), Ilorin (Kwara State), Bida (Niger State), Lafia (Plateau State), Gusau (Sokoto State), Ekiti-Akoko (Ondo State), Oyo North (Oyo State), Ayangba (Benue State) and Gombe (Bauchi State). Others were being planned for Anambra, Gongola and Cross River States. (See Table 6.2.)

These projects, as pointed out earlier, were, like those run by other international finance institutions, often included as part of the aid package, expatriate control, and exorbitant salaries, fringe benefits and allowances. In spite of huge budgetary allocations, no visible results had been produced by the time the Shagari administration was overthrown. A large percentage of the allocations went to ghost farmers, contractors, bureaucrats and foreign bank accounts. (See Table 6.3.)

The case of Kaduna State is typical. The state government in 1980 had cause to disagree with the terms of a World Bank loan which the Shagari administration had accepted. The Bank was actually to provide 40% and the

Table 6.2
World Bank Contribution to Seven Agricultural Development Projects

Project	Area (Km²)	Estimated number of families	Total Planned Cost (Naura million)	World Bank Loan (Naura million)
Funtua	7,500	88,000	39.0	23.4
Gusau	4,000	62,000	30.6	11.4
Gombe	6,450	65,000	30.7	12.6
Ayangba	13,150	125,000	64.0	21.0
Lafia	9,400	48,000	52.6	16.2
Bida	16,500	124,000	61.8	13.8
Ilorin	11,775	120,000	36.6	16.2

Source: Department of Rural Development, Federal Ministry of Agriculture, *Agriculture and Rural Development, Nigeria 1980 – Five Years Progress*, pp. 4 and 6.

Table 6.3
Capital Appropriations for Agriculture 1980-81 (Naira '000)

Project	1980 Appropriation	%	1981 Appropriation	%
Agricultural Development Projects (ADPs)*	34,432	4.1	75,098	8.1
National Accelerated Food Production Projects (NAFPPs)	4,000	0.5	4,000	0.4
Irrigation and Large Scale Food Projects*	613,161	72.7	710,516	76.2
Other Agricultural Expenditure	191,480	22.7	135,562	14.5

* Figure excludes ₦63,000 in 1980 and ₦50,100 in 1981 for sugar plants and estates controlled by the Federal Ministry of Industries.

Source: *Recurrent and Capital Estimates of the Federal Republic of Nigeria 1980* and *1981.*

federal government 60% of the total cost of the project. The conflict arose over the recruitment and remuneration of staff, which the state refused to allow the Bank to control, given the fact that its loan would be repaid eventually.

In a statement issued on the conflict by the Kaduna State Government, the Bank had wanted to appoint 45 of the major staff of the project and, in addition, stipulated: a) A salary of ₦40,000 per annum, tax free, and paid in foreign currency, in foreign banks; b) The payment of 7.8% of the gross salary as cost of living allowance; c) ₦773 per annum per dependant as dependant allowance; d) 25% of the gross salary as 'part-allowance'; e) 75% of their children's school fees to be paid abroad in foreign currency; f) Free air-conditioned and chauffeur-driven vehicle; g) Free air-conditioned and furnished-to-taste housing; h) Free electricity and water supply; i) Free trip return air ticket to anywhere in the world for annual vacation; and, j) 40 working days leave per annum. All these, according to the statement, would have cost the state government ₦12 million per annum, about a third of the cost of the project.[18]

It has been important to highlight this instance because it is one of the few that has ever come to public light in Nigeria. This was an unusual governor who was not so interested in the kickbacks which characterize contracts and negotiations in Nigeria and which became legitimized in the Second Republic. But more important, is the fact that the terms dictated by the Bank, which had the support of the Shagari administration, demonstrate very clearly the ways in which transnational interests contribute to draining foreign exchange, implanting administrative and financial obstacles in agricultural projects which ultimately perpetuate indebtedness and dependence and ensure, through the stagnation of such projects, continued food imports from which their home farmers and transnationals benefit. For, as the Managing Director of the Nigerian National Petroleum Corporation (NNPC) has put it:

> ... the bulk of our oil revenue is spent on the importation of various consumer goods, capital goods, rice and other agricultural produce which could be cultivated in Nigeria. Thus we earned our oil revenue only to use it to keep foreign farmers in employment and foreign industries going. In this way, even though there is evidence of substantial growth in the economy, this has not resulted in much development nor into any significant transformation of the economy.[19]

Finally, part of the policies of the Nigerian state as far as agriculture was concerned was to initiate a dependent food policy. Nigeria began to import food from all over the world — rice, wheat, millet, oil, every food item; from Singapore, the Ivory Coast, Brazil and Thailand to mention the not too popular ones. At one level, increasing food imports showed clearly that the numerous policies initiated by the government were not yielding positive results as the president had claimed. In addition, it showed very clearly one of the ways in which Nigeria was recycling its oil money which also contributes to its incorporation into world capitalism. (See Table 6.4.) The point is not that food imports were introduced under the Shagari administration; on the contrary, it was under his administration that imports crossed the two billion naira mark. Though budgetary allocations to agriculture were

Table 6.4
Nigeria Food Imports

Year	Amount (million £)
1960	23.9
1961	22.7
1962	23.5
1963	21.9
1964	20.6
1965	23.0
1966	25.8
1967	21.3
1968	14.2
1969	20.9
1970	28.8
	(million Naira)
1971	88.0
1972	75.0
1975	306.8
1976	404.1
1977	783.4
1978	1,094.0
1979	818.56
1980	1.56 billion Naira
1981	1.86 billion Naira

Source: Compiled from Central Bank of Nigeria, *Monthly Reports*; *West Africa*, 13 July 1981 and *Who is Responsible?* (Kaduna: PRP Directorate, 1982), p. 52.

large enough to stimulate increased production, the stimulus failed to come. In his 1982 budget, the sum of ₦999 million was allocated to the agricultural sector including the development of water resources. This allocation represented 13% of the capital budget. In his 1983 appropriation bill, the sum of ₦1.19 billion was allocated to agriculture, representing about 16.5% of the total budget. Of this total, the sum of ₦561 million was to be devoted to the exploitation of water resources. In spite of the increase, the food import bill crossed ₦2 billion and the food situation in the country reached alarming proportions, forcing warnings and appeals from members of the bourgeois class.

To take a few examples, Dr Michael Okpara, the Chancellor of the University of Benin, argued that the 'neglect of agriculture is the root of our economic problems' and warned that 'unless agriculture is made the leading sector of our economic effort, economic growth will continue to be a mirage'.[20] The National President of the Nigerian Chamber of Commerce, Chief

Adeyemi Lawson, also warned the government to address seriously the food situation which had deteriorated to alarming proportions. The chief asked: 'Why have the groundnut pyramids disappeared from the North? Why is it that Lever Brothers now import palm oil to make soap?'[21] Finally, the last Special Adviser to the President on Agriculture, Chief T.S.B. Aribisala, warned against the politicization of agricultural policies and programmes, the lack of cooperation between the federal, state and local governments and the low budgetary allocation to food production.[22] These warnings are not new. The power elites were not unaware of declining food production and rising food import bills. They were also aware of low allocations, under-spending and corruption which have militated against self-sufficiency. (See Table 6.5.) In fact, in the Fourth National Plan, 1980–85, while ₦6.5 billion was allocated to land transport, ₦3.9 billion for telecommunication, ₦2.83 billion for education, ₦1.05 billion for water resources and ₦964 million for water transport, only ₦837.3 million was allocated for agriculture.

In the light of the foregoing, one cannot but agree with Ray Ekpu that 'Shagari grew food on television, he provided qualitative education and shelter on television, he fought inflation and unemployment on television. . . .'[23] The susceptibility of the political leaders of the Second Republic to flattery and their manipulation of government-owned mass media for propaganda, meant an inability to evaluate critical opinions, perceive the reality and depth of social contradictions and initiate alternative policies.

Reaction of Producers
While it is true that in spite of short-paying rural producers, the Grain Boards in some cases paid the highest price for agricultural commodities in West Africa, their prices were not as high as those in the blackmarket or war-torn and drought-stricken areas of the Sahel. Thus, several producers withdrew from the market and smuggled their products across the border to neighbouring countries or sold to smugglers directly. There were others who withdrew from cash crop production and began to produce food crops in order to take advantage of the increasing food demand in the urban centres. But their efforts do not appear to have made much impact on food production levels.

Political manipulation of rural people, the displacement of producers by government and World Bank farm projects and the deliberate bias against agriculture and the rural areas in budgetary allocation and the provision of social amenities, forced many producers off the land to the urban centres. The construction boom — airports, army barracks, schools, expressways, oil pipelines, luxurious hotels and houses, etc. — which accompanied the oil boom also attracted rural skilled, semi-skilled and unskilled producers off the land — a continuing process inherited by the Second Republic. The neo-colonial educational system continued to teach youths to abhor rural areas and strive to remain in urban centres even as unemployed or under-employed persons. The total lack of basic amenities in the rural areas increased the drudgery of rural life and heightened the desire of peasants to ensure that their children moved to the 'bright' and 'attractive' urban centres.

Table 6.5
Decline in Agricultural Budgets (million Naira)

	1977-78	*1978-79*	*Decrease/Increase*
Federal	20.4	19.7	-0.7
Anambra	–	6.0	–
Bauchi	16.9	11.1	-5.8
Bendel	22.8	14.1	-8.7
Benue	21.0	13.7	-7.3
Borno	56.9	12.9	-44.0
Cross River	36.1	9.7	-26.4
Gongola	25.5	18.2	-7.3
Imo	30.0	10.5	-19.5
Kaduna	37.2	19.0	-18.2
Kano	35.2	7.1	-28.1
Kwara	9.6	6.3	-3.3
Lagos	–	11.4	–
Niger	4.4	13.7	+9.3
Ogun	–	7.3	–
Ondo	7.7	12.2	+4.5
Oyo	27.9	23.2	-4.7
Plateau	18.3	17.5	-0.8
Rivers	–	3.3	–
Sokoto	–	12.0	–
*Total**	*369.9*	*248.9*	*161.0*

* Escluding Anambra, Lagos, Ogun, Rivers and Sokoto States.

Federal Budget for Agriculture, 1972-76 (million Naira)

	1972	*1973*	*1974*	*1975*	*1976*	*Change 1975-6*	*Average annual change*
Current expenditure	12.4	13.4	24.6	36.8	18.5	-49.7%	24.9%
Capital expenditure	20.7	35.4	87.4	211.2	129.2	-38.8%	80.2%

Source: *African Business*, October 1978.

The consequent decline in agricultural output became reflected in the low purchases of the Grain Boards for cash crops and the high prices of food items in the local markets. For instance, in 1979, total groundnut production was estimated at 417,000 metric tonnes, but only eight metric tonnes reached the groundnut board. Between 1961 and 1970, the board's yearly purchase of groundnuts in Kano State was 357,000 tons; from 1971–75, this declined to 62,000 tons and from 1975 to 1980, it was less than 300 tons.[24]

The majority of the peasants displaced from their plots refused to take up wage employment on the World Bank and government projects. They collected their compensation, migrated to urban centres and took to petty trade. The constant use of the police against protesting peasants who have been denied their rightful compensation by the state generated severe contradictions between peasants and the state as well as its allies — transnational interests. There was also hostility between the urban family relatives of the peasants and the state. A typical instance of state violence against peasants was at Bakolori in Sokoto State where the peasants were massacred by members of the Nigeria Police Force for protesting against non-payment of compensation.[25]

The Deepening of a Dependent Food Policy

As noted earlier, the policy of food importation was not initiated under the Shagari administration. In fact, in 1981, Alhaji Shehu Shagari noted that: 'As of now, Nigeria does not experience intolerable and severe food shortages, but already there is ample evidence of food supply deficit which has grown at an alarming rate over the last couple of years'.[26] While this might have been an attempt to play down the reality of the food situation, conditions by 1981 had reached alarming proportions. The loans granted to 'farmers' and *farmers* had generally been diverted into other unrelated projects. The former because 'farming' was either part-time or a front for other activities and the latter because of the numerous problems of survival — high school fees, expensive health care, high house rents, electricity bills, and generally high cost of living. As a *Daily Times* editorial put it:

> Time was when over 95 per cent of Nigerians were farmers. But now massive education, rapid industrialisation and other paraphernalia of modern society have reduced this drastically ... Nonetheless, the percentage of the population who are still farming is put as high as 60. In spite of this, billions of naira is used every year to import food. This contrasts sharply with what existed about a decade ago when the country harvested more food than it could consume. . . .[27]

On the issue of loans to farmers specifically, the editorial had this to say:

> There is not much evidence to show that thousands of Nigerians who have been getting the loan conscientiously invested every kobo on agriculture. Certainly, some of the borrowers divert the money into other unrelated areas such as buying of prestigious cars, building of houses and even sometimes, marrying and throwing phoney parties.[28]

Unfortunately, for the Second Republic, major political positions were filled not on merit but on sycophancy and most of the advisers were either plainly ignorant or dedicated to the destruction of the government.

A typical example was the president's Special Adviser on agriculture, chief Theophilus Aribisala, who ignored the warnings and projections of the International Labour Office, the Food and Agricultural Organisation and the stark realities of the Nigerian situation.[29] Chief Aribisala[30] claimed as late as November 1983 that there was no threat of famine in Nigeria now or in the future. In addition, he dismissed the cry of governors in the northern parts, that agricultural output was being affected by drought and drew the ridiculous conclusion that food prices are 'systematically falling'. The adviser also claimed, to the surprise of most Nigerians, that the country produced 40% of the rice and 80% of the maize consumed in the country; if these percentages were correct the commodities were not available in the markets. A *Sunday Concord* editorial, reacting to these false claims noted among other things that:

> By asserting that food prices are 'systematically falling' he (the adviser) cast great doubts on whether Ribadu Road is actually in touch with what transpires in Oyingbo, Onitsha or Maiduguri markets. And this has been the greatest fear of most Nigerians. That things could not have been the way they are if our leaders know even one half of the nutritional hardships that face the ordinary man . . . the truth is that food is simply not there to be bought cheaply . . . The Federal Government appears to be grossly misinformed on this matter. With Aribisala's statement, it seems that the misinformation is going to be perpetual.[31]

However, if the government was not aware of the stark conditions in the markets, at least it was aware of the rising food bills which drained its foreign exchange earnings and which are a direct manifestation of its beautiful agricultural policies and programmes. In 1979, the food bill alone was ₦950 million. This increased to ₦1.56 billion in 1980, ₦1.86 billion in 1981 and has remained over ₦2 billion since 1982. These figures do not take into account the large quantities constantly smuggled into the country. From 1979, wheat imports began to take about ₦100 million annually. In 1982, Nigeria imported 200,000 tonnes of edible oil, and groundnut oil was imported from as far as Singapore. Rice imports alone constituted the largest single imported item. The food crisis reached such proportions that by early 1983 the government has lost its control over the importation process. Ministers and trade officials visited every part of the world seeking food and loans, particularly after the oil glut had reduced Federal revenues from $22 billion in 1980 to $9 billion in 1983. In December 1983, Nigeria imported 50,000 tons of granulated sugar and the Nigerian National Supply Company was expecting to take delivery of 300,000 cartons of condensed milk, 20,000 tons of rice and another 20,000 tons of rice, 6,000 tons of sugar and 5,000 bales of stockfish between December 1983 and January 1984.[32]

The austerity measures imposed by the Shagari administration in order to 'prevent the total collapse of the economy with all attendant consequences'[33] backfired when firms closed up, workers were retrenched, smuggling increased dramatically, prices of goods and services skyrocketted to unbelievable proportions, food became so expensive that *workers* could not afford two meals a day and hoarding became a thriving business. By December 1983, taking cognizance of the revolutionary pressures which the resultant inflation, unemployment, high crime rate, alienation and general disaffection had generated in society, the Shagari administration hurriedly issued import licences worth ₦42.5 million–₦5 million went to baby food, ₦5 million to vegetable oil, ₦10 million to frozen fish, ₦6 million to maize and ₦6 million to motor spare parts. Another ₦2 million went for motor batteries, ₦1.5 million for safety matches materials and ₦5 million for tube and tyre raw materials. Publishers and paper converters were granted ₦10 million. The point is not in the various sums but in the extent to which the measure demonstrates the crisis of food production. As usual, the state relied on the importation of food items. In 1982 alone, rice imports reached ₦400 million, fish ₦200 million, sugar ₦200 million and wheat ₦160 million.

The dependent food policy inherited and nurtured in the Second Republic was promoted by four major factors. The first, obviously, is the accumulative base of the dominant classes. Their involvement in the agricultural sector was often tenuous and served to provide them with needed capital to facilitate participation in other sectors. This is one of the most significant points often neglected in orthodox analysis of the problems of low agricultural productivity in Nigeria — the fact that the Nigerian bourgeoisie sees farming as a hobby or part-time vocation. The second point is in the fact that since 1973, with the oil boom, the comprador fraction of the bourgeoisie triumphed over other fractions and ensured that importation was superimposed over local production and self-reliance. To this end, the nation's import bill reached ₦1 billion *per month* in 1980 and ₦1.2 billion in 1982. Only the oil glut and increasing indebtedness forced the state to re-evaluate its policies. A third factor has to do with the unequal exchange relation between local dominant forces and transnational corporations. Thus, at a time when the United States and other Western powers were seeing food as a weapon of foreign policy, Nigeria was succumbing to the interests of transnational forces and locking itself into a dependent food policy on the West. Finally, the Shagari administration was overwhelmed by corruption, ignorance and mediocrity. It was incapable of pursuing a clear agricultural policy even in the short- and long-term interests of the dominant forces. The misuse of state power, corruption, ineptitude and reliance on propaganda and food imports ensured that fanciful programmes and speeches made little impact on hoarders and middlemen. These factors combined with a stubborn refusal to address the concrete problems of Nigeria's peripheral capitalism to promote rural decay, agricultural stagnation, migration to urban centres and the food crisis.

The Shagari administration was content to overlook these problems and contradictions, as well as neglect suggestions and criticisms from international and national organizations, primarily because it was determined to serve the interests of local compradors and transnational interests. For instance, the International Labour Office in its 1981 report on Nigeria noted that:—

> Food and non-food production seem to have followed the same path. Nigeria fell behind the rise in world agricultural output, even the performance in the African region. Although the growth opportunities for agriculture inherent in expanding domestic and foreign markets, abundance of land, generally enough labour, and improved technology were recognized, the need to exploit them through a transfer of resources from the booming non-agricultural sector has yet to be made the cornerstone of planning despite (or because of) the oil boom.[34]

The Organization also noted that in spite of state policies, the country's food balance-sheet calculations revealed the following problems all of which were worsened by the advent of the oil boom: (a) a national food deficit, (b) inadequate supplies of calories and proteins (especially animal protein), (c) a food deficit for particular periods or particular areas scattered over the country. The ILO concluded from its indepth survey that:

> Nigerian plans have always been biased against natural resource exploitation, especially agricultural resources ... A dramatic shift in resource allocation policy is therefore required to create and sustain effective agricultural programmes capable of reaching all parts of the sector and releasing development potential. In addition the oil policy of siphoning off agricultural surplus through Marketing Boards to the non-agricultural urban sectors needs to be completely abandoned, indeed reversed.[35]

The Shagari administration completely ignored these warnings. By the time it was overthrown in December 1983, the food conditions were at an unprecedented crisis level. As an oil worker put it,

> the Nigerian government has showed clearly that it hates the poor. A government that cannot provide enough food for the poor, does not deserve to be called a government. The corruption of the administration and its misplaced priorities have ensured that its policies have consistently worked against the poor majority.[36]

Conclusions and Suggestions

The Buhari administration is unlikely to fare better in the area of food production. Since it came to power it has made no specific or clear cut statement on the mobilization of peasants, the elimination of structural, political and social obstacles to expand agricultural production and the diversification of the country's revenue base. The recognition of problems inhibiting increased food and cash crop production in Nigeria is only one aspect of the problem. For instance, the *Guidelines to the Fourth National Plan*, noted quite correctly that 'the land tenure system has long been a bottleneck in the establishment'[37] of large-scale farms by private operators. It needs to be added, however, that the problem is not so much the non-involvement of 'private operators', but which private operators; where and how would they operate; what would be their relations with the state and the peasants? Would the involvement of these private operators be a deliberate weapon by the state to resolve spatial and social inequalities and re-direct the areas of emphasis in food production? So far, governments have paid lip-service to agriculture and food production. The Shagari administration inherited an already decadent agricultural system and because of its own ineptitude and bankruptcy, it could not make specific structural reforms. Even though food imports continued to increase, and in speech after speech the President and public officials continued to identify the numerous problems confronting food production, the issue and problem of local distribution was never addressed. Between 1979 and 1983, a few powerful 'rice barons' had emerged in Nigeria whose main tasks were to hoard imported food, especially rice, and influence the market prices. While such actions might have promoted a form of primitive accumulation, they also contributed to public alienation and therefore the background causes for the demise of the Second Republic. As a worker interviewed at Warri put it:

> The Shagari Administration can safely be described as the worst this poor nation has ever had. Hunger was everywhere and so was corruption and arrogance. How the government expected hungry workers to work hard is what my co-workers and I do not really understand. The aspect that hurt us more was the pattern of government officials continuously telling lies about food glut, low prices and so on on television.[38]

Even if one cannot place the entire blame of declining food production, agricultural stagnation and the distribution of hunger solely on the Shagari administration, the point remains that the totality of the system is run, shaped and nurtured by state policies and programmes. The hypocrisy of the administration was in no way different from that of its predecessors. Even if there had been attempts at implementing the peripheral suggestions, often short of suggesting structural changes, advanced by public officials and international organizations, the agricultural and food crisis would perhaps have been less severe.

A typical example is in the way the Shagari administration treated the 1981 International Labour Office's report on Nigeria. After an indepth study of practically all sectors of the economy, the ILO noted that the

> resource allocation policy confirmed the previous neglect of agriculture. Despite the (huge) work force in the sector, only 6.6 per cent of investment was allocated to it in the public sector programmes out of the total of 33 billion naira.[39]

Though the report was bold enough to suggest that only a different, indeed opposite, set of state policies could reverse current trends, a claim, unusual from such an international organization, the Shagari administration neglected its recommendations and warnings. Mr T. Aribisala, Shehu Shagari's Special Adviser on agriculture, on a major public forum in November 1983 identified the following problems of food production and agriculture in Nigeria: a) inadequate use of land and water resources; b) migration of young hands from rural to urban centres in search of white-collar employment; c) Nigeria's level of horsepower – 0.05% is lower than the minimum 0.5% on the farm to support the rate of national development; d) chaotic state of research institutes; e) inadequate funding of research work on agricultural production; f) incompetence of extension workers and researchers on the production of many food crops except cocoa and rubber; g) ineffective and inefficient opening of new land areas; h) farmers' lack of resources and capital to improve food production; i) inadequate investment on agricultural production; j) disintegration of the time-honoured extension services; k) the negative role of middle men; and l) rice importation.[40]

This is obviously a succinct analysis of the problems even if they have not been posed in objective class terms in order to expose the material basis of the contradictions. These problems have been with Nigeria since political independence and various governments have initiated only peripheral solutions to them. Thus, in Nigeria, it has become quite easy to identify problems, even solutions, but objective class interests have continued to influence and condition the initiation of public policy and programmes which have only deepened the crisis of agriculture. Aribisala in his celebrated discussion, of course, made some suggestions for improved agricultural, particularly food, output: a) procurement of agricultural inputs and distribution to farmers; b) increase in arable land area using high-yielding varieties of seeds; c) prevention of waste and losses taking place on land and in stores; d) re-organization of research institutes by giving them specific assignments with time scale; e) adequate funding of research into food to be provided to research institutes; f) provision of land clearing equipment for farmers; g) boosting of programme for maize, rice and soya bean production; h) training of enough farm management personnel; i) reactivation of agro-service centres in the states; j) building of simple dams and plenty of storage structures for food crops; k) provision of an assured market for all farm products; and [a rather ridiculous one] l) organization of competition among the states for food production.[41]

Taken together these suggestions are noble, even if, like the discussion of the problems, they neglect, deliberately, crucial structural and class problems. In a system of general public alienation and apathy as a result of neglect and pervasive corruption; and in a system where the bureaucratic machine is so slow and inefficient, these suggestions would not be worth the paper on which they are written. With the oil boom it became obvious that the problem of food production was not the unavailability of funds. Not after Nigeria has collected well over ₦60 billion in over 25 years of oil production and exportation. Even where relatively popular programmes are initiated, they have been pre-empted and rendered useless at the implementation stage, where the influence and corruption of comprador elements, their trans-national allies and the bureaucratic fraction of the bourgeoisie have come into play. Training extension service workers, importing tractors, improved seed-lings and so on, will not address increasing class differentiation in the rural areas; and the role and power of the 'absentee' or 'overnight' farmers, the selfish interests of aid-agencies and organizations and the negative policies initiated by the state at the same time.

The politicization of agriculture, food production, importation and dis-tribution under the Shagari administration operated at a level that has never been witnessed in Nigeria. Though huge quantities of food, especially rice and other provisions, were regularly imported — a bad policy in its own right — these were distributed along political lines. Holding the card of the ruling party, or being related to any high member of the ruling class, became a passport to 'capturing' huge quantities of imported food. These were then hoarded in buildings or warehouses, either to force up the prices or to be used to bribe hungry and, of course, angry electorates during elections. No matter what one thinks about why people drank and danced when the Second Republic fell, the attitude of top members of the ruling National Party of Nigeria in the area of food importation and distribution contributed to political alienation, industrial unrest, the distribution of hunger and the instability of the system. An editorial of the *Sunday Concord* on Aribisala's claims and statements during the discussion referred to earlier on captures part of the underlying problems of shallow public policy and programmes:

> The dialogue of our peasant farmers and the government has been a dialogue of the deaf. If the farmers must be mobilized, as Mr Aribisala agrees they must, then some efforts must be made in that direction. Right now there is no such effort. All that we hear are slogans and jingles which would never quieten millions of rumbling stomachs. .... Aribisala spoke of improved inputs and how the method succeeded in Mexico, Philippines, India and elsewhere. What we need is a success story within our borders, a success story on improved inputs for yam, cassava, plantain, cocoa, palm produce, cotton, soya beans and so on. We need a success story on access roads to our rural heartlands, on village electricity and water supply to take the farming burden off the tired back of aged and ageing villagers, so as to transfer that burden to the sturdier shoulders of our youths who are at present languishing in hunger and deprivation in the cities. We can also do with success stories in preserving our tomatoes, bananas and numerous other perish-ables that glut our markets seasonally but disappear subsequently. We need success stories on agricultural boards — grain, groundnuts, cocoa and so on — in their encouragement of farmers.[42]

The Shagari administration had no 'success story' to tell in any of the areas above. The few rich, particularly the 'rice barons', can tell stories of the wealth they amassed through hoarding, inflation of prices and the stealing of food meant for the public.[43] But the masses have stories to tell of hunger, malnutrition, kwashiorkor and other nutritional ailments.

Successes in the area of agriculture cannot be divorced from successes in other sectors of society — education, culture, industry, etc. — otherwise they would be only temporary. The need for an all round national ideology that will emphasize work, dedication, mobilization and education, reduce the existing unequal power and opportunity relations within and between rural and urban areas and emphasize self-reliance, is of cardinal importance to improved and integrated agricultural and food production. When Aribisala argued that Nigerian farmers must be mobilized and 'organized into groups and societies', he did not address some crucial issues: a) Under what ideological framework are these to be done? b) Who is to dictate the political and economic relations under which such mobilization is to take place? c) Are farmers the only group of people to be mobilized?, etc. These are issues which must be addressed, if successive regimes are to transcend making peripheral moves which would deepen contradictions and crisis within the rural areas and between it and other areas. Finally, as Hugh Byrne has noted:

> Food problems in Africa begin and end with politics. They begin with politics since problems of food production and distribution, the priorities concerning the crops to be grown and the price paid to the producers, all arise within the context of a world socio-economic system which defines goals, limits choices and ties less-developed states into a permanently unequal relationship with the developed capitalist states from which escape is difficult, if not impossible . . . The problems are *systemic*. It is only through an understanding of how the system operates and the extent to which food problems are a product of the structure and goals of the system, that real solutions can be put forward.[44]

Notes

1. General Olusegun Obasanjo, cited in *Exploitation and Utilisation of Resources for Social and Economic Development* (Lagos: NYASC Orientation Lecture Series, 1979), p. 9.
2. For details on the nature of the colonial agricultural system see G. Jan Van Apeldoorn, *Perspectives on Drought and Famine in Nigeria* (London: George Allen and Unwin, 1981); Dupe Olatunbosun, *Nigeria's Neglected Rural Majority* (Ibadan: Oxford University Press, 1975); and Sara S. Berry, *Cocoa, Custom, and Socio-Economic Change in Rural Western Nigeria* (Oxford: Clarendon Press, 1975).
3. Alhaji Shehu Shagari, New Year Broadcast to the Nation, 1 January

1981 and 'Historic Budget Proposals', *Nigeria Trade Journal*, 27, 2, 1980, p. 12.

4. Alhaji Shehu Shagari, Address to the Joint Session of the National Assembly, Lagos, January 1982.

5. Alhaji Ibrahim Gusau, ex-Minister for Agriculture, cited in *New Times* (Lagos), mid-October 1980, p. 35.

6. Federal Republic of Nigeria, *Third National Development Plan 1975–1980* (Lagos: Government Printer, 1975), Section 6, p. 35.

7. V.P. Diejomaoh, 'Rural Development in Nigeria: The Role of Fiscal Policy' in *Rural Development in Nigeria* (Ibadan: Ibadan University Press, for the Nigerian Economic Society, 1975), p. 103.

8. For empirical confirmations of these see 'Editorial', *Review of African Political Economy*, 13, May–August 1978; Tina Wallace, 'Agricultural Projects and Land in Northern Nigeria', *Review of African Political Economy*, 17, 1980; Bjorn Beckman, 'The World Bank and the Nigerian Peasantry: An Outline'. Paper presented to a Seminar on Peasants and other Petty Commodity Producers: Problems of Class Analysis, Organized by the AKUT Group for the study of Development Strategies, Stockholm, 1981.

9. Gavin Williams, 'Taking the Part of Peasants: Rural Development in Nigeria and Tanzania' in P.C.W. Gutkind and Immanuel Wallerstein (eds.), *The Political Economy of Contemporary Africa* (Beverly Hills: Sage, 1976), pp. 139–54.

10. 'Editorial', *Review of African Political Economy*, op. cit., p. 4.

11. Shehu Shagari, 1982 Budget Address to a Joint Session of the National Assembly, Lagos, December 1981.

12. Garri is a staple food item in Nigeria.

13. Shehu Shagari, 1982 Budget Address, op. cit.

14. Shehu Shagari, '1983 Appropriation Bill', reproduced in *Focus on Nigeria*, 1, 1, 1983, p. 10.

15. See Special Supplement on Nigeria, 'Shagari's Presidency Gathers Momentum', *New Times* , mid-October 1980.

16. Ibid.

17. Ibid.

18. See *New Nigerian*, Thursday, 20 November 1980 for the full text of the official statement.

19. Lawrence Amu, 'A Review of Nigeria's Oil Industry', Text of Public Lecture delivered to a 'Carefully Selected Audience', Lagos, 2 August 1982.

20. See Dele Olojede, 'Economic Problems — Neglect of Agric. Blamed', *National Concord*, 28 November 1983.

21. See 'Check Fall in Agric. Products Plea to Government', *Daily Times*, 28 November 1983.

22. See Raheem Mohammed, 'How to Produce Sufficient Food — Adviser', *Daily Times*, 8 December 1983.

23. Ray Ekpu, 'God is a Nigerian', *Sunday Concord*, 8 January 1984.

24. See Ambrose Bob-Manuel, 'Where are the Groundnut Pyramids?', *Daily Times*, 4 December 1983.

25. See 'Bakolori: Exploitative Capitalism at Work?', *The Sunday Triumph*, 4 July 1982.

26. Shehu Shagari, Address at the First Nigerian Agricultural Show,

Kaduna, 7 April 1981.

27. 'Loan to Farmers', *Daily Times*, 2 June 1983, p. 3.

28. Ibid.

29. See ILO, *First Things First: Meeting the Basic Needs of the People of Nigeria* (Addis Ababa: JASPA, 1981); 'African States Face Food Crisis', *Daily Times*, 14 November 1983; and Ambrose Bob-Manuel, 'Where are the Groundnut Pyramids?', op. cit.

30. See Dapo Aderinola, 'No Threat of Famine to Nigeria', *The Guardian*, 14 November 1983.

31. 'Aribisala Didn't Speak the Truth', *Sunday Concord*, (Editorial), 20 November 1983.

32. See Dafe Othinhiwa, 'Federal Government Issues ₦42.5 million Licences', *Daily Times*, 22 December 1983.

33. Shehu Shagari, National Day Address on the Occasion of Nigeria's 22nd Independence Anniversary, 1 October 1982.

34. ILO, *First Things First*, op. cit., p. 81.

35. Ibid., p. 95.

36. Field interview, Warri, August 1983.

37. Federation of Nigeria, *Guidelines for the Fourth National Development Plan, 1981–85* (Lagos: Government Printer, 1981).

38. Field interview, Warri, August 1983.

39. ILO, *First Things First*, op. cit., p. 81.

40. Aderinola, 'No Threat of Famine'.

41. Ibid.

42. See 'Aribisala Didn't Speak the Truth', op. cit.

43. Since the new military administration came into office, scores of warehouses filled with various food items and owned by the prominent politicians have been discovered all over the country.

44. Hugh Byrne, 'Food Problems in Africa', *Ufahamu*, IX, 3, 1979–80, p. 77.

7. Labour and Strikes

The Nigerian state has historically intervened in labour relations in order to promote so-called 'industrial peace' in the country. In reality, the rules and regulations often passed by the state and effectively enforced by the police have consistently promoted the power of employers (capital) and of the state over those of labour. Through the enactment of draconian and very punitive laws and decrees, the frequent and brutal use of the police against protesting workers, intimidation, victimization, scapegoatism and blackmail, the Nigerian bourgeoisie and state have attempted to incorporate and domesticate labour in Nigeria. In addition to these, through the use of periodic wage reviews, diversion of attention to peripheral issues and external affairs, the manipulation of ethnic, religious and state sentiments and the direct and indirect infiltration of trade unions, state and capital in Nigeria have sought to meet similar goals.

However, characteristic of the capitalist system, when a few own and control the means of production and exchange; and more so in peripheral capitalist economies where the local bourgeoisie is largely unproductive and the state largely pre-hegemonic, the policies of the state and the attitude of capital have deepened contradictions, heightened class alliances, consciousness and action amongst workers. Though there have been temporary setbacks for labour and successes for the state and capital, labour has constantly learnt from past mistakes and has sought to transcend ethnic, personality and other chauvinistic obstacles to labour unity and action. David Ojeli was reflecting on this background when he noted in 1977 that:

> It is no secret that seventeen years after Independence, certain employers have still not accepted the concept of trade unionism. As a result, they tend to treat union demands with levity, and are sometimes hostile to trade unions, employing all sorts of unorthodox methods to stultify union growth. Often letters from unions are not acknowledged, let alone meeting union demands even when such demands appear reasonable . . . worse still, implementation of agreements is unduly delayed and sometimes repudiated.[1]

In carrying out their anti-union activities, employers have received the open

146

or tacit support of the Nigerian state. Other than the constant call on Nigerian workers to be law-abiding, hardworking and obedient, and the constant use of the police against protesting workers, the state has enacted several laws which are directly aimed at domesticating labour and rendering 'union-power' meaningless.

Prior to the outbreak of the Nigerian civil war in 1967, the state relied on the labour control Acts, Ordinances and regulations, most of which had been passed by the fascist colonial state. These include the Trade Union Ordinance of 1938; the Trade Disputes (Arbitration and Inquiry) Ordinance of 1941; the Labour Code Ordinance of 1945 and the Wages Board Ordinance of 1957. These ordinances were partly responsible for the internal feuds, competition and crisis which plagued post-political independence trade unionism in Nigeria. For instance, the Trade Union Ordinance provided that five or more people, whose main purpose relates to economic matters, could form a trade union. This encouraged factionalism and the emergence of several splinter unions.[2]

Between the outbreak of the civil war and 1979 when the military returned to the barracks, the Nigerian state passed scores of draconian labour decrees which had the sole purpose of weakening the power of organized labour. While several decrees directly banned strikes, excluded certain persons from trade unionism, organized labour from politics and certain occupations from forming trade unions, no decree specifically addressed the labour control strategies and tactics of employers – retrenchment, dismissals, victimization and so on. These decrees include the Trade Disputes (Emergency Provisions) Decree 21 of 1968 and its 1969 Amendment through Decree 59 which directly banned any form of strike actions using as pretext the civil war and the need for national unity. After the war, the state did not repeal the decree. On the contrary, it passed in 1973, the Trade Unions Decree 31 (later amended through Decree 22 of 1978) which prohibited workers in the Nigeria Security Printing and Minting Company; Central Bank of Nigeria; Customs Preventive Service; Nigerian External Communications; and the Armed Forces and the Police from strike actions. The 1978 amendment barred them from establishing trade unions and empowered the Federal Commissioner for Labour to include workers from other establishments at his own discretion. The state also passed the Trade Disputes (Essential Services) Decree 23 in 1976 which defined practically all human activity in Nigeria as an 'essential service' and therefore barred from strike actions. Earlier, in 1975, the Petroleum Production and Distribution (Anti-Sabotage) Decree 35 had been passed to control strikes and protests in the oil industry on which the state was heavily dependent for revenues. This decree defined any strike action by oil workers (including oil-tanker drivers) as an attempt to sabotage the economy. It stipulated the death penalty or imprisonment without trial for such 'criminal' acts.

These decrees empowered the state and its agents to prosecute trade unions, proscribe them and prosecute union leaders for encouraging, publicizing or embarking on strike actions. The abolition of all existing labour centres, prohibition of foreign affiliation, the re-organization of the over 1,000 mushroom craft and house unions along industrial lines into one central labour organization, 42 industrial unions, 18 senior staff associations, 9 employers' associations and the introduction of the automatic 'check-off' method of dues collection were all part of promoting harmony between labour and capital under state guidance in a system which is heavily pro-capital. Efforts to impose pro-establishment unionists on the central labour organization — the Nigeria Labour Congress (NLC) — failed as a result of the determination of workers to decide their own affairs. Two points need to be made in relation to this brief background. First, the numerous decrees of the state and the autocratic character of the military government did not stamp out strikes and other forms of protest in the country. Even in instances where *overt* forms of protest were on the decline, the workers in response to the violent nature of the state and the need for survival, initiated numerous *covert* forms of protest.[3] In addition, in instances where the number of strike actions declined in number, the number of man-days involved increased substantially and these figures do not say anything about the hundreds of unreported, short, wild-cat strikes and protest actions all over the country, particularly in the private sector. Thus, the number of recorded strikes increased from 105 in 1973-74 to 354 in 1974-75, declining to 264 in 1975-76 and 153 in 1977-78. Workers involved in these actions increased from 41,527 in 1973-74 to 126,818 in 1974-75, declining to 122,546 in 1975-76 and 97,802 in 1977-78. However, the man-days lost increased from 148,130.1 in 1973-74 to 375,028.2 in 1974-75, 439,296.3 in 1975-76 and 448,335.7 in 1977-78.

A second point to note, however, is that the socio-economic conditions which were to mature in the Second Republic and significantly contribute to increasing worker protests, alienation and struggles had their roots in the periods before October 1979. To be sure, the high rate of corruption, arrogance of power, ineptitude and gross looting and mismanagement of the economy under the Shagari administration significantly promoted the inability to control workers or even to bribe them. However, the continued migration of people from the rural areas who put pressure on the limited urban amenities and increased crime levels as well as prostitution, problems of job insecurity, unemployment, poverty, low pay, inflation, scarcity of goods and services and generally high cost of living were all inherited (but deepened) by the Shagari administration. These problems, we must point out, are generally features of peripheral capitalism. This is not to say that they do not exist in developed capitalist formations; however, they are 'watered' down through the provision of all forms of social insurance, unemployment benefits and the use of the ideological and hegemonic powers of the state.[4]

Labour in the Second Republic

Nigerian workers, organized along industrial lines into industrial unions, had remained relatively dormant between 1978 when Decree No. 22 established the Nigerian Labour Congress as the only central labour organization and 1 October 1979 when the military returned to the barracks. What was to contribute to their militancy in the Second Republic revolved around the increasing crisis of Nigeria's peripheral capitalism and the utter neglect of working class problems by the Shagari administration. The extreme dependence on the oil sector and therefore the world oil market for foreign exchange earnings meant that fluctuations in the world price for oil were reproduced in the Nigerian economy.[5] Since the Shagari administration only addressed the issue of diversifying the revenue base of the state with limited enthusiasm, the precipitous decline in oil production, exportation and revenues in the 1980s meant an inability to mediate class contradictions effectively and keep development projects afloat. The first casualty of declining oil wealth were the workers. The crisis was, of course, deepened by the rabid corruption within the ranks of the dominant class, the politicization of development projects, misplaced priorities and poor policy projections and prescriptions.[6]

The condition of the working class in Nigeria during the Second Republic was, therefore, to put it simply, pathetic. The consequence of rural neglect reflected itself in the increased migration of rural dwellers to urban centres thus increasing the number of applicants for limited jobs available. The consequences of misplaced priorities and corruption were manifested in the inability of all the political parties (therefore state governments) to provide basic amenities for workers, pay their basic salaries and allowances as and when due or guarantee their security. The mismanagement of the oil wealth through the looting of public funds, high import bills and waste led to the need to impose stringent economic measures through the Economic Stabilisation Act in March 1982. The net impact of this Act was an increase in the retrenchment of workers as factories closed down partially or completely, though it is interesting to note that the majority of companies continued to declare huge profits in spite of the austerity measures.

In 1982, the Nigeria Labour Congress was forced to issue several warnings to the federal and state governments given the plight of workers. In declaring its 'FAR' and 'NOW' — Fight Against Retrenchment and Non-payment of Wages, the NLC demanded:

1. Right to Work
2. Regular payment of Wages
3. Social Security benefits
4. A stop to compulsory retirement
5. Full graduate employment
6. A stop to economic wastage.[7]

At one level these were the objective and immediate problems which were confronting the working class at that time. The problem of unemployment had risen to such an extent that graduate unemployment became a crucial issue of debate. As the NLC noted on the issue:

> ... the new phenomenon of lack of useful employment for school leavers and graduates of higher institutions, *many of them daughters and sons of working and ordinary people*, calls for concern. Resources cannot be spent on training youths only for them to be rendered useless by a wicked system that favours only a few Nigerians.[8]

Within the period under study, numerous stories were in the papers on the plight of unemployed school leavers, particularly university graduates who had to devise several means — legal and illegal — of survival. To be sure, the Shagari administration denied that graduate unemployment existed in spite of regular newspaper reports. Even while it agreed that retrenchment was taking place at an increasing pace, rather than devise ways of containing the problem, the Shagari administration argued that employers had a right to retrench workers in difficult periods and constantly warned unions to respect all the draconian labour decrees passed under the military which had been conveniently converted into Acts.[9]

The question of retrenchment was perhaps the highest manifestation of the administration's loss of control over the economy and the triumph of transnational interests and power over those of the state. To be sure, capitalist production requires a large pool of unemployed to promote the process of domesticating labour and cutting costs in order to increase profits as workers are retrenched and the workload increased for the few who are retained. The NLC provides figures, though hardly a day passed in the Second Republic without reports in the papers of a company laying off workers. Many transnational corporations seized the weakness and lack of direction of the Shagari administration to blackmail it by retrenching workers in order to obtain import licences or expand their expatriate staff quota. According to the NLC, between 1979 and 1982, 20,000 textile workers were retrenched. In the chemical industry, 1,000 lost their jobs, and 2,000 furniture, fixtures and wood workers, 3,000 workers of the food, beverage and tobacco industry and over 2,000 oil workers were retrenched between April and October 1982. R.T. Briscoe retrenched 1,000 workers; 2,500 workers in the shipping, clearing and forwarding industries were laid off and 5,000 from the footware and rubber industry:

> ... the working people of this country are deliberately made to bear the brunt of the [economic] crisis. Companies that retrench workers have shown themselves to be making profit ... Cadbury for example which has been at the forefront of bad industrial relation policies recorded a profit of ovef ₦3m in the first six months of this year [1982].[10]

As noted earlier, this is the area of contrast, where retrenching companies are declaring huge profits. (See Table 7.1).

Table 7.1
Profits Made by Selected Companies in Nigeria Pre-tax* (in Naira millions)

Company	Turnover		Profits	
	1982	1983	June 1982	June 1983
UTC (March each year)	396,456	311,520	39,664	22,233
Total	173,362	169,541	16,600	15,500
John Holt	301,046	138,809	17,405	5,254
	(September 1962)	(March 1983)		
Mobil	307,007	149,382	34,004	18,207
	(12 months)		(12 months)	
Food Specialities	–	–	3,155	5,489
Lever Brothers	–	–	5,971	4,321
Texaco	180,499	n.a.	23,603	n.a.
Nigerian Breweries	–	–	30,387	–
Guiness Nigeria Ltd.	–	–	8,870	12,217
SCOA	–	–	7,041	–
Agip	127,148	–	10,214	n.a.
Hoechst	24,036	27,737	1,865	2,390
UAC	380,421	387,983	18,893	15,307
	(9 months)	(March)	(September)	(March)
African Petroleum†	282,009	n.a.	15,002	n.a.

* All results are for the first six months of relevant years.
† After tax figures

Note: These are only *declared* figures.

Source: Various Nigerian newspapers; the *Financial Punch* is a particularly good source of data.

The question of non-payment of wages and salaries was a baby of the Shagari administration. Given the failure to find alternative sources of revenues, take cognizance of developments in the world oil market and the oil-consuming countries and the inability to check the corruption within the ranks of the bourgeoisie, the Second Republic found itself unable to pay workers their basic salaries. The tendency to keep public funds aside for electioneering campaigns, inflation of contracts, concentration of available resources on a few expensive prestige projects and dependence on foreign exchange-consuming policies, contributed to the inability to pay workers. The general socio-cultural consequences of these developments promoted the pauperization of the Nigerian working class in the Second Republic. In addition while on the one hand it promoted industrial unrest, it also promoted alienation, apathy and even helplessness among workers. Broken homes, children sent out of school, malnutrition, hunger, indebtedness and a total lack of hope in the future came to characterize the perceptions and expectations of the Nigerian working classes. In most states, in fact, in all the states, irrespective of political party, ideological positions and pretensions, workers were not regularly paid, some for up to six months and others for more than a year. However, governors, legislators and top bureaucrats collected their salaries, allowances and other claims as and when due:

> . . . poor working class families have been thrown into terrible misery, depression, deep debt and their children into increased malnutrition and hunger. In a public organisation like Bendel State Transport Services, workers have not been paid their wages for over a year. Some of them in the Lagos area got their June 1981 salaries in April 1982 and others their July 1981 salaries in August 1982. Consequently some of them have had their families broken and children lost to the streets.[11]

This was in 1982. By the end of 1983 when the Shagari administration was overthrown in a military coup d'etat, the situation had worsened. Hunger was clearly visible on the faces of workers in the cities. The so-called 'Green Revolution' which was expected to provide food had failed to perform the magic. The level of poverty and social dislocation arising from visible unemployment and the non-payment of wages in an inflation-ridden and mismanaged economy were reflected in the phenomenal increases in crime and prostitution, public protests, the lynching of thieves and suspected thieves and open hostility to the rich and prominent members of the ruling party. An oil worker interviewed in Lagos expressed a representative view thus:

> We workers have seen governments come and go. We were here before political independence. But to be frank with you, we have never had it so bad. How can people be so wicked and heartless and yet claim to be politicians, christians or muslims? This is not a question of corruption, it is sheer heartlessness. Under these uncertain conditions, how on earth can I work hard or remain honest and law-abiding when I don't know how I will pay my rent, feed my children or find money to buy clothes for my wife?[12]

The manner in which workers danced, drank and spent their meagre savings when the government was overthrown, is directly reflective of the level of frustration within the ranks of labour. In his 1983 May Day Address, the President of the NLC spent considerable time reflecting on the objective problems of Nigerian workers. The problem of 'mass retrenchment of workers' was still there and the problem of irregular payment of salaries and wages had taken a worse turn, teachers all over the country being the most affected:

> It is now fashionable, in these days of hyper-inflation, for employers of labour to refuse payment of wages to workers, as and when due. Indeed, it is wholly incredible that in these days of terrible hardships

for the working people, employers (Government and Private) could sit down on workers' salaries for upwards of six months. This clearly shows their utter insensitivity to the plight of workers.[13]

Hassan Sunmonu also noted: 'workers have had their wives desert them, because of their failure to cater for their basic needs' and that 'so many are indebted to shylock, hard-hearted, avaricious money-lenders'.

As far as the NLC was concerned, and this clearly represented the genuine views of the majority of workers, the advent of party politics had worsened the conditions of the Nigerian worker. This is not because party politics *per se* is bad but as a precipitate of the corrupt, comprador and mediocre nature of politicians in the Second Republic who were obviously anti-labour. In fact, at a time when several workers, earning the minimum wage of ₦125.00 per month, had not received their wages for several months, legislators all over the country who were sworn in only in October 1983 had all collected a minimum of ₦12,000 as car loans! As Sunmonu summarizes:

> It is now incontrovertible and manifestly evident, that the real as-pirations of our people for life more abundant and the provision of their basic needs and necessities of life, such as food, pipe borne water, electricity, decent housing and clothing, are daily eluding them. The great expectations that heralded the dawn of the return to democratic rule in Nigeria are now irretrievably being seen to be nothing but forlorn hopes. This is the crux of the matter. We all know better than before, the wide difference that exists between promises and fulfil-ments. For us, reality has knocked the bottom out of all claims at scoring impressive and astonishing success by this or that party in government.[14]

If nothing else, by the end of 1983, Nigerian workers had lost faith in the Shagari administration as a government capable of addressing the crucial problems of society.

Workers' Response to State Policies and Economic Crisis

The working class responded to the insensitivity of the Shagari administration and the deepening crisis of the Nigerian state and economy in several ways; while it is true that the economic crisis and the fear of retrenchment drove some workers and union leaders into cooperating with management, adopting an apathetic attitude to working class struggles and so on, the majority of workers came to learn several lessons. First, that, ultimately the trade union and the NLC represented the cource of strength, unity, mobilization and struggles against oppression and exploitation. Second, that in periods of economic contraction, management would initiate all sorts of strategies and tactics to domesticate labour, exploit them and divide their trade unions.

Third, that economic crisis and increasing working class consciousness bridge the gap between the interests of capital and the state as all efforts become geared to labour control and the maintenance of 'industrial peace'.

The attitude of the Shagari administration to labour enabled the NLC, which regards itself as the vanguard of the working class in Nigeria, to play a decisive role in the protection and advancement of working class interests in the country. Thus, through public lectures, seminars, press releases, communiques and rallies, the NLC constantly strove to mobilize workers and put pressure on the state and employers. In the process of finding solutions to the perennial problems of the working class, ultimatums were issued, strikes were supported, a general strike was organized and major debates were raised. For instance, the question of forming a labour party or supporting pro-working class candidates during elections was hotly debated all over the country. These activities won the NLC foes and friends within and outside the labour movement as the state-sponsored pro-establishment candidates for union positions, constantly invoked the labour control decrees which had been converted into Acts, used the police against protesting workers with impunity and moved to split the NLC in order to reduce its power and relative autonomy.

In his 1981 May Day broadcast to the nation, Alhaji Shehu Shagari said, among other things, that

> we need the full cooperation of the Nigerian Labour Movement. I regret to say that recent events within the trade union movement have given me considerable concern. Several strikes have taken place without the organisers using the machineries that have been established for resolving trade disputes. Workers in certain organisations performing essential services and who are prohibited by the provisions of the Trade Disputes (Essential Services) Act of 1976 from going on strike have gone on illegal strikes.[15]

In fact, in the first nine months of the Second Republic, as a precipitate of continued neglect of workers' problems, the country recorded 247 officially registered trade disputes involving 144,886 workers leading to the loss of over one million man-days. This did not include the hundreds of sporadic, short-lived and wild-cat strikes. In 1980, the country recorded a loss of 2,551,000 man-days in strikes involving 220,988 workers in 416 registered strike actions. Of this total, workers in the so-called 'essential services' declared 61. By 1981 when the economy was experiencing the full impact of the oil glut, the austerity measures and the consequences of mindless corruption, waste, and mismanagement, the President had enough reason to be concerned about the increasing spate of of strike actions by all categories of workers:

> ... but events in 1981 are likely to give far more cause for concern than the previous year. There was a general strike in Nigeria in May 1981, and there were several work stoppages before and after the

general strike. With the glut in the world oil market and with the con-
comitant decline in oil prices, workers' demands on the economy are
likely to generate more crises, not less . . . Yet, workers' wage gains
continue to be eroded by the soaring inflation, rising food, trans-
portation, and housing costs all of which is compounded by the
continuing drift to the urban centres from the rural areas . . .[16]

The succinct analysis above is official. In spite of this realization, the government 'made it clear that it will not tolerate militant prosecution of trade
disputes', and this 'appears to set government on a collision course with
labour. Labour-state relations are, as at now, anything but cordial'.[17]

In spite of these realizations, the state did little to address the roots of
contradictions which have promoted increased worker protest and militancy
in the country. Other than the *overt* forms of protest which featured daily
in the Second Republic, *covert* forms of protest — smuggling, absenteeism,
'sickness', sabotage, name-calling, stealing of public or company property,
time-keeping, drug abuse, lateness to work, misuse of employers' property,
etc., were resorted to by workers. But strikes were the most prominent and
immediate form of protest which were seen by the public as manifestations
of defiance:

> The only language that the government and private employers under-
> stand is the strike. Let them make more decrees and Acts, they cannot
> stop workers from going on strike. Let them establish more TV stations
> and newspapers, until they address the real problems of those who
> produce the nation's wealth, strikes and protests will continue.[18]

The intensity and dimension of worker protest in the Second Republic have
been so strong that Eddie Iroh concluded in an April 1982 piece that the
'Shagari administration has faced more crises in the labour front than any
other Nigerian government since 1960'.[19] This was not an exaggeration.

Before the military retired to the barracks in October 1979, the NLC
had issued a 21-day ultimatum to the Federal Military Government on
22 May 1979 on crucial issues affecting trade unions and labour in general.
The Congress demanded the lifting of the wage freeze, the abrogation of all
punitive labour legislation, the restoration of car loans and allowances and
an immediate review of rent and transport allowances to all categories of
workers. This action took the military by surprise, given the level of preparation for transition to civil rule and the need to avoid situations that might
prompt actions by factions of the military. Arrangements were quickly made
to negotiate with the congress and some agreements were reached which did
not really address the issues but were enough to prevent a strike.

The civilians who came to power in October 1979 treated the problems
of the workers with levity; while the legislators and executives restored car
loans and allowances as well as other benefits to themselves within weeks of
being sworn in, they failed to do the same for workers. Rather, they retained

all existing labour decrees and politicized statements and actions made or embarked upon by workers. As the economy deteriorated, the conditions of workers moved from bad to worse. In January 1980, the NLC issued another ultimatum threatening a general strike in March if the issues of car loans and allowances, housing subsidies and the abrogation of punitive labour Acts were not addressed. Though politicians in and outside the National Assembly tried to politicize the ultimatum, the National Economic Council (NEC) met over the issue and most of the demands were referred to the Industrial Arbitration Panel (IAP).

However, before the ultimatum was issued, the Congress had responded to the promises, manifestos and activities of all the political parties by preparing a major document in 1980 — *The Workers' Charter of Demands.*[20] This document, which had the support of the 42 industrial unions which constituted the Congress, was widely circulated and read by workers. It was presented to the federal government on 22 February 1980. This document, though essentially populist in nature, can be said to have contributed significantly to the background on which the 1981 general strike was called. It demanded the establishment of a 'Welfare State', a call which obviously sees the possibility of a level of partnership between labour and capital. Our research at the NLC has however revealed that this particular demand was heavily influenced by moderate elements within the National Executive Council of the Congress. Nonetheless, the Charter reflected the reality of the problems confronting the average worker which might have had their roots in the military era but had not been addressed by the Shagari administration. The document also provided the workers with a common critical perspective on Nigeria's political economy.

In summary, the Charter recognized the fact that

> the trade union organisation represents an irreparable instrument for winning, defence, extension and guarantee of economic, social and cultural rights of workers in their everyday life in place of work and in society.

In addition, it argued that the so-called indigenization policy of the various governments had only succeeded in expanding the ranks of 'Nigerian exploiters'. It therefore called for fundamental 'structural changes' in the national economic and social order so as to facilitate the process of workers' liberation from conditions of exploitation, misery and poverty. The required 'structural changes', according to the Charter, would culminate in 'bringing the economy under the ownership and control of the workers and masses'. Finally, the Charter made comments on other aspects of society, foreign policy and politics and called for changes in the *'laissez-faire* formula of development through profit and competition' which 'has created growing and unacceptable inequalities'. It called for a ₦300 minimum wage, rent subsidy for all categories of workers, free medical care, improved housing, industrial democracy, the payment of car loans and allowances and the abrogation of existing punitive labour Acts among other demands.

The 'radical' picture presented thus far must not hide the limitations of the Charter and the contradictions within the Congress. Essentially, the Charter calls for the establishment of a 'Welfare State', which in reality is only a shade better (?) than the existing peripheral capitalist system. It is possible to conclude, on the basis of interviews with affiliates of the NLC, that the Charter was a compromise document of various ideological groups and positions within the NLC's NEC. As S.O.Z. Ejiofor, the General Secretary of the Civil Service Technical Workers' Union, has argued:

> The NLC Charter of Workers' Demands is at best a social democratic reformist document. It is very evasive on the issue of ownership and control of the means of production. It is very much influenced by the depoliticisation policy of the congress. Nevertheless, it provides a necessary reference for assessing congress policy position on workers' welfare. It is obvious that the propertied class and the state which they control will see the demands as excessive and extravagant. We know that workers never achieve anything without struggle. No employer will voluntarily make concessions.[21]

This observation above raises some of the critical issues and problems to which the NLC and Nigerian workers had to respond in the Second Republic – the question of political neutrality; the question of voluntary concession to workers by the state and propertied class; and the question of the ownership and control of the means of production.

Within the NLC, that is, its principal officers, they are clear on these issues. That the means of production and exchange should be under the control of the working class is agreed upon. They are also agreed on the fact that capitalism can never concretely and permanently address the problems of the working class, even less meet their aspirations. That workers and their unions cannot be politically neutral in a peripheral capitalist society where everything is politicized and politics is seen as a 'do-or-die' affair, is also agreed upon. But the NLC has to contend with the ideological positions and sympathies of 44 other affiliated unions, the majority of whose leaders can be described as simply reactionary. Though the Charter was presented to President Shagari on 22 February 1980, in his 1980 May Day Address, the President of the NLC Hassan Sunmonu declared that:

> The great lesson (of May Day) is that workers will not achieve anything except through struggle, unity and solidarity . . . the NLC is the vanguard of the working class in Nigeria and the champion of the oppressed and exploited . . . Our objective is to ensure that class and property will be wiped out of our society once and for all time. In the final end of the struggle, there should be no poverty because there will be no capitalism.[22]

The President and members of the NLC were called communists and political enemies of democracy in Nigeria. The campaign against the congress was championed by some union leaders, particularly in the Nigeria Civil Service Union and the Labour Editor of the *Daily Times* both of whom had the full support of the Nigerian state and top officials of the Federal Ministry of Labour, Manpower Development and Productivity.[23] In reply to the accusations, the NLC president said that

> the drift of trade unionists and other intellectuals into the Marxist camp is due, among other things, to frustration with the way democracy is being practised and the sight of misery, squalor and want in the midst of plenty.[24]

And in an interview with another official of the Congress on this issue the following response was given:

> We are not bothered by these labels and names. At a level they demonstrate how successful we have been in presenting the cause and problems of Nigerian workers to the State and employers. Exploiters and reactionaries, irrespective of where they may be are usually scared of people who articulate fruitful and progressive positions. Perhaps if we had ignored our historical role in society, side tracked our constitution, formed all sorts of alliances with the ruling parties, ignored workers and so on, we might have been seen as heroes, democrats and God-fearing leaders. I think we have generated fear and crisis within the ranks of the reactionaries, the struggle just has to continue.[25]

At the first negotiations with the civilian administration (on issues which had been raised under the military and negotiated with the Supreme Military Council in May and July 1979) over the famous five points demands, in March–April 1980 the congress won some concessions from the state. The Shagari administration agreed to: (1) implement all previously negotiated collective agreements; (2) lift the wage freeze which the military had imposed in its last budget; (3) restore vehicle loans and basic allowances; (4) restore housing allowance to all categories of worker; (5) restore transport allowance for all workers; and (6) make legal a national minimum wage for Nigerian workers. Actually, by the time the February 1981 NLC Delegates' Conference was held in Kano, the Shagari administration had not seriously implemented any of the agreements above. In addition, the campaign between so-called 'democrats' and 'Marxists' at the Conference was so intense that only few unionists considered the implications of a unanimous decision to call a nation-wide strike in May 1981 in response to the attitude of the federal government to the general problems of workers and more specifically the March–April 1980 agreements. The state officials who had attended the Conference were so preoccupied with ensuring victory for the pro-establishment candidate, the president of the Civil Service Union, that they, too, ignored the implications of the strike decision.

The 1981 General Strike

The strike was a specific congress response to the attitude of the Shagari administration towards workers in general. Its success, in spite of logistical problems, stemmed from the deep level of alienation and anger which had been generated as a result of the failure of the political parties to fulfil election promises, the non-payment of wages, the increasing high cost of living and the failure of the federal government to fulfil its promises to workers.

The general strike began on 11 May 1981 and was called of on the 12th though many workers did not return to work until the 14th and 15th. Prior to the strike, the mass media gave it wide publicity, there were efforts to politicize it and the government-owned mass media attempted to blackmail the leadership of the NLC into calling off the strike action. Even where newspaper editorials conceded the inhospitable living conditions of Nigerian workers and the delaying tactics of the government on crucial areas of nego- tiation, they failed to recognize the fact that the Nigerian workers had only resorted to 'the only language which the government understands', without which it would not negotiate seriously. In a letter from the General Secretary of the National Union of Petroleum and Natural Gas Workers (NUPENG) to all Zonal Offices and principal officers of the Union, the reasons for the strike were stated as: 1) national minimum wage of ₦300.00; 2) car and motor-cycle loans; 3) 33 1/3 tax from end of service benefits; 4) collective agreements not to go to the Ministry of Labour for approval; 5) the abolition of NPF (National Provident Fund) or a balance sheet and early payment of contributions to contributors.[26] In a press statement issued by the NLC on 5 May 1981 and signed by the President and Secretary-General, the issues at stake were put at three:

1. national minimum wage
2. total restoration of vehicle advances and basic allowances
3. that minimum pension should not be less than the national min- mum wage.[27]

In the statement, the NLC made it clear that the ₦300.00 minimum wage was negotiable only to the extent that whatever was agreed to would 'ade- quately allow an average worker to live a decent life'. It also declared that

> the present administration (Shagari's) abolished the Price Control Board and substituted what it called Price Intelligence Unit, which does not control prices but only monitors price increases. It is no wonder that prices started to gallop ever since at the expense of workers and the poor masses of the country. Congress would soon expose those benefitting from these uncontrolled and uncontrollable price increases, and who shamefully turn round to blame Nigerian workers for causing inflation.[28]

On the issue of restoring car loans and allowances, the 5 May press statement declared that the demand was 'not negotiable' and argued that

> both the Governments of the Federal Republic of Nigeria and the National and State Assemblies have no moral right to refuse the total restoration of vehicle advances and basic allowances when they have given themselves vehicle advances and fantastic basic allowances, ranging from ₦10,000.00–₦12,000.00 with ₦250.00 monthly basic allowance. The workers who are the producers of the wealth of this country deserve the best considerations in the sharing of the wealth they so created.

On the issue of minimum pension, the congress declared that it considered it a

> shame on everybody that older men and women who have served this country to the best of their abilities are in their old age when they can no longer work, still be paid the shameful present minimum pension of ₦33.00 per month.

Finally, commenting on state manipulation of the mass media and the infiltration of pre-establishment unions, the NLC statement concluded:

> Congress remains unruffled by the use of the Government-controlled mass media to distort, malign and castigate the legitimate rights and demands of Nigerian workers. The use of trade union quislings can never stop the winning of legitimate demands of Nigerian workers. Those who are doubting the seriousness and commitment of Nigerian workers will only have themselves to blame come 11th May 1981.

In fact, the NLC suspected the possibility of the state using the police to force its President to make a statement on television, calling on workers to return to work. Thus, workers were generally informed through 'appropriate channels' that should such a situation arise, and the President was 'not smiling then, they should disregard whatever he says on television'.[29]

The strike, to say the least, was very successful. It took place all over the country and in pro-establishment unions, the rank and file defied their leaders and joined in the general strike. Where workers reported for work, they remained idle and discussed politics. In a very comprehensive nation-wide situation report, the government-controlled *New Nigerian* noted that virtually every aspect of society from the National Assembly to the airports and hospitals were affected directly and indirectly.[30] Essential services, which were barred from all forms of strike actions by the Essential Services Decree No. 23 of 1976 and even oil workers, for whom Decree No. 35 of 1975 had prescribed a death penalty or imprisonment of not less than 21 years for going on strike action, joined in the general strike. A worker interviewed at Warri, commented on the general strike thus:

The strike really shook the government and employers. They had all under-estimated the power of the NLC and the various unions. We workers are united irrespective of the activities of traitors and the constant use of the police. We shall continue to struggle. The strike is our major weapon and no amount of government propaganda or police brutality will stop us from struggling to overthrow oppression, degradation and exploitation.[31]

The state responded to the May general strike with repression, the arrest of workers and union leaders, the use of the mass media to misinform the rank and file and political blackmail. The most astonishing aspect of the use of the mass media was in the case where announcements were made to the effect that the strike had failed and activities were going on smoothly. And the workers concerned in these activities were at home hearing this on television!

Other than the NLC strike which prompted increased efforts from the National Assembly and the Nigerian Employers' Consultative Association to destabilize and split it, workers resorted to independent forms of protest against injustices suffered from the state. Legislators were attacked, houses of assembly were invaded, alliances were formed with other social groups and pronouncements and criticisms against the state and its functionaries became radicalized. Demonstrative of the plight of workers, even after the general strike, is the typical case of workers of the Bendel State Transport Service where they had not been paid their wages for over a year by November 1981. They were forced to demonstrate in November, 'carrying twelve mock coffins'. And, according to the report on the demonstration, the workers,

> . . . alleged that twelve workers of the company had died of starvation as a result of non-payment of salaries. 'Some of us have almost been deserted by our wives because there is no money to maintain them, while our children have been forced to go a begging' . . . Many of the workers were now squatting with relatives while some sleep in broken down buses in the company's premises after being driven away by their landlords for failure to pay their rent.[32]

Unfortunately for the Nigerian state and bourgeoisie, and reflective of the unproductive and crisis-ridden nature of Nigeria's peripheral capitalism, the glut in the world oil market affected the economy and made nonsense of all attempts to rationalize private capital accumulation through state subsidy. Oil revenues declined as a result of declining production and exportation of oil. Internal and external debts increased tremendously, all the states and the Federal Government began to record budgetary defects, food could not be imported and contractors and workers could not be paid regularly. These developments, in a system which was already anti-labour, only prompted all sorts of responses from the working classes.

In 1982, the country was almost completely paralysed by industrial actions. The depth of anger expressed by workers, the unrelenting support from the NLC to the struggles of its affiliate unions and the high level of organization and unity demonstrated by the rank and file, even in unions where the leadership was obviously pro-establishment, embarrassed the government and threatened the fragile hegemony and stability of the state. In March 1982,

> the country's entire electricity and power facilities were shut down as members of the Electricity and Gas Workers' Union downed tools in a sudden industrial show of anger that plunged all of Nigeria into darkness.[33]

This lasted for over a week. Members of the bourgeoisie who relied on their personal generators were slow to respond to the strike. The electricity workers were joined a week later by members of the Civil Service Technical Workers' Union 'after the government had ignored their 21-day ultimatum' for the implementation of agreements reached on improved conditions. They were joined by radio and signals technicians in the civil aviation service and this almost grounded Nigeria Airways. Water supplies were shut off and engineers and pilots went on a work-to-rule at Nigeria Airways. As Eddie Iroh notes:

> It was a week in which Nigeria's federal authorities appeared confused and helpless as the whole country lay paralysed. . . . While there was considerable public displeasure over the precipitate action of the striking workers, there was no applause for the manner in which the authorities seemed to have reneged on the incomes and bonus agreement, or for the Federal Government's lack of haste in tackling what is the most effective industrial action since the civilian administration came to power . . .[34]

Rather, the state and its agents embarked on propaganda and outright lies to explain away the power failure such as the lack of sufficient water at Kainji Dam and technical hitches. The Federal Minister for Mines and Power, Mohammed Hassan, rather than placate the workers by addressing their grievances, described the strike as 'illegal' and threatened the workers. This action only 'worsened the mood of the angry strikers', especially when they were threatened with mass dismissals.

It is indeed difficult to identify a sector of the economy which did not embark on a major strike action (not to mention work-to-rule actions) in the four years of the Second Republic. The Academic Staff Union of Universities embarked on one that lasted over ten weeks and totally disrupted the calendar of the Universities. Medical doctors, Magistrates, oil workers, technological students, nurses and teachers all over the country (primary and secondary levels inclusive) went on several strike actions. Marketwomen, schoolchildren and housewives were not left out of the protest actions as they struggled for their own rights or on behalf of unpaid and pauperized husbands, fathers and teachers. Austin Ogunsuyi describes a typical situation in Bendel State where an extravagant, corrupt and obviously confused administration was unable to pay any group of workers for several months:

> About 200 women and 50 school children stormed the Bendel State House of Assembly and almost disrupted proceedings, some members of the house were harassed while the gate to the assembly was destroyed by the mob, who claimed to be protesting... the non-payment of teachers' salaries by the state... The women barricaded the gate and attacked the vehicles of some legislators.[35]

By mid-1983, it was obvious that the depth of alienation among the workers was enough for them to work for the overthrow of the Second Republic. In fact, one can argue that the only reason why the workers did not overthrow the system was because the NLC as a body lacked a political programme, especially the control over the means of coercion. Other than raising peripheral debates on supporting so-called pro-labour candidates or the formation of a labour party, not much work had been done in the areas of education and organization to achieve these ends. This is in spite of the swift reaction from the state and members of the various employers' associations. The retrenchment of workers worsened in 1983. About 60 workers were sacked by the state-owned Ogun State Radio Corporation; by November 1983, 15,000 workers of the printing industry were being threatened with retrenchment and 17,000 metal workers had lost their jobs. The latter figure represented about 58% of the total organized workers in the industry. The usual excuse for these actions was the lack of raw materials, import licences and foreign exchange facilities. Workers also responded to these actions by adopting several forms of overt and covert actions identified earlier with increasing levels of organization, co-ordination and sophistication. In Anambra State alone, there were 34 officially recorded strikes between September 1979 and June 1983 involving 110,570 workers, leading to the loss of 677,442 man-days or 2,743 workman-years. By the time the Shagari administration was overthrown the NLC had lost faith in it and concluded that it was a 'directionless, corrupt, wicked and absolutely anti-worker government'.[36] It called on the 'governments of the federation to surrender voluntarily to the working people of this country if they can no longer govern'.[37] Of course, history teaches us that no ruling elite has ever or will ever voluntarily relinquish political power to opposing factions of its class, not to talk of the working class.

State Response to Working Class Militancy and Action

When the Shagari administration first came into power in October 1979, it realized the potent and actual power of the working class. It also realized the organizational capacity of the NLC. The compulsory check-off system, the ₦1 million starting-off grant and the long period of 'consolidation, organization and stock-taking' had provided the NLC and its affiliates with enough base on which to struggle on behalf of the rank and file. However, characteristic of bourgeois democracies and politics, the hope was that union leaders, particularly those at the NLC, would hustle after political party cards, contracts and favours from prominent politicians and these would be enough to get them to compromise their positions. Of course, the administration overlooked the fact that, even where the leadership could be incorporated, the rank and file of Nigerian workers had reached a level where they could effectively by-pass the leadership if the issues at stake were crucial enough.

Thus, the government relied on three major policies to keep workers in line and promote 'industrial peace'. First, it relied on the constant invocation of the labour decrees passed by the military which had been conveniently converted into Acts of law. Second, it relied on strengthening the hands of capital by putting the police at the disposal of employers, providing them with cheap indigenous and expatriate labour, condoning the policy of retrenchment and even attempting to privatize some public corporations. Finally, the state initiated moves to split the NLC by allowing the creation of more central labour organizations and abolishing automatic check-off which were aimed at creating disunity within the labour movement. Other strategies of blackmail, incorporation through bribery and other methods were only employed to ensure the effectiveness of the strategies above.

The Shagari administration did not succeed in any of these policies to any extent which can be interpreted as affecting worker unity. The open support which the conservative and obviously pro-establishment President of the Nigerian Civil Service Union received (not the Civil Service Technical Workers Union) at the 1981 Delegates' conference in Kano where Hassan Sunmonu was overwhelmingly re-elected by the workers demonstrates clearly the fact that ultimately it is the workers who decide on who leads them. The beautiful speeches made on behalf of Mr David Ojeli by agents of the state and capital at the conference and the campaign against Sunmonu about his Marxist sympathies did not affect the perception of workers. In interviews with over 250 oil workers all over the country, 100% praised Sunmonu's efforts, declared their support for only *one* central labour organization and even felt the NLC was 'not radical enough'.[38] And the National Union of Petroleum and Natural Gas Workers is one of the most powerful unions in the country.

The NLC condemned efforts to sell public corporations to capitalist and transnational elements by the Shagari administration. It argued that the sale of these public corporations would promote 'economic slavery and pauperization of the nation'. In addition, it would amount to using public funds to enrich a few individuals at the expense of the nation:

> what is needed is a radical re-organisation under public ownership; to want to re-organise under private control is to ensure that accruing profit goes into private pockets and this will lead to retrenchment

in the public sector and will bring untold hardships to the working people of this country.[39]

However, the most formidable response by the Shagari administration was in the effort of the National Assembly to split the NLC. This move was spearheaded by Mr Edet Bassey Etienam, who, while in the Federal House of Representatives, served as the chairman of the Committee on Labour. His one-man battle against the NLC is an irony in the sense that Mr Etienam was himself a former labour leader who was on leave of absence from his union, the Customs and Excise and Immigration Staff Union of Nigeria. The successful organization of the 11 May 1981 general strike, the refusal of the NLC leadership to compromise its radical position and the obvious interest in protecting a system which favours employers against workers, influenced the zeal with which efforts were made to: 1) establish a multiplicity of central labour organizations; 2) allow the establishment of mushroom and ineffective house/craft unions; 3) abolish automatic 'check-off' system; and 4) introduce an anti-strike bill which would severely bureaucratize the process of decision making within unions.[40]

The open support for the policies above encouraged some union leaders to form a so-called 'Committee for Democratic Trade Unions' (CDTU) which workers constantly refer to as 'Committee for Destruction of Trade Union Unity'. The labour editor of the *Daily Times*, Mr Umoh James Umoh also took it upon himself to run down the NLC and expost the 'Marxists' and 'Democrats' among them, while Mr Etienam used every means to present the existing arrangements as 'illegal' and 'undemocratic'. Even Chief Adisa Akinloye, the national chairman of the National Party of Nigeria, campaigned openly for support for the bills which were aimed at splitting the congress.[41]

These appeals and efforts failed. The bills did not pass through the National Assembly and the NLC has remained intact. The point remained, however, that the Nigerian state refused to address the issues responsible for industrial actions in the country and preferred to pursue peripheral and political issues:

> It [was] a feature of the Shagari Administration not to address the roots of problems even when they were obvious. The government was too deeply engrossed in corruption, ethnic and religious parochialism, waste and subservience to imperialist pressures that structural and fundamental changes were alien to it. Even if the National Assembly had passed the bills, it did not immediately mean workers would rush to form new central labour organisations.[42]

Conclusions: the Need for a Political Programme

No matter how radical workers are within their industries, they can at best develop a 'trade union consciousness'. The overthrow of the exploitative system would be unattainable unless concrete political programmes are set out and pursued. It is the dream and wish of any bourgeois system to domesticate labour and if possible make the existence of trade unions impossible. In advanced capitalist formations, the state and bourgeoisie try to rationalize worker exploitation through the provision of all forms of insurance schemes. The competition and corruption which plagued Nigeria's Second Republic could not have allowed any serious or rational attention to be paid to the need to minimize class contradictions and struggles in Nigeria. Nonetheless, 'insurance programmes' are only temporary and cosmetic solutions to more fundamental structural contradictions arising from the nature and pattern of production and exchange in the system. In a political economy where ethnicity, religious parochialism, corruption, waste and ineptitude are entrenched; where state policies more often than not end up in reproducing poverty; where institutional inefficiency and decay slows down the process of policy initiation and implementation and the process of accumulation is subsumed under imperialist interests, the interests of workers on the one hand and those of employers and the state on the other, are inevitably contradictory.

The NLC would inevitably be forced either through the increasing consciousness of its leadership, increasing attacks from the state and bourgeoisie or popular pressures from the rank-and-file to develop a concrete political programme. Obviously, it has demonstrated in the Second Republic the power of organized labour. Prior to the 1983 general elections, the position and pronouncements of the NLC forced the federal government to advance loans totalling ₦539 million to the 19 state governments in order to facilitate the payment of workers' salaries. But such pressures, in sensitive periods alone, are not enough. While the state can be expected to continue its tactics of infiltration, manipulation, pressure, blackmail and direct intervention, and employers can be expected to forge stronger alliances with the state while initiating autonomous domesticating policies within industry, the NLC must continue to consolidate, expose pro-establishment unionists, get to the rank-and-file, deepen the content of its worker educational programme, step up the mobilization of the rank and file and develop a *political* programme:

> As presently constituted the NLC is a huge compromise of ideological positions, and it is consequently disabled from pursuing a radical, proletarian cause. This is why it has been unable, despite its militant rhetoric to place before the Nigerian masses a clear programme to combat the bourgeoisie *politically*. Although the NLC *Charter of Demands* yearns for the establishment of a Welfare State, it says nothing about how workers can organise *autonomously* to bring this about. Trade unions emerged in history as organisations to challenge the domination of employers or owners of capital.[43]

This critical perspective also exists within the NLC and it influences debates, decisions and actions. Though the *Charter* is not a programme of political struggle there is no evidence that the NLC has developed such yet. If the mistakes of the past and the 'raw deal' suffered under the Shagari adminis-tration are not to be repeated even in worse proportions, then the need for serious organizational work cannot be overlooked.

Finally, the NLC would be making a grave mistake to expect much from the Buhari administration. The regime has so far not made any *serious* pro-nouncement on the need to re-structure the economy and society. In any case, most of those in power today were present between 1966 and 1979, when the military passed all the anti-labour decrees. Some even participated in the formulation of such policies. Also, they have their own specific ideological sympathies. As a right-wing coup led by bourgeois fractions in the armed forces, all one can expect are palliatives which would rationalize the process of domesticating labour in Nigeria.

Notes

1. David C. Ojeli, 'Promoting Industrial Peace in Nigeria', *Labour and Development*, 31–33, September 1977, p. 19.

2. For details see Tayo Fashoyin, *Industrial Relations in Nigeria: Development and Practice* (London: Longman, 1980) and Wogu Ananaba, *The Trade Union Movement of Nigeria* (London: Hurst, 1969).

3. For details on overt and covert strategies and tactics of protest, see Robin Cohen, 'Resistance and Hidden Forms of Consciousness Amongst African Workers', *Review of African Political Economy*, 19, 1980.

4. See H. Braverman, *Labour and Monopoly Capital: The Degradation of Work in the Twentieth Century* (New York: Monthly Review Press, 1974).

5. For details see Julius O. Ihonvbere and Toyin Falola, 'The Re-cycling of Petro-Naira and Nigeria's Incorporation into World Capitalism', forthcoming.

6. Alhaji Shehu Shagari admitted this much in his 23rd Independence and Inauguration Address to the Nation, 1 October 1983.

7. Text of Press Release by the Nigeria Labour Congress (NLC) reproduced in *Liberation News*, 1, 3, February 1983, pp. 1 and 8.

8. Ibid.

9. The Minister for Labour, Mr Osamor, made this declaration to oil workers, when in early 1983 they complained to him personally over the issue of retrenchment of workers in the oil sector.

10. Press release in *Liberation News*, op. cit.

11. Ibid.

12. Field interview with a member of the National Union of Petrol-eum and National Gas Workers (NUPENG) Lagos, 12 November 1983.

13. Comrade Hassan Sunmonu, 1983 May Day Address (Lagos: NLC Secretariat, 1983), p. 2.

14. Ibid.

15. Alhaji Shehu Shagari, '1981 May Day Address' (Lagos: Executive Office of the President, 1981).

16. 'Labour Problems', *Periscoping Nigeria* (Ottawa: Nigeria High Commission), 2, 1, 1982, p. 57.

17. Ibid.

18. Interview with an official of the Nigerian Labour Contress, Yaba, Lagos, October 1983.

19. Eddie Iroh, 'Nigeria: Unions Flex their Muscles', *Africa*, 128, April 1982, p. 34.

20. Nigerian Labour Congress, *Workers' Charter of Demands Prepared and Presented to the Federal Government of Nigeria* (Lagos: NLC Secretariat, February 1980).

21. 'Trade Unions Cannot be Neutral in Politics – An Interview with Comrade S.O.Z. Ejiofor', *Socialist Forum* (Ile-Ife), 3, June 1981, p. 17.

22. Comrade Hassan Sunmonu, '1980 May Day Address' (Lagos: NLC Secretariat, 1980).

23. For samples of the works of the Labour Editor of the *Daily Times*, see his 'Labour Notes' every Monday issue of the *Times*, centre pages and his two articles in *West Africa*, 26 May 1980 and 2 June 1980.

24. *West Africa*, 23 June 1980, p. 1108.

25. Interview with an official of the NLC, Yaba, Lagos, October 1983.

26. Field document, Letter to all NUPENG Officers and Offices signed by the former General Secretary, Mr A.E. Otu.

27. Field document.

28. Ibid.

29. Field interview with NLC official, Yaba, Lagos, October 1983.

30. See 'National Services Partially Disrupted', *New Nigerian*, 12 May 1981; 'Strike Day – 40 Unions Taking Part Says NLC', *Daily Sketch*, 11 May 1981 and 'Confusion: Few Turn Up', *Nigerian Tribune*, 14 May 1981.

31. Field interview with an oil worker, Shell-BP Depot., Warri, August 1983.

32. Andrew Isibor, '1,000 Workers of Bendel Transport Service Demonstrate', *New Nigerian*, 19 November 1981, p. 13.

33. Eddie Iroh, op. cit.

34. Ibid.

35. Austin Ogunsuyi, '200 Women Storm Bendel Assembly', *The Nigerian Observer*, 17 February 1982, p. 1.

36. Interview at the Headquarters of the NLC, November 1983.

37. 'Perform or Hand Over to Workers! NLC Tells 20 Governments', *Labour Champion* (official monthly newspaper of the NLC.), 001, 1983, p. 1. *The Labour Champion* was established to counter the negative coverage provided by government and capitalist-controlled newspapers. It is also expected to contribute significantly to popular mobilization and education.

38. The findings of this research would appear soon in Julius O. Ihonvbere, 'Labour, Transnational Oil Corporations and the State in Nigeria's Oil Industry', PhD thesis, Department of Political Economy, University of Toronto (Summer 1984).

39. Nigerian Labour Congress, 'Statement on Plans to sell Public Corporations' reviewed by Tony Masha, 'NLC Flays sales of Government Companies', *Sunday Times*, 6 November 1983, p. 1.

40. For the NLC's position on these developments see NLC, *The Need to Sustain One Central Labour Organisation (BLC) in Nigeria: Workers of*

Nigeria Unite and Organise. (Lagos: NLC Secretariat, n.d.); Tony Masha, 'Nobody can split NLC — Osunde Fumes', *Daily Times*, 25 September 1983, p. 3; and Adekunle Oyebanji, 'Resist Moves to Split NLC, Labour Unions Told', *New Nigerian*, 4 December 1981, p. 2. For other criticisms of the effort particularly of Mr Etienam's crusade against the NLC see *The Guardian*, (Editorial), 'Etienam Against the NLC', 14 September 1983, p. 8.

41. See NLC Document, ibid.

42. Interview with an official of NUPENG, Lagos, NUPENG Headquarters, November 1983.

43. 'Ruling Class War Against Workers: The Current Moves to Split the NLC', *Socialist Forum* (Ile-Ife), 4, December 1981, pp. 24–5.

8.   External Relations

Introduction

The linkage between crises and contradictions within the economy and foreign policy initiatives and action was clearly manifest in Nigeria's Second Republic. The weak nature of the Nigerian state, the dependent accumulative base of the bourgeoisie, increasing class contradictions and struggles, combined with pressures from the metropolitan bourgeoisie to compel the Shagari administration to pursue a complacent and, in fact, reactionary foreign policy. Not only did oil production and exportation on which the Shagari administration was dependent for foreign exchange earnings decline precipitously, the unmet expectations from the politicking between 1979 and 1983 as well as corruption, mismanagement and inefficiency, all fuelled by the need to pay expensive political debts, affected the conduct of the country's foreign policy. In addition to these, it is essential to note the increasing class consciousness and militancy of organized labour, increasing worker–peasant alliances, the intensity of intra-bourgeois class crises and the re-integration of Nigeria into the world capitalist system. In the process of this re-integration, Nigeria moved from the position of a semi-peripheral, Newly Industrializing Country (NIC) to that of a classic peripheral country once again — dependent on foreign loans, food imports and very vulnerable to external pressure and manipulation.

Though the civilian government was in power for only four years, a lot happened to justify a critical study of its foreign policies as well as the extent to which internal economic conditions and developments influenced such policies. Other than the decline in oil production, exports and revenues, on the internal side, we can also note the effects of agricultural stagnation, rural decay, urban restlessness, inflation, political violence and the second elections and various institutional and policy conflicts and disagreements between the states and the federal government, oil and non-oil states, oil and non-oil bourgeoisies and the various political parties. On the external front, the South African and Namibian issues still remain, relations with ECOWAS member States, the expulsion of 'aliens', the Ghanaian, Camerounian and Chadian issues have also come and gone but their imprints remain on Nigeria's foreign policy chart. Finally, relations with the great powers were also affected not only by the nature of politics and the ideology of the ruling party but also by the economic contraction and the apparent failure of Nigeria to emerge as a Newly Industrializing Country.

Internal Contradictions in the Second Republic

The Second Republic has been beneficial to Nigerian social science in two major ways. First, the numerous contradictions and the inter- and intra-class conflicts have forced orthodox analysts to move away from description, the emphasis on institutions, personalities and 'major developments' to focus on and conceive the Nigerian society as a totality. While the majority of these orthodox works have abandoned the modernization and institutionalization models, they have been careful to flirt with dependency formulations while clearly staying away from materialist approaches. The second benefit of the Second Republic is in the extent to which it has come to legitimize radical (political economy, Marxist and dependency) models and perspectives on the Nigerian society. This has intensified debates which have moved beyond ethnicity, statism, military versus civilian rule, etc. Increasingly, in the area of foreign policy, analysts are accepting the links between the domestic economy and foreign policy objectives.[1]

It is quite valid to argue that Nigeria's foreign policy, in spite of the general fundamental objectives of non-interference, respect for the sovereignty of other countries, the evaluation of international issues on their merit and the sovereign equality of all states, has fluctuated with regimes, 'ideology' and the level of social contradictions. Thus, in the First Republic Nigeria's foreign policy was conservative and reactionary. The vacillations and outright hostility of the government to progressive forces reflected the country's precarious political arrangement, the economic domination by foreign interests, the unavailability of resources and the perceptions and beliefs of the feudal-aristocratic fraction of the power-elite that captured political power in 1960. To Ibrahim Gambari, 1960–66 was a period of 'uncertainty and timidity', while to Gordon Idang, the period witnessed a high level of inconsistencies, a lack of enthusiasm for radical-nationalist positions, a cautious and conservative approach to anti-colonial policy, gradualism and legalism.[2]

The experiences of the civil war, the command character of the military, the nature of the new political arrangement in which the centre became more powerful than the states, and more importantly, the billions of petro-naira collected from oil exports after 1972, enabled the military leaders to pursue a relatively vigorous and active foreign policy. To these factors one must also add the changing perceptions of the dominant social forces who wished to see the country emerge in the sub-region and continent as a sub-imperial power, if not in actuality, i.e. based on actual and demonstrated military and economic might, at least at the level of influence, rhetoric and propaganda. Thus, a deliberate and persistent policy of propaganda aimed at projecting the country as the 'spokesnation' and 'leader' of the continent was systematically launched after the civil war in 1970.

Unlike in the First Republic, the security problems of the country were exposed by the war. The military leaders realized that the country's stability and security could not be divorced from those of the sub-region or the continent. Thus, South Africa became a 'special area' of interest to the government. At the sub-regional level, the creation of the Economic Community of West African States (ECOWAS) became the high point of relations with Nigeria's neighbours. The oil money lubricated the process of achieving the country's external objectives through the granting of soft loans, donations, technical aid and other forms of financial assistance to African States.[3] Internally, the military passed scores of decrees against labour and other non-bourgeois forces in order to further incorporation and domestication.[4] Efforts were made to reduce friction between foreign and domestic capital through the indigenization decrees which defined the spheres of interest of both in the economy. But problems of rural and institutional decay, social contradictions, inefficiency, corruption, misuse of state power and general mismanagement of oil rents generated forces of instability which mediated the depth of foreign relations. Thus, in spite of Nigeria's so-called dynamic foreign policy prior to October 1979, the military confined this exclusively to press conferences, declarations, financial contributions and propaganda. Yusufu Bala Usman captured the limitation of this approach to foreign policy when he queried:

> What is good about a foreign policy because it involves a lot of motion, whether aeronautically, orally, or even financially? Motion and 'dynamism', in themselves, separate from objectives can only be regarded as desirable if foreign policy is seen essentially as an airport, conference and state visit affair. In other words, a show.[5]

The point however remains that at the time the Shagari administration came to power on 1 October 1979, it inherited *specific* internal and external situations, problems and contradictions.

At the broad level, it inherited a new political mix with five different competing and conflicting (but not contradictory in ideology, strategy and objectives) political parties. The views of each party on foreign policy and the domestic economy differed, though none advocated the radical restructuring of internal power and exchange relations. The 1979 Constitution equally imposed some limitations on the powers of the executive president while stipulating some broad foreign policy objectives. Thus, though the constitution vested powers over external policy in the federal government, Section 5(3)(a) restricted the powers of the President in relation to war with another country. Here, the President could not declare war with another country without the approval of the National Assembly. Senate approval was also required under Section 5(3)(b) before the President could send any members of the armed forces on combat duty outside Nigeria. Furthermore,

Section 12(1) stipulated that the National Assembly must sanction, through law, any treaty signed by Nigeria with another country. Section 74(2) restricted the power of the President from spending any money from the Consolidated Revenue Fund without the approval of the National Assembly, and, according to Section 157(4), heads of Nigeria's Diplomatic Missions must be approved by Senate. Thus, it is clear that the National Assembly could, under the Second Republic, determine not only the nature and composition of Nigeria's external relations but also the extent of an executive President's success. Where the President did not enjoy a clear majority in the National Assembly and could not strike a working relationship with other parties in the form of an accord, then such a President, given the 'winner-takes-all' nature of Nigerian politics, was unlikely to succeed in either domestic or foreign policies. This is notwithstanding the broad declaration of the same constitution in Section 19 that:

> The state shall promote African unity, as well as total political, economic, social and cultural liberation of Africa and all other forms of international co-operation conducive to the consolidation of universal peace and mutual respect and friendship among all peoples and states, and shall combat racial discrimination in all its manifestations.[6]

While this declaration restates the broad angles of Nigeria's foreign policy, it does not capture or even pretend to capture the internal and external conditions that would enable the state to execute the stated goals. Even the five objectives of the *Four Year Development Plan* of 1970 which was subsequently incorporated into the 1979 constitution are so broad and utopian (given objective socio-economic and political problems and contradictions) that governments since 1970 can hardly claim to have even recognized the means with which they can be achieved. These objectives are: 1) a united, strong and self-reliant nation; 2) a great and dynamic nation; 3) a just and egalitarian society; 4) a land of bright and full opportunities for all citizens; and 5) a free and democratic society.

Without doubt the attainment of these five objectives would set a very credible and viable base on which to pursue an effective foreign policy. Under the Second Republic, Nigeria, to say the least, moved further and further away from these objectives. Mounting internal contradictions and crises in the world economy have combined to disrupt well-laid plans where corruption did not already undermine the meagre efforts of the government.

The high level of alienation and contradiction that the policies of the ruling party at the centre as well as those of the various parties in the states generated effectively mediated even the effort to keep up the propaganda, generosity and 'dynamism' inherited from the Murtala-Obasanjo regime in 1979.

It is important to note the views of the six political parties on foreign policy issues. The National Party of Nigeria which controlled the central government throughout the Second Republic emphasized a creditable defence policy, the national interest, world peace and order and the intensification of the struggle against apartheid in Southern Africa. It would not re-open relations with Israel until it severs all ties with South Africa and withdraws from all Arab lands. In addition, the principles of foreign policy inherited from the military will all be retained. The Unity Party of Nigeria, on the other hand, would start by opening up diplomatic relations with Israel 'whose expertise we need badly'. The leader of the party promised to stay at home, and to withdraw Nigeria from OPEC. The party also promised to act swiftly and decisively against neighbouring countries who 'try Nigeria's strength' and would drastically reduce the number of visits to Nigeria by foreign dignitaries. The Nigeria People's Party emphasized non-alignment, good neighbourliness, not to 'inherit the prejudices of any particular nation' in the Middle East, not to open relations with Israel unless it stops servicing the war machines of South Africa and, depending on conditions, to withdraw Nigeria from OPEC. The Great Nigeria People's Party felt it was wrong for Nigeria to 'throw its weight around in Southern Africa'. It would retain the then existing pattern of foreign policy but modify some methods, and would commit Nigeria to the collective decisions of the OAU. The People's Redemption Party was against the re-opening of relations with Israel because of its Zionist policies and connections with South Africa. It promised to pull Nigeria out of the Commonwealth because British wealth was certainly 'not common', supply the teeth to the OAU which it described as a toothless bull-dog and work for the creation of an African High Command. These positions were stated in 1979 and remained unaltered during the 1983 general election-eering campaigns. The Nigeria Advance Party, which became the sixth registered political party, paid more attention to internal issues but promised to deal with imperialist and neo-colonialist forces that exploit Nigeria, team up with progressive African nations to fight colonialism and racism and defend Nigeria's interest within international organizations.

It is evident therefore, that the positions of the parties were congruent on certain issues and divergent on others. But these differences influenced the way the ruling party's foreign policy was evaluated, supported or criticized. However, the point must be made that there are other fundamental constraints other than these constitutional ones which militated against a dynamic and progressive foreign policy in Nigeria's Second Republic. If these constraints were not there, competition, power struggles and corruption within the ruling party, increasing organization, consciousness, militancy and action within the ranks of non-bourgeois classes, the mismanagement of the oil economy and efforts to re-integrate the country into the world capitalist system by transnational interests would still have been other factors prevent-ing the Shagari administration from pursuing far-reaching external policies.

When the NPN took over the reins of the federal government on 1 October 1979, the Nigerian economy was already on the brink of collapse. Inflation was well over 30%, unemployment and labour unrest were on the increase and the import bill was over ₦600 million per month. The urban construction boom and dependent food policy which accompanied the oil boom had attracted hordes of skilled, semi-skilled and unskilled labour from the rural areas into the urban areas. Food imports in 1979 were ₦818.8 million, oil production stood at 2.4 million barrels per day and revenue from oil exports was ₦8,880.9 million.[7]

However, within four years of taking over the reins of power and the privilege of presiding over the spending and allocation of oil rents on which the state had become exclusively dependent for revenues, things gradually became worse for the economy. The monthly import bill reached one billion naira per month barely one year after taking over the reins of office.[8] The country by May 1981 experienced a general strike. Industrial disputes increased. Though revenues from oil increased to $22.4 billion in 1980, food imports also increased to ₦1.56 billion in 1980 reaching ₦1.86 billion in 1981. Total exports declined by 34.5% from the level in the first half of 1981 to about ₦4 billion in the first half of 1982. By the end of August 1983, the country's external debt stood at ₦16 billion. To make matters worse, the high level of corruption and misplacement of priorities by the various state governments led to a situation where most could not pay workers for up to six months, their basic salaries and allowances. This intensified the contradiction between labour and the state. As the debt of the centre increased, the various state governments were equally in debt. The nineteen state governments collectively owed over ₦5 billion externally, with Imo State incurring the highest of ₦341.20 million. (See Table 8.1.) In fact, revelations by newly elected governors in 1983 in some of the states showed that the ₦5 billion figure did not capture the extent of the debt by any means.[9]

The deteriorating condition of the Nigerian economy under the Second Republic was so severe by April 1982 with the glut in the world oil market that the country had to rely on Saudi Arabia and OPEC to put pressure on the oil companies to keep lifting Nigerian oil. In addition, the Shagari administration was forced in April 1982 to introduce the Economic Stabilization Act and consequently imposed 'austerity measures' at home. At this time foreign reserves which had reached ₦5.6 billion in 1980 and ₦6.4 billion in early 1981, plummeted to ₦1.1 billion in 1982, and further declined below ₦1 billion in 1983. Part of the 'austerity' and rather panicky measures also included the expulsion of 'illegal aliens', the prohibition of the importation of a wide range of goods, and the ban on employment and promotions. With the decline in oil production, mass retrenchment began in all major companies and corporations particularly those severely affected by the ban on importation. In 1981, the International Labour Organization (ILO) had come up with a report which not only noted that 'much acute' poverty still existed in Nigeria but also that the lot of the majority in the rural and urban areas had worsened since political independence. The report also noted the mismanagement of oil rents, the widening gap between rich and poor, the poor agricultural policies and the dangers inherent in the dependent food policy. It cautioned against the risks of replaying the Iranian or Ghanaian scenarios in Nigeria.[10]

Table 8.1
External Debts* of State Governments as of March 1983

State	External Loan (Naira million)
Anambra	318.60
Bauchi	229.00
Bendel	210.55
Benue	266.00
Borno	167.30
Cross Rivers	210.04
Gongola	199.17
Imo	341.93
Kaduna	111.40
Kano	212.93
Kwara	228.40
Lagos	275.00
Niger	157.10
Ogun	84.66
Oyo	334.60
Ondo	250.80
Plateau	339.60
Rivers	189.80
Sokoto	302.12

* The new governments following the August/September 1983 elections are currently in the process of revealing the true extent of debts owed by the various states.

Source: Federal Ministry of Finance, Lagos.

Alhaji Shehu Shagari noted the very fragile political foundation on which he was to base his administration in his inaugural address in 1979:

> The problems of creating a national government, a viable economic base and the integration of various ethnic groups in Nigeria in fairness and without acrimony, overwhelmed the first republic. These problems are still with us. And it is our determination to do our utmost best to contribute to their resolution . . .[11]

In 1980, the President overlooked these problems, the declining rate of oil exports and revenues and the heightening of socio-economic contradictions in Nigeria to state that:

> At independence, when economically this nation had so little, Nigeria did not hesitate to commit itself politically as well as financially to the

struggle for the liberation of Africa. Today, Nigeria is economically better off, and the present administration has no hesitation in further-ing the commitment of this nation to the struggle for the total liber-ation of the remaining parts of Africa that are still under colonial and white racist minority rule. Nigeria's support will be diplomatic, moral and material, it will be financial. In short, it will be total.[12]

At one level, this declaration was very much in line with positions inherited from the military in terms of using internal resources to back up foreign policy goals and actions. But the declaration, in view of the problems high-lighted thus far, particularly the increasing alienation of the poor majority, can be regarded as out of tune with the objective realities of the country. The fact that the single source of food, foreign loans, technology, expertise, investors was the oil industry on which the economy was dependent and perhaps more importantly, that the market for Nigeria's oil was the Western world, was enough to mediate the ability to employ autonomously local resources in support of foreign policy objectives. The persistence of inflation, housing problems, political competition, unemployment, police brutality, corruption in high places, job insecurity, lack of basic amenities, in short mass poverty, meant that the government could not rely on mass or popular support for foreign policy objectives. And finally, the declining revenues meant that its hitherto relative financial autonomy, ability to seek alternative markets, the attractiveness of its local market, generosity to poorer African states and liberation movements, all in the external arena, were gone. On the internal level, this intensified the struggle within the bourgeois class to cap-ture or corner whatever was left (or was coming in) of the oil money. In addition, the state could no longer lubricate the edges of class contradictions and struggles through sinecure positions, periodic wage and salary reviews and the granting of patronage. In his October 1983 Independence Day Broadcast to Nigerians, President Shagari had emphasized the gloomy nature (and future) of the economy:

> More than ever before, I ask for your continued co-operation and understanding because the magnitude of the task ahead of us demands nothing less. Although there are brighter prospects in the economic sphere, the situation is still far from normal . . . Indeed, our oil export earnings, which reached a peak of 22.4 billion in 1980, declining to an estimated $9.6 billion in 1983. Moreover the exportable surplus of oil production is being gradually reduced by the growing domestic con-sumption of refined petroleum products. With the fall in oil revenues, the country is now faced with a growing shortage of foreign exchange. At the same time, our manufacturing sector, which is unhappily import-oriented, continues to weaken.[13]

It is therefore against this economic background that we examine foreign policy objectives and goals under the Shagari administration, particularly the extent to which developments in the oil industry which had by 1980 become the 'main source of government revenue and foreign exchange earnings'[14] affected foreign policies.

Oil, Contradictions and the Return to a Subservient Extra-African Policy

The nature of the dominant political parties in the Second Republic, the escapist nature of their programmes and the accumulative bases of the various factions/fractions of the bourgeoisie which dominated policy-making institutions and positions throughout the life-span of the Second Republic showed clearly that positions on extra-African issues were going to be subservient to Western imperialist interests. The Nigerian dominant class, particularly its ruling fraction, as in the First Republic, fell prey to the paternalism and vain propaganda of Western diplomats, statesmen and media who emphasized the country's so-called wealth, power, democracy, reasonableness, peaceful and cooperative nature of the leadership and the need to show example through accommodating leadership. Hence, Andrew Young, who under the Carter Administration in the United States had used his African descent to hoodwink a lot of African leaders, wrote in 1981 that 'Nigeria is in some important respects Africa's most powerful nation'.[15] To Young and other commentators who constantly based the calculation of Nigeria's power on its oil wealth, the former US Ambassador to the UN explained this position further:

> . . . Nigeria is playing an increasingly influential role in the political and economic policies of other African countries. As a consequence of its oil wealth and OPEC membership, Lagos exercises considerable leadership in the OAU and dominates ECOWAS. Nigeria's resources and zealous commitment on Zimbabwe made it a mutual partner with the frontline states at various stages of the negotiations for a settlement. . . .[16]

To be sure, the extent to which the pattern of recycling oil rents – on armaments, food and capital goods imports, corruption and storage of public funds in foreign banks, etc. – has influenced Nigeria's role as an agent of conservatism and reaction within the organizations mentioned above among others is often conveniently overlooked or underplayed. Nigeria's constant vacillatory or inconsistent positions are actually deliberate policy positions aimed at not taking positions on issues that critically affected the Western powers. While Nigeria did not openly go against the Eastern bloc as was the case in the First Republic, the enthusiasm of the Shagari administration was obviously directed towards the interests of the Western bloc – the source of its loans, food, weapons and other imports. Analyses of Nigeria's 'defensive radical' posture on African affairs and the seemingly indeterminable (indefinable?) position on non-African issues, which neglect (deliberately) the relationship between the *nature* of the sub- and super-structures have often missed the dynamic points of Nigeria's foreign relations. As Stephen Wright has rightly noted, 'the neo-colonial nature of the Nigerian economy is a major constraint . . . the economy is open to manipulation by non-Nigerian forces, particularly the multinational companies',[17] who usually operate in the interests of their home governments at a certain level.

In the Second Republic, the relatively 'independent' approach to non-African issues inherited from the military in October 1979, practically gave way to a subservient and generally diversionary one. To be sure, the nature of the economy and society had a lot to do with the inability of the peripheral state and comprador bourgeoisie to deepen what had been inherited from the military. In 1976 the Adebayo Adedeji Commission had recommended six elements of Nigeria's national interests, which were accepted by General Obasanjo in June 1976 and subsequently upheld by Shagari. Three of the recommendations had a lot to do with relations with the world. These were

> the achievement of collective self-reliance in Africa and the rest of the developing world; the promotion and defence of social justice and respect for human dignity; and the promotion and defence of world peace.

Olajide Aluko has rightly argued that given the nature and context of the economy, particularly the dependence on the Western world and low level of political integration, these objectives are not realizable.[18] Bolaji Akinyemi, arguing largely along similar lines, has concluded that 'there is a limit to the retaliatory acts Nigeria can take against industrialized countries for violating her national interests because she needs the transfer of technology'.[19] Akinyemi does not capture the essence of Nigeria's relative weak position in relation to the Western powers, because the root of this weakness lies in the commitment of the Nigerian bourgeoisie to the maintenance of a peripheral capitalist economy through the concretization of unequal exchange arrangements with the Western powers. The conspicuous and extravagant life style of this dominant class, its corruption, subservient mentality and largely unproductive nature makes it predisposed to accepting junior positions as agents, shareholders, managers, legal advisers and so on in transnational interests.[20] The oil industry on which the bourgeoisie and state had become dependent is dominated by Western companies — Shell, Gulf, Mobil, Exxon, Elf, Pan Ocean etc. (Table 8.2 shows how they dominated oil production.)

Segun Osoba explains the internal dimension of this major contradiction in the production and accumulation process in Nigeria:

> The contradiction between the national bourgeoisie and the masses in Nigeria hinges on the operation of international finance capitalism

179

Table 8.2
Crude Oil Production by Companies for a Typical Month: July 1982

Company	% Contribution to Total Production
Shell	50.19
Gulf	19.55
Mobil	8.39
Agip	10.27
Elf	7.28
Texaco	1.75
Pan Ocean	0.36
Ashland	1.56
Phillips	0.09
Tenneco	0.56

Source: Nigerian National Petroleum Corporation, *Monthly Petroleum Information, July 1982*, p. 2.

> of the national bourgeoisie. But the national bourgeoisie is not able to resolve this contradiction in favour of the masses of its people and against its foreign imperialist principals. It is also not able to come out openly and tell the Nigerian people that its true commitment is to domestic and foreign capitalist exploitation of the human and material resources of the nation.[21]

The Shagari administration, as the governing arm of the bourgeoisie, conveniently overlooked how substructural (internal) contradictions and relations of production and accumulation combined to influence policies towards the outside world. On the contrary, the government focused attention on the United Nations, the New International Economic Order, problems of technology transfer and terms of trade with developed countries. Even in these broad superstructural aspects the rhetoric was louder than concrete achievements. The *nature* of the bourgeoisie and dependent and distorted economy have continued to expose the fragile base on which the loud proclamations and boasts are based. Thus the great powers never took Nigeria too seriously.

On issues such as the Palestinian problem, re-opening of diplomatic relations with Israel and the South African connections of the Western powers, where Shagari was relatively consistent, the government was unable to make a radical break with efforts to appease the West. It was very inconsistent on relations with the Arab world, the Israeli issue and even in relations with the Western friends of South Africa. These factors immediately negated whatever 'progressive' posture the Shagari government can be seen to have adopted occasionally at international conferences. Like other administrations before it, the Shagari administration firmly believed that a dialogue with the Western powers and a tinkering here and there with the existing power and exchange relations would bring about a just and equitable world order. The Shagari administration also extended the scope of the country's foreign policy commitments to embrace the world:

> We in Nigeria believe that so long as one inch of African territory is occupied territory, we remain in bondage, and that wherever a black or African is oppressed, we share the indignity. Nigeria shall work relentlessly to uphold the dignity of the black race anywhere in the world.[22]

Though inspiring, the statement above is only rhetoric. What could Nigeria under Shagari, given its peripheral location and role in the world capitalist system and more relevantly, declining oil revenues and foreign reserves and increasing indebtedness have done about blacks in the West Indies or the USA? After his inauguration in 1979, Shagari, in his address to the Lagos Diplomatic Corps on 9 November 1979, declared that Nigeria 'shall continue to do everything in [its] power to eliminate apartheid from our continent and to defend the dignity of man everywhere'.[23]

In his criticisms of the Western world, Shagari was 'radical'. Perhaps, this was also an attempt to reflect the growing discontent at home with Western exploitation of the Nigerian economy. In 1980, the former President noted that 'we are victims of mass exploitation . . . it is unrealistic for the developed world to sustain their standard of living by buying our raw materials cheaply and selling us their manufactured goods at high prices determined unilaterally by them.'[24] And in line with General Obasanjo's very radical criticism of complaints over the presence of Cuban troops in Africa, Alhaji Shagari explained, from a Nigerian perspective, the position of the non-aligned movement on issues concerning either the West or East thus:

> . . . the West is more imperialist by nature, from its own history and background. Most non-aligned countries have been victims of western imperialism. But in Africa, what bothers us more than anything is apartheid in South Africa, colonialism in Namibia and neo-colonialism. We know these evils are being supported and promoted by the West and not by Russia. So if there is any impression that we are soft towards Russia it is because Russia too is soft on us over these issues which we consider of grave importance.[25]

If Shagari realized this fact, what did his administration do either to challenge or at least distance itself from Western imperialism? We have noted the dominant position of Western interests in virtually all sectors of the economy and the structured re-integration of Nigeria into world capitalism in the current post-OPEC period. The administration hardly took any measure of consequence to challenge Western domination and imperialism. Rather, compromises with transnational interests were sought and links with the West intensified within the context of an internal and external unequal exchange arrangement.

The policies of the Shagari administration towards Israel did not differ from those of previous administrations though debates within the country on the issue of re-opening of relations can be grouped into four. First, those who noted Israel's South African links and condemned Zionist policies in the Middle East, and thus argued that relations should not be re-opened. The second group noted that, irrespective of the normalization of relations between Israel and Egypt, since the OAU had not officially sanctioned the re-opening of relations, Nigeria could not follow the example of Zaire or Liberia. The third group noted that Nigeria 'badly needs' Israel's technological and other assistance in the process of economic development. The Middle East issue is an Arab problem and Nigeria could not afford to inherit the prejudices of any nation. The fourth position was the one which argued that Nigeria's policy towards Israel was hypocritical and exposed the double standards in the refusal to re-open diplomatic relations. This position condemned Israel's expansionist, aggressive and sometimes racialist posture in world politics. It also condemned the economic and military connections between Israel and South Africa which it saw as a security risk to Africa. But opposition to the official position hinged on two points. First, why single out Israel? What had Israel done with South Africa that France, West Germany, Iran, Saudi Arabia, Zaire, Britain and the United States did not do? If Nigeria was going to sever diplomatic relations on the grounds of linkages with South Africa, it must be extended to cover all the culprits. The second point was that, though the government claimed to have no diplomatic relations, Israeli firms continued to operate profitably in Nigeria. These firms, particularly in the construction and oil sectors, won government contracts. These facts have forced observers to conclude that the failure of Nigeria to renew relations with Israel, while good on its own merits, was severely influenced by the following factors:

(i) The Islamic religion to which the former President subscribes in spite of the fact that Nigeria is a secular state;[26] (ii) the influence of the strong pro-Arab and pro-Islamic lobby in Nigeria championed by members of the northern aristocracy to which top members of the ruling party belonged; (iii) the desire to maintain the radical posture of the military regime before it; (iv) to maintain the pro-Palestinian position of Nigeria which was strengthened under the Shagari administration; (v) since the objective political, military and economic realities of Nigeria in the Second Republic meant that the administration could not take on any major power over the Southern Africa issue, Israel which had full connections with South Africa and the West served that purpose; and (vi) to retain Nigeria's claim to leadership and initiative in the continent, the Israeli issue was just one aspect of the moves to re-establish that position.

At the July 1980 OAU Summit in Freetown, Alhaji Shagari made categorical statements on 'The Middle East Situation' when he expressed 'Nigeria's continuing concern for peace and justice in the Middle East, particularly with regard to the inalienable right of the Palestinian people to self-determination and a national home'. At the same Summit, on Israel, the former President declared:

> Nigeria condemns without reservation Israel's continuing occupation of Palestinian and other Arab territories in complete violation of Security Council resolution 242 and other related resolutions of the United Nations Organization. We cannot support any decision or act on the part of Israel to change the status of the old city of Jerusalem. Nor shall we accept any unilateral action by Israel to alter the character of the occupied Arab territories by planning Jewish settlements in them.[27]

Israel went ahead and carried out some of these acts and Alhaji Shagari and his administration could do nothing about it. In fact, some African states such as Liberia and Zaire have been re-opening or strengthening diplomatic relations with Israel. What is more, Israel did (and still does) not depend on Nigeria for anything and whether it (Nigeria) accepts certain acts or not, their impact on the Israeli state is minimal. In fact, Nigeria was unable to question the links between Saudi Arabia and South Africa, yet Nigerian Muslims flocked to Mecca every year to perform the pilgrimage while Nigeria involved itself in negotiating various loans with the Saudis. In an interview, former President Shagari restated his administration's stand on the Middle-East question:

> We are not isolating Israel, but we are working on principles. Our position is that the decision to break with Israel was not that of Nigeria alone; it was an OAU decision taken unanimously by all African countries. You are no doubt aware that the reason for breaking relations with Israel was not just because of the Middle East, a question which was basically the concern of the Arabs. We acted as Africans because of Israel's continued co-operation with racist South Africa. Israel has further intensified this co-operation with South Africa and we, as Africans have continued to be horrified by this attitude. Israel . . . has a quarrel with Africa as well. . . . It is true that they have been able to settle with Egypt on their withdrawal. But there still remains the Palestinian issue which is extremely important and serious. We believe that the Palestinians deserve to have their own homeland returned to them. . . . The whole attitude of Israel in the international community is that of defiance.[28]

Though Nigeria joined OPEC in 1971 and at various times was ahead of Libya in oil production, its position within OPEC was undefined. The military leaders under whose rule the country became a world oil producer and exporter mismanaged the huge oil rents collected from oil exports. In addition, the military leaders, within limits, were able to employ oil as a major foreign policy weapon particularly in establishing Nigeria as a so-called 'giant' in Africa, initiating and establishing ECOWAS, sponsoring and hosting scores of international festivals, jamborees and conferences, and donating very generously to African countries and movements. However, under the Shagari administration, Nigeria became identified and regarded as the 'weak link in OPEC'. The fragility and vulnerability of the country's economy exposed it to pressures from transnational oil corporations and the Western powers. Nigeria equally became one of the 'rebel states' that lowered oil prices below OPEC agreed levels. These developments were generally prompted by the need for more foreign exchange and dependence on revenues from oil exports. When the transnationals put pressure on Nigeria, the Shagari administration had no choice but to seek the assistance of conservative states like Saudi Arabia, thus exposing itself to pressure and penetration from other angles.

The border skirmishes between Nigeria and Cameroun in 1981 was another instance in which, though internal opinion was divided, the unreliable and fragile basis of Nigeria's foreign policy in the Second Republic was exposed. In addition, Nigeria's response was severely conditioned by the desire not to confront France. Though Cameroun had taken over a few Nigerian villages, attacked Nigerian army units and flouted efforts to win apologies or compensation, the administration could at best appeal to the OAU to whip Cameroun into line. Internally, there were calls for either an invasion of Cameroun or the use of the army to recapture Nigerian villages from the Camerounians. Generally, particularly because of the diplomatic disrespect demonstrated by Cameroun which had sent a very junior Minister to Nigeria on the issue, Nigerians felt it was essential for the government to 'test its soldiers' externally, teach Cameroun a lesson or practicalize its claim to be the 'giant of Africa'. It is possible that the recourse to the OAU over the issue was rational, but more important is the fact that the Shagari administration was scared by the politicization of the issue at home, and the wide level of public disaffection at that time due to the rising cost of living, scarcity of goods, unemployment and general political dissatisfaction. Thus, the government was not prepared to risk a war in which an initially supportive public could not be relied upon to give continued support.

In fact as far back as March 1981, the *Nigerian Tribune* reflected on the internal situation in its condemnation of President Shagari's visit to the United Kingdom:

> President Shagari's current state visit to the United Kingdom is, to say the least most unpatriotic and thoroughly condemnable. The mission is unpatriotic because the President has demonstrably shown, by the visit that he is rather unmoved by the untold suffering and agony of the people he swore on oath to serve ... We vehemently condemn the mission for its timing ... Since about two weeks ago the country's health care delivery system has been ground to a total halt as a result of

the industrial action by doctors. ... To leave the shores of Nigeria at this [sic] trying times, as the President has done, when the doctors' case is far from being resolved and with the death toll attendant upon it, amounts to a very clear abdication of President Shagari's constitutional responsibilities.[29]

It is the type of unfavourable internal conditions highlighted by the *Nigerian Tribune* that militated against any idea of resolving the Camerounian issue through war. These internal conditions bedevilled the foreign policy actions of Nigeria between 1979 and 1983.

Oil and Responses to African Issues in the Second Republic

The leadership in the Second Republic were convinced beyond any doubt that Niberia was the most powerful country in the continent. To this end, its leadership role was constantly stressed while its confused and sometimes reactionary responses to developments in the African continent were rationalized and explained off as resulting from the need to show good leadership and example. In the country's Fourth National Development Plan, 1981–85, the Shagari administration, expressing an idealist position had noted with careless optimism:

In a world economy that is basically reliant on oil, Nigeria's economic and strategic importance is enormous ... Increasingly, Nigeria's wealth and position has immensely enhanced her political and strategic importance in Africa and world politics. A strong member of OPEC, a pioneer and stabilizing force in the OAU, a member of the Non-Aligned Nations, a co-founder of ECOWAS, Nigeria is slowly but assuredly emerging as a major factor in the global power calculus.[30]

While the availability of oil has been the major indicator of Nigeria's power and importance in world politics, the ability to employ this effectively has been consistently mediated by the structural problems highlighted in the preceding sections. However, the Nigerian power elite has always presented alternative rationalizations for its failures, inconsistencies and weaknesses. Essentially, in the defunct Second Republic, there was more emphasis on a positive international morality, legalism and so-called leadership by example which in real terms meant subservience to the West, taking ambivalent positions or contributing to problems through abstentions. As Alhaji Shagari explained this:

Our foreign policy [which] has been meticulously geared towards promoting good neighbourliness ... adherence to the provisions of international law ... precluded [and] hasty recourse by us to military response in ... situations until all diplomatic pressure failed.[31]

Table 8.3
Destination of Nigeria's Crude Oil Exports for a Typical Month: July 1982

Country	% of Total Exports	Revenues (Naira)
USA	46.74	338,263,714
France	11.85	82,481,994
West Germany	9.08	64,574,678
Curacao	5.82	42,112,502
Italy	5.65	40,145,706
Sweden	5.46	38,491,505
Netherlands	4.17	30,030,825
Canary Islands	2.66	19,171,761
Bahamas	2.57	18,843,518
Ghana	2.25	14,843,518
Belgium	1.48	10,096,824
Portugal	1.46	10,208,670
Sierra Leone	0.53	3,824,857
Uruguay	0.46	3,136,941

Source: Nigerian National Petroleum Corporation, *Monthly Petroleum Information, July 1982*, p. 36.

In spite of this commitment to international law, developments in the African continent within the brief life-span of the Second Republic tested Nigeria's power, influence and claim to the continent's leadership. Major (even if rhetorical) positions were adopted on crucial issues which were often determined by the *nature* of the Nigerian economy. In addition, developments and contradictions within the economy forced the government to initiate some measures internally, which nonetheless affected foreign policy issues. For instance, the retention and efforts to enforce punitive labour laws and the imposition of austerity measures (see chapters on economy and labour) affected the level of dynamism with which foreign policies were initiated and pursued. Zimbabwe became independent, the struggles in Namibia and South Africa continues, the problem in Eritrea and Western Sahara remains, the OAU is yet to find unity and consensus, and ECOWAS remains plagued with major problems particularly those of finance, commitment and the equitable distribution of costs and benefits. The emergence of Master Sargent (now Major General) Samuel Doe in Liberia and J.J. Rawlings in Ghana, the border problems with Cameroun and the crisis in Chad also elicited some reactions from the civilians. Responses were generally conditioned by an objective look at internal problems, the depth of the crisis and the extent to which Nigeria could mobilize internal human and material resources as well as its international 'status' and influence to project its interests.

Within the African continent, it can be rightly contended that three major

External Relations

issues or problems confronted the Shagari administration in the Second
Republic: (a) that of maintaining Nigeria's interventionist and expensive
commitments in the West African region; (b) the Southern Africa problem;
and (c) the maintainance of unity within the OAU. At these levels and,
perhaps, other African issues, the Shagari government retained one policy
inherited from the Murtala/Obasanjo regime — diplomatic and rhetorical
commitment to the liberation of Africa. One does not need to look too far
to argue that given the distorted and crisis-ridden nature of Nigerian society
and its peripheral location and role in the world capitalist system, it could
make very minimal contributions to the liberation of other societies. Given
Nigeria's military weakness in every sense of it, the corruption within the
bourgeois class and dependence on the Western world, the level of vulnerability to external forces is high. In addition, the import and dependence
syndrome has continued to render Nigeria very susceptible to penetration,
manipulation and pressure. Even the dependence on oil wealth significantly
exposes the country to external blackmail and pressures from its major
customers and the home governments of the foreign oil companies which
dominate the industry in terms of technology, capital, high-level manpower
and information supplies. Nonetheless, the President and his cabinet were
very convinced that Nigeria was not only influential in world politics but
could in fact be seen as an 'emerging super-power' if not already a world
power. The basis of this assumption included the huge population of over
80 million and thus its large internal market, its standing army of about
146,000 and the failure to realize that the position Nigeria enjoyed in its
relations with America under Jimmy Carter was by no means permanent.
More important than the above were the failure to realize and evaluate
correctly the internal and external limits to Nigeria's power and the assumption that with oil wealth Nigeria had automatically become rich and powerful.
Alhaji Shagari restated this point in 1980:

> ... oil has become a weapon in international politics. I am on record
> as saying that we shall use all weapons at our disposal, including oil if
> it become unavoidable, to pursue and fight for the interests of Nigeria.[32]

Though this declaration was made in the United States of America it was
obvious to analysts that the use of the oil weapon would hurt Nigeria more
than its enemy. In addition, the ability to employ the oil weapon might not
receive unanimous or popular support at home while it would even be dependent on the co-operation of foreign oil companies and Nigerian comprador
elements.

In May 1980, at a meeting in Lomé, Togo, of the Authority of ECOWAS
Heads of State or Government, Shagari declared:

> I have on several occasions expressed publicly the foreign policy of
> my administration. Africa and African interests constitute the centre
> piece of our foreign policy. We are committed to the total liberation

187

of Africa and the establishment of a fair and just economic order. We are determined to create an environment in which the African can realize his full potential, enjoy the fruits of his labour, and exercise full control over the resources with which God has blessed this continent.[33]

At this level the Shagari administration attempted to pursue the lines which the military had established in its policies towards Southern Africa. It remained committed to the rather complex and contradictory programme of supporting armed struggle and peaceful negotiations concurrently in Southern Africa. Unfortunately, the administration was unable to keep up the level of financial assistance to liberation movements and liberated territories because of internal commitments and declining revenues. In 1980, a ₦10 million grant to Zimbabwe was severely criticized by the National Assembly as being beyond the powers of the executive president. Like the previous administrations, the Shagari government was very careful not to undertake measures which would either alienate the major powers supporting South Africa or those that would create conditions where it would be necessary to make military commitments. In fact, the policy of supporting armed struggle and negotiations was underscored by the need to remain influential in Africa, friendly with liberation movements and liberated territories and the Western powers. In a speech at the Annual Dinner of the Nigerian Institute of International Affairs in 1980, the former President reiterated Nigeria's support for the armed struggle in Southern Africa when he stated that Nigeria remains

> committed to support armed struggle to liberate Namibia and bring an end to racism in Southern Africa. We are supporting and will continue to support the liberation fighters. We will not sacrifice this commitment for any other cause.[34]

At the OAU Summit in Freetown, July 1980, Alhaji Shagari spoke on Southern Africa:

> We must not relent in our struggle against the forces of apartheid. We should re-affirm the legitimacy of the struggle of our oppressed brothers in South Africa by giving our full material, diplomatic and moral support to the National Liberation Movement as well as to those Front Line States under South Africa attack and harrassment. Their struggle is also our struggle. We must strive for the total elimination of the apartheid regime and the exercise of the right of self-determination by the people of South Africa as a whole.[35]

At this Summit, the President was even confident enough that 'Namibia must be independent next year' — 1981. In his goodwill message to Zimbabweans on the occasion of the country's independence, he argued that Nigeria's 'opposition to racism is not mere rhetoric'. In fact, every major conference, speech and lecture was an opportunity to re-state Nigeria's opposition to apartheid in Southern Africa.

On the Namibian question and the related issue of Cuban troops in Angola, the Shagari administration which had earlier in 1979/80 condemned efforts to link the territory's independence to the withdrawal of Cuban troops from Angola made an about-turn. The new policy, which in spite of the successive failures of OAU peace-keeping forces, advocated the withdrawal of Cuban troops and the replacement by OAU forces, was influenced by pressures from the IMF and the United States to which the Shagari administration was heavily indebted.

In his 1983 foreign policy address at the Nigeria Institute of International Affairs, the president attempted to whitewash this position, but the point remained that Nigeria was unable to make any concrete proposal beyond the use of an inexistent and imaginary African Defence Force, the mobilization of an undefined and unreliable public opinion and an appeal to the morality of racist elements in South Africa and imperialist forces in the Western bloc.[36] Even the usual rhetoric, by December 1983, meant very little to those involved in the Southern Africa struggle:

> Shagari, it ought to be recalled, also anchored his foreign policy in theory at least, on the centrality of Africa. He also made verbal pretensions to operating a dynamic foreign policy. Yet Shagari's foreign policy served decidedly anti-African interests, and was the antithesis of dynamism, except we define African interests as corresponding to imperialist interests, or dynamism as consisting of globe-trotting.[37]

Thus, Nigeria in the Second Republic had a queer and peculiar definition of African interests. The extent to which its postures became congruent with those of the Western powers was clearly reflected in its inability to influence both African and non-African nations.

Nigeria decided to go nuclear, not just because of the possible economic and other benefits derivable from the effort but also because South Africa had acquired the nuclear capability. Along this line, not only did Nigeria condemn South Africa but also the Western countries which aided it in acquiring nuclear weapons. As the one-time Minister of Defence, Professor Iya Abubakar explained:

> Nigeria is a great country and it needs a strong, invincible and unassailable defence capability. It is only when she has become a nuclear power that she can boast of that status. Moreover, as long as protagonists of apartheid have access to nuclear capability Nigeria should, as of necessity, endeavour to acquire it at any price. Nigeria will go in for the best that is available and on terms that will neither offend nor compromise her independence and sovereignty.[38]

During his visit to the United States in October 1980, the President, in his address to the 35th Session of the United Nations General Assembly, criticized the great powers for aiding South Africa's acquisition of nuclear weapons. At the annual dinner of the NIIA, Shagari noted:

> There have been some reports recently in some sections of the international media about South Africa's acquisition of the nuclear bomb. These reports further confirm the long documented sordid design of the white minority government of nuclear blackmail. Back in 1968, South Africa refused to be a signatory to the Nuclear Test Ban Treaty. Now, her Western allies have surreptitiously co-operated with her to add to her arsenal, this most lethal weapon known to mankind. This clearly portrays the hypocrisy and the double-standard of these powers in their African policies. . . . Let me also call the attention of apartheid South Africa's collaborators to the unsavoury consequences of their action on the socio-economic development of Africa. . . . If apartheid South Africa, with the connivance of the Western democracies, fires the gun to start the arms race in Africa, the consequences will be too dreadful for world peace in general and African security in particular.[39]

The internal human and even material resources to acquire and service nuclear reactors do not exist in Nigeria. More important than this is the fact that if Nigeria were to succeed in forcing the Western powers to choose between it and South Africa, the West is likely to choose the latter. Not only is it of strategic importance to them but they have reaped billions of dollars as profits from centuries of economic connections. But by retaining the sanctions of the previous regimes and the fiery rhetoric of the Murtala/Obasanjo regime, the Shagari administration kept alive the momentum of opposition to apartheid. It should however be noted that these sanctions have had limited effects. Trade between the two countries has historically been very insignificant. South Africa gets Nigeria's oil through third parties and it is militarily superior to Nigeria.[40] Though Nigeria has been a very 'safe' and distant frontline state, it can hardly take any serious military or economic action against either South Africa or its Western allies. Other than the former's military superiority and limited historical economic contacts, the domination of the Nigerian economy and culture (taste, education, world-view etc.) by Western transnational interests means that the best Nigeria can do is to confine its attacks to propaganda, conference centres and summits. Hence threats issued by the civilian administration to foreign corporations were hardly taken seriously given the comprador and dependent role of the Nigerian bourgeoisie:

> We have no desire whatsoever to interfere in the affairs of any nation. But we have the right to determine who will take part in our economic prosperity. We cannot be expected to allow any nation or any organisation by whatever description to prosper in their involvement in our

nation's economy only to turn around and use that prosperity to strengthen apartheid South Africa.[41]

While this threat linked internal economic arrangements and relations with foreign policy, the Shagari administration was unable to take any measure to demonstrate its commitment to this line of action, even though scores of companies with South African connections operate in Nigeria and even won contracts from the government. The Shagari administration even dismantled the limited restrictions on foreign participation in the economy while its mismanagement of oil rents facilitated the process of the country's re-integration into the periphery of the world capitalist system. Even, when the President boasted at the 35th Ordinary Session of the UN General Assembly that

> Nigeria will no longer tolerate the provocations by South Africa or the dialatory tactics of her allies in the Western bloc with regard to self-determination and majority rule in Namibia,

it was obvious that it was nothing more than a UN Speech.[42]

In the West African sub-region, the Shagari administration had no choice but to uphold the commitments of the military to the survival of the Economic Community of West African States (ECOWAS). Nigeria contributes 32% of the annual budget and hosts its secretariat in Lagos. The protocol on labour mobility has promoted the movement of thousands of West Africans to Nigeria. Because Nigeria is a disarticulated neocolonial branch-plant economy, it could not accommodate the extra surplus labour. The net consequence was urban pressure, unbridled exploitation, crime wave and unemployment. The aliens did not introduce these problems though in some areas their presence intensified them. The tendency was to blame all problems on the so-called aliens who were at the same time exploited as prostitutes, house-helps, casual labourers, etc. Blaming government inadequacies on aliens served as a good diversionary tactic to the government and even though they had long been coming into Nigeria, it was not until 1983 that they were expelled. At this time, it had become a way of scoring a cheap political point, blaming the problems of the economy on the presence of aliens while at the same time, it diverted the attention of Nigerians (though only temporarily) away from domestic issues.

Nigeria's new interventionist and rather expensive sub-regional policy was occasioned by the security problems exposed by the civil war. The establishment of the community at great cost to Nigeria (financially) was part of the attempt to change the isolationist policy of the First Republic.[43] In his first participation in the deliberations of ECOWAS Heads of State or Government in May 1980, Shagari declared that his administration 'shall continue to give full support to the Community in the realization of its goals and objectives'.[44] It was however doubtful if Nigeria could continue to bear much of the burdens of the Community or serve as a 'core state' given the deteriorating economic conditions at home. It aided the Sahelian states financially, invested in projects and provided 90-day credit facilities for those buying its crude oil. Nonetheless, President Shagari was unable to reconcile himself to drastic political changes in Liberia and Ghana. The expulsion of aliens made a 'big dent' in Nigeria's image in the sub-region in which most people had come to look up to it. The fact that the so-called third category of illegal immigrants — 'professionals, and technical workers such as doctors, teachers, engineers etc.' were allowed to remain and 'regularize their stay' is clear manifestation of the underlying reason for the expulsion.[45] Liberia seized the opportunity to expel 'aliens' and some ECOWAS member states condemned the suddenness of the act.

The Shagari administration, in view of declining revenues and restlessness within the ranks of non-bourgeois forces internally, was forced to take the extreme measure of expelling the aliens. The decision not to allow Master-Sergeant Doe of Liberia to attend the ECOWAS meeting in Lome and the OAU Economic Summit in Lagos has been seen as due to Nigeria's 'big voice' in the process of arriving at the moves. In fact, in an interview with *Africa Now*, President Shagari did not hide his hatred for the Doe administration:

> . . . soon after the coup in Liberia, there was an economic Summit meeting of the OAU in Lagos. Soon after Sgt. Doe had massacred the leaders of Liberia, he wanted to come and attend the OAU meeting in Lagos and we thought that that was an opportunity to discuss the issue concerning recognition of governments formed by people of such temperament, leaders who were blood thirsty. Leaders who had done despicable acts to the embarrassment of Africa, just after washing their bloody hands would walk into the OAU meeting and sit and dine with other leaders of Africa.[46]

In the case of Ghana when Rawlings refused to stop the execution of corrupt leaders and politicians not only did oil stop flowing to Ghana due to 'technical problems', there was a rumour that Nigeria planned to invade Ghana. In addition, some Ghanaians who claimed to be policemen and had fled from the 'bloodthirsty' Rawlings government, were given wide exposure in the Nigerian media. Ghana was also asked, in spite of its terrible financial position, to pay up the oil debts it owed the Nigerian National Petroleum Corporation (NNPC). This plot backfired. For one thing, these reactions were precipitates of the desire to prevent whatever radical ideas Doe and Rawlings were spreading from getting to Nigeria. Both men were exceedingly popular among non-bourgeois forces in Nigeria and in buses and market places, people were often heard asking: 'where is our own Rawlings?' The hostility of the OAU was part of the factors which forced Doe back into the full orbit of US hegemonic interests and Rawlings into an alliance with Libya. The expulsion of aliens which affected mostly Ghanaians was later to be seen by Ghanaians and other observers as a way of putting pressure on the 'budding revolution'.[47]

Nigeria's worst diplomatic reverses were suffered in Chad. Those reverses were not only in terms of the direct humiliation which Nigeria and its armed forces suffered at the hands of Chadian factions first under the military and then as part of the OAU peace-keeping forces under the Shagari administration, but in the inability to act decisively as Libya was to do in Chad. The military administration had unilaterally encouraged the Chadian factions of Hussein Habre and Goukouni Waddeye to sign a Peace Accord in Lagos on 21 August 1979. This accord agreed on the establishment of a broad-based Transitional National Union Government headed by Waddeye as President and Habre as Defence Minister pending the return to civilian rule. Nigeria even sent troops to N'Djamena unilaterally to aid in the process of transition. This move, which was far beyond the capacity of the Nigerian army — logistically and in terms of securing and maintaining the proper understanding of the factions — was a huge disaster. Nigerian lines were crossed by the rebels with impunity. Colonel Magoro, who led the operations, was to reflect:

> ... the explosive situation in N'Djamena, the Chadian capital, left no time for rigorous preparations of our troops for normal peace-keeping operations ... the performance of these functions had attendant problems ... frustration, extreme provocation, uncertainty, and selfishness. Under such situation, self discipline, exercise of patience, endurance and persuasion became the only weapons available to Nigerian troops.[48]

Colonel Magoro also described the peace-keeping operation as a 'hasty entry and withdrawal', noted the language problem which created a communication gap between Nigerian troops and Chadians and concluded that there was a 'lack of proper briefing on the factional leaders and their factions' while there was 'the lack of a legal instrument spelling out the status of Nigerian troops'.[49] Bolaji Akinyemi, the former Director of the NIIA, summarized initial efforts in Chad thus:

> Nigeria's initial efforts which involved the sending of a peace-keeping force to Chad was a failure. It was flawed right from the word go. It was hastily conceived and it was ill conceived. There was no status-of-forces agreement with the Chadians, the troops were not properly briefed as to their mission and those sending them did not have the correct perception of what a peace-keeping mission was all about ... it did not take long for the Chadians to realise that the Nigerian peace-keeping mission lacked credibility.[50]

The Shagari administration, while favouring Hussein Habre, completely shied away from attempting another unilateral peace-keeping mission. Rather, it worked hard within the OAU to direct attention to the crisis which was sending thousands of refugees into Nigeria daily. The resultant OAU Peace-keeping Operation was a disaster. The OAU forces were attacked and had to be withdrawn in haste. As Shagari explained, Nigeria was not prepared to risk another unilateral action in Chad. Its participation under the OAU had been at Nigeria's expense. The Shagari administration even had to 'assist the other contingents from Senegal and Zaire with some logistics and food'.[51] Nigeria under Shagari continued to call for the implementation of the Lagos Accord which the Chadian factions long regarded as dead and in spite of the reverses of the OAU peace-keeping efforts, calls were made that another peace-keeping operation be sent.

By the time Libya intervened on the side of Waddeye in June 1980, it had mapped out its own strategic, religious and economic interests in the country and region. It was invited by the Transitional Government which Habre had attacked with French assistance. Libya routed the forces of Habre, chased him out of Chad and helped to establish Waddeye as head of the Transition Government as agreed to in the Lagos Accord, thus saving the OAU from disgrace. On 6 January 1981, the two countries (Chad and Libya) announced that they were merging into one state. Nigeria took this rather badly given Libya's foreign policy pronouncements and interventionist attitude in the continent.[52] It saw Libya's presence in Chad as a major security problem especially as Libya was militarily superior. Libya had been tested externally, if anything it proved it could do what the OAU and Nigeria could not do in Chad by routing the forces of Habre. Tom Imobighe has described Nigeria's reaction thus:

> ... the merger proposal drove Nigerian leaders into an uncontrolled diplomatic frenzy; so much so, that they were knocking on the doors of both friends and foes in an attempt to find a solution to the Libyan problem. In the process, the Nigerian government took the embarrassing step of sending the External Affairs Minister, Ishaya Audu, to France to work out a common military intervention in Chad. . . .[53]

The absurdity of the diplomatic move is further explained thus:

> It is difficult to understand how France could have convinced the Minister that the French objective in Chad was to allow the Chadians to be in a position to manage their own affairs when all along France's intervention had constituted the greatest impediment to the peaceful resolution of the conflict. Apparently the Minister seems oblivious of the fact that France maintains a ring of military bases around Nigeria and by that token constitutes the greatest threat to Nigeria.[54]

In spite of the two major diplomatic moves made by Nigeria which led to the Lagos Conference in December 1980 and the Lome Conference of 14 January 1981 which called on the withdrawal of Libyan troops and the conduct of general elections, peace has continued to elude Chad, and Libya not only snubbed overtures from Nigeria but was invited to Nigeria in 1983. During the visit, the Libyans violated all known security measures by bringing into the country their own soldiers to protect Colonel Gaddafi.

Perhaps, Nigeria's greatest test was during the crisis within the OAU over the convening of the 19th Summit. Nigeria's specific interest in support of Habre in Chad was not because he was better than Waddeye, but because the latter had Libya's support, and this prevented Shagari from taking an objective look at the issue. However, the greatest setback was in Nigeria's inability, in spite of huge oil rents, donations and loans to other African, particularly ECOWAS member, countries, to use its influence to get enough attendance at the Tripoli meeting. President Shagari, in spite of criticisms at home, refused to attend the August 1982 Summit. When he finally attended the November Summit, he could not convince other recalcitrant African leaders to attend and a quorum was not formed. This was in spite of the fact that Shagari was said to have personally telephoned unrepresented African leaders. Eight of those who eventually failed to attend were ECOWAS members. Tunde Obadina has noted on this issue:

> The previously assumed capability of Nigeria to convince absenting African leaders to participate in the OAU Summit has been tested. The result was that the giant of Africa was shown to have little weight on the continent. She could neither by treat nor by reasoning persuade even one of the rebel African heads of state to fly to Tripoli and save the OAU from embarrassment and eventual collapse.[55]

At the Summit the Nigerian delegation lobbied to get a so-called compromise solution which recognized Habre's right to occupy Chad's seat. On Western Sahara, another thorny issue,

> the Shagari administration's soft pedalling and refusal to recognise the Saharawi Arab Democratic Republic has not sufficiently distanced itself from the West's position of outright support for Morocco,[56]

though, officially, Nigeria remains committed to the idea of a referendum and UN intervention to resolve the crisis. Reviewing Nigeria's performance in Chad, on Western Sahara and at the 19th OAU Summit, Obadina concludes:

> It is evident that the Shagari administration fears Qhadafi more than it fears Reagan. . . . What was certainly revealed in Tripoli is the unsavoury fact that Nigeria does not have the power in Africa that many have ascribed to her. She is in a sense a leader without followers. It may be said that a bulldog without teeth should not bark too loudly because it might be called upon to scare off a fearless attacker and thereby be exposed as useless. The giant of Africa was last month (November 1982) called upon to counter the reactionary attacks on African unity and in the process displayed her gummy growl to the world.[57]

The contributions of the 'giant of Africa' to the failure to host the OAU Summit in Tripoli obviously had a lot to do with its sympathy with American (and Western bloc) hostility to Gaddafi and Libya. Shagari, like most of the satellite African states, cashed in on the Saharawi Democratic Republic and the Chadian issues among others to deny Gaddafi the Chairmanship of the OAU:

> Shagari dictated a style of foreign policy based on waiting for the rest of Africa to take positions, and then casting a lot with the majority — a majority that was often, as in the case of Gaddafi's chairmanship of the Organisation of African Unity (OAU), stupid. For to deny Libya leadership of the OAU was to oblige imperialist interests to an astonishingly ludicrous degree.[58]

The inability of Nigeria under Shagari to command the respect of other African (particularly ECOWAS) states on issues concerning the continent stems from three interrelated factors. First, Nigeria could not (and has not been able to) serve effectively as an alternative to the Western donor countries. The inability to do what Libya did in Chad or to respond effectively to Cameroun's provocations in spite of popular calls at home as well as the country's obvious military weakness, have all exposed the fact that Nigeria cannot be militarily relied upon in time of emergency. A second point is that, the increasing economic crisis at home and the apparent reactionary and conservative nature of the ruling fraction of the Nigerian bourgeoisie also meant an inability to maintain the false posture, propaganda and extravagance which the Shagari administration had inherited from the military. Finally, Nigeria's deepening re-integration into the world capitalist system and dependence on the Western powers meant that when issues involved these powers, Nigeria had to tone down its aggressiveness, at least when compared to the heyday of Nigeria's foreign policy under Murtala Mohammed.

Finally, Nigeria's African policy in the Second Republic hardly lived up to the standards set by the military. In fact, it was escapist and diversionary. Real issues were avoided and broad utopian goals far beyond the country's capacity such as world peace and stability and the 'total liberation of Africa from colonialism, racism and neo-colonialism' were pursued. In the case of Chad, Cameroun and even the problems of ECOWAS, rather than address the issue of French imperialism, the Shagari administration, in spite of popular opinion at home, tried to forge alliances with France:

> In Chad and Cameroon, for example, it is obvious that the root of the crises is French imperialism. If Nigeria were consistent in its foreign policy aims, it should long ago have started an intensive propaganda and diplomatic campaign to make the presence of French troops in Africa, especially in neighbouring countries, an international issue. Nevertheless, despite threats of reprisals against Western countries who continue to deal with South Africa, Western firms continue to enjoy a great deal of patronage from the government. This can be seen in the

contract awards for some of Nigeria's most sensitive projects like the multi-million dollar Naira Ajaokuta and Aladja Steel Mills, and the planning and construction of the new capital at Abuja.[59]

It is indisputable that Nigeria's unequal relationship with the West has over time (and will continue) to mediate its ability to win and retain credibility in African and world affairs. Though Shagari re-iterated the fact that Africa is the centre piece of Nigeria's foreign policy, deteriorating economic conditions at home, poverty and underdevelopment, lack of resoluteness and consistency cost Nigeria, particularly in the Second Republic, the position of a Newly Industrializing Country (NIC) which it attained with its contribution to the independence of Angola.

Conclusion

As soon as the army retired to the barracks in October 1979, it became obvious that Nigeria was not going to chart a new course in international politics, if not only for the bourgeois nature of the political party that captured federal power but also for the deteriorating conditions within the economy and in the world capitalist system. Between 1979 and the end of 1980 the Shagari administration tried to keep alive the propaganda and rhetorical postures and gestures it inherited. The depth of social contradictions internally and the nature of external pressures were such as to mediate such efforts. By the end of 1980, the propaganda and rhetoric had mellowed down significantly. Increasing mismanagement, corruption and misplacement of priorities drew a very sharp and critical response from the ILO in 1981. Of course, there was no evidence that the warnings and messages of the organization were heeded.[60] Rather, the dependence on oil continued, the rural areas and agriculture remained neglected and no attempt was made to involve the majority of the people in the planning processes in the country. The net result of this decay, inefficiency, ineffectiveness, poverty and social violence were increasing class contradictions, alienation and erosion of popular support, even those earlier mobilized on ethnic, religious and other chauvinistic grounds.

The country's trade relations continued to be completely tied to developments in the Western world. Given the dependence on oil wealth, the US remained the single largest market for this mono export (see Table 8.3). The efforts to raise huge loans from Western financial markets, the petty capitalist disposition of the members of the ruling political party and the internal conditions, particularly food imports and dependence on the West, not only served to mortgage the future of Nigeria but also helped to water down whatever *status* or influence the military was able to win among the community of nations:

The contribution of our indebtedness to financial institutions controlled by forces of imperialism to our dormant foreign policy cannot be discounted. Shagari was ready to go cap in hand negotiating loans from these financial institutions, especially those run by America, thereby limiting his scope for any radical manoeuvres in foreign policy: America, and other imperialist forces, thus became an inevitable factor in our foreign policy considerations. Nigeria paid a political price for the economic assistance it got.[61]

J. Bayo Adekson, reflecting on Nigeria's foreign policy and particularly its preparedness for autonomous peace-keeping operations in Africa, has argued that 'Nigeria is largely underdeveloped, ill-equipped and backward in military technology. She depends heavily on external and imported military technology and lacks domestic facilities comparable to those of Egypt and South Africa. . . . A large military establishment is needed as a supplant to lack of technology . . .'[62] The problem with Nigeria is certainly not the size of its army or military establishment. With over 146,000 men in the army, it ranks as one of the biggest in the continent. The ultimate question rests on the ability of the state to define clear and attainable national objectives, mobilize and sustain internal support and disengage itself from a rather noisy yet expensive foreign policy. Bolaji Akinyemi has reflected on the need for Nigeria to come to grips with the declining import and impact of the rhetorical approach to foreign policy:

> It seems then, expedient for the Nigerian government to make up its mind. The missionary phase, the hortatory phase of its militant foreign policy is over. It should be prepared to use military means to do two things — (a) either to stop other African states using military means to achieve their unilateral foreign policy objectives in Africa or, (b) using military means to achieve its own foreign policy objectives in Africa. . . . Nigeria cannot afford to stand idly by. Else she would then be condemned to merely recognising fait accomplis, and rationalising the success of other African countries. Eventually, this would not be in the national interest of Nigeria.[63]

While the position above might be calling for a clear definition of Nigeria's role in world politics, it contains a suicidal recommendation which is the precipitate of wrong premises, perceptions and therefore projections. Nigeria's ability not to 'stand idly by' would be a direct precipitate of how much it is able to relate internal (domestic) development to international (foreign) relations. How can a peripheral capitalist, inflation and crisis-ridden dependent economy with a weak state presided over by an inept, corrupt, unproductive and decadent bourgeois class talk of rising beyond rhetorics in its foreign policy? These are crucial areas that analysts must address. Under the Shagari administration, the dismal failure to address internal problems was very well reflected at the external level:

There is an undeniably positive relationship between domestic policy and foreign policy. Shagari recorded such a dismal failure in foreign policy because his domestic policy was also in shambles. He often abdicated pressing domestic problems even as he put on the illusive toga of the leader of Africa, winging from one country to another, hobnobbing and signing cultural agreements. Such was the pedestrian nature of his vision.[64]

The Shagari administration did not heed advice. The inept leadership was incapable of controlling the intensive contradictions within the ranks of the opposing parties. The suggestions and criticisms of the opposing parties were born out of the desire to win access to state power and preside over the allocation of national resources. Where the government recognized the consequence of internal disunity and economic and social disarticulation, as well as its military weakness to serve as the leader of Africa, little was done to generate an internal base with which to promote the 'total liberation' of Africa to which Nigeria claimed to be unrepentantly committed. The Shagari administration, just before it was overthrown by the military, admitted its failure in the area of foreign policy. It equally came to the conclusion that the country's role in foreign affairs was declining in its impact. Unfortunately, the new 'dynamic foreign policy' promised within ECOWAS, the OAU and UNO as well as in the 'fight against colonialism, neo-colonialism, racism and apartheid' could not be mounted given changing internal power and social configurations and crises.[65]

In addition, Nigerian leaders have been wise enough to realize that the country is of little or no immediate strategic importance to the great powers. The Western powers have been very unreliable as friends, as was demonstrated during the civil war; and other than the large market and oil there is little else that the West would need Nigeria for. The issue of confronting South Africa militarily is out of the question. Even in the cases of Ghana, Libya, Cameroun and Chad the leaders did not risk any serious military option not only for fear of the unpredictability of local support but also because of a desire not to alienate or come into conflict with the external forces behind these countries.

Nigeria's re-integration into and continued peripheralization in the world capitalist system will continue to militate against a viable and autonomous foreign policy in the next two or more decades. There are as at present limited exit options for the Nigerian state. Having spent all its non-military options (financial contributions, denunciations, propaganda, rhetoric and material support), it will soon be faced with the direct military alternative in Southern Africa, Chad and other trouble spots on which Nigerian leaders have expressed concern. At this level, the military weakness, internal poverty and contradictions will caution against such a possibly disastrous venture. On the other hand, given increasing internal contradictions, the Nigerian power-elite can attempt to create a diversion by demonstrating its strength and 'dynamism' with a small and weak African state. Here, Nigeria must be ready to confront a great or much more prepared middle power. This option does not hold much potency for Nigeria.

The democratic experience did at best unleash forces and factors of contradictions and conflict which will continue to militate against a vigorous foreign policy. In Nigeria, politics is not concerned with mobilization, education, provision of amenities and so on. Rather, it is an avenue to wealth, influence and power, and an opportunity to punish recalcitrant and 'rebel' elements and communities and forge alliances which serve chauvinistic or other selfish interests. This sort of politicking is unlikely to generate forces of awareness, patriotism and mobilization in support of foreign policies. The increasing alienation and restlesssness of the working class and intra-class struggles only serve to deepen the negative results of the 'democratic exercise' which did not live long. Military dictatorship, after a few years generates its own contradictions and cannot mobilize the necessary local base for a consistent and progressive foreign policy.

The failure of Nigeria to emerge as a Newly Industrializing Country (NIC) and the evident decline in its influence and status in Africa and the world at large coupled with the crisis in the world oil market which has completely devastated the economy while generating contradictions of dangerous proportions, means that the leadership would have to initiate accommodating policies if it is to reproduce itself. The acceptance of IMF conditions for assistance, the devaluation of the Naira, the decision to sell off some state parastatals and involve international finance institutions in the agricultural sector at great financial and social costs are just a few cases in point.

The new military administration has described itself as an off-shoot of the populist-nationalist Mohammed/Obadanjo regime of 1975–79. It has also promised to revitalize Nigeria's foreign policy, introduce a new sense of direction, make Africa the centrepiece of the country's foreign policy and maintain cordial relations with other nations. In his first New Year Day Broadcast to the nation, General Buhari, the new military leader stated the foreign policy of the regime thus:

> The Federal Military Government will maintain and strengthen existing diplomatic relations with other states and with international organisations ... will honour and respect all treaty obligations entered into by the previous governments.[66]

In his address to a world press conference in Lagos on 5 January 1984, General Buhari made a similar point, emphasizing the guiding principles of Nigeria's foreign policy:

> I wish to re-affirm that Nigeria will continue to honour its international commitments at the multi-lateral and bi-lateral levels. We will maintain cordial relations with friendly countries based on mutual respect,

sovereign equality and non-interference in the internal affairs of each other.[67]

Whatever the expectations of the new military leadership, in so far as no structural changes have been made in the economy, it is doubtful if it can mount a fundamental and progressive i.e. anti-imperialist foreign policy in Africa. No change has taken place in the ideological disposition of the ruling class. Its military fraction which is currently in power has so far avoided the crucial questions relating to contradictions arising from Nigeria's peripheral capitalism and the country's location and role in the world capitalist system. The unequal and exploitative relations of production and exchange which have bred apathy, alienation, violence and contradictions in the past have been maintained. We have no reason to expect the 31 December coup to be the last in Nigeria's history even if we think that it is likely to be the last 'bloodless' one. Nonetheless, the factors and forces which have historically compromised Nigeria's foreign policy position in Africa and beyond have remained constant since political independence. As the country's one-time Federal Commissioner for External Affairs, and now Nigeria's Permanent Representative in New York, Major-General Joe Garba, once put it,

> a nation's foreign policy is as successful as its internal policies are equally successful. In other words, no nation can successfully pursue its foreign policy objectives without comparable success in its domestic policies.

In light of this observation which we share, cosmetic solutions to structural contradictions and crisis arising from the country's distinctive historical experience and the context and directions of class struggles, cannot provide a viable and reliable background on which to mount a 'dynamic' and *progressive* foreign policy.

At this level, two scenarios are possible. Either the state enters into a military alliance with the West in order to get enough support to control internal opposition elements and organizations and gain assistance in its foreign policy objectives or it could intensify its alliances with transnational corporations in order to promote a Brazilian model of growth without development. Neither option will increase Nigeria's power or influence. Not only are the social and economic costs too high, the contradictions they generate are often deep enough to herald the emergence of alternative perceptions, expectations, strategies and tactics of struggle and society. Perhaps, out of the current contradictions, crises and struggles, a new order will emerge which will manifest new directions and policy in Nigeria. Until then, the custodians of state power and members of the bourgeoisie, in a rather curious contract, have agreed to overlook internal contradictions in the struggle to 'share the national cake' or win access to state power.

Notes

1. Compare for instance the collection in Henry Bienen and V.P. Diejomaoh (eds.), *The Political Economy of Income Distribution in Nigeria* (New York: Holmes and Meier, 1981) and Okwudiba Nnoli (ed.), *Path to Nigerian Development* (Dakar: CODESRIA, 1981). See also Chapter 1 for more details.

2. Ibrahim Gambari, 'Domestic Political Constraints on Progressive Foreign Policy for Nigeria', *Nigerian Journal of Political Science*, 2, 1, June 1980, p. 25; and Gordon Idang, *Nigeria: Internal Politics and Foreign Policy 1960-66* (Ibadan: University of Ibadan Press, 1973), pp. 120-6. See also Chapter 2 above.

3. This process has been dubbed 'spraying diplomacy' to denote the extent to which grants, loans and donations were made to sometimes unworthy projects. See Chapter 4 for details.

4. Two major examples are Decree No. 23 of 1976, the Trades Disputes Essential Services Decree, which completely banned strikes from virtually all human activity in Nigeria and Decree No. 15 of 1977, the Petroleum Production and Distribution (Anti-sabotage) Decree, which defines industrial actions in the oil industry as a criminal offence.

5. Yusufu Bala Usman, *For the Liberation of Nigeria* (London: New Beacon, 1979), p. 190.

6. All citations are from *The Constitution of the Federal Republic of Nigeria 1979* (Lagos: Government Printer, 1979).

7. For details on economic conditions under the military, see Oyeleye Oyediran (ed.), *Survey of Nigerian Affairs 1976-77* (Lagos: Macmillan, 1981) and Alhaji Shehu Shagari, 'National Day Broadcast Message to the people of Nigeria on the Occasion of the Twentieth Anniversary of Nigeria's Independence and 1st Anniversary of the Executive Presidency', Lagos, October 1980.

8. Alhaji Shehu Shagari, ibid.

9. For details of these economic problems, see *Who is Responsible? The Nigerian Worker and the Current Economic Crisis* (Kano: PRP Directorate, 1981); 'Entering the Debt Circle', Concord Editorial, *National Concord*, 21 July 1983; 'How Big is Nigeria's Debt?', ORICOM Special Report, *The Guardian*, 19 July 1983; J.K. Randle, 'Nigeria's Economy: A Desperate Disease', *National Concord*, 11 July 1983 and Iyiola Faloyin, 'Economic Implication of IMF Loan', *The Punch*, 25 October 1983 and 27 October 1983.

10. See International Labour Office, *First Things First: Meeting the Basic Needs of the People of Nigeria* (Addis Ababa: JASPA, 1981).

11. Alhaji Shehu Shagari, 'Inaugural Address to the People of Nigeria, October 1, 1979' (Lagos: The President's Office).

12. Alhaji Shehu Shagari, 'Address at the Annual Dinner of the Nigerian Institute of International Affairs', Lagos, 1980.

13. Alhaji Shehu Shagari, 'Address to the People of Nigeria on the Occasion of the Country's Twenty-Third Independence Anniversary, October 1, 1983'. For another very frank discussion of the crisis of the economy and the extent of vulnerability to external pressures, see Lawrence Amu, *The Oil Glut and The Nigerian Economy* (Lagos: NNPC Public Affairs Division,

1983).

14. *News From Nigeria* (Ottawa: Nigeria High Commission, 31 January 1981), p. 3.

15. Andrew Young, 'The United States and Africa: Victory for Diplomacy', *Foreign Affairs*, 59, 3, 1981, p. 654.

16. Ibid., pp. 655–6.

17. Stephen Wright, 'Limits of Nigeria's Power Overseas', *West Africa*, 21 July 1981, p. 1685.

18. See Olajide Aluko, 'Necessity and Freedom in Nigeria's Foreign Policy', *Nigerian Journal of International Affairs*, 4, 1–2, January–June 1980.

19. Bolaji Akinyemi, 'Introduction' in B. Akinyemi (ed.), *Nigeria and the World: Readings in Nigerian Foreign Policy* (Ibadan: Ibadan University Press, 1978), p. xi.

20. For details see Segun Osoba, 'The Deepening Crisis of the Nigerian National Bourgeoisie', *Review of African Political Economy*, 13, 1978 and 'The Nigerian Power Elite, 1952–1965' in P.C.W. Gutkind and Peter Waterman (eds.), *African Social Studies: A Radical Reader* (New York: Monthly Review, 1978), and Ikenna Nzimoro, 'The Political and Social Implications of Multinational Corporations in Nigeria' in Carl Widstrand (ed.), *Multinational Firms in Africa* (Uppsala: SIAS, 1975).

21. Segun Osoba, 'The Deepening Crisis . . .', op. cit., pp. 74 and 77.

22. Alhaji Shehu Shagari, 'Address at the 35th Ordinary Session of the UN General Assembly', op. cit.

23. Alhaji Shehu Shagari, 'Reply to an Address on behalf of Members of the Lagos Diplomatic Corps', 6 November 1979.

24. Alhaji Shehu Shagari, 'Address to the First Economic Summit of the Organisation of African Unity', Lagos, 28 April 1980.

25. *Shagari in Conversation*, op. cit., p. 40.

26. The importance of this point is borne out in the fact that during the August/September electioneering campaigns, Alhaji Shagari called on all Moslems not to vote for non-Moslems whom he condemned in the harshest language.

27. Alhaji Shehu Shagari, 'Address to the Summit Conference of the OAU, Freetown, Sierra Leone', op. cit.

28. *Shagari in Conversation*, op. cit., pp. 39–40.

29. Editiorial Opinion, *Nigerian Tribune*, 18 March 1981.

30. 'Nigeria's Fourth National Development Plan: Advertisement', *Financial Times*, 17 March 1981, p. 5.

31. Alhaji Shehu Shagari, 'Annual Foreign Policy Address', *Nigerian Forum*, 1, 6, August 1981, p. 204.

32. Alhaji Shehu Shagari, 'Nigerian Oil as a Weapon', *West Africa*, 24 March 1980 and *Africa Currents*, 19/20, Spring/Summer 1980, p. 43.

33. Alhaji Shehu Shagari, 'Address to Heads of State or Government of ECOWAS Member States, Lome, Togo', May 1980.

34. Alhaji Shehu Shagari, 'Speech at the Annual Dinner of the Nigerian Institute of International Affairs', op. cit.

35. Alhaji Shehu Shagari, 'Address to the Summit Conference of the Organisation of African Unity, Freetown, Sierra Leone', 1 July 1980.

36. See Alhaji Shehu Shagari, Text of Annual Foreign Policy Address,

on the Occasion of the 1983 Patron's Dinner of the Nigerian Institute of International Affairs, December 1983.

37. 'Towards a Dynamic Foreign Policy', Editorial, *National Concord*, 9 January 1984, p. 2.

38. Interview with Professor Iya Abubakar, Nigeria Defence Minister by Enukora Joe Okoli, *West Africa*, 19 May 1980. See also E. Joe Okoli, 'Nigeria Going Nuclear?', *West Africa*, 10 November 1980 and 'Nigeria's Military Capacity', *Africa Currents*, 21/22, July–August 1980, pp. 7–8.

39. Alhaji Shehu Shagari, Speech at Annual Dinner, op. cit.

40. For details of comparative military strength of Nigeria and South Africa see *Root* (London), Special Issue of Nigeria (1981). The table shows very clearly South Africa's military superiority. See also Olajide Aluko, 'Necessity and Freedom in Nigeria's Foreign Policy', *Nigerian Journal of International Studies*, 4, 1–2, January–June 1980 where he compares Nigeria and Libya. He concludes *inter alia* that 'Not only can the armed forces not support and supply any active operation anywhere in Southern Africa, they were even unable, especially the Nigerian Airforce, to provide air cover for our troops sent to Chad early in 1979, and to flush out by air attacks the Chadian dissidents that were harassing Nigerians along the Northern-Eastern border with Chad between October and November 1980.' (p. 11).

41. Alhaji Shehu Shagari, Speech at Annual Dinner, op. cit.

42. Alhaji Shehu Shagari, Address to the 35th Session of the UN General Assembly Reproduced in *New Times*, mid-October 1980, p. 13.

43. Details of these can be found in Julius O. Ihonvbere, 'Integration in a Dependent Regional Economy; Goals and Problems of ECOWAS', unpublished MA Research Essay, The Norman Paterson School of International Affairs, Carleton University, Ottawa, May 1981; and Olatunde Ojo, 'Nigeria and the Formation of ECOWAS', *International Organization*, 34, 4, 1980.

44. Alhaji Shehu Shagari, Address to Heads of State or Government of ECOWAS Member States, Lomé, Togo, May 1980.

45. See Federal Government, Clarification Statement on the Expulsion of Illegal Aliens from Nigeria (Lagos: Office of the President, 1983).

46. Interview with Alhaji Shehu Shagari by Peter Enahoro, Editor of *Africa Now*. Reproduced as *Shagari in Conversation* (n.d. and no publisher), p. 41.

47. See Julius O. Ihonvbere, 'External Pressures on the Budding Revolution in Ghana', Text of Public Lecture Under the Auspices of UMOJA: York African Students Association, York University, Canada, 3 March 1983; Tunde Obadina, 'Nigeria: A Leader Without Follower', *National Concord*, 6 December 1983; Bimbo Osifeso, 'Nigeria's Foreign Policy in Disarray', *Sunday Times*, 7 February 1982; Jide Kutelu, 'Towards a Dynamic Foreign Policy', *The Punch*, 25 October 1983 and Ade Fagbemi, 'Our Foreign Policy Muddle', *The Punch*, 15 July 1983.

48. Colonel M. Magoro, 'Nigeria's Peace-Keeping Role in Chad' in *Peacekeeping* (Lagos: Nigerian Institute of International Affairs, n.d.).

49. Ibid.

50. Bolaji Akinyemi, 'Chad: The Lessons for Nigeria', *Nigerian Forum*, 1, 1, March 1981, p. 8.

51. Alhaji Shehu Shagari, Interview with Peter Enahoro, op. cit.

52. An excellent discussion of this can be found in Tom Imobighe, 'Libyan Intervention In Chad: Security Implication for Nigeria', *Nigerian Journal of International Studies*, 4, 1/2, January–June 1980.

53. Ibid., p. 31.

54. Ibid.

55. Tunde Obadina, 'Nigeria: A Leader Without Follower', op. cit.

56. Ibid.

57. Ibid.

58. 'Towards a Dynamic Foreign Policy', op. cit.

59. Edet Inwang, 'Foreign Policy: Seeking the Break-even Point', *South* (Special Issue on Nigeria), February 1982, p. 58.

60. See ILO, *First Things First*, op. cit.

61. 'Towards a Dynamic Foreign Policy', op. cit.

62. J. Bayo Adekson, 'Nigeria's Preparedness for Peace-Keeping . . .', op. cit., pp. 53–6.

63. Bolaji Akinyemi, 'Chad: Lessons For Nigeria', op. cit., p. 13.

64. 'Towards a Dynamic Foreign Policy', op. cit.

65. See Alhaji Shehu Shagari, 'Twenty-Third Independence Day Anniversary Broadcast to the Nation, October 1, 1983'.

66. Major General M. Buhari, New Year Day Broadcast to the Nation, Lagos, 1 January 1984.

67. Major General M. Buhari, Address to a World Press Conference, Lagos, 5 January 1984.

9. The 1983 Elections and the Coup

Campaigns for the August–September 1983 general elections started as soon as the results of the 1979 elections were announced. In pronouncements, speeches, articles and actions by politicians and appointed officials, efforts were made to present and sell party programmes to states under the control of opposing parties. State governors tried as much as possible, through deed and otherwise, to convince their people that they were lucky and wise to have voted for the party in control of the state. However, and in spite of these efforts, it was obvious that alignment and re-alignment of class forces, particularly along political lines between October 1979 and August 1983 would severely affect the nature and outcome of the final elections held under the Second Republic.

The rabid corruption of political office-holders, the failure of some state governors to perform, personality clashes, intra-party feuds, conflicts between some state governments and the federal government and clashes resulting from efforts to superimpose the political party's constitution and structure over the power and authority of elected officials were bound to impact upon the 1983 elections. Moreover, the desire to manipulate the power of incumbency in order to remain in power, the challenge to incumbent officials by alienated or opposition elements in the struggle to win access to the state and its resources, the desire to expand the power and sphere of interest of particular parties and the subsequent registration of a sixth political party were also major factors which affected the 1983 elections. Finally, the nature of the country's economy and soicety, which by 1983 had shown cracks and conflicts were to become campaign issues that were expected to affect not only the pattern of voting but also the need of the political parties to come out with more concrete solutions and 'promises'. The consequences of export concentration, the contradictions of Nigeria's peripheral capitalism, the precipitous decline in oil production and exportation and therefore national revenues and foreign reserve, inflation, unemployment, increasing indebtedness (internally and externally), high crime rate and scarcity of essential commodities, particularly food, were very crucial in terms of factors and forces that affected the 1983 elections.[1]

These conditions equally compelled the incumbent powers to devise strategies and tactics for not only retaining power but also ensuring their survival after the elections. It is therefore possible to identify six major internal conditions which affected the outcome of the 1983 general elections.

The obvious non-performance and arrogance of power displayed by almost all the 19 state governors and the federal government immediately comes to mind. Admittedly, in some of the states, there were efforts to address the real problems affecting the masses, e.g. Lagos and Kano states. But in the majority of the states, where the governments, irrespective of political party, did not pursue selfish and class-based interests, the leadership busied itself with prestige projects, propaganda, political victimization within and outside its party in order to eliminate opposition or divert public funds to foreign bank accounts. This apparent corruption and ineptitude convinced the majority of people that, unless the federal government employed extra-legal means such as coercion, there were bound to be major changes in most states if the people were allowed to exercise their franchise honestly. In Bendel State for instance, the constant battle between the speaker of the House of Assembly and the governor, even though both were of the UPN, the corruption of elected and appointed officials amd a total neglect of 'non-political' issues such as the payment of salaries, employment, health services, etc., and the wastefulness of the UPN governor demonstrated to all that the 1983 elections in the state was not going to be easy for the incumbent governor given large-scale public disaffection. In Kaduna state, where the NPN-dominated Assembly was determined to remove the PRP governor, over politicization of issues, and myopic perspectives on the need for development as it affects the majority, virtually grounded the state as the House of Assembly put all possible impediments on the path of the executive, culminating in the governor's impeachment. It was the electorate that was to vote in the 1983 elections that suffered directly from this intra-bourgeois class conflict in the State.

A major development arising from the above was the dismally neglected living conditions of the people. (See the chapter on labour.) Given the deterioration all over the country in the provision of basic and essential services, the non-payment of workers' salaries and the mismanagement of the economy which prompted the imposition of 'austerity measures' in 1982, it was obvious by August 1983 that parties that did not perform were going to be badly affected by the alienation of the public. The non-payment of workers' salaries and wages was also expected either to contribute to an apathetic response to the whole exercise or to effect a radical shift in allegiance. The apathetic response to the calls of Fedeco to voters to register for the elections was a pointer in this direction which forced politicians to intensify efforts at winning support away from rival parties.

While only five political parties had contested the 1979 elections, a sixth party, the Nigeria Advance Party (NAP), was registered to contest the 1983 elections. In certain quarters it was believed that the NAP, which never got over its identity problems in spite of flirtation with socialist rhetoric, was registered by Fedeco to take some votes away from the UPN. The registration of the NAP was also expected to attract the youths, particularly the increasing number of unemployed school leavers who were most likely to be frustrated with the existing five political parties.

Between October 1979 and August 1983, intense intra-class contradictions and conflicts within the ranks of the bourgeoisie had led to several alignments and re-alignments of class forces. The new coalitions were prepared for major confrontations with the ruling party if only to facilitate their struggle to win access to state power and national resources. Thus, a lot of 'decampings', mostly from the UPN to the NPN and vice versa, 'expulsions' for anti-party activities and 'declarations' in line with the 'wishes' of certain communities took place, particularly between November 1982 and August 1983. These 'declarations' became intensified after the primaries had been held by all political parties for the election, selection or re-nomination of party candidates. In states where certain elements felt that the process of re-nomination had been rigged or where they had failed to win re-nomination away from incumbents, the general tendency was to 'decamp', usually to the rival political party. The UPN in Bendel, Oyo and Ondo states suffered from this development. Given the relative influence of these 'decampees', it was expected that elections were going to be conducted in a very tense environment as former 'comrades' confronted each other on conflicting party platforms. In addition, 'decampees' usually claimed to be decamping with their 'teeming supporters' and this was expected to affect the pattern of voting.

The level of preparedness of the Federal Electoral Commission (Fedeco) itself was another major factor that was expected to affect the elections.[2] In several respects, the delay in passing the Electoral Law had affected the ability of the Commission to begin its arrangements for the elections on time. In spite of this, it raised a lot of doubts in the mind of the public when it produced a very shoddy and suspicious electoral list in which the names of prominent politicians were missing. Prior to that, the number of registered voters produced by the Commission had been condemned all over the country except by members of the NPN, as incredible (see Table 9.1). In fact, in Oyo state, Governor Bola Ige was registered as a female voter, and Governor Mbakwe's name was omitted from the Imo list. This prompted the latter to remark that the British colonial masters should return to rule Nigeria. By the time the elections were two months away, polling booths had not been constructed in several places, electoral officers had either not been appointed or trained properly and even a month away to the elections, the corrected voters list was not out for public scrutiny. When the final list came out, political parties were asked to purchase it for ₦1.6m, thus restricting its use to the rich parties. In addition to this, the Commission decided to alter the pattern of the election; rather than begin with the House of Assembly elections and end with that of the president, it reversed the order. This move aroused the suspicions of other parties and the public who believed that whichever party won the presidency was bound to have undue advantage (the so-called bandwagon effect) over the other elections. Fedeco also decided to count the votes at the polling stations rather than the collating centres. To ensure the success of this exercise it bought 400,000 hurricane

Table 9.1 Percentage Increase in Registered Voters for 1979 and 1983

| State | Registered Voters | | | | † 1963 (in '000) | Population | | Percentage increase in 16 years |
	*1983	1979	Difference	Percentage increase		† 1979 (in '000)	Difference (in '000)	
Kano	7.60m	5.10m	2.50m	49.02	5,775	8,625	2,850	49.3
Kaduna	6.74m	3.40m	3.34m	98.24	4,090	6,115	2,025	49.5
Oyo	5.14m	4.50m	0.64m	14.22	5,208	7,770	2,562	49.2
Sokoto	5.12m	3.70m	1.42m	38.38	4,539	6,771	2,232	49.2
Imo	4.52m	3.40m	1.12m	32.94	2,998	4,472	1,474	49.0
Borno	3.58m	2.70m	0.88m	32.59	2,998	4,472	1,474	49.2
Anambra	3.53m	2.60m	0.93m	35.77	3,596	5,365	1,769	49.2
C. River	3.36m	2.40m	0.96m	40.00	3,478	5,188	1,710	49.2
Bendel	3.15m	2.30m	0.85m	36.96	2,461	3,671	1,210	49.2
Ondo	3.06m	2.40m	0.66m	27.50	2,729	4,071	1,342	49.2
Rivers	3.01m	1.40m	1.61m	115.00	1,719	2,581	862	50.1
Gongola	2.96m	2.20m	0.76m	34.55	2,606	3,887	1,281	49.1
Bauchi	2.68m	2.08m	0.60m	28.85	2,432	3,628	1,194	49.2
Benue	2.40m	1.05m	1.35m	128.57	2,421	3,621	1,194	49.2
Lagos	2.23m	1.80m	0.43m	23.89	1,444	2,537	1,093	75.7
Ogun	1.85m	1.60m	0.25m	15.63	1,551	2,555	1,004	64.7
Plateau	1.54m	1.60m	0.06m	-3.75	2,026	3,022	996	49.2
Kwara	1.31m	1.08m	0.23m	21.30	1,715	2,587	872	50.8
Niger	1.28m	1.04m	0.24m	23.08	1,194	1,782	588	19.2
FTC	.21m	–	0.21m	–	–	–	–	–
Total	65.30m	47.40m	17.90m	37.76	55,661	83,728	28,067	97.96

Source: * Fedeco; † National Population Bureau
Note: 1963 estimates are derived from the census taken at that date. Subsequent years' figures are projections by the National Population Bureau.

lanterns at a cost of ₦1.5 million. The public criticized the exorbitant cost and doubted if kerosene would be provided and at what cost. The situation was not helped when retired Colonel Ayo Ariyo, the Electoral Commissioner for Bendel state, declared that August was an 'unrealistic' date for any election given the unpreparedness of Fedeco.[3] Whatever the real or imagined problems of Fedeco the general feeling was that it was being teleguided by the NPN-controlled federal government and that it had to be watched closely if the elections were to be 'free and fair'.

In spite of the declarations of all the parties against rigging and violence before, during and after the elections, it was obvious to the electorate that these were empty declarations. The extent to which individuals, parties and organizations were to support or organize violent actions would be determined by how desperate they were to win or how much they felt cheated by the rival party.[4] Though malpractices in elections are not novel to Nigerians, the stakes in the Second Republic were high given the nature of the presidential system and the fact that whoever controlled the centre, controlled national resources and thus, the viability or otherwise of most states. In addition, control of the centre also opened avenues for more contracts and opportunities to pay political debts at public expense.

The attack on the UPN entourage in Modakeke area of Ile-Ife in Oyo state, the Maitatsine riots in Kano, the violent political incidents in Lafia and Bida and the use of thugs and 'vanguards' which were fully armed, all pointed to the possibility of violence during and possibly after the elections. The situation was so tense that the leaders of the six registered parties held a meeting in Lagos in June specifically on the question of violence. At this meeting, they all declared their commitment to a 'fair, free and non-violent election'. They also agreed to assist in defusing the tense political atmosphere in the country. Specifically, they resolved that, (i) the meeting of one party must not be disturbed by another party, (ii) police permits should be issued to one party at a time in any town, (iii) when a party was campaigning in a town, the vehicles of other parties must not ply the route of the party authorized to hold a rally, (iv) where two parties had police permits to conduct a rally in a town, the leaders must ensure that their supporters were kept apart and, (v) they urged the police force not to support any political party and to promptly investigate all suspected cases of crime.[5] The leader of the Nigeria Advance Party refused to sign the final communique. But it was obvious to observers that these leaders, particularly at rallies, had very limited control over their supporters. In any case, given the stakes of the system, and the need to 'unseat' the NPN, violence was a factor on which the weaker parties relied indirectly. Thus, it was widely feared that two developments were possible in relation to violence and the 1983 elections: either voters would stay at home for fear of their lives and this would affect certain parties more than others or voters would come out and quickly retire indoors. Both were to happen. The politicians made statements aimed at scaring supporters of the opposing parties in order to ensure that only their supporters came out to vote. Nonetheless, even if Fedeco's voters' register, which inflated the country's population astonishingly, was to be accepted; a comparison of the number of registered voters against that of actual voters would show that many people refused or were prevented from exercising their franchise (see Table 9.1).

The role of the police was perhaps one of the single major factors that affected the nature of the elections. The police force in Nigeria has never been known to defend the cause of the poor or to be really neutral in politics. It is also known to be ridden with corruption and ineffectiveness. However, its behaviour between 1979 and 1983 convinced the average citizen that the majority of the police officers were card-carrying members of the ruling NPN. Other than the frequent massacres of peasants (as was the case in Bakolori, Sokoto state), students and workers, most of the state police commissioners operated as military governors and had the belief that they had the power to determine the future of any politician. The period before and after the election saw the inspector general of police constantly on television in full combat uniform warning the public not to invite 'massacres' by protesting against announced election results. To make this threat credible, leave was cancelled for all officers, top-level meetings were constantly held, armoured tanks were provided in some states, notably those opposed to the NPN and about 65,000 policemen were given para-military training and fully equipped for anti-riot duties. In fact, any visitor to Nigeria shortly before the elections would have concluded that the country was preparing for war. This conclusion would have been strengthened by the presence of soldiers at all roadblocks all over the country searching all passing vehicles. The NPN leaders were, of course, confident of the support of the police for it never issued any statement or criticism of the force, but the other parties constantly cautioned the public against possible (and actual) collusion between the police, the Fedeco and the NPN to rig the elections.

A final factor that affected the conduct of the 1983 election was the attitude of the Nigerian press. On any given day, the country could boast of 27 daily newspapers, about 30 radio stations and almost the same number of television stations, about 50% of these having come into existence since 1979. Most of these media were owned by either the states or the federal government and to the extent that the journalists were public servants, they had lost the power to be objective in their reports. The federally-controlled media were the first to declare for the NPN and their role in presenting the true picture of the ailing economy, covering achievements in non-NPN states as well as in contributing to public education and mobilization before the elections had forced the majority of non-hard core NPN supporters to boycott federally-owned media sources.[6] The attacks against the federal government, particularly the exposure of corrupt practices by top NPN members while of course, covering up the misdemeanours of other parties by non-NPN state-owned media forced the then minister for communications to threaten to close down state-owned television and radio stations as they constituted a threat to 'peace and stability'. In all, except for the handful of 'independent' newspapers, *The Punch*, *The Guardian* and the *National Concord*, which tried to remain 'objective' even while defending the cause of a class society, Nigerians were fed with varieties of falsehood and propaganda before, during and after the 1983 elections. The role of the Nigerian media was severely restricted not only by the corruption and mediocre nature of some journalists but also by the constant threats from the various governments, law-suits and police invasion of media houses all in the effort to ensure conformity with the 'truth'.

Thus, in the period before the actual electioneering campaigns took off, the country was in a state of flux. Uncertainty permeated every nook and corner of society. The public was unsure of whom to believe or trust. Rumours of violence, counter-violence, coups d'etat, even of foreign invasion were rife all over the country and politicians, depending on the extent to which such rumours favoured them, did much to intensify the fears. While in other societies elections are seen as periods to spotlight new leaders, change bad government and representatives, exercise one's franchise and demonstrate the people's will, in Nigeria before and during the 1983 (as in previous) elections the situation was quite different. The police behaved as if it was preparing for war against a great power. The politicians behaved as if politics was the only possible avenue of human existence or survival and it was a do-or-die affair. To the politicians, where violence and threats could not compel the electorate to support them, bribery was certain to do it. In the alternative, the people's will could be neglected and the 'required' or desired results announced. The contradictions within and between the various political parties and contradictions between the people and the elite intensified the depth of the competition for political power, increased the stakes, both actual and imagined, and made more brutal the strategies and tactics of struggle.[7]

It was obvious before the election that the PRP as a political party was going to remain an exclusively Kano-based party. The death of its leader Aminu Kano; the impeachment of Balarabe Musa in Kaduna State and his disagreements with the PRP, the 'decamping' of S.G. Ikoku to the NPN; the emergence of the PPP embracing Michael Imodu, Abubakar Rimi and Balarabe Musa initially and the subsequent 'decamping' of Rimi to the NPP all pointed to the bleak fate of the PRP.

The UPN had lost some of its 'strong men' in Oyo and Ondo states, as well as in Bendel to the NPN. The non-performance of the party in Bendel also contributed to fears that the rival NPN would win the state. Everything came to rely on the charisma of the party's leader — Chief Obafemi Awolowo. The party also hoped to benefit from the rabid corruption of the ruling party and the economic crisis of the country. In Borno state, where the UPN had championed the cause of Alhaji Shugaba, the GNPP majority leader who had been illegally deported by the ruling NPN, the UPN also hoped to win, especially as the GNPP governor had declared for the party. In Sokoto, Cross River and Rivers states, the UPN was equally hopeful.

The NPP was confident it could win Kano given the declaration of the populist Abubakar Rimi for the party. It also hoped to win Benue State with

Paul Unongo as its gubernatorial candidate. It was, in any case, confident that it would retain Imo, Amambra and Plateau states.

The ruling NPN was not really sure where it could win. Many NPN governors initially refused to campaign alongside Alhaji Shehu Shagari because of feared public hostility to the president given the nature of the economy. In Sokoto state itself the incumbent president had to rely on the manipulation of religious and ethnic sentiments to win support for the incumbent governor and himself. Since it faced stiff opposition in all States, the NPN relied on the police, government-owned and NPN-controlled media, Fedeco officials and the use of thugs (more than any other party) to retain its former states and win over those under the control of opposing parties. As for the GNPP and NAP, it was clear to all before the election that they would play only a nuisance role, but would win no state.

The situation in the country was, therefore, so tense and in several ways so uncertain that the *Nigerian Democratic Review*, a radical reformist (at least in its maiden issue) journal, projected the following as likely before or during the elections: 1) Fedeco might postpone the 1983 elections, but this will be difficult to do on the basis of the constitution. 2) The presidential election might come first. A military coup might happen after the presidential elections. 3) Direct and 'armed extra-constitutional intervention' may happen before any election.[8] The *Review* also expected the possibility of a military intervention which would mark the end of the Second Republic and 'set in motion a re-enactment or a second edition of the 1966–79 history of Nigeria' before the August elections.

To be sure, none of these projections came to pass, exactly as predicted but to a very large extent, they reflected the depth of contradictions, violence and fear which had permeated the body politic of the nation prior to the August elections.

The growing tendency towards fascism had been clearly demonstrated in the country by the ruling NPN. While other parties had certainly victimized opponents in the various states, the NPN employed its control over national resources, the government-owned media and armed forces to expand and defend its interests, even if it meant violating sections of the constitution. The celebrated case of Alhaji Shugaba Abdulrahman Darman, majority leader of the Borno State House of Assembly, who was unceremoniously and illegally abducted from his home and deported on 24 January 1980 by the Shagari administration demonstrated to many observers the extent to which the state could go. The abduction and detention without trial of Dr Patrick Wilmot, who had promised to aid the administration in concretizing its foreign policy rhetoric by exposing all Nigerian companies with South African connections was another case in point. The massacre of defenceless peasants in Bakolori, Sokoto state, the frequent murder of students in and outside their campuses, attacks on workers and constant invocation of punitive labour Acts and so on, are areas where the ruling NPN and to a lesser degree (probably only because they did not control the centre), the other parties, created conditions which were bound to affect the elections.[9]

To be sure, the NPN had mapped out its own strategies. It realized that it had to contend with powerful forces. The economy was in a shambles and it was necessary to play all possible political cards if it was going to demystify the opposing parties, especially the UPN. Seven major strategies were adopted, among others: (i) the nomination of 'powerful' candidates in some non-NPN states. For instance, Samuel Ogbemudia in Bendel was a good match for the UPN incumbent, Ambrose Alli, who had performed poorly in office; (ii) influencing Fedeco and the police was another strategy. While all the parties were obviously involved in this game, the NPN had more resources and power to capitalize on this strategy; (iii) intimidation of the electorate through the use of the police; (iv) incessant use of the national television, to such an extent that nothing but the NPN or news about the NPN occupied about 70 per cent of daily air time, (v) the manipulation of figures and the use of money to bribe the electrate, (vi) the neglect of crucial campaign issues and concentration on peripheral and non-issues; the pardon granted to Yakubu Gowon and Odumegwu Ojukwu were obviously political to the extent that the NPN government spent public funds to welcome the latter (who arrived first) and encouraged him to join the party. He was immediately made a state vice-chairman of the party and even allowed to contest a senatorial seat. The hope was that with the 'Ojukwu factor', combined with the other factors — Okpara, Ikweme, etc. — which sprang up here and there, the eastern states were bound to go NPN.[10] The expulsion of 'illegal aliens' must also be seen as having serious political implications. Without doubt, given the poor state of the economy, it was essential to raise issues which would divert the attention of the public. It had also been widely believed that some rival parties had distributed voters' cards to the 'aliens' and others were organizing alien-gangs to disrupt the elections or cause violence after the elections. But, in spite of the economic problems in the country, it paid all the parties to ignore their structural roots and pay lip service to those facing the electorate on a daily basis:

> The economic conditions agitated no minds. The death seizure of large and small businesses, development projects, social amenities, the scarcity of commodities and the upward spiral in the cost of all essentials of day-to-day living, including food at its most basic, all these intolerable of social existence which were attributable to financial mismanagement and rampant corruption of Shagari's government, widely and consistently published, none of these featured at all in the campaign manifestoes of the various political parties.[11]

The UPN, on the other hand, realised quite well that the NPN would employ all the powers — legal and extra-legal — at its disposal to remain in power. Unfortunately, the leadership did not fully acknowledge this until after the elections. But as part of its own strategy, (i) It re-nominated all its incumbent governors, a mistake, at least in the case of Bendel. However, this policy led to the 'decamping' of some aggrieved elements who saw the

NPN as an alternative to the UPN, a fact which says much for the bankrupt ideological convictions and commitments of UPN stalwarts; (ii) Unlike during the 1979 elections, the UPN picked a Northerner as running mate to Chief Awolowo. But as in 1979, Alhaji Kura was an unknown figure in Nigerian politics and made no impact whatsoever on the UPN's fortunes in the North. (iii) The UPN Director of Organization, an ebullient and articulate 'socialist', Ebenezer Babatope, moved around the country helping with mobilization, education, debates and exposure of NPN atrocities. In some cases, this backfired as people wondered if UPN members in the state would rely 'on the man from Ibadan', to help with their local polities if the party came to power. (iv) Consistent comments were made on the economy and the corruption within the NPN. To be sure, these were done at a 'safe level', the core of the system must be preserved even if the party was determined to make the capitalist system humane. For instance, Awolowo came up with the ridiculous statement that, if he became president, he would not probe anyone, because such a probe 'will be a futile exercise since money embezzled by certain functionaries of federal government can never be recovered'.[12] This position was criticized as evidence of fear not to expose corruption within the UPN and, in fact, as evidence of faith in the ability of a heavily pillaged system to regularize itself. (v) The UPN struck a deal with a so-called committee of concerned citizens who are based in the north.[13] This committee used to be called 'the Northern Group' and, by and large, its influence was more imaginary than real.

According to an address to a World Press Conference by the Committee's Spokesman, Dr Datti Ahmed, Chief Awolowo agreed to the following in order to win their support: The Committee (a) was to provide the UPN with a respectable and acceptable running mate to Chief Awolowo; (b) mobilize support for the UPN so that it would win at least 25 per cent in the 10 northern states; (c) was to organize respectable candidates for elections in the north; (d) was to recommend those to participate in the federal government should Chief Awolowo win the election. Chief Awolowo, on behalf of the UPN, also agreed, if he won the election, to bridge the north-south educational gap, encourage religious freedom and the teaching of morals and religion in schools, support the performance of Hajj by Muslims, promote agriculture particularly in the north, promote friendly relations with all countries and not automatically re-open relations with Israel, develop Abuja as the nation's capital and ensure that the north gets some of the 'key positions and ministries so that the participation of the Northern part of the country will be seen in the North as obvious and important'. The point in this pact is that at one level it demonstrates the extent to which bourgeois elements are breaking down the region, religion and ethnic barrier while on the other hand it shows the UPN as ready to compromise its objectives e.g. on Abuja and foreign policy, just to extend its influence to the northern part of the country.

As the 6 August date for the presidential election moved closer, each party tried to play its last card or trick or spring its last surprises. Each party claimed it would win in all the states. 'Final appeals' were made to the electorate and soldiers joined policemen at roadblocks all over the country.

The Elections

No one, except perhaps members of the defunct NPN, would argue that the 1983 elections were fair and free. Even then, the NPN members would only argue this in private unless they wished to argue that victimization, the use of fake policemen, polling agents, the manipulation of Fedeco officials and policemen, the alteration of election figures and the use of thugs are. indicators of a free and fair election. The point is not that the other parties did not rig. The extent of rigging was directly proportional to the amount of resources, access to political power, influence over Fedeco officials and the police, available to any political party. There is hardly a state where the results can be regarded as genuine. As Obafemi Awolowo put it,

> ... there was rigging in 1979, ... this time ... the rigging was so massive it would have taken a month just to prepare the case; to collect the facts and figures. In Sokoto, Bauchi and Borno they didn't allow the people to vote at all. In some places they did cast some votes, but in most of the polling stations, about 85 per cent of them, they didn't allow the people to vote. The polling agents were driven away from practically all of the polling stations, but in most of the stations the people who came to cast their votes were driven away, and if they refused to go they teargassed them. That happened in Sokoto and it happened in Borno, where even Governor Goni himself was teargassed.[14]

If these complaints reflected the anguish of a defeated candidate, then General Buhari's views reflect those of an army officer trying to justify military intervention in politics:

> ... the people could only look forward to a change in their circumstances by the installation through the mechanism of the ballot box of a government with a more purposeful and responsible leadership [*sic*, as against that provided by the NPN].
> The conduct of the 1983 elections dashed that hope since ... that election could be anything but free and fair.[15]

These positions, nonetheless, reflected the reality of the 1983 elections.
Wole Soyinka, while acknowledging the involvement of all the parties in election malpractices, places the blame on the ruling NPN:

> Discredited, condemned and rejected, even loathed by the majority of Nigerians, the National Party of Nigeria, buoyed by the image-building of its leader by the Western press — meek, unassuming, detribalised,

the guarantor of peace and stability etc. etc. ad nauseam — went confidently ahead to commit the most breathtaking, in sheer scale, electoral fraud of any nation in the whole of Africa. At every level from acts of brutal ejection of the opposition at the polling booth by 'law-enforcement' agencies to the simplest but most daring motion of all, swapping the figures at the very point of announcement — the scale of the robbery is unprecedented, truly mind-boggling. Wherever all other measures failed, the Secretaries to the States Electoral Commissions simply announced the wrong figures or else, the Federal Commission in Lagos announced the forgeries . . .[16]

In an editorial, probably written the day before the change of government, the *National Concord* warned:

In conducting the forthcoming local government elections, slated for this month (January 1984), we should ensure that the bloodletting, arson and rigging that marked the 1983 elections are not allowed to recur. . . .[17]

The fact however was that an 'election' did not take place in 1983; rather a 'selection' was carried out through a strong alliance between the police, Fedeco officials and members of the ruling NPN with the latter supplying the money.[18] Alhaji Waziri Ibrahim, who was to challenge the results of the presidential election in court, called the elections 'Fedeco Awards'. To cite Chief Awolowo again:

. . . the election was rigged on a big scale in 1979 and massively rigged in 1983. Apart from the NPN hard core, everyone recognized that the elections have been rigged. And what is more, apart from two or three newspapers that are owned by the Federal Government or an NPN leader, all of the other newspapers condemned the elections and reflected the unhappiness of the people on the 23rd anniversary of the country. It is the first time that elections have been won in such a massive manner and nobody rejoices. . . .[19]

The real problem, other than the factional and fractional struggles within and between the dominant classes and their political organizations, was the fact that all the parties offered almost nothing to the electorate during the electioneering campaigns. Abuses, ethnic and religious jingoism, mediocre comments, lies and propaganda dominated speeches. There was little or no mobilization or public education. No one wanted to analyze and expose the roots of contradictions and crisis in the society. The NPP offered nothing different from its usual 'democracy', 'freedom and equality', employment and education. The UPN gracefully retreated from its 1979 slogan of 'democratic socialism' as its goal and concentrated on free education, health care, rural development and full employment. These programmes had created problems, failed to take off or had been badly handled in the five UPN states between 1979 and 1983. The other parties promised little beyond the vague — food, shelter, clothing, etc. The NAP stuck to its radical rhetoric to fight neocolonialism, imperialism and capitalism. It also promised to promote freedom, provide revolutionary education, etc.[20] It lacked the ability to conceptualize the society in clear and objective class terms. Its focus was excessively superstructural and its mechanism of struggle, elitist. In all, the politicians saw and treated the electorate as objects of manipulation and not of participation:

> What seems to have been demonstrated is that Nigerian politics has not changed much from what it was in the First Republic. Politicians refuse to play the game by the rules, they try to cheat in their drive for power and when they are defeated, they take the results with bitterness, and very often show excessive enthusiasm for putting their own or their parties' interests above the national interest.[21]

This position is not too far from that of *The Guardian*, which, writing under the title 'Season of Anomy', noted:

> Whatever else the events of August may mean, the one thing they most certainly do not portend is a triumph for democracy. Foreigners may indulge in supercilious cackles about our robust devotion to multi-party democracy. But self-knowledge, and our own self-esteem do not, or at least ought not to, permit such delusions on our part. If the elections so far held prove anything, it is this: that our institutions are fragile, and that they will continue to be so for as long as we ourselves regard them as structures to be cynically manipulated.[22]

These views capture very well why the ruling party (in particular) did not give any consideration to its biased politicization of the police, its open display of corruption and even mediocrity:

> Shagari's anti-tribalism was no doubt proven when he campaigned in his home state Sokoto and appealed so crudely to both religious and tribal sentiments . . . His tolerance has been underscored by his constant threats to use a 'big stick' on those who opposed him, his habit during the campaigns in hostile states, of warning that such states would continue to lose benefits because of their 'confrontational' attitudes . . . Let me assure you that there is no Nigerian child living today who does not know that Shehu Shagari has complacently presided for four years over the most unscrupulous and insatiable robbery consortium that the nation has ever known.[23]

General T.Y. Danjuma, the retired Chief of Staff of the Nigerian army equally argued in an interview that:

Democracy had been in jeopardy for the past four years (1979–1983). It died with the 1983 elections. The army only buried it. They didn't kill it. The politicians killed democracy . . .[24]

The retired general also argued that though all the political parties participated in rigging the 1983 elections, 'the greatest offender was the NPN. The NPN had the largest gathering of the worst human beings that Nigeria could produce'.[25]

The point on democracy and the 1983 elections is an important one. Throughout the elections, even during the campaigns, the ruling NPN continued to emphasize 'peace and stability'. It was obvious to observers that 'peace and stability' were required in order to enable the NPN 'to rule for ever', and further capitalist exploitation of the masses. The tendency was to present 'democracy' as meaning the 'conduct of elections', irrespective of the *nature* of the elections. The politicians neglected the fact that democracy and politics other than meaning *popular* participation in the organization of parties, the selection and election of representatives, also meant the provision of food, shelter, health care, public safety and other basic needs required by the majority:

> The poor state of the Nigerian economy has inevitably developed into a major issue in the country's coming elections. Foreign exchange problems, import licence difficulties and import prohibition have led to production cut-backs in local manufacturing plants, shortages of many consumer goods and higher prices. These developments would be god-sent news to opposition politicians anywhere, and in Nigeria much capital has been made of them.
>
> Sadly, however, the discussion of the economy's problems so far has not transcended the level of politicking. The first objective usually is to find a scapegoat, of whom there are many; then rosy solutions are offered, which cannot stand close examination. The rhetoric then tries to confuse the issues and all too frequently succeeds in merely diverting attention from the basic problems.[26]

This pattern of politicking characterized the 1983 elections. It was therefore impossible for the political parties to expose the structural roots of ethnic and religious chauvinism, political violence (organized and otherwise), economic mismanagement, corruption and general political instability. As the results of the elections started trickling in after the August 6 presidential voting exercise, so did reports of violence, the absence of voting in several places, allegation of police brutality and complicity in election-rigging and other malpractices. The point, however, was that the results confirmed the worst fears of the public – those outside the ruling NPN and the expectations of those in the NPN (Tables 9.2, 9.3, 9.4, 9.5 and 9.6 show the election results).

The level of dissatisfaction with the results of the election, particularly

Table 9.2
Results of the 1983 Presidential Election

State	GNPP	%	NAP	%	NPN	%	NPP	%	PRP	%	UPN	%	Total Votes
Anambra	36,163	3.2	27,511	2.38	385,297	33.26	669,348	57.79	16,103	1.39	23,859	2.06	1,158,283
Benue	19,897	3.05	10,573	1.62	384,045	38.83	152,209	23.31	6,381	0.98	79,690	12.21	652,795
Bendel	11,723	1.06	8,653	0.79	452,776	41.17	53,306	4.85	7,358	0.67	566,035	51.46	1,099,851
Borno	179,265	24.96	15,698	2.19	348,974	48.60	26,972	3.76	26,996	3.76	120,138	16.73	718,043
Bauchi	37,203	2.09	18,979	1.07	1,507,144	84.57	65,258	3.66	54,564	3.06	98,974	5.55	1,782,122
Cross River	16,582	1.29	10,967	0.85	696,592	54.18	46,418	3.61	8,229	0.64	606,922	39.43	1,285,710
Niger	12,984	3.01	8,182	1.90	272,086	65.17	112,971	26.23	8,736	2.03	15,772	3.66	430,731
Kwara	7,670	1.26	6,056	1.00	299,654	49.25	16,215	2.66	3,693	0.61	275,134	45.22	608,422
Ogun	6,874	0.55	2,862	0.23	43,821	3.47	5,022	0.40	4,449	0.33	1,118,033	95.00	1,261,061
Ondo	11,629	0.63	10,566	0.58	366,217	20.03	20,340	1.11	7,052	0.39	1,412,539	77.26	1,828,343
Oyo	15,732	0.67	9,891	0.42	885,127	37.66	34,852	1.48	9,174	0.39	1,396,226	59.39	2,351,000
Plateau	18,612	2.85	10,490	1.61	292,606	44.86	280,803	43.05	11,581	1.77	38,210	5.86	652,302
Imo	52,364	3.29	32,684	2.06	398,463	25.07	1,064,436	66.99	18,370	1.16	22,648	1.43	1,588,975
Gongola	25,530	3.47	37,318	5.07	282,820	38.44	148,055	20.13	81,205	11.04	160,720	21.85	735,648
Sokoto	46,752	1.65	22,152	0.72	2,605,935	91.83	63,238	2.23	24,280	0.85	75,428	2.66	2,837,786
Kaduna	80,862	3.80	37,396	1.75	1,266,894	59.28	225,919	10.58	300,476	14.02	225,878	10.57	2,137,398
Kano	35,252	2.95	14,209	1.19	383,398	32.19	274,102	22.98	436,997	36.63	48,494	4.06	1,193,050
FCT	1,103	–	977	–	127,372	–	4,156	–	641	–	1,102	–	135,351
Rivers	12,981	0.96	15,061	1.11	921,664	67.88	151,558	11.16	4,626	0.34	251,825	18.55	1,357,715
Lagos	11,748	0.72	8,636	0.53	126,165	7.28	119,455	7.28	6,570	0.40	1,367,807	83.38	1,640,381
No. of States won (25%)	NIL		NIL		16		4		1		7		

Table 9.3
Federal House of Representatives 1983 Election Results

State	NPN	UPN	NPP	PRP	Total Constituencies
Anambra	15	–	14	–	29
Bauchi	20	–	–	–	20
Bendel	18	2	–	–	20
Benue	15	–	4	–	19
Borno	24	–	–	–	24
Cross River	26	2	–	–	28
Gongola	21	–	–	–	21
Imo	10	–	20	–	30
Kaduna	33	–	–	–	33
Kano	33	–	2	41	46
Kwara	9	5	–	–	14
Lagos	–	12	–	–	12
Niger	8	–	2	–	10
Ogun	–	12	–	–	12
Ondo	–	–	–	–	22
Oyo	–	–	–	–	42
Plateau	10	–	6	–	16
Rivers	14	–	–	–	14
Sokoto	37	–	–	–	37
Abuja	1	–	–	–	1
Total	264	33	48	41	450

with the presidential and gubernatoral, is reflected in the level of protests and violence all over the country, especially in Borno, Benue, Plateau,[27] Oyo, Ondo and Anambra states. It was also reflected in the number of court actions instituted by defeated candidates who, even in spite of little confidence in the courts, still saw it as the last chance of fighting a semi-fascist political organization, the NPN.

Generally, political and other trade organizations and unions were dissatisfied with the conduct and results of the election. The air of suspicion was so strong that even top members of the NPN which won a 'landslide' victory through the help of the 'bandwagon effect', 'the peaceful, honest and sincere' style of the president, and the desire of the masses to 'break with the old ethnic organizations', could not rejoice in public. In fact, top NPN members had to warn their supporters to suppress their joy over the results of the election. The Nigeria Labour Congress (NLC) described the election as 'heavily rigged'. As one official put it:

> We know what democracy means. It goes just beyond voting and campaigns. The 1983 'selection' was badly done. Only a fool will say we had an election. While all parties rigged the election, the ruling

Table 9.4
Results of the 1983 Senatoral Elections

State	No. of seats	NAP	GNPP	UPN	NPN	PRP	NPP
Anambra	5	–	–	–	1	–	4
Bauchi	5	–	–	–	5	–	–
Bendel	5	–	–	–	5	–	–
Benue	5	–	–	–	5	–	–
Borno	5	–	–	–	5	–	–
Cross River	5	–	–	–	5	–	–
Gongola	5	–	–	–	5	–	–
Imo	5	–	–	–	–	–	5
Kaduna	5	–	–	–	5	–	–
Kano	5	–	–	–	–	5	–
Kwara	5	–	1	2	2	–	–
Lagos	5	–	–	5	–	–	–
Niger	5	–	–	–	4	–	1
Ogun	5	–	–	5	–	–	–
Ondo	5	–	–	4	1	–	–
Oyo	5	–	–	–	5	–	–
Plateau	5	–	–	–	2	–	3
Rivers	5	–	–	–	5	–	–
Sokoto	5	–	–	–	5	–	–
FTC	1	–	–	–	1	–	–

Source: *Daily Times*, 1 October 1983, p. 17.

> NPN employed gestapo and mafia tactics to win its 'landslide'. Once
> again, this shameful display of affluence, power and mediocrity should
> alert Nigerian workers to the need for a workers' party that will take
> over the means of production and exchange.[28]

The Academic Staff Union of Universities was equally critical of the conduct and results of the elections. On these, the union noted:

> ... whereas the members of the ruling class are wallowing in stinking
> opulence, the masses of the working people have increasingly been over-
> burdened by economic and social hardships. The people had hoped that
> the 1983 elections would enable them to replace the corrupt and rich
> politicians responsible for this state of affairs. But these high expec-
> tations have been dashed by the shameful manipulation of the electoral
> process to reimpose the same notorious people responsible for the
> hardships. Thus the right of the people to have responsible govern-
> ments and a dignified living has been denied.[29]

Table 9.5
Results of the 1983 Gubernatorial Elections

State	*Candidate*	*Party*
Anambra	C.C. Onoh	NPN
Bauchi	Tatari Ali	NPN
Bendel	S. Ogbomudia	NPN
Benue	Aper Aku	NPN
Borno	Ashak Jarma	NPN
Cross River	Donald Etiebet	NPN
Gongola	Bamanga Tukur	NPN
Imo	Sam Mbakwe	NPP
Kaduna	Lawal Kaita	NPN
Kano	Bakin Zuwo	PRP
Kwara	C. Adebayo	UPN
Lagos	Lateef Jakande	UPN
Niger	Awwal Ibrahim	NPN
Ogun	Bisi Onabanjo	UPN
Ondo	M. Ajasin	UPN
Oyo	V. Olunloyo	NPN
Plateau	Solomon Lar	NPP
Rivers	M. Okilo	NPN
Sokoto	Garba Nadama	NPN

NPN:	12	PRP:	1
UPN:	4	NPP:	2

Source: *Daily Times*, 1 October 1983, p. 17.

The ASUU also noted that that 'shameful performance' of Fedeco was 'inexcusable', given the fact that unlike in 1979 when it spent about ₦30 million to conduct similar elections, in 1983, it spent over ₦600 million '(about one-tenth of the national budget) to produce results unacceptable to very large sections of the electorate'.[30] In addition, Fedeco was accused of:

> ... operational deficiencies such as the ordering of excess election materials (ballot boxes, papers, and unreliable voters' register), indecision on lanterns; dubious division of authority amongst electoral officers; undisguised tampering with results in favour of some candidates and against others, and delays in announcing results.[31]

On the police force, ASUU noted that its 'leadership . . . was openly partisan and among other things did make statements that were clearly calculated to intimidate and frighten opposition parties'.[32]

These criticisms were not different from those made by students' unions,

Table 9.6
Voters Response to the Presidential and Gubernatorial Elections (1983): Total Votes Cast

State	Presidential	Governorship	Variance
Anambra	1,138,273	1,869,192	730,919
Bauchi	1,722,127	2,365,419	643,292
Bendel	1,099,851	1,838,887	739,036
Benue	652,302	942,567	290,265
Borno	719,043	1,094,449	375,406
Cross River	1,285,710	2,541,413	1,255,703
Gongola	735,648	1,071,468	335,820
Imo	1,588,975	1,656,455	67,480
Kaduna	2,137,398	3,255,194	1,117,796
Kano	1,193,050	1,682,766	489,716
Kwara	608,423	872,039	263,616
Lagos	1,640,381	1,759,434	119,053
Niger	430,695	656,572	225,877
Ogun	1,271,061	1,357,378	86,317
Ondo	1,818,343	2,356,154	537,811
Oyo	2,351,000	2,840,190	489,190
Plateau	652,302	896,347	244,045
Rivers	1,357,715	2,337,451	979,736
Sokoto	2,837,787	3,459,586	621,799

Source: *The Guardian*, 12 September 1983, p. 7.

trade and professional unions and other organizations in the country in general. The 'landslide victory' of the ruling NPN gave people little cause to rejoice or to expect an improvement in living standards. General Danjuma in his discussion of the elections noted that, given the way the election was massively rigged 'by a combination of the police, the party officials, and some of the Fedeco appointees', it was inevitable that a 'gunslide' was bound to follow the 'landslide victory' of the NPN.

The Aftermath and the Coup

Three major reactions were made to the elections: (1) litigation, (2) violence and (3) apathy. In all, these reactions demonstrated the extent to which people were unwilling to accept the results of the elections whether they were by defeated candidates or the electorate.

The court cases exposed the fact that in several cases the courts were not (and cannot be) neutral in politics. Even Chief Obafemi Awolowo, who is a Senior Advocate of Nigeria (SAN), refused to go to court over the results of the presidential elections, though he claimed to have sufficient evidence to show that the election was rigged by the NPN, the police and Fedeco agents. Among other reasons, he mentioned the fact that 'the judiciary has been terribly corrupted'.[33] The efforts of the GNPP leader, Alhaji Waziri Ibrahim, to get the results of the presidential elections nullified, were dismissed as frivolous and lacking merit.[34] The point raised by his lawyer against the draconic time-limit of 30 days set by the Electoral Act within which all appeals must be filed, was also dismissed as an 'academic point'.

Over sixty per cent of the governorship results were contested in the courts. The most prominent of these were in Oyo, Anambra and Ondo states where the incumbent governors were 'defeated'. There were equally challenges to Fedeco results in Bendel, Benue, Imo, Kaduna, Niger, Plateau and Rivers states. The election tribunals in many of the states dismissed the appeals on so-called 'technical grounds', only to have the Supreme Court order a retrial and sometimes with a directive that a different tribunal be reconstituted. In Bendel state, the tribunal threw out Professor Ambrose Alli's petition on the grounds that the relief sought was not available on the basis of the facts pleaded. In Benue, where Paul Unongo had challenged the re-election of Aper Aku, the tribunal struck out the petition claiming that the appeal had been filed on the wrong forms. Both cases were overturned by the Supreme Court. In other cases, it was either that the case was 'not ripe for hearing' or the appeal had some 'defects'. In all, there seems to have been the belief that all litigations had to be cleared by 1 October, as if a governor or representative not sworn in on that date could not later assume office and perform his or her duties. It, however, provided partisan tribunals and courts with the excuse to dismiss genuine cases.

In Ondo state, the tribunal reversed Fedeco results arguing that the scores had been inflated, and declared the incumbent UPN governor Chief Michael Ajasin the winner. In Anambra state, there was a split decision in favour of the incumbent Jim Nwobodo of the NPP against C.C. Onoh of the NPN. In Oyo state, there was also a split decision against the incumbent Bola Ige of the UPN in favour of the NPN's Omololu Olunloyo on the grounds that the former did not prove 'falsification beyond reasonable doubts'. However, at the Supreme Court to which the three cases later went, Ajasin retained Ondo state for the UPN, Anambra went to the NPN and so did Oyo. The retrials ordered for the two other interesting cases — Bendel and Benue — had not been concluded by the time the military took over.

Violence greeted the results of the elections all over the country, in spite of the court battles within the ranks of the dominant classes. While some of these violent reactions were obviously sponsored by defeated candidates or parties, there is no doubt that some were spontaneous reactions to some glaringly impossible results announced by Fedeco. In Oyo, Niger, Anambra, Plateau, Imo, Benue and Cross-River states, violent clashes were reported. In states where violent actions were not reported, a situation of uneasy calm existed as rallies, meetings, street processions, even night outings were banned by the police. The carnage, particularly in Benue, Oyo and Ondo states resulted in the loss of hundreds of lives, the burning of properties and the decimation of certain political organizations.

Rather than address the crucial issues involved in these reactions, the NPN-controlled federal government tried to blackmail opposing parties, repress and intimidate the electorate and divert debates around whether the violence was organized or spontaneous.[35]

Finally, there was the apathy of the general public even after the violent reactions had died down. People just could not believe that the NPN could have successfully managed to get away with the malpractices. Phrases and labels were coined to describe the nature of the elections, which were frequently referred to as 'selections' or 'Fedeco Awards'. For others, since it was obvious that the NPN had re-installed itself in power, there was no alternative but to join in the looting of national resources, corruption and search for easy access to wealth with little work. There was thus a rush for NPN membership cards after the elections.

This rush was heightened with debates in the papers of the possibility of establishing a fascist one-party state.[36] The arrogance of power displayed by top NPN functionaries further drove home the fear that even for one's personal safety, it was wise to become NPN. The NPN national secretary, Uba Ahmed, for example, on 27 August called a world press conference during which he made a number of allegations against the UPN, particularly Chief Onabanjo, the governor of Ogun state and Chief Awolowo. He warned the Shagari administration that the UPN was already on the road to 'treasonable felony' and suggested that the state had to act quickly against the party and its leaders.[37] Just before the election to the Senate, the *National Concord* warned Nigerians on the possibility of a one-party state:

> Two choices stare Nigerians in the face today as they go to the polls: succumb to the NPN's political machine and vote for a one-party state or rescue our democratic dispensation by voting for a broad based legislature.... In the August 6 Presidential elections, NPN's President Shehu Shagari was returned with an awesome majority. A week later, the NPN garnered 13 States with its control representing more than two-thirds of the country. If therefore the NPN takes two-thirds of the seats in the National Assembly the nation would have taken the last irretractable step toward a one-party state.[38]

This debate, more than anything, reflected the inherent fear in the country — a fear of the ruling NPN with its powerful police force and mobile policemen in particular. This fear prevented Nigerians from debating or analyzing the *nature* and material conditions which condition the emergence and operation of a single party in any country. The fear of the possibilities of a one-party state was not helped when top NPN members started boasting that there were only two parties in Nigeria — the NPN and the army or that the NPN would rule for ever. Nonetheless, the issue of a one-party state like those of violence, democracy, OPEC and the economy were encouraged by the interplay of class forces, the use of state power and precipitates of class contradictions and struggles.[39]

However, in spite of the jubilation that took place within the ranks of top NPN members, a heavy air of uncertainty still hung around all statements, movements and activities. People were quite sure something had to happen with the high rate of inflation, armed robbery, prostitution, hunger, corruption, scarcity of food, election violence and affluence of top members of the ruling NPN. The problem was that the nature and timing of what was to happen could not be predicted. During the swearing-in ceremony of the president, security was tightened, invited dignitaries all wore bullet-proof vests, some arrived very late and speeches were short. These were all because people expected a coup or violent public reaction. However, newspapers generally predicted the possibility of a military coup in the country. For example, *The Punch*, 1 October 1983, noted that there was really little to celebrate on the occasion of the country's twenty-third independence anniversary and second inauguration ceremony, given the fact that the waste, recklessness and abuse of power of the past four years (October 1979–October 1983) showed that the country had learnt little or nothing from its turbulent past. It concluded that nothing demonstrated this situation more than 'the just concluded elections'.

In the periods before, during and after the elections, the *Nigerian Tribune*, which was in fact the official paper of the UPN, continued to remind Nigerians of the words of John F. Kennedy that 'those who make peaceful change impossible make violent change inevitable'. In its 1 October issue, it accused the ruling NPN of abuse of office, nepotism, inefficiency and all sorts of corruption and of having rigged the 1983 elections. The editorial concluded that, given the *nature* of the party, its leaders and the government, the NPN government was 'assuming office on borrowed time'. In fact, before these statements and predictions were made, the Kano-based *Sunday Triumph* had noted in its 21 August 1983 edition, that the conduct of the presidential election was such that 'violent change was inevitable and that Shagari and the NPN must be reminded in the event they forgot of the consequences of the rigged elections in 1965'.

Other than the newspapers, by the time Shahu Shagari was sworn in in October 1983, the majority of Nigerians knew that in spite of police intimidation, the spreading of 'oil naira', even in the face of biting austerity, propaganda through the *Daily Times, New Nigeria* and the Nigeria Television Authority as well as expensive, glossy and heavily doctored paid supplements in international magazines, the NPN government could not survive until 1987. The only problem was: What sort of change? Could it be the Latin American, Ethiopian, Liberian or Ghanaian styles? These were crucial given the variations in the *nature* of the various military regimes in these places. Except in Ethiopia, where Colonel Mengistu declared a socialist state, carried out land reforms, mobilized peasants and rural producers into co-operatives, created a people's militia and so on, the others violently eliminated top politicians and former leaders, failed to carry out structural transformations and ended up re-integrating their countries deep into the orbit of Western imperialism. The statement above does not imply undisguised approval for the attitude of the Ethiopian government which maintains an imperialist presence in Eritrea and has systematically eliminated the communists in the country. But for Nigerians after 1 October 1983, when violent reactions, court litigations and abuses had all failed, anything was certainly better than the ruling NPN government.[40]

Why the Coup was Carried Out

Each military regime in the Third World has a litany of accusations it can always levy against any system it has overthrown. Experience has shown however that ultimately, the military can hardly be seen as a solution. The populist approach often adopted as soon as power is seized — hard statements, imprisonment or dismissals, even execution of corrupt businessmen and politicians and a few popular actions, soon die down as the military leaders confront the realities of a Western-dominated, structurally distorted, poor, peripheral capitalist formation.

When in the early hours of 31 December, four years and three months after the military had handed over power to civilians, news of another coup reached the public, there was jubilation. People drank, danced and sang all over the country that the decadent, corrupt, and directionless politicians had been wiped off the face of Nigeria's political life. People called for 'military rule for ever'. Others called for *war* on politicians, the execution of all legislators, ministers, governors (many were willing to let go Jakande of Lagos) and top party men.[41] Yet many remarked that unless 'we do like Rawlings, Shagari and his men will come back'. Two immediate points need to be made in relation to these positions. First, the new military regime, though the actors had not fully come to light by then, never declared any ideological position. In fact, by the time the Supreme Military Council was named and Major-General Muhammed Buhari emerged as head of State, it was clear that this coup was a right-wing coup of Generals and Brigadiers. More important is the fact that people generally failed to realize (and expose) the nature and role of the coup in the stabilization of the status quo and the re-constitution, through violent intervention, of the interests of the Nigerian bourgeoisie. To be sure the fractions and factions of the bourgeoisie had gone amok in their undisguised corruption and ineptitude; it required the intervention of the military wing of this class to redirect efforts towards class unity and survival. Thus, once again the genuine struggle of workers, peasants, students and the unemployed was hijacked by comfortable military officers, only because they had the organization and weapons to do so.[42]

A second point that needs to be made is that while the reasons given for the coup are quite valid and in fact justified, and were indeed well received by the public, the reasons did not in any way address the crucial structural and fundamental roots of contradictions, crises and underdevelopment in

Nigeria. The coup leaders did not see the problems of corruption, nepotism, waste, unproductiveness of the bourgeoisie, retrenchment and unemployment, social insecurity, etc., as direct and indirect manifestations of the distinctive nature of Nigeria's peripheral capitalism as well as its dependent location and role in the international division of labour. In so far as the coup plotters neglected these facts, their class nature is easily identifiable, if not their *factional* (as against fractional) allegiance. In addition, the fact that they can only provide at best populist, yet temporary, solutions to deep-rooted structural contradiction (as against problems) is easily identifiable. And here lies the possibility of another coup as a result of (a) public disenchantment with the rate at which the 'goods' are delivered and (b) by more impatient middle or junior officers who see the current regime as unable to move decisively against the ousted politicians except in the recovery of a tiny aspect of the looting that had continued for four years. It is important to bear these points in mind while discussing the reasons or rationalizations provided by the coup plotters. In fact, the general impression arising from debates in the newspapers, interviews with retired and functioning top military officers, is that the December coup was executed to pre-empt a 'junior officers' coup which would have been very bloody. Although, compared to other sectors of society, the Shagari administration had not neglected the army, there were certainly some cleavages within it. The old complaints about northern domination of key army positions have not exactly died out. To be sure, more 'progressive'—or rather nationalist conscious—young officers are beginning to emerge at the middle levels. Shagari ensured that defence expenditures were not cut and most of those holding top positions in the government today were promoted by his administration.

Whatever cleavages existed within the army before the coup have deep historical roots, but were intensified by the unequal access to promotions, contracts and other opportunities within and outside the army. In any case, the junior and lower ranks felt the brunt of the decaying economy much more than did the officer corps.

In the very first announcement by Brigadier Sanni Abacha (later to be appointed General Officer Commanding 2nd Mechanised Division) which started at about 7 am on 31 December, the Shagari administration was accused of imposing a 'grave economic predicament and uncertainty' on Nigeria. It was also described as 'inept and corrupt':

> I am referring to the harsh intolerable conditions under which we are now living. Our economy has been hopelessly mismanaged. We have become a debtor and beggar-nation. There is inadequacy of food at reasonable prices for our people who are now fed up with endless announcements of importation of foodstuffs. Health services are in shambles as our hospitals are reduced to mere consulting clinics, without drugs, water and equipment. Our educational system is deteriorating at an alarming rate. Unemployment figures, including the graduates, have reached embarassing and unacceptable proportions. In some states,

workers are being owed salary arrears of eight to 12 months, and in others there are threats of salary cuts, yet our leaders revel in squander-mania, corruption and indiscipline, continue to proliferate public appointments in complete disregard of our stark economic realities.[43]

It was for these reasons, and 'after due consultation' the armed forces 'in discharge of (their) national role as the promoters and protectors of our national interest decided to effect a change in the leadership of the government of the Federal Republic of Nigeria . . . '.[44] That is exactly what it was, a 'change in leadership', but over *the same structures, institutions, class and production relations, external linkages and class contradictions and struggles*.

The ease with which the coup succeeded (with only one casualty)[45] is evidence of how lax the security of the Shagari administration was and the general disaffection within and outside the armed forces.

In his maiden broadcast to the nation, the head of state, General Buhari, highlighted the reasons for the coup.[46] Generally, they were not different from those given by Sanni Abacha except that there was more emphasis on the rigging of the elections and the death of democracy and the mismanagement of the economy. In his address to a World Press Conference in Lagos on 5 January 1984, the General noted:

The otherwise buoyant economy of the first two fiscal years 1979/80 and 1980 was allowed to run down through mismanagement. Not only was there an inadequate response to the global recession caused by the world-wide oil glut . . . but measures designed to curb Nigeria's vulnerability to the vagaries of the oil market were applied in a half-hearted manner.[47]

The General also accused the various governments of the defunct Second Republic of having 'failed to provide even the minimum of good government' and as unable to deal decisively with fraudulent acts, arson at public buildings, corruption, indiscipline, smuggling, armed robbery, etc. As for the legislative arm of the defunct Second Republic, it was in no way better than the corrupt and decadent executive arm. According to the general, the

legislators, however, were in no position to check the drift of the Executive since where they were not active collaborators, they were pre-occupied with other things of no benefit to the people whom they represented.[48]

Finally, the general observed, that between 1979 and 1983, the 'planlessness, downright incompetence and irresponsibility which characterised the previous four years continued'. Specifically on the elections, General Buhari, in his New Year Day Broadcast to the nation, on 1 January 1984, highlighted the linkage between the elections and the coup:

The last general elections could be anything but free and fair . . . There is ample evidence that rigging and thuggery were related to the resources available to the parties. This conclusively proved to us that the parties have not developed confidence in the presidential system of government.[49]

Other justifications were provided by the plotters to win legitimacy and therefore support from the public. So far, neither their justification nor policy statements demonstrate in any way that the military leaders realize the structural roots of Nigeria's underdevelopment, instability and crises. In fact, the tendency has been to continue to focus on the manifestations of these fundamental structural contradictions and distortions such as corruption, military coups, inefficiency, waste, etc. Though General Buhari was able to identify the linkage between the level of development of productive forces and the nature of politics, his prescriptions were escapist, diversionary and reflective of the petty-bourgeois right-wing character of the coup. The identification:

While corruption and indiscipline had been associated with our state of underdevelopment, these twin evils in our politics have attained unprecedented height over the past four years. The corrupt, inept and insensitive leadership in the last four years has been the source of immorality and impropriety in our society, since what happens in any society is largely a reflection of the leadership of that society.[50]

The prescription:

With no corruption in all its processes, this government will not tolerate kickback, inflation of contracts and over-invoicing of imports et cetera. Nor will it condone forgery, fraud, embezzlement, misuse and abuse of office and illegal dealing in foreign exchange and smuggling.[51]

Conclusion

The developments within the economy, intra-class and political party conflicts and class alignments and re-alignments between the inception of the Second Republic in 1979 and the 1983 elections affected the nature and conduct of the election itself. By and large, these developments and (re)-alignments were precipitates of the distinctive nature of Nigeria's peripheral capitalism as well as of the country's location and role in the world capitalist system. The obvious break down of rationality in Nigerian politics shortly before and after the 1983 elections and the dismal state of the economy, provided enough excuse for the bourgeois fraction in the military to intervene in the long-term interests of the Nigerian bourgeoisie in order to stabilize the system. Since the coup, no structural changes have been made to the system.

The contradictions of the system have not been addressed. The distinctive nature of Nigeria's peripheral capitalism as well as the unequal relations between the Nigerian bourgeoisie and its foreign allies have not been addressed.[52] To be sure, the coup eliminated all possibilities for expanding 'democratic space' in order to facilitate popular struggles and involve workers, peasants and students in decision-making and implementation bodies. Ultimately, the point must be made, that military coups cannot provide solutions to fundamental contradictions which were historically determined and whose reproduction has revolved around entrenched class interests. Nigeria's experiences since the first January 1966 coup support this assertion.

Notes

1. See 'Workers still face Cruel Times', *National Concord*, 20 October 1983, p. 1; C.O. Ibie, 'Reflections on Nigeria's Economic Policy', *The Guardian*, 1, 2 and 3 December 1983; Udunna Ullegbu, 'The Culprits of Austerity', *Daily Times*, 31 May 1983; Xton Bugnor, 'Reviving the Economy – A Challenge for All', *Daily Times*, 31 March 1983; Achike Okafo, 'Pricing the Masses out of Market', *Daily Times*, 13 July 1983; 'Austerity Stays till 1980', *The Punch*, 30 November 1983; 'Darker Days Ahead, Experts Take a Hard Look on Nigerian Economy', *The Punch*, 30 November 1983; David Dafinone, 'Woes Betiding a Nation's Economy', *National Concord*, 28 November 1983 and T. Ogonibe, 'How to Revitalise the Nigerian Economy', *Daily Times*, 15 September 1983.

2. See 'The Electoral Act: Vote Counting and the Press', *West Africa,* 4 July 1983.

3. See *West Africa*, 20 June 1983, pp. 1446–1447; *West Africa*, 1 August 1983, pp. 1747–1762.

4. See *West Africa*, 1 August 1983, p. 1751.

5. See *West Africa*, 27 June 1983.

6. See 'Turbulent Seas of Opinions', *West Africa*, 10 October 1983.

7. See 'What are the Politicians Offering?', *West Africa*, 13 June 1983.

8. See 'Nigeria '83: Political Crisis and Fedeco's Arbitration', *Nigerian Democratic Review*, 1, 1, March 1983, pp. 8–10.

9. See 'Alhaji Shugaba Interviewed', *West Africa*, 26 July 1982; and Wole Woyinka, 'The 1983 Elections and the Foreign Press', *The Guardian*, 10 September 1983.

10. See 'Ojukwu in Politics', *The Guardian* (Editorial), 25 August 1983 and 'Ojukwu in Defeat', *The Guardian* (Editorial), 26 August 1983. For criticisms of the NPN's strategies and tactics during the 1979 and 1983 elections see Wole Soyinka, op. cit., Nnamdi Azikiwe, 'History Will Vindicate the Just', *Daily Sketch*, 31 August 1983; 'UPN Reviews Elections', *Nigerian Tribune*, 18 August 1983 and 'ASUU Writes Ovie Whiskey Electorate's Verdicts Have Been Falsified', *Daily Sketch*, 31 August 1983.

11. Wole Soyinka, op. cit.

12. See *West Africa*, 27 June 1983.

13. See 'Our Pact With Awo – Committee of Concerned Citizens'. Text of an address to a World Press Conference. Reproduced in *Nigerian*

1983 Elections and the Coup

Tribune, 5 August 1983. This was just a day before the presidential elections. It was obvious that neither the committee nor the UPN was seriously hoping that the 'Pact' would make any difference.

14. 'Awolowo Interviewed', *West Africa*, 21 November 1983, p. 2674.

15. Major General M. Buhari, Text of an Address to a World Press Conference, Lagos, 5 January 1984.

16, Wole Soyinka, op. cit.

17. 'Nineteen-Eighty Four', *Sunday Concord* (Editorial), 1 January 1984.

18. The writings of Ray Ekpu, Yemi Ogunbiyi, Dele Giwa, Niyi Osundare, Allah-Dey and the editorials of all non-government owned papers, exposed the nature of this Police-Fedeco-NPN alliance between May and December 1983.

19. 'Awolowo Interviewed', op. cit.

20. See NAP's political adverts before the elections and 'Things Have Just Got to Change' (Lagos: NAP Secretariat, 1983).

21. 'Trials and Tribulations', *West Africa*, 10 October 1983, p. 2347.

22. 'Season of Anomy', *The Guardian* (Editorial), 24 August 1983.

23. Wole Soyinka, op. cit.

24. General T.Y. Danjuma (Rtd), '12 2/3 Dented our Image'. Text of interview with A. Ogan, *The Guardian*, 22 January 1984, p. 3.

25. Ibid.

26. 'Keeping Nigeria on Track', *West Africa*, 27 June 1983, p. 1487. In fact, members of the NPN like Dr Doyin Okupe, tried as much as possible to de-politicize the nature of the economy during the elections. See 'Austerity Measure Not a Campaign Issue', *Daily Times*, 5 July 1983, p. 5.

27. See Labanji Bolaji, 'Miracle of Oyo '83 Elections', *The Guardian*, 28 October 1983; and reports on violence all over the country particularly between 1 August and 4 October 1983. *The Punch, Nigerian Tribune, Daily Sketch, Nigerian Herald, Satellite, Triumph, National Concord* and *The Guardian* are specially recommended.

28. Field interview, Nigeria Labour Congress Headquarters, Yaba, Lagos, November 1983.

29. Academic Staff Union of Universities (ASUU), National Executive Council Communique, 'The 1983 Election Crisis, Dangers Ahead and the Way Out', n.d., p. 2.

30. Ibid.

31. Ibid.

32. Ibid., p. 3.

33. 'Awolowo Interviewed', op. cit. See also 'Awolowo's Last Throw', *Africa Now*, May 1983, pp. 14–16,

34. See 'Waziri Fails Again', *West Africa*, 3 October 1983 and 'Litigation and Nigerian Democracy', *West Africa*, 12 September 1983, p. 2100. All Nigerian dailies carried reports of the Court decision. It was dismissed with ₦2,400 costs. Earlier on 5 September 1983, the presidential election petition tribunal had dismissed the petition with ₦3,000 costs.

35. See *West Africa*, 3 October 1983; *West Africa*, 10 October 1983; Claude Ake, 'The State of the Nation', Address to the Yearly Conference of the Nigerian Political Science Association, Jos, July 1983; 'October 1 1983', *National Concord* (Editorial), 1 October 1983; and 'Those whom the

gods would destroy, they first make mad', Text of Wole Soyinka's statement to the Press in Europe and America reproduced in *The Guardian*, 10 September 1983.

36. See 'Averting a One-Party State', *National Concord* (Editorial), 20 August 1983, and Edak B. Ene-Ita, 'A One-Party System of Government in Nigeria?', *The Guardian*, 18 October 1983. The debate heated up after October 1983. *The Punch, The Guardian, National Concord* and *Nigerian Tribune* are recommended for contributions to the debate.

37. All national dailies of 28 August 1983 carried Uba Ahmed's allegations on their front pages. For some replies see Gbolabo Ogunsanwo, 'Haba, Uba Ahmed', *The Guardian*, 4 September 1983, *Sunday Sketch* 4 September 1983; and 'No Secret Army in Ogun State', Text of Governor B. Onabanjo's Address at a World Press Conference, Lagos, 30 August 1983.

38. 'Season of Anomy', op. cit.

39. See Pini Jason, 'Come October, We shall all be Losers', 25 August 1983; Fred Ohwahwa, 'The Beneficiaries of the Second Republic', *The Guardian*, 25 August 1983; 'Violent Change Inevitable', *Sunday Triumph* (Editorial), 21 August 1983; and Olu Onagoruwa, 'What Legacy is Ovie-Whiskey Leaving?', *Sunday Tribune*, 28 August 1983.

40. Ibid.

41. The Jakande case could be likened to that of Alhaji Shagari. While many believe that they were perhaps honest, they argue that in so far as they complacently presided over a system which can hardly be described as incorruptible or democratic, they must be held liable for all the shortcomings of their respective governments.

42. See Sina Odugbemi, 'The Illusion of Change', *Nigerian Tribune*, 22 January 1984; Ayodele Fagbemi, 'A Letter from the Other Side to the Military Rulers', *Sunday Concord*, 15 January 1984; and Sully Abu, 'A Revolution Confiscated?', *The Guardian*, 23 January 1984.

43. Brigadier Sanni Abacha, Text of Coup Broadcast to the Nation, 31 December 1983.

44. Ibid.

45. The casualty was Brigadier Bako.

46. Major General M. Buhari, New Year Day Broadcast to the Nation, 1 January 1984.

47. Major General M. Buhari, Address to a World Press Conference, Lagos, 5 January 1984.

48. Ibid.

49. Major General Buhari, New Year Day Broadcast, op. cit.

50. Ibid.

51. Ibid.

52. Criticisms of the government have begun to emerge and certain sections of society are dissatisfied with responses to economic problems and the general treatment given to 'political criminals'. See Ola Balogun, 'No Half Solutions or Messy Compromises', *The Guardian*, 5 January 1984; see *The Guardian*, (Editorial), 'Must Not be a Mere Change of Guards', 3, 4 and 5 January 1984; Yemi Ogunbiyi, 'Memo to Brigadier Idiagbon', *The Guardian*, 26 January 1984 and Pini Jason, 'It will Soon be "Business as Usual"', *The Guardian*, 21 January 1984.

10. Conclusion: Political Instability and Economic Underdevelopment Since Independence

Nigerian social science has traditionally suffered from theoretical and critical poverty. In terms of quantity and quality, the majority of works have been escapist, shallow and orthodox. The dominance of the orthodox school has maintained a tendency to concentrate on the use of outmoded methodologies, models and approaches long discarded in other societies. It has also led to analysis, prescriptions and projections which not only reinforce the status quo but in fact promote the deepening and reproduction of the contradictions of Nigeria's peripheral capitalism. The recent emergence (or revitalization) of the tiny (but quite strong) radical (even Marxist) *genre* has stimulated debates within and between the various schools of thought and forced the orthodox school to refine its methodology and re-conceptualize the reality of the Nigerian formation. Thus, this school has moved somewhat away from 'modernization', absorbing concepts such as 'class', 'state' and others popularized in the 'political economy' *genre*.

However, the damage has already been done. The influence of the orthodox school has continued to affect perception and praxis. There continues to be concentration on personalities, economic growth, foreign investments, foreign aid, constitutional matters and other peripheral aspects of society. Indeed, the orthodox approach, through its ideological influence has succeeded in whipping up a high degree of distrust and fear for radical (not to mention Marxist) methodologies, analysis and prescriptions. The largely ahistorical nature of orthodox approaches has thus been unable to capture the distinctive substructural contradictions of the Nigerian society. Other than the superstructural (and often diversionary) focus of this approach, it has continued to emphasize problems instead of contradictions, harmony and compromise instead of conflict and struggle, and its prescriptions have revolved around the possibilities of finding accommodation within the world capitalist system, rather than self-reliance, restructuring of the existing order and autonomy.

The poverty of Nigerian social science, despite the efforts of the radical school, is evidenced in the poor quality of the products of the country's institutions. The ideas, models and methodologies imbibed from the institutions have been useless when confronted with the contradictions and crises of Nigeria's distorted and disarticulated formation. By and large, the institutional decay and inefficiency, corruption, high crime rate, military coups, prostitution, political mediocrity and adult delinquency, to mention a few of the problems which have been persistent since independence, are explained in terms of the 'wicked', 'lazy' or 'average' Nigerian. In its most sophisticated forms, ethnicity, religion or region of origin is employed in the attempt to explain problems of political intolerance, violence and instability, the continued reproduction of poverty, even in the face of increasing budgets and national revenues, and the continued vulnerability of the Nigerian system to military coups. At one time, the reason advanced was that of the 'illiteracy' of politicians. Then university lecturers, lawyers and other educated elements were involved in decision-making and implementation processes. The contradictions in fact became deepened. Then, it was thought that the creation of more states would do the trick. The creation of twelve states in 1967 and 19 in 1976 have lessened some tensions but also generated other contradictions and problems. Finally, it was thought that the problem was with the British parliamentary model which had come with political independence in 1960 and had failed to prevent a military coup in 1966. Then, the country tried an expensive American presidential model. As we have seen, this model in spite of efforts to ensure its survival, was susceptible to overthrow by the army. In spite of regimes, constitutions and personalities (civilian and military, parliamentary and presidential), the country has hardly witnessed any development. The living conditions of the majority of Nigerians, as the International Labour Office (ILO) recently noted, have worsened in several respects. Problems of rural decay, absolute poverty, unemployment, rural-urban migration, alienation, the oppression of workers, waste, inefficiency and corruption have continued to grow in geometric proportions. In addition, the country's peripheral role in the world capitalist system and the internal form of this role evidenced in the domination of the local economy by vertically integrated hegemony-seeking transnational corporations, have deepened over the years.

The analysis above means that there is a serious defect in Nigeria's intellectual and academic tradition. It means that the real roots of Nigeria's problems have not been generally addressed, exposed and attacked. We can thus identify defects in the following areas among others:

    1) a poor exposition of the nature of Nigeria's distinctive history and historical experience. Of particular importance here would be the nature and consequences of the contact with Western imperialism and the structural incorporation into and peripheralization in the world capitalist system.

    2) the distortive and disarticulative impact of colonialism on the Nigerian formation, the interplay of class forces, the politics of decolonization and the programmed transition to neocolonial dependence. Of importance here is how these factors affect Nigeria's continued role in the world capitalist system as well as affect contemporary efforts at class and systemic reproduction.

    3) the social origins and nature of social classes, the forms of political

domination, class contradictions and struggles. The overt and covert forms of class struggle, intra- and inter-class struggles, strategies and tactics of class reproduction, fractional and factional antagonisms and struggles. The impact of these on the 'manifestations' — corruption, violence, inefficiency, etc. need to be exposed here.

4) the origins, form and nature of the Nigerian state and 'tendencies' within it have received limited attention. In fact, Nigeria (unlike Kenya and Tanzania, even Ghana) has not benefited much from the vigorous debate on the nature of the postcolonial state. The instability of the state, its pre-hegemonic nature, its vulnerability to attacks from non-bourgeois forces, its relative autonomy and so on, have not been effectively addressed.

5) the relationship between the Nigerian state and agents and forces of Western capitalism has received a fair amount of treatment. The forms of investment, strategies of domination and domestication of labour, methods of exploitation and repatriation of resources, influence on the state and incorporation and control of local bourgeois elements, while they have been studied, have not received a systematic attention.

These are some aspects which must be studied in order to comprehend the nature of the Nigerian state and society, the roots of instability, contradictions and poverty. Fortunately, the failure of orthodox prescriptions and projections as well as the crisis of the Nigerian state and economy have called into question the usefulness of this school. In recent times, members of the Nigerian bourgeoisie (aided by orthodox intellectuals) have attempted to explain off the problems of the Nigerian society and state as resulting from indiscipline and the oil boom or oil glut. The last coup d'etat is explained in terms of ambition within the ranks of the officers and politicization of the armed forces. There is certainly some truth in this, but the explanations are diversionary and superficial. Why is the Nigerian bourgeoisie or decision-maker consistently undisciplined? Why has the Nigerian ruling class been unable to manage effectively the huge oil rents it has collected since 1973? Is it only in Nigeria (as in other peripheral capitalist societies) that the army is politicized or that ambitious army officers exist?

We would particularly wish to pay theoretical and practical attention to problems of the state, hegemony and coups. This is because, unlike in the case of the economy, labour and culture, these aspects have suffered from much superficial interpretations and analysis. It is crucial to explain why certain societies are stable while others are not. It is also important to explain not only why some societies are vulnerable to coups but also why they cannot manage the economy consistently. The problem of state and class hegemony is crucial for an understanding of the contradictions, crises and instability of the Nigerian state and social formation. Unfortunately, there have been almost no serious efforts to theorize along these lines.

Antonio Gramsci's concept of hegemony provides a basis for comprehending the nature and crisis of the Nigerian state since political independence in 1960. The point is to present arguments that will demonstrate

that the best way to understand the Nigerian state's crisis and its vulnerability to military coups, like other Third World states, is to locate the crisis,
and the coups in particular, in the inability of the Nigerian bourgeoisie to
create a viable hegemony in the social formation. Our position is that the
bourgeoisie has been unable to constitute itself into a hegemonic class
because of its peripheralization in the world capitalist system, its tenuous
relation to production, the domination of the Nigerian economy by international capital and the consistent challenges it has faced from other social
classes in the country.

Military coups as part of this crisis can be understood not from the various
peripheral theories or motives that dominate the literature but as part of the
strategy of the dominant social classes to retain control of the social formation in times of crisis resulting from challenges to the weak or pseudo-
hegemony imposed by the dominant classes. Coups are also the precipitates
of contradictions between the dominant classes and international capital.
These contradictions result from the internal reproduction of the crisis of
capitalism at the centre of the world system or from efforts by a faction or
fraction of internal dominant forces to extend control over the accumulation
processes in the economy.

We shall begin with a brief discussion of the concept of hegemony as
advanced by Antonio Gramsci in the *Prison Notebooks*. We then look at
the hegemonic crisis of the Nigerian state and conclude by looking at military
coups as a specific instance of hegemonic crisis in peripheral capitalist
societies using the Nigerian example.

The Concept of Hegemony in Gramsci

In the *Prison Notebooks*, Gramsci notes that a social group can be supreme
at two levels which are interrelated. The first is at the level of control over the
coercive instruments of the state — this is the level of class 'domination'.
The second is the level of moral and intellectual leadership exercised by the
dominant class through which it imposes its will on society without the use
of force — this form of domination or supremacy is exercised through state
institutions in 'civil society'. Civil society encompasses the educational,
religious, social and cultural institutions through which the dominant class
'releases' into the social formation ideas and beliefs which in actuality reflect
and encompass its interests but are presented as the interests of the society
at large. It is this latter form of manifestation of class supremacy that constitutes hegemony. The use of state power and coercion does not constitute
hegemony because it is often resorted to when a dominant social class cannot
impose its will and values on society in other ways.

Hegemony therefore would refer to an

> order in which a certain way of life and thought is dominant, in which
> one concept of reality is diffused throughout society, in all its in-

stitutional and private manifestations, informing with its spirit all tastes, morality, customs, religious and political principles, and all social relations, particularly in their intellectual and moral connotations.[1]

When a hegemonic order prevails in a social formation, the supremacy or domination of the hegemonic class is established, maintained and reproduced through consent over other social classes. This domination is imposed through the penetration of all aspects of society and manifested in the general acceptance of the world-view of the dominant class and the interpretations that this class gives to social reality.

The concept of hegemony does not preclude the control over the institutions of the state, particularly the means of coercion, by the hegemonic class, rather the control over these areas is concretized or protected and rationalized through the mediation of conflicts and contradictions through the use of subtle and 'normal' forms of control. The masses are made to believe in a so-called national interest without raising questions as to why that interest, when did it become the national interest, why did it become the national interest, who made the decision to make that interest the national interest and so on. The masses are made to believe in God as the final judge who can be relied upon to decide in favour of the poor and oppressed. The national flag, national anthem and other symbols come to acquire a special place in the thoughts and activities of the masses. They are made to believe in the 'neutrality' of the judicial system, the protective powers of the police and army, the existence of freedom in the society for all and the fact that eventually every one would 'make it'.

In short, the masses become victims of an all pervasive ideology of 'false consciousness': false in the sense that in reality the consciousness which they employ in the overall reproduction of the social formation is the consciousness of the ruling class. Though Marxism traditionally recognizes the possibility of imposing false consciousness on the oppressed through the institutions of civil society, the adherence to the consequences of the division of labour, i.e. the generation of social contradictions and class conflicts between the owners of property and the non-owners, has led to a neglect of other methods of rationalizing contradictions without resort to violence by dominant classes. In advanced capitalist societies, even when order breaks down the hegemonic classes do not resort to force immediately. When the crisis is eventually resolved through whatever means, the dominant classes attempt to rationalize the contradictions and the use of force through 'normal' channels such as the court system. Through these means the hegemonic classes in capitalist societies can divert, thwart, delay or redirect the content and intensity of class struggles. Equally, in peripheral capitalist societies, attempts can be made in this direction in order to rationalize the peripheralization of the economy in the world capitalist system and promote capital accumulation. Peasants can be made apathetic, workers can become very conservative or made to direct their energies into effective collective bargaining for bread and butter issues. 'Socialist' parties, trade unions and 'radical' intellectuals can begin to believe in the possibilities of capturing political power through *democratic* means, i.e. by participating in general elections or serving in bourgeois cabinets. At this level, class struggle is domesticated perhaps with occasional ruptures, and a particular form of emotional acceptance of the status quo in a manner dictated by the dominant class reigns supreme.

It is important to point out that these institutions can exist and dominant classes can adopt numerous strategies and tactics aimed at instituting bourgeois hegemony on the social formation. The success achieved in the process will be determined by the accumulative base of the dominant classes, the nature and power of the state, the role and location of the social formation in the world capitalist system, the level of class consciousness, the tradition of popular resistance and class struggle, the frequency with which the state employs coercion and the depth of social acceptance of the hegemonic institutions and structures.

The acceptance of an effective hegemonic class is demonstrated in either of two ways. First, it could involve an active participation in the process of reproducing the domination of the hegemonic class, e.g. the creation and sustenance of a personality cult, the active acceptance, defence and preparedness to sacrifice for certain beliefs and ideas imposed on the society and public demonstration of confidence and support for the regime and all it stands for. Active demonstration could also include outright hostility to alternative ideas or direct opposition to radical political parties, revolutionary movements, radical newspapers, intellectuals and groups. The second demonstration of acceptance could be 'passive'. While this would imply inactivity, it is in reality a form of acceptance often manifested in failure to challenge the institutions and ideas of the hegemonic class, failure to support alternative ideas and movements and the demonstration of moral and political apathy as a result of the power of the propaganda or actual power of the hegemonic class.

It is the position of this work, however, that at no point in the history of societies can hegemony, no matter how well entrenched, be permanent and free from challenges. This implies that hegemony cannot be imposed on all citizens at any point in time: there will always be challenges from various sectors of the society and it will not prevent crisis within the ranks of the hegemonic class itself. However, while these developments or challenges can be regarded as contributing to the development of alternative perceptions of social realities, unless they transcend the mechanisms which aid the reproduction of bourgeois hegemony and are directed at overthrowing it, they can hardly qualify for consideration as challenges. It is interesting to note that the bourgeois state itself thrives on crises, it requires them in order to demonstrate the fact that it is 'democratic' and that it permits alternative methods of expressing dissatisfaction provided this is done *within* the dictates of the law. It is only when the hegemony of the dominant class at the level of material production and at the level of the superstructure (the state and civil society) or in other words, its world-view, institutions and structures is effectively challenged through the creation of an alternative world view which permeates society and overtakes that of the 'hegemonic' class that we can talk of *challenge* or the development of a *counter-hegemony*.

At this point the intellectuals of the dominant group begin to lose their grip on the minds of the public, institutions lose their sanctity, conflicts within the ranks of the dominant social class get out of control, the agents of the state, especially the police and the army, become unreliable and the spontaneous consent hitherto enjoyed by the dominant class withers away. Thus the historical bloc imposed on the society begins to give way to a new historical bloc. When two or more historical blocs co-exist within a social formation, then we have a contradiction of historical blocs. The faction that commands the support of the agents of coercive institutions at this level can either win temporary or permanent dominance over the others. If the dominant class still controls the loyalty of the police and armed forces, outright police measures can be resorted to, a state of emergency can be declared or alternatively the armed forces can move in to seize power for itself in a coup d'etat.

Where a state is unable to use force on a consistent basis and the dominant class is incapable of imposing its will on society for a variety of reasons, it experiences a permanent crisis leading to the seizure of political power by factions or fractions of the dominant class. In peripheral capitalist societies, with underdeveloped structures and institutions where the state is controlled by a techno-comprador class (the technocrats, bureaucrats and compradors) the military is usually the fraction that seizes political power for itself or on behalf of the bourgeoisie. The reason why the military succeeds in this effort has nothing to do with its level of organization or its modernizing role in the society. Rather, it succeeds because of its historical development, an institution that was created and nurtured to use violence on behalf of imperialism and more importantly, its control over the weapons of war.

The Hegemonic Crisis of the Nigerian State

The literature on the postcolonial state emphasizes the role which the state assumes not only in the mediation of class struggles but more importantly in the overall reproduction of the social system.[2] In the course of the debate regarding the nature of the postcolonial state, concrete efforts have been made to identify and present the corollary of the advanced capitalist state by presenting the state as 'overdeveloped', 'central', 'relatively autonomous' and as possessing 'overdeveloped apparatuses'. In this regard, the bureaucracy of the postcolonial state, its decisive role in the economy and the direct and indirect influence of metropolitan bourgeoisies on it have been highlighted. The central role of the military and the role of the state in the protection and extension of the interests of the dominant classes have also received attention. Hamza Alavi who set the tone of the debate premises his arguments on:

the historical specificities of the post-colonial societies, a specificity which arises from structural changes brought about by the colonial experience and alignment of class and by the superstructures of political and administrative institutions which were established in that context, and secondly from the radical realignment of class forces which have been brought about in the post-colonial situation.[3]

Thus, the bottom line of the argument is that the colonial state set the basis of the power of the postcolonial state. The structure and institutions inherited at the attainment of political independence though overdeveloped for the postcolonial state, had their roots in the colonial period. Finally, the relatively autonomous role of the postcolonial state, coupled with the domination of an over-extended state apparatus, facilitated the super-imposition of state power over the allocation of scarce resources in the name of economic development. This control over society's resources makes the postcolonial state the focus of capital accumulation and class competition and struggles.

To a very large extent the debate on the nature of the postcolonial state has been escapist and time-wasting. The use of given categories sometimes fails to capture the peculiarities of the underdeveloped social formations of the Third World. In addition, the state in postcolonial societies is treated as given and attempts are made to understand its nature through the attitudes of state functionaries. Relative autonomy and centrality as well as state interventionism are in no way peculiar to the postcolonial state. If 'over-development' of the state is the product of the extensive institutions inherited from colonialism, one could make an argument for the fact that indigenous elites have been involved in the initiation, operation and reproduction of the state before political independence. In fact, it is difficult to accept the idea of an 'overdeveloped' state since this would tend to suggest a 'normal' size for a state. Because colonialism is employed as a starting-point without using the processes of decolonization as well as the interplay of class forces in this period as dynamic points for understanding the continuity inherent in the class role of the state, the literature on the postcolonial state has remained incapable of presenting the postcolonial state for what it is.

The postcolonial state is essentially an underdeveloped and dominated crisis-ridden state type. True, it inherited the institutions of colonialism, it did not inherit the ability of the colonial state to use force and manipulations without any moral or public censure. It also did not inherit the central role of the colonial state in the international division of labour, nieither did it inherit the finances, metropolitan support (militarily or otherwise) and the ideological backing of metropolitan bourgeoisies. Rather, in the programmed transition to political independence, its peripheralization in the world capitalist system and domination (internally) by foreign capital were concretized. The tenuous relation of the dominant classes that captured state power to productive activities meant not only a reliance on the productive activities of the metropolitan bourgeoisie but also the 'indigenization' of the unequal exchange system implanted by imperialism. The failure of colonialism to revolutionize completely the forces of production in the colony meant that various powerful forces were left un-unified by capital and therefore, remained outside the sphere of control inherited at independence. Finally, the dependence on foreign aid, political protection and assistance in all respects by the postcolonial state coupled with the domination of the social formation by a world-view which was not initiated by the internal bourgeoisie but originated from the metropole meant an inability to impose effectively a hegemonic view on other social forces or to mediate effectively class contradictions and struggles. This explains the frequent resort to the use of force, unlike the advanced capitalist state, and the perpetual instability resulting in military coups or civil disorder. As Gramsci puts it: ' "State" should be understood not only [as] the apparatus of government, but also [as] the "private" apparatus of "hegemony" or civil society'.[4] And as Lenin put it,

> the state is the product and manifestation of the irreconcilability of class antagonism. The state arises where, when and insofar as class antagonism objectively cannot be reconciled. And conversely, the existence of the state proves that the class antagonisms are irreconcilable.[5]

In order to capture the nature, power and crisis of the state in postcolonial societies, therefore, it is essential that we return to a historical understanding of the role of imperialism and colonialism in restructuring the social formation, class forces, class alignments and re-alignments, the content and direction of class struggles and finally, provide a clear analysis of the class forces in the specific society. Marxism does not need to be challenged to do these. We shall attempt to highlight aspects of this and the way they aid an understanding of the crisis of hegemony faced by the Nigerian state following political independence in 1960.

The Nigerian State and its Postcolonial Version

Colonialism as a logical extension of imperialism imposed the colonial state to protect and reproduce the interests of the metropolitan bourgeoisie. In the Nigerian case, the British ruling class was directly responsible for fashioning the structure and power of the colonial state. The colonial state was supreme within the colony: it controlled the use of force, had the support of the metropole and unlike in the period of informal empire when imperial capital secured its interests indirectly and through informal means, the colonial state was very interventionist. By 1900, the Royal Niger Company had laid the foundation which in conjunction with the introduction of formal institutions were to contribute to the systematic exploitation of Nigeria. The starting-point was the subjugation of the pre-capitalist social formation to foreign capitalist interests, the programmed effort to deny and distort the history of the peoples of Nigeria and the imposition of an alternative world-view which reflected the interests of the imperial bourgeois class. Following this, the colonial state which as we have argued represented the interests of the British ruling class, through several agricultural, fiscal, spatial, political, educational and religious policies, endeavoured to reorganize the economy towards a capitalist mode of production. Since colonialism did not need to create a capitalist state in Nigeria in order to obtain raw materials for British industries or control and protect the market for the metropole, it introduced elements of capitalism but not capitalism.

The colonial period distorted the Nigerian economy, introduced new relations of production and accumulation, introduced a new world-view and integrated the peripheralized economy of Nigeria into the international division of labour. It is however very important to highlight three aspects of the colonial society which throw some light on the focus of this chapter. The first is the educational policies of the colonial state, the second is the underdevelopment of Nigerian entrepreneurship in this period or rather the confinement of the emerging bourgeois class to commercial activities and third, the creation and role of the military in this period.

Missionary groups were in the forefront of the educational system in the colonial period. The colonial state assumed a largely supervisory role and ensured that the establishment of institutions and the content of the curriculum did not contravene colonial policies. Education in Nigeria as in other colonies was an important ideological weapon of the state because it served as an avenue for disseminating the values of the metropolitan bourgeoisie. Essentially, the system was structured to provide the colonial system not with scientists, top bureaucrats or administrators but with interpreters, clerks, messengers, station masters, sanitary inspectors, dispensers and house boys. The limited goals of the educational system are evidenced in the fact that for mainly political reasons the British government, working through the Colonial Office, ensured that the northern part of the country was largely isolated from the influences of the missionaries. In addition, when the colonial state became directly involved in the school system in the 1920s, it ensured that the content of the curriculum effectively denied the existence of Nigeria's history while the glory and virtues of the Queen and British Empire served as the core of the system.

The important point to emphasize, however, is that for the few who had access to higher or middle level education the system was aimed at, and it succeeded in, creating a so-called philosophy of 'educated gentlemen ... the refined elite ... that select group, of like mind, who form the cream of society, leaders necessarily chosen and trained for the purpose and not a spontaneous outgrowth of a whole people participating in their attempt to solve problems'.[6] This system greatly served to ease the incorporation of the Nigerian social formation into the world capitalist system. It also ensured that those who were to become the intellectuals of the dependent capitalist system would be products of this educational system. In addition, the

244

colonial educational system served to reconcile the world-views of the colonial bourgeoisies with those of the emerging bureaucratic and commercial class in Nigeria.

The colonial system did not need to create a viable capitalist system in the colony in order to promote capital accumulation. In fact, if the colony was to serve as a source of raw materials and a market for the products of British industries, it was necessary to ensure that the colony never achieved a self-sustaining productive capacity. The educational system described earlier had laid a foundation for diverting the attention of the emerging educated class to the service sector. The imposition of state monopoly on the purchase of farm products ensured that the peasants received much less than the world price of their products thus leaving them with no funds to invest in rural industries. The use of licensed agents by the state enabled the internal elite to accumulate capital by short-paying the peasants. But they could not invest in production because the colonial state initiated and implemented several measures to ensure that production did not take place in the colonies, linkages were not allowed into areas that would fundamentally challenge the domination of the economy by foreign capital. As Gavin Williams has put it, the British, 'through their control of the political process of decolonization, promoted class and power relations which would ensure the continued domination of Nigeria by international capitalism.'[7] Thus, the underdevelopment of Nigerian entrepreneurship was promoted at this time but consolidated at the attainment of political independence.

The consolidation of the domination of the Nigerian economy was possible because of the weak role of the indigenous classes and the dominant role of international capital which had the support of the colonial state. As Segun Osoba has also put it:

> ... several of the unsophisticated indigenous industries had to close down or continue to run at a loss because their crude products could not compete effectively with the cheaper and finer articles being imported into the country by the foreign firms ... [a] disastrous fate ... befell most of the Nigerian-owned banks, described by a top Federal Government official as 'mushroom' institutions with signboards across derelict windows.[8]

The consequence of the colonial policies in relation to industrial production therefore included the dependence of the Nigerian bourgeois class on the state for capital accumulation through the granting of sinecure posts in government and public corporations, the award of inflated contracts and the granting of loans for existing and non-existent projects. In addition, foreign capital, beginning with the granting of internal self-government in 1952, voluntarily initiated a programme of incorporation. Through this, indigenous power elites were incorporated as advisers, legal representatives, counsellors, shareholders, sole distributors and major representatives by foreign firms both as a means of rationalizing their participation and domination of the economy and as a form of 'political insurance'. This trend was so pronounced at the beginning of the First Republic that a Senator was forced to cry out that:

> The trend now is to call every company a Nigerian company. That is, somebody is appointed from the outside, a Nigerian, one foolish man, who is usually given a big salary, so that they can call the company Nigerian. He has nothing to do with the company.[9]

The postcolonial relations of production and accumulation that were imposed on the Nigerian social formation in 1960 were such as to convert the Nigerian state into a regulator of the interests of foreign capital and indigenous elites. The result of this arrangement is well put by Gavin Williams thus:

> Expatriate domination of investment opportunities and sources of capital accumulation inhibits the accumulation and re-investment of capital by indigenous entrepreneurs who lack the resources to compete with vertically integrated multinational corporations. Consequently, indigenous entrepreneurs became compradors (i.e. intermediaries between expatriates and the indigenous polity and economy).[10]

From the analysis thus far, it is evident that the Nigerian economy at independence had not changed much even though the civil service was 'Nigerianized', and the postcolonial state acquired the tenuous capacity to mediate class conflicts through the use of patronage, violence and other means. The tenuous relation of the Nigerian bourgeoisie to production meant that the state itself was controlled by a techno-comprador class that was in turn dominated by foreign capital or the international bourgeoisie.

The problems which faced the postcolonial state went beyond the socioeconomic and political fragmentation and distortion which the colonial state had created in its efforts to establish firm control to include the release of hitherto suppressed intra-class conflicts primarily within the ranks of the dominant class. The challenges posed to the state by other social classes, the manipulations of international finance capital and the inability of the dominant social classes to create a new world-view or maintain the world-view of the colonial state (for reasons already discussed) all combined to galvanize the seizure of political power by a fraction of the bourgeois class in 1966, i.e. the army.

The third aspect that must be examined which is an integral part of the Nigerian state is the army. The major point here is that colonialism was established in Nigeria through the use of uncontrolled force. The subjugation of the indigenous peoples and the imposition of the world-view of the metropolitan bourgeoisie as well as the operation of the colonial superstructure — the collection of taxes, the conscription of forced labour, the seizure of land or the conversion of farmers into cash crop producers were all achieved through the use of force by the colonial state. Though the British government prided itself as practising so-called indirect rule, the system was in actuality more direct than indirect. In the first place, the colonial government never wasted time or hesitated to make its rule direct by 'showing the flag' whenever or wherever certain communities or individuals failed or refused to contribute labour to public projects, pay taxes or produce required cash crops. Secondly, the indigenous officials and traditional rulers who collaborated with the colonial authorities were in fact part of the colonial superstructures. If this position is valid, recognizing the fact that most of them shared the world-view of the colonial power, then one can argue that colonial rule was always direct.

To make this rule direct and effective, the colonial state in the first instance relied on the aura of the metropolitan state as well as the armed might of the metropole. In the second instance, partly to save costs and partly because of the need to institute a process of creating an indigenous military institution that would be groomed to rely on the metropole or at least protect the interests of the metropole, the colonial state created an internal military machine. The recruitment initially focused on minority elements and outcasts and was later extended to include other social groups especially the royal or feudal and new middle-class elements. Generally, these were groups who had specific interests to gain in the new relations of accumulation, interests to protect or grudges to settle. It can therefore be understood why the colonial police and army were very brutal on their own people and why the military took the sides of the dominant classes after political independence. The role played by the military in the colonial period largely laid the basis for the role it plays in the postcolonial period. Many of the first generation officers could not as at present understand why they should not continue to play exactly the same role especially now that the government was being Africanized.

Finally, in this section, it is important to note that the crisis of hegemony that faced the postcolonial state arose from the distortion of the social formation in the colonial period, the peripheralization of the economy in the international division of labour, the domination of the economy by foreign capital, the relegation of the indigenous power elite to commercial and exchange activities, the relative power of other social classes, the inability of the postcolonial state to create and impose an alternative world-view on the other social classes and the intra-class conflict that characterized the politics played by the power elite following independence. The crisis of hegemony also had its roots in the exclusion of the majority from plan initiation and implementation, the attempts to preserve the colonial relations of production and accumulation e.g. the continued use of Marketing Boards, the increasing level of organization, militancy and consciousness among the working class, the frequent use of force by the postcolonial state in the face of popular protests, the massive rate of corruption, ethnic chauvinism, religious bigotry, opportunism, political brigandage and the use of state power and institutions to divert public funds into private pockets and accounts.

All the above and many others combined to throw the Nigerian social formation into perpetual crisis. The use of vague and shallow ideological tools, the preservation of the neocolonial educational system and the intensification and expansion of the system of patronage did not serve to reduce the challenges to the state and bourgeoisie. At this level the military could intervene for three major reasons. First, it could intervene to protect the interests of the dominant class especially when it becomes clear that the opposition from other social classes has reached a level where they have created a counter-hegemonic force on the society, where the opposition commands the support of the majority or where the social order has broken down due to the inability of the dominant class to maintain control over capital accumulation and the distribution of patronage. The military could also intervene to advance and consolidate its own interests. In this regard it acts not as an opposition to the ruling class but as a replacement within the established mode of accumulation. This could be done because the ruling class has neglected the military, over-extended its functions or because the military wishes to instil new vigour into state institutions, strengthen the alliance between it and international capital or contribute to the emergence of a fascist state. This happens where the social origins of the officers are different from those of the ruling class, though this is not a necessary condition always. The final reason why the military might intervene arises from the desire by progressive forces to use the military either as part of a larger social movement on the side of a larger social movement or in isolation.

In peripheral capitalist societies, the ability of the military to capture political power has been demonstrated again and again even within the same country and within short intervals. The possibility of outside forces, internal or external, using the military to capture political power has also been demonstrated. Thus it is possible for revolutionary forces to infiltrate the army and use it in the overthrow of the social order, demystify the army by the creation of a people's militia and creating institutions for popular mobilization, participation and defence. As revolutionaries, such an intervention is more likely to succeed when the hegemony of the dominant class is under attack, even if no counter-hegemony has been developed; this is important because of the likely developments following the take-over of power.

We shall now turn to the final part of this chapter, the intervention of the military in Nigeria and attempt to argue that, the coups that have taken place are precipitates of the first type rather than the last two, i.e. intervention on behalf of the dominant classes as a result of challenges to the state.

Military Interventions in Nigeria

Before we discuss military interventions in Nigeria, it is essential to make some comments on existing attempts to analyze the causes of military coups in the Third World. Attempts to do this have sometimes strayed into the area of 'grand theorizing', providing cosmetic and escapist explanations and therefore inadequate solutions. There are in fact two major schools of thought. While their theories might not be essentially wrong, they do not appear to capture the fundamental basis of military intervention in peripheral capitalist social formations. Thus, they have relied on attitudinal, institutional or cultural approaches to the comprehension of the motives behind coups.

The Janowitz school[11] argues that there are certain characteristics inherent in the nature of modern military organizations which dispose the military to intervene in politics. The army is conceived as an 'ideal type' characterized by certain organizational features. This school argues that African armies (to narrow down the focus) as an outgrowth of the European colonial armies and with their officer corps trained by ex-colonial powers are, *ipso facto*, modern institutions. The officers, they argue, while in training have imbibed certain qualities such as a puritanical ethic, professionalism, dedication, nationalistic ethos and an ingroup cohesion which will make them act in unity and decisively in the execution of military or political functions. The skills acquired in training coupled with a high sense of national identity, managerial ability as well as the fact that the military is recruited from the middle and lower middle classes all go to explain the unity, strength and decisiveness of the military in the emerging states. In addition to the above, the fact that the training of the officer corps of the military takes place abroad, the equipment of the armies with modern weapons and the organizational discipline of the military makes it the most modern sector of society which creates a 'competence gap' between the military and other sectors of the society. This technical and administrative superiority enables the military to abhor political corruption and inefficiency, therefore when the politicians fail to perform well, the military intervenes to correct the problems.

The position of the Janowitz school is unhistorical and can be criticized on several methodological and conceptual grounds. The nature of military intervention in the African continent as well as the performance of the military in office have disproved every idea this school has advanced in its attempt to explain military intervention. The analysis of the military and its role in society is undertaken without regard to the social environment in which the military is located, the history of the military and the role and location of the specific social formation in the international division of labour. Moreover, the Janowitz school appears to have been heavily influenced by the structural organization and contemporary role of the military in advanced capitalist societies. It is not valid to claim that there is cohesion or unity among African armies, or else how do we explain the various coups and counter-coups? It is equally suspect to emphasize the technological and administrative superiority of the army over the civil service because it is false. The idea that the army is nationalistic, less prone to corruption and possesses managerial ability cannot be supported by empirical facts.

A look at the historical origin of African armies will show that they were not recruited from the so-called middle or lower middle classes. In fact, under colonialism careers in the military were generally looked down upon and it never attracted the best talent in the society even after political independence. The best talents were in the public service and private sector. The military in Africa was never composed of educated men to such an extent that they monopolized administrative or managerial abilities. In fact, as case after case has shown, the military has had to rely on the civil servants to run the state. The varying cyltural backgrounds from which they are drawn coupled with the fact that postcolonial regimes trained their soldiers in a vast array of countries — capitalist and communist — meant that the military lacked common myths, symbols, comprehension of their role in society and the relationship between the military and other social classes. To argue that at independence the military was the only modern sector is also false considering the fact that when the colonial powers effected a political transfer of authority, the new states had adopted state assemblies, established universities and research centres, created civil services, police forces, courts, political parties and adopted new constitutions. Finally, if we are to accept the idea of cohesion and organizational effectiveness of the military as derivative of the training and exposure to foreign influences as valid, the Janowitz school must explain why all advanced capitalist states are not under military rule considering the fact that these qualities are more visible and better entrenched in these societies. The Janowitz school would therefore appear to have abstracted the military from the mode of production, the relations of production and in fact, the whole history of the specific societies and imposed it on the dynamics which in reality are products of the domination of these societies by metropolitan capital. This domination which limits the accumulative capacities of indigenous classes creates a condition where the state is unable to meet the demands of other social classes. The resultant competition for the scarce resources coupled with the inability of the dominant classes to create and impose a hegemony on the social formation lead to instability and conflict and the military can intervene for either of the three reasons already advanced.

A second school of thought which we shall call the Huntington school emphasizes the nature of society in general in an attempt to explain military coups and intervention in politics.[12] According to Samuel Decalo, this school stresses the

> societal and structural weaknesses — institutional fragility, systemic flaws and low levels of political culture — which act as a sort of magnet to pull the armed forces into the power and legitimacy vacuum.[13]

Samuel Huntington, a powerful proponent of this position has argued that:

> the most important causes of military intervention in politics are not military but political and reflect not the social and organisational characteristics of the military establishment but the political and institutional structure of society.[14]

The bottom line of the argument of this school is therefore that political institutions as instruments for mediating societal conflicts or resolving societal contradictions are weak and ineffective. This ineffectiveness allows other social forces to begin to make crucial demands which the imported institutions and corrupt politicians cannot satisfy. In such a situation of institutional fragility and inability to operate society effectively, the only institution capable of saving the country and resolving the contradictions because of its modernity is the army.

An extension of this position is that because of the absence of a legitimate and effective political institution(s), social forces confront each other with little restraint. The army which has been standing by as in the praetorian state because of its 'prestige, responsibility and the material resources'[15] moves in to restore order. Thus military intervention is only part of a general syndrome in societies where the contradictions in the objective demands of social groups are unresolvable by political institutions inherited from the colonial experience.

The arguments of the Huntington school are certainly an improvement on the ideas advanced by the Janowitz school in terms of recognizing the activities of the army as an aspect of the structure and contradictions of society. However, it is still defective as an explanation of the dynamics that prompt military intervention in politics, especially in Africa. In the first place, there appears to be a tautological problem in that society is praetorian because political institutions are ineffective and political institutions are ineffective because society is praetorian. In the words of Huntington:

> praetorian societies . . .are caught in a vicious circle. In its simpler forms the praetorian society lacks community and this obstructs development of political institutions. In its more complicated forms, the lack of effective political institutions obstructs the development of community.[16]

In addition to this problem of tautology, the Huntington school appears to neglect the fact that political institutions — their nature, efficiency, composition, size, function and so on — are determined by more fundamental structures and processes. In short, the nature of political institutions is conditioned by the mode of production and the use to which societal institutions are put cannot be divorced from the accumulative *base* of the dominant social classes and the class struggle in society. Hence, the gap between rich and poor, corruption in high places, rural-urban migration, unemployment and underemployment, the erosion of institutional legitimacy, low level of social integration, minimal or absence of political participation and the absence of a strong and dynamic bourgeoisie cannot be brushed aside as the Huntington school attempts to do.

The notion that the military in Africa is a modern elite capable of leading the societies and that the problems of the African continent are such that only militarism can resolve them appears to be well entrenched in the thoughts of this school. La Palombara who subscribes to the analysis of this school has asserted that 'in many of the new states what development does occur will be managed by the military bureaucracy'.[17] This assertion fails to explain how and with what resources the military is expected to carry out this development. If the problems of underdevelopment are not resolved in class terms by the military, there is no way they can be expected to escape the contradictions between social classes in the struggle to control the state and therefore preside over the allocation of resources. Samuel Decalo provides an accurate critique of this school when he argues that:

> It is both simplistic and empirically erroneous to relegate coups in Africa to the status of a dependent variable, a function of the political weaknesses and structural fragility of African states and the failings of African civilian elites.[18]

Thus once again we are left with the explanation of military intervention in either of the three conditions identified at the end of the second section of this chapter.

Other than the Janowitz school and the Huntington school there are other specific motives often identified or emphasized by various commentators which can (or cannot) be fitted into the two major schools. Eric Nordlinger for instance asserts that 'the protection of corporate interests is decidedly the most important interventionist motive . . .'.[19] This includes issues of promotion, wages, over-extension of functions, politicization, and political penetration, budgetary strangulation, demobilization, supplies, military autonomy, dismissals and so on. Taken as they are, these are very valid sources of discontent and capable of motivating a coup. But they must all be explained and comprehended within the political economy or particular social formations for them to be of any analytical use. It is only in this way that we can explain why similar situations, e.g. budgetary strangulation and over-extension of services, do not cause military coups in the developed social formations.

Samuel Decalo emphasizes a host of issues which include 'corporate, ethnic and personal grievances'. In fact, he states explicitly that:

> detailed examination of motivations for coups reveals that the main weakness of attempts to explain them by pinpointing major areas of systemic stress is that insufficient weight is placed on the personal motives of ambitious or discontented officers who have a great deal of freedom and scope for action in fragmented, unstructured and unstable political systems.[20]

The problem with Decalo's position is that he fails to explain why the political systems are 'fragmented, unstructured and unstable'. The failure to do this diverts the analysis into areas of personal motivations and ambitions without explaining the fact that such motivations are rooted in the material foundations of society. As Eze Ogueri II has put it.

> People who are satisfied with a political system have no reason to stage a coup on the contrary it is people who are so unhappy and dissatisfied as to wish to make the supreme sacrifice in order to save the nation and its people.[21]

Even then, we cannot divorce the sources of unhappiness and dissatisfaction from the nature of socio-economic and political arrangements within a specific social formation. Professor C.E. Welch, writing on Ghana, for instance, points to the 'combination of widespread economic malaise with intra-military grievances'[22] which hastened military intervention. Ruth First contends that in the same instance, it was the private army of Nkrumah 'which more than any other single grievance, ignited the military into coup d'etat action'[23] while Bob Fitch and Mary Oppenheimer regard military intervention as a direct manifestation of an international neo-colonialist strategy. This position is supported by Leo Huberman and Paul Sweezy in their foreword to the book.[24]

These attempts do not go any further than the ones advanced by the other two schools of thought already discussed. Locating the problems of military intervention or the motives for military intervention at the international level neglects the internal contradictions which enable international conspiracies to succeed. To this end, such explanations cannot highlight the reasons why such conspiracies have succeeded in some social formations more than five times while they have failed in others.

The inadequacy of the explanations advanced thus far demands that we return to the Marxist notion of historical materialism for a more comprehensive and dynamic understanding of the causes of military coups in underdeveloped social formations. Historical materialism asserts that legal relations, forms of state, social consciousness, power relations and so on can be comprehended not in isolation but by tracing them to their roots in the material conditions of life i.e. to the system of material production in society. Historical materialism also asserts that in all existing societies, the process of production, exchange and consumption determines the social and class structure as well as their specific juridical, political and ideological forms. Finally, it asserts that 'the history of all hitherto existing society is the history of class struggles'.[25]

To comprehend the basis of political instability, dependent accumulation and military intervention in Africa, therefore, we must begin the analysis from the period when the continent was incorporated into the world capitalist system, the restructuring of the political economy of the continent to meet the needs of the metropole, the arrest of the natural process of state formation, the creation of 'alien' social structures, institutions and the introduction of new relations of production. It is also important to note the undeveloped social classes as well as the partial transformation of the precapitalist mode of production, the grouping of different ethnic groups into single units without regard to cultural and historical differences and the structuring of the economy into one-crop exporters. In the light of these transformations and developments, political independence in Africa witnessed the inheritance of a very fluid state of affairs – a weak state, institutions with low legitimacy, absence of an autonomous dynamic for growth and development and therefore the inability to meet the promises of the nationalist period or the demands generated by the euphoria of self-rule. Political instability resulting in military intervention in this period must therefore be seen as manifestations of inherent contradictions in the struggle by dominant 'power elites' to consolidate their position, put down challenges to their power and expand their accumulative base.

Part of the struggle within the ranks of this dominant bourgeois class arises from the desire to emerge as a strong national bourgeoisie and the struggle to create a strong state from the heterogeneous superstructure left behind after colonialism. But in a society where more than two modes of production co-exist, where foreign capital is fully entrenched, where no strong state exists to resolve the contradictions between social classes and where no dominant ideology exists, military intervention can be regarded as inevitable – inevitable to the extent that the monopolization of the tanks, guns, bombs and bullets by the soldiers puts them ahead in the race and concretizes their bid for power among other social classes. It is only this fact that enables it practically to 'hijack' the struggles by trade unionists, students, peasants and other oppressed groups for political power in the society.

The Nigerian experience validates our argument so far. When self-government was granted to the regions in 1952, the geo-political entity called Nigeria operated as three separate countries – the East, West and North. The regional centres even at independence were more powerful than the federal centre; in fact, the top political figures were regionally and ethnically based. The struggle to accumulate, consolidate and expand the acquired spheres of influence gradually generated a state of insecurity and confusion in the country. The situation is very well put by Roger Murray thus:

> Most of the post-colonial successor regimes have been unable to stabilise themselves morally or institutionally. They have on the contrary displayed a fragility, incompetence, lack of authority, and corruption which rendered their function as political holding companies, companies for foreign capital, a good deal less effective than might have been wished.[26]

In Nigeria, politics became a zero-sum game, a kind of primitive accumulation was introduced and the competition within the ranks of the dominant classes assumed proportions which the weak state structure inherited at independence could not support. It is essential to point out that the struggle at this period related more to the efforts by the regional 'power elites' to carve out for themselves economic and political spheres of influence than with an attempt to challenge the dominant role of foreign capital. In the process, ethnic and religious differences were manipulated or where they did not exist, the differences were artificially generated and magnified. The institutionalized means for overcoming or mediating the strains that emerged from this situation were inadequate and, as Billy Dudley noted, 'so inadequate were these means that stress and strain had led by November 1965, to conditions best described as near anarchy'.[27] In addition to this institutional problem, the military had been heavily politicized especially by the competition between the Prime Minister and the President to control the army. Rumours about the intentions of particular ethnically based political parties to use the army against other ethnic groups were rampant in the country and especially within the army. The issue of corruption was an open one, bribes were given and received in the open, political offices were being sold, ministers were heard to boast in public about the fat size of their foreign bank accounts. In the midst of mass poverty, illiteracy, unemployment and hunger, they rode in long luxurious American cars protected by thugs. Elections were rigged especially in the Western Region in 1965, intra-party conflicts assumed proportions leading to disarray in the ranks of the regional bourgeois classes, and the trial, conviction and imprisonment of the petty-bourgeois leader of the Action Group did not help matters.

Given the unsteady state of affairs, the wanton destructions of lives and property by the agents of the politicians and political parties, the inability to keep public services functioning, the indiscriminate use of state power by politicians and the free use of force on civilian populations by the police, it became very clear that the politicians did not have any hegemonic influence left, that they were incapable of mediating the contradictions within their ranks, the contradictions between them and other social classes and finally that they were incapable of creating a suitable climate for capital accumulation by foreign capital and internal dominant classes. To drive home this point, the workers staged numerous strike actions, working to rule, demonstrations and riots; the market women and students joined and so did the peasants who became very insecure as the political thugs ravaged the countryside.

It was at this point that the Nigerian army 'hijacked' the struggles of the workers against the corrupt and ineffective civilian regime in January 1966. The army was able to do this not because it was more modern, educated or sophisticated but because it controlled the means of violence. Thus when the first coup led by Major Chukwuma Kaduna Nzeogwu took place it was expected.

No one doubts Nzeogwu's sincerity, though he did not stay in power long enough to put his ideas into practice and unfortunately he is not alive today to expand on the ideas with which he planned the coup along with his associates.[28] However, in his broadcast statement he declared:

> Our enemies are the political profiteers, swindlers, the men in high and low places who seek bribes and demand ten percent, those that seek to keep the country divided permanently so that they can remain in

> office as ministers and V.I.P's of waste, the tribalists, the nepotists
> . . . we promise that you will no more be ashamed to say you are a
> Nigerian.[29]

In an interview, Nzeogwu also declared that

> we had a short list of people who were either undesirable for the future
> progress of the country or, by their position at that time, had to be
> sacrificed for peace and stability.[30]

He called the coup a 'revolution' and stated that it was carried out in the
name of 'Nigerianism', and that they had wanted to 'gun down all the big
wigs'.[31]

We think this is a classic instance when the military intervenes in politics
to protect itself and its own interests using populist slogans and efforts to
buy its way into power by taking actions in the name of the nation. In the
first place 'Nigerianism' is no ideology though it could buy a regime some
breathing-space. Secondly, Nzeogwu came to power without any clear-cut
programme that would ensure that other 'big wigs' did not or would not
replace the ones they had planned 'to gun down'. By July 1966, the rightist
forces within the Nigerian army had taken full control and put an end to
Nzeogwu's disturbing populist rhetoric.

Even under the military, the inherent contradictions in the peripheral
capitalist social formation remained. The state did not become stronger,
irrespective of the Decrees passed by the military and attempts to reconcile
the warring factions of the Nigerian bourgeoisie. The unstable state of affairs
resulted in the civil war which lasted until 1970.[32] It is interesting to note
that the civil war did not solve the problems of the Nigerian bourgeoisie or
demonstrate the 'modernity', 'sophistication' and 'abhorrence of corruption'
among the military. By the time Yakubu Gowon was overthrown in another
military coup in 1975, the same reasons of tribalism, corruption, lack of
direction, wastefulness and arrogance which had been levelled against the
politicians in 1966, were made. It is however important that the same objective conditions under which the military intervened in 1966 existed in 1975
when a faction of the military intervened. The mismanagement of oil
revenues had created a spiralling inflationary condition, the wage review
undertaken worsened the situation; the government engaged in a series of
internal and external prestige projects; journalists, lecturers, students, trade
unionists were detained or molested by the soldiers; the police used its
emergency powers indiscriminately; corruption reached the pre-1966
level; the government lacked a rural development programme, a factor which
increased rural-urban migration; and with the oil boom the state initiated a
dependent food policy. In addition, bureaucratic inefficiency, port con-
gestion, and institutional decay reached their highest points in the nation's
history.

The response of the workers, peasants and students, despite the emergency powers of the police, the numerous decrees of the army and the ban on industrial action by workers, followed the pre-1966 pattern. Demonstrations, riots, strike actions and other forms of protest took place virtually every day. It became clear to the faction of the military that intervened that the Gowon administration had lost its legitimacy and power. The world-view which it represented had broken down completely and the workers and peasants through formal and informal alliances were beginning to constitute an alternative power bloc which had to be nipped in the bud. This galvanized the military into action. Brigadier Murtala Mohammed who emerged as the leader of the coup (he was also involved in the coup of July 1966), justified the coup by declaring that:

> ... the affairs of state, hitherto a collective responsibility became characterised by lack of consultation, indecision, indiscipline and benign neglect.[33]

Other reasons advanced by the new Mohammed regime included the failure of Yakubu Gowon to remove the state governors from office as he had promised to do, the widespread allegations of graft, misuse of public funds, complaints of ostentatious living, flagrant abuse of office and deprivation of people's rights and property, perversion of time-honoured procedures and norms, desecration of traditional institutions, the humiliation of highly respected traditional rulers and so on.[34] These allegations were all very true. In fact, by the time Yakubu Gowon was overthrown, he had lost the support of virtually every class in the society. The politicians had withdrawn support because he reneged on his promise to return the country to civilian rule in 1976. The military governors, realising that they still had some time to stay in office, began to loot the public treasury as fast as possible and this led to the emergence of anti-corruption crusaders all over the country, while students, market women and peasants resented the limited attention paid to their problems and complaints.

Mohammed was assassinated by Bukar Dimka who led an unsuccessful coup in 1976. Dimka accused the Mohammed regime of going communist even when the regime had made no structural changes in the relations of production and accumulation and had not taken any step to redefine the role and location of Nigeria in the international division of labour. Olusegun Obasanjo who came to power following the assassination of Mohammed virtually returned the country to the Gowon era but managed to prevent other coups until the new civilian regime came to office in 1979.

At this stage it is perhaps essential to examine the point raised by Bob Fitch and Mary Oppenheimer on imperialist conspiracy as a cause of military intervention in Africa.[35] We have already argued that the two writers must be able to explain why imperialist conspiracies succeed in some social formations and fail in others. In addition, the ability of imperialism to manipulate internal social classes and the officer corps of the army in particular must be located in the integration and role of the social formation in the world economy, a role which is essentially reflective of the internal class configuration, production and accumulation patterns and the content and direction of class struggles.

In the Nigerian situation, it is difficult to ascertain the direct role of Western powers in the various coups beyond the level of their domination and exploitation of the economy as a fundamental factor responsible for the continued underdevelopment of the economy and the continued reproduction of social contradictions and struggles. However, the role of the British High Commissioner and American Ambassador in providing advice to Yakubu Gowon after the July 1966 coup and their efforts to ensure that Murtala Mohammed did not become head of state because of his secessionist ideas are known.[36] The unresolved nature of the contract between Buka, Suka Dimka and the British High Commission following the assassination of Mohammed in 1976 has continued to intrigue analysts. The attitude of the British government to the initial overthrow of Gowon and the consequent assassination of Mohammed who was accused of 'going communist' have convinced a lot of Nigerians that Britain was interested in assisting Gowon to regain power. But the situation in Nigeria prior to each coup (except the unsuccessful coup of 1976) was such that no outside power was required to encourage a well armed group to seize political power. As Murray has aptly put it:

> The fragility of authority in contemporary tropical Africa, is, of course, related to the fundamental but unbalanced transformations of the economy and society catalysed by administratively supported capitalism. Partial and unfavourable integration into the world market system has detonated a radical restructuring of society and the emergence of contradictions which in most of Africa are only now beginning to crystallize demographic upsurge, imbalance between education and employment opportunities, rural depopulation, widening income differentials and social fissures, violation of cultural values etc.[37]

When the military decided to retire 'voluntarily' from active politics in October 1979, it handed power to a conservative fraction of the bourgeoisie just as the colonial powers had done in 1960. The military had assumed that a new constitution, a new anthem and pledge, new states and local governments, indigenization decrees defining spheres of interest and influence, etc., would guarantee stability and accumulation. But these assumptions had not addressed in any manner the systemic contradictions which have prompted political disintegration and crisis in the past. The Shagari administration was unable, in spite of the human and material resources available to it, to mediate class contradictions and impose a viable hegemony on society. Like the military and civilian governments, the Shagari administration was easily susceptible to another coup d'etat.

It is interesting, however, to note that the December 1983 coup which marked the end of Nigeria's second experiment with bourgeois democracy, took place at a time of intense class struggles and active challenges to the state. The high level of public indignation against the state, arising from the contradictions of Nigeria's peripheral capitalism, posed a major threat to both short- and long-term interests of the bourgeoisie. Given the consequences of unmet basic human needs and neglect, non-bourgeois forces were beginning to form alliances, constituting a counter-hegemony against the state and bourgeoisie. Strikes, demonstrations and violent resistence were only overt indicators of this challenge. Thus, once again, the struggles of workers and peasants was practically 'hijacked' by a fraction of the armed forces with interests congruent to those of the custodians of state power in the Second Republic. The intervention was carried out in order to stabilize the system which was obviously disintegrating, thus creating room for the emergence of alternative 'blocs' of power. The intervention, by the bourgeois fraction of the armed forces (generals, brigadiers and colonels), also checked (even if temporarily) the political hopes of radical (even if nationalist) fractions within its ranks (majors, captains and other lower ranks). The class position of the Buhari regime is evidenced in the fact that its solutions to the numerous problems of the Nigerian formation have not shifted significantly from those it inherited from the Shagari administration.

Finally, from the actions of the military in office, it is evident that intervention took place when the unstable world-view of the dominant social classes (military or civilian) was subjected to fundamental and persistent challenges from below. Thus, the interventions can be interpreted as an aspect of the ongoing class struggles in Nigeria. The coups were planned and executed by the military elite — majors, colonels, generals, brigadiers and so on, who in terms of status, income and office, are part of the Nigerian bourgeois class. On coming to power they did not alter the social relations of production and accumulation and they did not attempt in any serious way to wage a fundamental struggle against foreign domination and imperialism. The military, on the contrary, proceeded to rationalize the participation of foreign capital in the economy by defining spheres of interest, through the indigenization decrees to take just one example, and through numerous partnerships with foreign capital in the establishment of industries, breweries, banks and other facilities. The army was converted into an avenue for rapid capital accumulation just as the civilians had done with politics in the pre-military period. Efforts were also made to initiate and impose an alternative world-view on the society, a world-view which, using Nigerian symbols like a new political arrangement, a new constitution and local government structure, a so-called new foreign policy,[38] the introduction of a National Youth Service Corps and so on, was in reality a reflection of the world-view of the international bourgeoisie which still dominated the economy.[39]

Ultimately, the point must be made that military organizations are part of the political forms of a society. Each stage of social progress within societies has therefore produced military organizations that fundamentally reflect its needs, ideas, class configuration and struggles and culture. The nature and structure of the military and the points of intersection between the interests of the military and those of factions or fractions of the dominant class is also dependent on the mode of production and accumulation. These points of intersection of interests ultimately determine and condition the role the military ascribes to itself, the specific interests it is expected to play in society and the frequency with which it intervenes in politics.

Military intervention in Nigeria has been part of the struggles to establish a strong bourgeois state. Thirteen years of military rule certainly led to the emergence of a stronger centre (this was greatly aided by the civil war and the oil boom which followed) and a more organized techno-comprador class. The bottom line is that the domination of the economy by foreign capital has never been challenged.[40] What the military regimes have done in Nigeria include the attempts to establish Nigeria in the West African sub-region as a sub-imperial power, initiate a dependent food policy, create conditions for the near-total dependence on oil revenues and restructure the labour movement with the hope of imposing a pro-establishment leadership on it. Finally, there is no reason not to expect more military coups in Nigeria given the extent to which the Nigerian state has been integrated into the world capitalist system. The net impact of this integration has been the internal reproduction of the crisis of capitalism at the centre of world accumulation. The situation has not been helped by the near-total dependence on the oil sector which is dominated internally by the international oil majors. This dependence on oil revenue has meant the generation of major contradictions in the economy whenever the price of oil fluctuates at the world level. In addition, the pattern of state expenditure, the massive level of corruption, the gross inefficiency of the civil service and parastatals, the frequent resort to violence and the arrogance of power which followed the oil boom, have all characterized politics and political competition in contemporary Nigeria.

From our discussion thus far we have demonstrated that the pattern of production and accumulation, the level of utilization of production forces and the nature of society are direct precipitates of the nature of the state, dominant classes and the direction and intensity of class struggles. Distorted and disarticulated formations can hardly expect any level of serious stability. In societies where a level of 'stability' is maintained or in which coups have not taken place, such as in the Ivory Coast, Sierra Leone and Zambia, the leaders have maintained themselves in power in four ways: (1) systematic physical elimination of opposition forces and the manipulation of the so-called existing 'democratic' processes, (2) the establishment of a vast administrative system made up of friends, in-laws, relations and other close aides in order to ensure a form of loyalty, (3) heavy expenditure on security and defence and the domestication of the leadership cadre of the armed forces through bribery, marriage bonds and blackmail and (4) the forging of strong alliances with imperialist powers who, while exploiting the country, provide spies, agents, and also maintain a direct or indirect military presence. Nonetheless, these regimes have only forcibly *imposed* their domination and 'hegemony' on their societies and have therefore not been free from overt and covert challenges.

Other than the instability of the state as arising from the lack of hegemony in 'civil society', and the unproductive nature of the bourgeoisie as arising from its domination by foreign capital, political stability and development *cannot* (and has indeed never) taken place in peripheral formations in so far as they remain tied to the capitalist metropoles.

At the internal level, the need to·*overthrow* and completely restructure the existing modes and relations of production, revamp and de-colonize the educational system, establish popular nd democratic institutions and eliminate transnational influences on the pattern of decision-making must be paramount if *development* as against mere *growth* is to take place. In so far as growth continues to be the focus of planning, a process which ensures that the rich and their foreign allies continue to accumulate at the expense of the poor majority, all talk about stability, development, progress and initiative would remain rhetorical. Planning *must* address the needs of the majority. The masses of workers, peasants, market women and students *must* be involved in the initiation and implementation of plans in order to make them accept the plans and policies as well as be committed to their success. The dissipation of energy, wastage of public funds in the formation and operation of political parties by a few bourgeois elements who then try to 'sell' the party to the public cannot promote stability. Where the system can afford the luxury of a multi-party system, the people *must* determine the programmes, select their own candidates and have constitutional rights to remove representatives who fail to perform. No country can expect stability and development by flirting with the capitalist ideology and seek to rationalize the brutality of the system with some public programmes. As history affords us of no example of a peripheral capitalist society that has become *capitalist*,[41] the only alternative is a socialist option which is dedicated to independence from imperialism and all its institutions and agents and committed to democracy, self-reliance and progress. Brazil, Mexico, South Korea and other so-called Newly Industrializing Countries (NIC) afford us nothing admirable to aspire towards. The social, economic and psychological costs of their dependent development has promoted fascism, brutalization of rural peoples and workers, poverty, indebtedness and fully mortgaged their future to the dictates and needs of Western imperialist countries. The so-called cry in Nigeria that the Japanese example has to be copied is often hinged on ignorance and attempts to divert attention. After the 1868 Meiji Restoration in Japan, a strong and local *productive* (as against a distributive) bourgeois class, supported by a strong state, emerged to promote internal investment and accumulation. The state also regulated the influence of transnational forces on the Japanese economy. In addition, it is essential to note that the Japanese formation was never colonized, distorted and underdeveloped. Any comparison with the decadent, ostentatious, lazy and complacent mentality and nature of the Nigerian bourgeoisie today will show that it represents the situation in Latin America in the early periods and its corollary in Japan cannot be found.

It is of course obvious that the current custodians of state power in

Nigeria are not predisposed to a socialist option. In fact they are likely to resist such a move. The constant massacre of protesting students, workers, farmers, the draconian labour laws and the rapid expansion of security agencies even in peace time are pointers in this direction. This is the more reason why Nigerian social science must become more critical and relevant. Labour must be encouraged to forge alliances with student and peasant organizations. The linkages outside specific organizations already exist. These alliances must begin to develop critical political programmes while organizing, mobilizing and acting along class lines. The organizations themselves must evolve democratic structures. Progressive intellectuals and professionals must wage a *war* against their status-quo oriented colleagues and expose the ideological content of proverbs, songs, the news media, propaganda as well as demystify the 'intellectual gurus' of the crisis-ridden capitalist system in contemporary Nigeria.

While the strategies and tactics of a socialist Nigeria cannot be provided here as we believe that this *must* be done by the people in their separate and collective organizations, we remain convinced that certain developments can be projected for Nigeria's future. More military coups are likely to be possible but would be bloodier. In other words, the last 'bloodless' coup Nigeria would experience in its history is likely to be the last one led by General Buhari. The crisis of the economy and society would continue to deepen as the government continues to pursue the manifestations of more structural contradictions. These crises would deepen the content and direction of class struggles, forcing the state to repress workers, popular groups and institutions. This reaction would force non-bourgeois forces to organize politically and develop critical overt and covert means of resistance and survival. The clash of forces is likely to kindle a serious interest in Nigeria from the Western powers. Given Nigeria's influence (not power) in Africa, particularly in West Africa, its resources, population and potentials, a socialist Nigeria is definitely a threat to imperialist exploitation of the continent. This is why progressive forces must and cannot underestimate the possible level of support from the West. However, such support would mean the need for a counter-source of support and this could internationalize the nature of the struggle for a democratic Nigeria. If we are to learn anything from Cuba, Angola, Mozambique, Iran, Guinea-Bissau, Nicaragua, Libya, Ethiopia, Vietnam and other parts of the world where the forces of Western capitalist domination and exploitation have suffered defeats, there is little reason to expect the Nigerian scenario to differ.

Finally, we recognize that these are long-term projections. We also recognize the possibility of delays, diversions and the numerous obstacles to organization, consciousness, mobilization and struggle. However, over two decades of so-called self-rule have made very little difference in the lives of Nigerians, and as most people would say in reaction to deepening crisis and poverty: 'who eats democracy?', 'we want food, jobs and shelter'. The future of Nigeria, its stability and development, would lie in the ability to provide these within a *democratic*, equitable, self-reliant and independent system.

Notes

1. Gwyn Williams, 'The Concept of "Egemonia" in the Thought of Antonio Gramsci', *Journal of the History of Ideas*, 21, 1960, p. 587.

2. See Michela von Freyhold, 'The Post-Colonial State and its Tanzanian Version', *Review of African Political Economy*, 8, January–April 1977; John Saul, 'The State in Post-Colonial Societies: Tanzania', *Socialist Register 1974* (London: Merlin Press, 1974); Bharat Patanker and Gail Omvedt, 'The Bourgeois State in Post-Colonial Formations', *The Insurgent Sociologist*, IX, 4, Spring 1980; Hamza Alavi, 'The State in Post-colonial Societies: Pakistan and Bangladesh', *New Left Review*, 74, July–August 1972; Colin Leys, 'The Overdeveloped Post-colonial State: A Re-evaluation', *Review of African Political Economy*, 5, January–April 1976; and W. Ziemann and M. Langendorfer, 'The State in Peripheral Capitalist Societies', *The Socialist Register, 1977* (London: Merlin Press, 1977).

3. Hamza Alavi, op. cit., p. 59.

4. Antonio Gramsci, *Prison Notebooks* (New York: International Publishers, 1980), p. 261.

5. V.I. Lenin, *State and Revolution* in his *Collected Works* (Moscow: Progress Publishers, 1971), p. 267.

6. P.U. Okeke, 'Background to the Problems of Nigerian Education', in Okechukwu Ikejiane (ed.), *Education in Nigeria* (New York: Praeger, 1965), p. 10.

7. Gavin Williams, 'Nigeria: A Political Economy' in Gavin Williams (ed.), *Nigeria: Economy and Society* (London: Rex Collings, 1976), p. 28.

8. Segun Osoba, 'The Nigerian Power Elite, 1952–65' in Peter Waterman and Peter Gutkind (eds.), *African Social Studies: A Radical Reader* (New York and London: Monthly Review Press, 1977), p. 369.

9. Senator Nwafor Orizu cited in ibid., p. 374.

10. Gavin Williams, 'Class Relations in a Neo-Colony: The Case of Nigeria', in Peter Waterman and Peter Gutkind (eds.), op. cit., p. 284.

11. See Morris Janowitz, *Military Institutions and Coercion in the Developing Nations* (Expanded Edition of *The Military in the Political Development of New Nations*, (Chicago: University of Chicago Press, 1977) and John J. Johnson (ed.), *The Role of the Military in Underdeveloped Societies* (Princeton: Princeton University Press, 1962).

12. See Samuel P. Huntington, *The Soldier and the State* (Cambridge: Harvard University Press, 1967); S.E. Finer, *The Man on Horseback: The Role of the Military in Politics* (Harmondsworth: Penguin, 1975); Samuel P. Huntington, *Political Order in Changing Societies* (New Haven: Yale University Press, 1968); and E.W. Lefever, *Spear and Scepter* (Washington: Brookings Institute, 1970).

13. Samuel Decalo, *Coups and Army Rule in Africa: Studies in Military Style* (New Haven: Yale University Press, 1976), p. 7.

14. S. Huntington, *Political Order*, op. cit., p. 194.

15. Eric Nordlinger, *Soldiers in Politics: Military Coups and Governments* (Englewood Cliffs: Prentice Hall Inc., 1977), p. 3.

16. S. Huntington, *Political Order*, op. cit., p. 237.

17. Joseph La Palombara, *Bureaucracy and Political Development* (Princeton, N.J.: Princeton University Press, 1963), p. X.

18. Samuel Decalo, *Coups and Army Rule in Africa*, op. cit., p. 13.
19. E. Nordlinger, op. cit., p. 79.
20. S. Decalo, op. cit., p. 21.
21. Eze Ogueri II, 'Theories and Motives of Military Coups D'etat in Independent States', *Afrika Spectrum*, 3, 1973, p. 282.
22. C.E. Welch, 'Praetorianism in Commonwealth West Africa', *Journal of Modern African Studies*, 10, 2, 1972, p. 208.
23. Ruth First, *The Barrel of the Gun: Political Power in Africa and the Coup d'etat* (Harmondsworth: Penguin, 1979), p. 197.
24. Bob Fitch and Mary Oppenheimer, *Ghana: End of An Illusion* (New York: Monthly Review Press, 1966).
25. K. Marx and Frederick Engels, *The Communist Manifesto* (New York: Pocket Books, 1964), p. 57.
26. Roger Murray, 'Militarism in Africa', *New Left Review*, 38, July-August 1966), p. 43.
27. Billy Dudley, *Instability and Political Order: Politics and Crisis in Nigeria* (Ibadan: Ibadan University Press, 1973), p. 100.
28. Some of the officers who participated in the January 1966 coup have just begun to provide the public with their versions of how the coup was planned, why it was planned and why it failed. See for example, Adewale Adegboyega, *Why We Struck: The Story of the first Nigerian Coup* (Ibadan: Evans Brothers Nigeria Limited, 1981) and Ben Gbulie, *Nigeria's Five Majors: Coup d'etat of 15th January 1966 First Inside Account* (Onitsha: Africana Educational Publishers, 1981).
29. Cited in John St. Jorre, *The Nigerian Civil War* (London: Hodder and Stoughton, 1972), p. 38. See also A.H.M. Kirk-Greene, *Crisis and Conflict in Nigeria* (Oxford: Oxford University Press, 1971), p. 71.
30. Cited in Billy Dudley, op. cit., p. 103.
31. Ibid., p. 107.
32. Denis Brutus has argued that to 'explain the Nigerian conflict in terms of tribal rivalries and antagonisms is one level of superficiality, but to say as Wole Soyinka says that it was more than that, it was the collapse of humanity, of human beings behaving in some atavistic fashion, seems to be merely another level of superficiality. Any failure to take into account the rivalries, the economic rivalries of multinational corporations, of the oil interests, of Western powers causes one to end up with superficial interpretations', 'Cultural Liberation and the African Revolution', in Immanuel Wallerstein (ed.), *World Inequality* (Montreal: Black Rose Books, 1975), p. 155.
33. General Murtala Mohammed, *Daily.Times*, 31 July 1975.
34. Ibid.
35. Bob Fitch and Mary Oppenheimer, op. cit.
36. See John de St. Jorre, op. cit., pp. 71-72.
37. Roger Murray, 'Militarism in Africa', op. cit., p. 44.
38. See Julius O. Ihonvbere, 'Resource Availability and Foreign Policy Change: The Impact of Oil on Nigeria's Foreign Policy Since Independence', *Afrika Spectrum*, 1982 and his 'Foreign Policy of Dependent States: Oil and Nigerian Foreign Policy 1962-1982', *Indian Political Science Review*, January 1984. Other symbols adopted by the Nigerian state and bourgeoisie include a new national anthem and pledge to be sung/recited by school

children every day, selection of national heroes, and the introduction of national merit awards. The same governments rendered these symbols value-less by concentrating the awards on members of the bourgeois class many of whom had been publicly disgraced for corruption and abuse of office, and the frequent use of force to solve minor problems. Examples include the violent suppression of the Agbekoya Farmers revolt in 1969, the killing of students in 1978 (now almost an annual affair) and the massacre of farmers at Bakolori in 1980. For more on the class structure in Nigeria, the politics of idiosyncracy and accumulation, the class war on the Nigerian masses and the response or challenges to state power see Julius O. Ihonvbere, 'The Political Economy of the Rentier State: Oil and Class Struggles in Nigeria', paper at the 12th Annual Conference of the Canadian Association of African Studies, University of Toronto, May 1982.

39. See Bade Onimode, 'Imperialism and Multinational Corporations: A Case Study of Nigeria' in Aguibou Yansane (ed.), *Decolonisation and Dependency – Problems of Development in African Societies* (Greenwood Press, 1980) and his 'A Critique of Planning Concepts and Methodology in Nigeria', *Review of Black Political Economy*, 7, 3, Spring 1977. See also Claude Ake, *Revolutionary Pressures in Africa* (London: Zed Press, 1978); Ola Oni, 'A Critique of Development Planning in Nigeria', *Review of African Political Economy*, 4, November 1975; Ikenna Nzimiro, 'The Political and Social Implications of Multinational Corporations in Nigeria' in Carl Wid-strand (ed.), *Multinational Firms in Africa* (Uppsala, 1975) and Otonti Nduka, 'The Rationality of the Rich in Nigeria', in Peter Waterman and Peter Gutkind (eds.), *African Social Studies*, op. cit.

40. It is important not to overlook the linkages between the civilian power elite and the military officers before and after every coup d'etat. In the Nigerian case a careful analysis has revealed that in several instances, the two 'factions' (of the same class) had similar social backgrounds, belonged to the same open and secret club and had absorbed the same world-views. This explains, to some extent, why military intervention in Nigeria has always been on behalf of the ruling class. The military, because the coups are planned 'secretly' (some members of the ruling class have been known to have encouraged the officers), often come to power without any plan. This creates a heavy reliance on the bureaucracy, the super permanent secretaries, the intellectuals of the 'overthrown class' and foreign advisers usually the American or British Ambassadors and High Commissioners. The bottom line is that the class alliance between the military and the 'overthrown class' and the administrative weaknesses of the officers creates a situation where they come to rely on the very same individuals they had overthrown. The panels, boards, committees, commissions of inquiry and so on are often chaired or staffed by the very individuals who had been displaced.

41. What we have in mind here is the fact that *peripheral* capitalist economies are largely crisis-ridden and unproductive formations. They are suppliers of raw materials and markets to the *centre* of world capitalism. The hopes of bourgeois elements in the periphery that real capitalist develop-ment and accumulation will take place has so far not been validated with any historical example.

Appendix

Unlimited Liability Company

Chairman, wetin you dey find for home?
We tink say you still dey overseas
Ah, I forget, it's getting near the time
For a meeting of all the shareholders

Chairman, you sabi waka o
We look for you from Tokyo to New York
In Bulgaria, they say you just commot
Your executive jet pass us from Argentina

Chairman, dis meeting go hot o
Your Directors done chop all we money
While you dey shake hands with Kings and Presidents
Your business partners done shake the Treasury loose

Each time they sneeze, millions of naira go scatter
When they snore, the bank itself go shake
Mobilisation fee is the other of the day
The contractor collect, take we money and run away

My eye se wonder the other day for Yola
When your Directors meet for society wedding
Private jet and helicopter na de fashion
Mercedes na dash to their favourite singers

Forty aeroplanes, all private, fly in the guests·
Each Director and wife spray at least twenty thousand
When money finish at midnight they open the bank
For brand-new Naira to continue the lovely spray

> Chairman, palava dey o
> For dis meeting of all the shareholders
> While you de hobnob with Kings and Presidents
> Your Company Directors done labe tan
>
> You say you fit be Chairman
> You lobby to be Chairman
> You say you go try for me o
> You swear you go try for me o
> Make meself I tanda small
> Make I get small sugar for my tea
> Se mi jeje, se mi jeje etc. etc.

Chairman, dis Naira be like you
Both of you dey waka soyso tey
While you de toast Kings and Presidents
Common gari done become luxury

Chairman, no to say I vex
I be just a common shareholder
I never say I want butter for my bread
I fit to drink my tea without sugar

But Chairman, something dey worry me
Dis Naira, e still be Naira so?
De ting one Naira buy yesterday
Twenty Naira no fit buy am today.

I never tell you de story of London Airport
Where the Customs grab your company Director
Six million Naira dem find inside in briefcase
Crisp and new, straight from our Naira mint.

Your Excellency — they give am in proper title —
You be Mobile Bank, or Nigerian Mint in transit?
Your Director laugh, e laugh e nearly collapse
E say, White Boy, make you no waste my time.

For dis small portmanteau na in you dey open your mouth?
Ship containers, na others, na   dey take load cash
London or Frankfurt go give us foreign exchange
They love our Naira, so wetin be your concern?

When we done do a shopping according to our status
Minor luxuries like private jets
The same Naira, at double devaluation
Returns by containers to where it started from.

We're friends with the Bank of England and all of Europe
And the good old U.S. of America
Shareholder, take your time, you hear?
Why you dey shout so, come in and shut the door.
If na matter of butter dey worry you
I go fill your mouth with cake and jam

Shareholder, you no wan chop?
There is still room in the company caucus
Your cheeks go robust like we very own
Milk and honey and sugar for your tea

Abi you wan suffer for ever?
Abi you wan kuse for ever?
You no want your own to better?
You no wan ride Mercedes?
Come in then and shut your mouth
Make a put some sugar for your tea
       Se mi jeje se mi jeje etc. etc.

Chairman, e don spoil from the start
That time you chose your Legal Adviser
We tell you say na bribery'e sabbe
Still you give am de job on super-scale.

Another Director is a Wanted Man
He commit rape for Washington D.C.
He run come home, you give am bigger post
As Director of a chain of newspapers

Chairman, what of Iron and Steel
Wey you tell us big profit go commot?
Two point One billion na in you spend so far
E done vanish for inside Kainji damn

How many billion you spend to clear the bush
Where you say you wan grow food for chop
Soil erosion na in alone dey grow
Common farmer do better on in own

How many many I go talk o
How many many I go shout o
What of that Two point Eight billion
Wey you take play Hide and Seek o?
Make you take yourself commot
Unless you give me my share of Two point Eight

> Se mi jeje, se mi jeje etc. etc.
> Me too I want some gari
> Share-de-gari, share-de-gari
> Share-gari, Share-gari, Share-gari etc. etc.

Etike Revo Wetin?

Chorus:
I love my country I no go lie
Na inside am I go live and die
I know my country I no go lie
Na im and me go yap till I die

I love my country I no go lie
Na inside am I go live and die
When e turn me so, I twist am so
E push me, I push am, I no go go.

I wan begin with history
That war we fight in recent memory
When music wey come from barrel of gun
Was: We must keep the nation one
Me I tink I get cancer for me eye
I dey see double, dat's de reason why
When I look, na two I see
Make I explain, I tink you go gree.

Make you no worry, both country be friends
Even when they fight, they soon make amends
When one back dey itch, de other go scratch
One lay egg, de other go hatch.
Eggs na eggs but some are rotten
But make a tell you, some are golden
I tell you my country no be one
I mean, no to yesterday I born

One go proud, the other so meek
One go hide, the other go seek
One go slap, the other go turn cheek
And soon they are playing Hide and Seek.

They're lovely twins of whom I speak
Mr. Country Hide and his brother Seek.
One country hide two point eight billion
'E tell Country Seek, Brother, carry on
Seek from Turkey to China Sea
The more you look, the less you see

You tief one kobo dey put you for prison
You tief ten million, na patriotism
Den go give you chieftaincy and national honour
You tief even bigger, dem go say na rumour
Monkey dey work, baboon dey chop
Sweet pounded yam – some day e go stop!

One time we stack the groundnut so high
Like pyramid nearly reach the sky.
Palm oil de flow from here to London
Cassava, plantain, our fruits be champion.
Our cocoa compete with that of Ghana
Mouth dey water to look we banana.
Yam wey thick like wrestlers' thighs
Which rice get fame like Tapa rice?
But now to eat, na half my budget
Food dey cost like golden nugget
De rain wey fall from open skies
'E only float Presidential Rice.

> Brother Hide, where all dis food disappear
> My belle dey rumble, abi you no hear?
> Brother Seek, keep scratching in the city slums
> Me, I content with petrol drums.

The day dem bring Green Revolution
Country Seek tink say e get salvation
E give a shout, e tink at last
Green Revolution go end in fast.
Education is good for me and you
So let's give praise where praise is due
Green Revolution was most educative
And coincidentally most lucrative
Education alone cost one quarter the budget
To teach the farmer what he never forget
Posters left, and right, and centre
Green Revolution by Government Printer.

But that was nothing but chicken feed
A nation in need is my friend indeed
Summon the Chief Chemical Analyser
To spell out the magic of fertilizer
Country Seek, hear me, I no be miser
Millions dey hide for fertilizer.

One time each day na Regatta Day
A thousand ships in Lagos Bay
As if to say na naval display
By all the nations for Seamen's Day
But me, I tink na naval blockade
By angry nations for debts unpaid.
Country Seek, go look for foreign aid,
Dis no ceremonial parade

Our budget finish for demurrage fee
Cement de choke we mouth for sea.

The Russian astronauts flying in space
Radioed a message to their Moscow base
They said, we are flying over Nigeria
And we see high mountains in built-up area
Right in the middle of heavy traffic
Is this space madness, tell us quick!
These facts were fed to the Master Computer
Which soon analysed the mystery factor.
That ain't no mountain, the Computer said, snappish,
It's just a load of their national rubbish.

Bottomless pits na we favourite project
You fall inside, you done land erect.
You're made for life, no more worry
Play the game and you won't be sorry.
A bottomless pit is a mighty creation
In every corner of our lovely nation
Choose your project, give it a name
Construction, destruction, it's all the same.
Inside Kaduna, two bottomless pits
Smash some innocent lives to bits
Low-cost housing became mass graves
One man chops while the other grieves.
As for Abuja, billions dey roll
And vanish for ever in the Capital Hole.

In this our country all is free
To starve to death, you don't pay a fee.
The water tap is free to pour
Or take a vacation for a month or more.

Electricity supply na part-time vocation,
One day show then a month vacation
Meat grow maggots, fish dey smell
You leave your soup for frig e go swell
The doctor wey begin operation
Na candle light go finish in session
The mortuary beg, come take your body.
NEPA no dey spare your soul or body.
But one man's curse is another's blessing
Some day Country Seek go learn in lesson
While e dey cook by light of the moon
Country Hide done turn generator tycoon.

One morning time I wake for my bed
And the radio say, I sick for my head
No, make I talk true, de ting wey e mention
Na someting call etika revolution
Etika revo kini?

    Etika revolution.
Etika revo how much?
    Etika revolution
Make a take small snuff make a clear my head
E be like say I still asleep for my bed
Etika revo wetin?

    Etika revolution
Make a drink gari small make my stomach swell
When man belle flatee no fit hear well
Etika revo how?
    Etika revolution
Etika tiko wetin
    Etika revolution

Dis snuff never strong, my head never shack
Bring dat ogogoro before white turn black
Na tief carry load, na im call policeman
Na who ban imported? Na who break the ban?
Etika revo why?
    Etika revolution
Corner-corner revo wetin?
    Etika revolution
Me a go revo dem head o!
    Etika revolution
Etika chop-chop
    Etike, etike

Etika millionaire: Etike, Etike
Etika champagne: Etike, Etike
Etika Swiss Account: Etike Etike
Etika private Jet: Etike, Etike
Elokomita: Etike, Etike.

Dey wan rob church, so they call prayer-meeting
When all eyes close, dem do their ting
Dem say no licence, but who dey smuggle
Whose belle dey swell while we dey struggle
Na who loot de nation, na who dey shed
Crocodile tears – I beg, drop dead!
When they shoot poor farmers for Bakolori dam
Mr. Crocodile Tears, he don't give a damn
Country Seek my brother, leave corner-side
Don't let them take you for another ride:
Etika revo wetin? DROP DEAD!

Bibliography

Oral Sources

The success of this work owes very much to the assistance and co-operation of several peasants, workers, intellectuals, students and politicians. To all our informants in Lagos, Warri, Kaduna, Benin, Enugu, Ore, Port-Harcourt and other places, we are especially very grateful.

People were very willing to comment on virtually all activities of the Second Republic; their willingness was owed largely to their frustration and disappointment.

Government Publications

(Federal publications, Government Printer, Lagos, except where noted. Classified materials are not cited.)

Annual Budgets
The First National Development Plan, 1970-74.
The Second National Development Plan, 1975-80.
Guidelines For Local Government Reforms (Kaduna: Government Printer, 1976).
An Introduction to the New System of Local Government Council System in the Western State of Nigeria (Ibadan: Government Printer, 1971).
Report of the Interim Revenue Allocation Review Commission (Apapa: Nigerian National Press Ltd; 1969).
Report of the Technical Committee on Revenue Allocation (Lagos, December, 1978).
Report of the Constitution Drafting Committee. Containing the Draft Constitution, Vol. 1 (Lagos: Federal Ministry of Information, 1978).
Central Bank of Nigeria, *Annual Report and Statement of Accounts*, 1960-1983.
Central Bank of Nigeria, *Economic And Financial Review.*
Federal Office of Statistics, *Economic Indicators*
Federal Government Views on the Report on the Industrial Enterprises Panel, 1976
Report of the Public Service Review Commission, Main Report, 1974.
Recurrent and Capital Estimates of the Government of the Federal Republic of Nigeria, 1981.

Central Bank of Nigeria, *Monthly Reports.*

The Oil Rich Rivers State: Account of Mineral Exploitation and Production (Ministry of Information, Office of the Governor, Port-Harcourt, 1967).

Government Role in the Nigerian Oil Industry (Lagos: Federal Ministry of Information n.d.).

Report of the Judicial Commission of Inquiry into the shortage of Petroleum Products (Lagos, 1976).

Management Agreement on the First Nigerian Crude Oil Tanker (Lagos, 1976).

Federal Military Government Views on the Report of the Judicial Commission of Inquiry into the shortage of Petroleum Products (Lagos, 1976).

Agreement Between the Government of the Federal Republic of Nigeria and Shell-BP Petroleum Development Company Limited of Nigeria 12 May, 1971.

Report of the Fact Finding Mission on Petroleum Revenue and Miscellaneous Matters on the Petroleum Industry (Lagos, 1969).

Proceedings of the Tribunal of Inquiry into the Activities of the Trade Unions (Adebiyi Proceedings) 1976.

First Report of the Wages and Salaries Review Commission (The Adebo Report) (Lagos, 1970).

Report on the Reorganisation of the Dock Labour Industry in Nigerian Port (The Ayida Report) (Lagos, 1969).

Report of Grading Team on Grading Posts in the Public Services of the Federation of Nigeria, 1966.

The Federal Military Government's Views on the Report of the Tribunal of Inquiry into the Importation of Cement, 1976.

White Paper on the Second and Final Report of the Wages and Salaries Review Commission, 1970-71, 1971.

The Attack on Inflation; Government Views on the First Report of the Anti Inflation Task Force, 1975.

Federal Military Government's Views on the Investigation of Farms Owned by Mr. S. O. Ogbemudia and Alhaji Bako (Lagos, 1976).

Federal Military Government's Views on the Report of the Panel of Inquiry into the Purchase of Leyland Buses for FESTAC from British Leyland (Lagos, 1978).

Proceedings of the Foster-Sutton Tribunal of Inquiry. (2 Volumes, Lagos, 1957).

Nigeria's Principal Economic and Financial Indicators, 1970-77 (Central Bank of Nigeria, Lagos, 1978).

Nigeria Year Book – 1970-1978 (Federal Ministry of Information).

Articles

Aboyade, O. and Ayida, A., 'The War Economy in Perspective', *Nigerian Journal of Economic and Social Studies*, 13, 1971.

Aboyade, O., 'The Economy of Nigeria' in Robson, P. and Lury, D. (eds.), *The Economics of Africa* (London: Allen and Unwin, 1969).

Adekson, J., 'The Nigerian Military and Social Expenditure' in *Democracy in Nigeria: Past Present and Future*, proceedings of the 5th Annual Conference of the Nigerian Political Science Association held at Ife, 1978.
———— 'Machiavelli and the Military: The Prince and the Psychology of Empty Power' in *Planning Strategy For Nigeria in the Eighties* (NISER and Federal Ministry of Economic Development, 1980).
Adeogun, A., 'The Legal Framework of Industrial Relations in Nigeria', *Nigerian Law Journal*, 3, 1969.
Akindele, R.A., 'The Conduct of Nigeria's Foreign Relations', *International Problems*, 12, October 1978.
Alavi, H., 'The State in Post-colonial Societies: Pakistan and Bangladesh', *New Left Review*, 74, July–August 1972.
Aluko, S.A., 'Nigeria Federal Finance: A General Review', *Quarterly Journal of Administration*, IV, 2, January 1970.
Aluko, S.O., 'The Civil War and Nigerian Foreign Policy', *Political Quarterly*, April 1971.
Anglin, D.G., 'Nigeria: Political Non-Alignment and Economic Alignment', *Journal of Modern African Studies*, 2, 2, 1964.
———— 'Brinkmanship in Nigeria: The Federal Election of 1964–65', *International Journal*, Spring 1965.
Arrighi, G. and Saul, J., 'Socialism and Economic Development in Tropical Africa', *Journal of Modern African Studies*, 6, 2, 1968.
Arrighi, G., 'International Corporations, Labour Aristocracies and Economic Development in Tropical Africa', in R. Rhodes (ed.), *Imperialism and Underdevelopment* (New York: Monthly Review Press, 1970).
Bennett, V.P., 'Patterns of Demilitarisation in Africa', *Quarterly Journal of Administration*, IX, 1, 1974.
Byrne, H., 'Food Problems in Africa', *Ufahamu*, IX, 3, 1979–80.
Caccia, G., 'Nigeria: Oil Plot or Oil Glut?', *Journal of African Marxists*, 3, 1983.
Campbell, I., 'The Nigerian Census: An Essay in Civil-Military Relations', *Journal of Commonwealth and Comparative Politics*, XIV, 3, 1976.
Cohen, R., 'Nigeria's Labour Leader No. 1: Notes for a Biographical Study of M.A.O. Imodu', *Journal of the Historical Society of Nigeria*, 5, 2, 1970.
———— 'Nigeria's Central Trade Union Organisations: A Study Guide', *Journal of Modern African Studies*, 9, 3, 1971.
———— 'Resistance and Hidden Forms of Consciousness Amongst African Workers', *Review of African Political Economy*, 9, 1980.
Dadieh, C.K. and Shaw, T., 'The Political Economy of Decision-Making in Africa: The Cases of Recognition of Biafra and MPLA', *International Political Science Review*, 5, 2, April 1984.
Dare, L.O., 'Dilemma of Military Disengagement: The Nigerian Case', *Nigerian Journal of Economic And Social Studies*, 16, February 1974.
———— 'The Patterns of Military Entrenchment in Ghana and Nigeria', *African Quarterly*, XVI, 3, 1977.
———— 'Military Withdrawal From Politics in Nigeria', *International Political Science Review*, 2, 3, 1981.
Decalo, S., 'Military Coups and Military Regimes in Africa', *Journal of Modern African Studies*, 11, 1, 1973.

Dubley, B.J., 'The Military and Development', *Nigerian Journal of Economic and Social Studies*, 13, 2, 1971.

Enahoro, A., 'Address by the Commissioner for Labour to the First Meeting of the Reconstituted National Labour Advisory Council', *NECA News*, March 1973.

Essang, S.M., 'Patterns of Labour Absorption in Southern Nigerian Plantations', *Economic Bulletin of Ghana*, 4, 2, 1974.

Essang, S.M. and Olayide, S.O., 'Economic Development or Income Distribution? A False Dilemma', *Nigerian Journal of Sociology and Anthropology*, 1, 1, 1974.

Fajana, F.O., 'The Nigerian Union of Teachers: A Decade of Growth, 1931–40', *Nigeria Magazine*, 110–12, 1974.

———— 'Intra-Industry Wage Differentials', *Journal of Developing Areas*, 9, 4, 1975.

Feit, E., 'Military Coups and Political Development: Some Lessons from Ghana and Nigeria', *World Politics*, 20, 2, January 1968.

Frank, A.G., 'The Sociology of Development and the Underdevelopment of Society', *Catalyst*, 1967.

Freeman, David H., 'Work in Nigeria: A Corner-Stone of Meeting the Needs of People', *International Labour Review*, 120, 6, 1981.

Freund, B., 'Oil Boom and Crisis in Contemporary Nigeria', *Review of African Political Economy*, 13, 1979.

Freyhold, M., 'The Post-Colonial State and its Tanzania Version', *Review of African Political Economy*, 8, January–April 1977.

Gambari, I., 'Domestic Political Constraints on Progressive Foreign Policy for Nigeria', *Nigerian Journal of Political Science*, 2, 1, June 1980.

Gutkind, P.C.W. *et al*, 'Political Consciousness of the Urban Poor in Ibadan', *Cahiers d'Etudes Africaines*, 57, 1975.

Herskovits, Jean, 'Nigeria: Africa's New Power', *Foreign Affairs*, January 1975.

Hinchcliffe, J.K., 'Earning Determinants in the Nigerian Textile Industry', *Comparative Education Review*, 20, 1, 1976.

Hoogvelt, A., 'Indigenization in Kano', *Review of African Political Economy*, 14, 1980.

Ihonvbere, J., 'Resource Availability and Foreign Policy Change: The Impact of Oil on Nigeria's Foreign Policy Since Independence', *Afrika Spectrum*, 1982.

———— 'Foreign Policy of Dependent States: Oil and Nigeria Foreign Policy, 1962-1982', *Indian Political Science Review*, January 1984.

———— 'Foreign Capital and Economic Integration in the Third World: The Economic Community of West African States Revisited', *Africa Quarterly*, 22, 1, 1982/83.

Imobigbe, T., 'Libyan Intervention in Chad: Security Implication for Nigeria', *Nigerian Journal of International Studies*, 4, 1, January–June 1980.

Jackson, Sam, 'Hausa Women on Strike', *Review of African Political Economy*, 13, 1978.

Joseph, R.A., 'Affluence and Underdevelopment: The Nigerian Experience', *Journal of Modern African Studies*, 16, 2, 1978.

Karp, Mark, 'Export Concentration in Nigeria', *Journal of Developing Areas*, 14, April 1980.

Keay, E.A., 'Legal and Constitutional Changes in Nigeria under the Military Government', *Journal of African Law*, 10, 2, 1966.

Kraus, J., 'Nigeria Under Shagari', *Current History*, 81, March 1982.

Lazar, von A. and Duerstein, A.L., 'Oil and Development and Planning: Implications for Nigeria', *Energy Policy*, December 1976.

Leys, C., 'The Overdeveloped Post-colonial State: A Re-evaluation', *Review of African Political Economy*, 5, January–April 1976.

Lubeck, Paul, 'The Value of Multiple Methods in Researching Third World Strikes: A Nigerian Example', *Development and Change*, 10, 2, 1979.

Madujibeya, S.A., 'Between Oil Wealth and Petronaira', *South*, February 1982.

———— 'Oil and Nigeria's Economic Development', *African Affairs*, 75, 300, July 1976.

Mazrui, A.A., 'Nigeria and the United States: The Need for Civility, the Dangers of Intimacy', *Orbis*, 25, 4, 1982.

Mayall, James, 'Oil and Nigerian Foreign Policy', *African Affairs*, 75, 300, July 1976.

Mejak, M., 'Nigeria's Foreign Policy: Commitment to Non-Alignment and African Unity', *Review of International Affairs*, 34, 20, February 1983.

Murray, R., 'Militarism in Africa', *New Left Review*, 38, July–August 1966.

Nafziger, Wayne, 'The Economic Impact of the Nigerian Civil War', *Journal of Modern African Studies*, 10, 2, 1972.

Nwaueze, R.O., 'Impact of Military Rule on Nigerian Trade Union Movement (1966–1980)', *Indian Journal of Industrial Relations*, 16, 4, 1981.

Nwogu, E.D., 'Oil in Nigeria', *Nigerian Geographical Journal*, 3, November 1960.

O'Connell, J., 'The Inevitability of Instability', *Journal of Modern African Studies*, 5, 2, 1967.

Ogueli, E., 'Theories and Motives of Military Coups d'Etat in Independent States', *Afrika Spectrum*, 3, 1973.

Ogunbadejo, O., 'Nigeria's Foreign Policy under Military Rule', *International Journal*, 25, 4, 1980.

Ojeli, D., 'Promoting Industrial Peace in Nigeria', *Labour and Development*, 33, 33, September 1977.

Okigbo, P.N.C., 'Economic Implications of the 1979 Constitution of the Federal Republic of Nigeria', in *The Political Economy of Nigeria, Proceedings of the 1982 Annual Conference of the Nigerian Economic Society*.

Ojo, M.O., 'Food Supply in Nigeria, 1960–1975' in Central Bank of Nigeria: *Economic and Financial Review*, 15, 2, 1977.

Ojo, O.J.B., 'Nigeria and the Formation of ECOWAS', *International Organization*, 34, 4, 1980.

Okolo, J.E. and Langley, E.W., 'The Changing Nigerian Foreign Policy', *World Affairs*, 135, Spring 1973.

Oloku, O., 'Impact of Management Nationality on Worker Commitment to Employment in Nigeria', *Journal of Management Studies*, 9, 2, 1972.

Onah, J. and Iwuji, E.C., 'Urban Poverty in Nigeria', *South African Journal of Economics*, 44, 2, 1976.

Oni, O., 'A Critique of Development Planning in Nigeria', *Review of African Political Economy*, 4, November 1975.

Onimode, B., 'Economic Development and Class Struggle in Nigeria', *Nigerian Journal of Economic and Social Studies*, 20, 3, 1978.

────── 'A Critique of Planning Concepts and Methodology in Nigeria', *Review of Black Political Economy*, 7, 3, 1977.

Osoba, S.O., 'The Nigerian Constitution and the Nigerian Working Class', *Positive Review*, 1, 3, 1973.

────── 'Trade Unions: Does the New Constitution Discriminate?', *New Horizon*, 4, 4, 1979.

Otobo, Dafe, 'The Nigerian General Strike of 1981', *Review of African Political Economy*, 22, 1982.

Oyediran, O., 'Local Government in Southern Nigeria: The Direction of Change', *The African Review*, 4, 4, 1974.

────── 'Participation in the Nigerian 1976 Local Government Election', *The Nigerian Journal of Economic and Social Studies*, 19, 1, 1977.

Patanker, E. and Omvedt, 'The Bourgeois State in Post-Colonial Formations', *The Insurgent Sociologist*, 14, 4, 1980.

Peace, A., 'Industrial Conflict in Nigeria' in E. de Kadt and G. Williams (eds.), *Sociology and Development* (London: Tavistock, 1974).

Peil, M., 'A Civilian Appraisal of Military Rule in Nigeria', *Armed Forces and Society*, 2, 1, 1975.

Phillips, A.O., 'Revenue Allocation in Nigeria, 1970–80', *Nigerian Journal of Economic and Social Studies*, 17, 2, July 1975.

Phillips, A., 'The Concept of Development', *Review of African Political Economy*, 8, 1977.

Post, K., ' "Peasantisation" and Rural Political Movements in Western Africa', *European Journal of Sociology*, 13, 1972.

Sada, Phillip O., 'Urban Growth and Development in Nigeria', *Tropical Geographer*, 38, 1974.

Samoff, J., 'On Class, Paradigm and African Politics', *Africa Today*, 29, 2, 1982.

Saul, J., 'The State in Post-Colonial Societies: Tanzania', *Socialist Register, 1974* (London: Merlin Press, 1974).

Schatz, S.P., 'Crude Private Neo-Imperialism', *Journal of Modern African Studies*, 7, 4, 1969.

────── 'Nigeria's Petro-political Fluctuation', *Issue*, 11, 1 & 2, 1981.

────── 'The Nigerian Economy Since the Great Oil-price Increases of 1973–79', *Africa Today*, 29, 3, 1982.

Shaw, T., Review article on 'Foreign Policy, Political Economy and the Future: Reflections on Africa in the World System', *African Affairs*, 79, 315, 1980.

Stremlau, J.S., 'The Fundamentals of Nigerian Foreign Policy', *Issues*, 11, 1 & 2, 1981.

Teriba, O., 'Nigerian Revenue Allocation Experience, 1952–65: A Study in Intergovernmental Fiscal and Financial Relations', *Nigerian Journal of Economic and Social Studies*, 8, 3, November 1966.

Vayrynen, R., 'Economic and Military Position of Regional Power Centres', *Journal of Peace Research*, 16, 4, 1979.

Warren, B., 'Imperialism and Capitalist Industrialisation', *New Left Review*, 81, 1973.

Waterman, Peter, 'Communist Theory in the Nigerian Trade Union Move-

ment', *Politics and Society*, 3, 2, 1973.
———— 'Industrial Relations and the Control of Labour Protests in Nigeria (The Hague: Institute of Social Studies, 1977).
———— 'Consciousness, Organisation and Action Amongst Lagos Port Workers', *Review of African Political Economy*, 13, 1979.
Welch, C.E., 'Praetorianism in Commonwealth West Africa', *Journal of Modern African Studies*, 10, 2, 1972.
Williams, G., 'The Concept of "Egemonia" in the Thought of Antonio Gramsci', *Journal of the History of Ideas*, 21, 1960.
———— 'The Social Stratification of a Neo-Colonial Economy: Western Nigeria' in C.H. Allen and R.W. Johnson (eds.), *African Perspectives*, (Cambridge: Cambridge University Press, 1970).
———— 'Imperialism and Development', *World Development*, 6, 1978.
Young, A., 'The United States and Africa: Victory for Diplomacy', *Foreign Affairs*, 59, 3, 1980.
Ziemann, W. and Langerdorfer, M., 'The State in Peripheral Capitalist Societies', *The Socialist Register, 1977* (London: Merlin Press, 1977).

Books

Achebe, C., *The Trouble With Nigeria* (Enugu: Fourth Dimension, 1982).
Adamolekun, L. And Gboyega, A. (eds.), *Leading Issues in Nigerian Public Service* (Ife: Ife University Press, 1981).
Adedeji, A. and Rowland, I., *Local Government Finance in Nigeria: Problems and Prospects* (Ile Ife: University of Ife Press, 1972).
Adegboyega, A., *Why We Struck: The Story of the First Nigerian Coup* (Ibadan: Evans Brothers Nigeria Ltd., 1981).
Agboola, S.A., *An Agricultural Atlas of Nigeria* (London: Oxford University Press, 1979).
Ajibola, W., *Foreign Policy and Public Opinion: A Case Study of British Foreign Policy Over the Nigerian Civil War* (Ibadan: Ibadan University Press, 1978).
Ake, C., *A Political Economy of Africa* (London: Longman, 1971).
———— *Revolutionary Pressures in Africa* (London: Zed Press, 1978).
———— *Social Science as Imperialism: The Theory of Political Development* (Ibadan: Ibadan University Press, Second edition, 1982).
Akinyemi, B.A. (ed.), *Nigeria and the World: Readings in Nigerian Foreign Policy* (Ibadan: Oxford University Press for the NILA, 1978).
Akinyemi, A.B., Cole, P.D. and Ofonagoro, W., *Readings On Federalism* (Lagos: Nigerian Institute of International Affairs, 1979).
Aluko, O., *Essays in Nigerian Foreign Policy* (London: George Allen and Unwin, 1981).
Ananaba, W., *The Trade Union Movement in Nigeria* (London: Hurst, 1969).
Apeldoorn, G.J. van, *Perspectives on Drought and Famine in Nigeria* (London: George Allen and Unwin, 1981).
Arikpo, O., *The Development of Modern Nigeria* (London: Penguin, 1967).
Awa, E., *Federalism in Nigeria* (Berkeley and Los Angeles: University of California Press, 1964).
Awojobi, A., *Nigeria Today* (Lagos: John West, 1980).

Awolowo, O., *Path to Nigerian Freedom* (London: Faber and Faber, 1947).
––––––– *Thoughts on Nigerian Constitution* (Ibadan: Oxford University Press, 1966).
Ayida, A. and Onitiri, H., *Reconstruction and Development in Nigeria* (Ibadan: NISER, 1971).
Ayida, A.A., *The Nigerian Revolution* (Ibadan: Nigerian Economic Society, 1973).
Bello, Ahmadu Sir, *My Life: The Autobiography of Alhaji Sir Ahmadu Bello, Sardauna of Sokoto* (Cambridge: Cambridge University Press, 1962).
Bienen, H. and Diejomaoh, V.P., *The Political Economy of Income Distribution in Nigeria* (New York: Africana, 1981).
Biersteker, E.J., *Distortion or Development: Contending Perspectives on the Multinational Corporations* (Cambridge Mass: MIT Press, 1978).
Blum, A.A. (ed.), *International Handbook of Industrial Relations: Contemporary Developments and Research* (London: Aldwych, 1981).
Braverman, H., *Labour and Monopoly Capital: The Degradation of Work in The Twentieth Century* (New York: Monthly Review Press, 1974).
Cohen, R., *Labour and Politics in Nigeria* (London: Heineman, 1974).
Coleman, J.S., *Nigeria: Background to Nationalism* (Berkeley and Los Angeles: University of California Press, 1958).
Collins, P.D. (ed.), *Administration for Development in Nigeria* (Lagos: African Education Press, 1980).
Davison, R.B., *Industrial Relations Decrees: Questions and Answers to Explain the Law* (Zaria: ABU Press, 1977).
de Kadt, E. and Williams, G. (eds.), *Sociology and Development* (London: Tavistock, 1974).
Dudley, B.G., *Parties and Politics in Northern Nigeria* (London: Frank Cass, 1968).
––––––– *Instability and Political Order: Politics and Crisis in Nigeria* (Ibadan: Ibadan University Press, 1973).
Dunn, J. (ed.), *West African States: Failure and Promise* (London: Cambridge University Press, 1978).
Echer, C.E. and Liedholm, C., *Growth and Development of the Nigerian Economy* (East Lansing: Michigan State University Press, 1979).
Ekundare, R.O., *The Economic History of Nigeria, 1860–1960* (London: Methuen, 1973).
Essien-Ibok, A., *Political Repression and Assassination: A Tribute to the Late Dr Bala Muhammad* (Kano: Research Unit, Governor's Office, 1983).
––––––– *Towards a Progressive Nigeria* (Kano: Triumph Publishing Company, 1983).
Evans, P., *Dependent Development: The Alliance of Multinationals, State and Local Capital in Brazil* (Princeton: Princeton University Press, 1979).
Fagbamigbe, O., *Selected Speeches of Obafemi Awolowo*, 3 vols. (Akure: Fagbamigbe Publishers, 1981).
Fashoyin, T., *Industrial Relations in Nigeria: Development and Practice* (London: Longman, 1980).
Finer, S.E., *The Man on Horseback: The Role of the Military in Politics* (London: Pall Mall, 1962).
First, R., *The Barrel of the Gun: Political Power in Africa and the Coup d'Etat* (Harmondsworth: Penguin, 1970).

———— *Power in Africa* (New York: Pantheon Press, 1970).

Fitch, B. and Openheimer, M., *Ghana: End of an Illusion* (New York:Monthly Review Press, 1966).

Foley, Gerald, *The Energy Question* (Harmondsworth: Penguin, 1976).

Fransman, M. (ed.), *Industry and Accumulation in Africa* (London: Heinemann, 1982).

Freund, Bill, *Capital and Labour in the Nigerian Tin Mines* (London: Longman, 1980).

Gambari, I.A., *Party Politics and Foreign Policy: Nigeria Under the First Republic* (Zaria: Ahmadu Bello University Press, 1980).

Gbulie, B., *Nigeria's Five Majors: Coup d'Etat of 15th January 1966: First Inside Account* (Onitsha: Africana Educational Publishers, 1981).

Gramsci, A., *Prison Notebooks* (New York: International Publishers, 1980).

Gutkind, P.C.W. and Waterman, P. (eds.), *African Social Studies: A Radical Reader* (New York: Monthly Review Press, 1977).

Gutkind, P.C.W. , Cohen, R. and Copans, J. (eds.), *African Labour History* (London: Sage, 1979).

Gutteridge, W., *Military Institutions and Power in the New States* (New York: Praeger, 1964).

Heilbronner, R.L., *Between Capitalism and Socialism: Essays in Political Economy* (New York: Vintage Books, 1970).

Heyer, J., Roberts, P. and Williams, G., *Rural Development in Tropical Africa* (London: Macmillan Press, 1981).

Hill, Polly, *Population, Prosperity and Poverty: Rural Kano 1900–1970* (Cambridge: Cambridge University Press, 1977).

Huntington, S.P., *The Soldier and the State* (Cambridge: Harvard University Press, 1967).

———— *Political Order in Changing Societies* (New Haven: Yale University Press, 1969).

Idang, G., *Nigeria: Internal Politics and Foreign Policy 1960–1966* (Ibadan: University of Ibadan Press, 1973).

Ikejiani, O. (ed.), *Education in Nigeria* (New York: Praeger, 1965).

Institute of Administration, University of Ife, *The Future of Local Government in Nigeria: The Report of the National Conference on Local Government, April–May, 1969* (Ile Ife: University of Ife Press, 1969).

International Labour Office, *First Things First: Meeting the Basic Needs of the People of Nigeria* (Addis Ababa: JASPA, 1981).

Iyayi, Festus, *Violence* (London: Longman, 1979).

Janowitz, M., *The Military in the Political Development of New Nations: A Comparative Analysis* (Chicago: University of Chicago Press, 1964).

———— *Military Institutions and Coercion in the Developing Nations* (Chicago: University of Chicago Press, 1977).

Jeffries, R., *Class, Power and Ideology in Ghana: The Railwaymen of Secondi* (Cambridge: Cambridge University Press, 1978).

Jemibewon, D. Brigadier, *Combatants in Government* (Ibadan: Heinemann Educational Books, 1978).

Johnson, J.J. (ed.), *The Role of the Military in Under-Developed Countries* (Princeton: Princeton University Press, 1962).

Jorre, J. de St., *The Nigerian Civil War* (London: Hodder and Stoughton, 1972).

Kilby, Peter, *Industrialisation in an Open Economy, Nigeria 1945-1966* (Cambridge: Cambridge University Press, 1969).

Kirk-Greene, A.H.M., *Crisis and Conflict in Nigeria: A Documentary Source-Book, 1966-1970*, 2 volumes (London: Oxford University Press, 1971).

Kirk-Greene, A.H.M. and Rimmer, D., *Nigeria Since 1970: An Economic and Political Outline* (London: Hodder and Stoughton, 1981).

Legum, O., Zartman, I.W., Langdon, S. and Mytelka, L.K., *Africa in the 1980s: A Continent in Crisis* (New York: McGraw-Hill Book Company, 1979).

Lenin, V.I., *Collected Works* (Moscow: Progress Publishers, 1980).

Lewis, W.A., *Reflections on Nigeria's Economic Growth* (Paris: 1967).

Lieuwen, E., *Generals Vs Presidents: Neomilitarism in Latin America* (New York: Praeger, 1964).

Lloyd, P.C., *The New Elites of Tropical Africa* (London: Oxford University Press for International African Institute, 1966).

Luckham, R., *The Nigerian Military 1960-67* (Cambridge: Cambridge University Press, 1971).

Levefer, E.W., *Spear and Scepter* (Washington: Brookings Institute, 1970).

Madunagu, E., *Problems of Socialism: The Nigerian Challenge* (London: Zed Press, 1982).

Mazrui, A., *Protest and Power in Black Africa* (New York: Oxford University Press, 1970).

Mackintosh, J.P., *Nigerian Government and Politics* (Evanston: Northwestern University Press, 1966).

Miners, N.J., *The Nigerian Army, 1956-1966* (London: Methuen, 1971).

Mohammed, B., *Africa and Non Alignment: A Study in the Foreign Relations of New Nations* (Kano: Triumph Publishing Co., 1982 edition).

Marx, K. and Engels, F., *The Communist Manifesto* (New York: Pocket Books, 1964).

Muffett, D.J.M., *Let Truth Be Told: The Coups d'Etat of 1966* (Zaria: Hudahuda Publishing Company, 1982).

Nigerian Labour Congress (NLC), *Workers' Charter of Demands Prepared and Presented to the Federal Government of Nigeria* (Lagos: NLC Secretariat, February 1980).

———— *The Need to Sustain One Central Labour Organisation (NLC) in Nigeria: Workers of Nigeria Unite and Organise* (Lagos: NLC Secretariat, n.d.).

Nnoli, Okwudiba, *Ethnic Politics in Nigeria* (Enugu: Fourth Dimension, 1978).

———— (ed.), *Path to Nigerian Development* (Dakar: CODESRIA, 1981).

Nordlinger, E., *Soldiers in Politics: Military Coups and Government* (Englewood Cliffs, N.J.: Prentice Hall Inc, 1973).

Nwankwo, A., *Can Nigeria Survive?* (Enugu: Fourth Dimension, 1981).

Olatunbosun, D., *Nigeria's Neglected Rural Majority* (Ibadan: Oxford University Press, 1975).

Oni, O. and Onimode, B., *Economic Development of Nigeria: The Socialist Alternative* (Ibadan: Nigerian Academy of Arts, Sciences and Technology, 1975).

Onimode, B., *Imperialism and Underdevelopment in Nigeria* (London: Zed Press, 1982).

Onyemelukwe, C., *Problems of Industrial Planning and Management in Nigeria* (London: Longman, 1966).

———— *Men and Management in Contemporary Africa* (London: Longman, 1973).

Osoba, O. and Usman, Y.B., *A General Report on the Work of the Constitution Drafting Committee: A Minority Submission*, August 1976.

———— *Minority Draft Constitution*, August 1976.

Oyediran, O. (ed.), *Nigerian Government and Politics Under Military Rule, 1966–79* (London: Oxford University Press for NIIA, 1979).

———— (ed.), *Annual Survey of Nigeria Affairs, 1975* (Oxford University Press for the Nigerian Institute of International Affairs, 1979).

Palombara, J. (ed.), *Bureaucracy and Political Development* (Princeton, N.J.: Princeton University Press, 1963).

Panter-Brick, S.K., *Nigerian Politics and Military Rule: Prelude to Civil War* (London: Institute of Commonwealth Studies, 1970).

———— (ed.), *Soldiers and Oil: The Political Transformation of Nigeria* (London: Frank Cass, 1978).

Peace, Adrian, *Class, Choice and Conflict in Nigeria* (Hassocks: Harvester Books, 1979).

Pearse, Andrew, *Seeds of Plenty, Seeds of Want, Social and Economic Implications of the Green Revolution* (London: Clarendon Press for United Nations Research Institute for Social Development, 1980).

Pearson, Scott R., *Petroleum and the Nigerian Economy* (Stanford: Stanford University Press, 1970).

Pearson, S.C. and Cownie, J., *Commodity Exports and African Economic Development* (Lexington: D.C. Heath, 1974).

Peil, M., *Cities and Suburbs: Urban Life in West Africa* (New York: Africana Publishing Co., 1981).

Post, K.W.J., *The Nigerian Federal Election of 1959* (London: Oxford University Press, 1963).

Post, K.W.J. and Jenkins, R., *The Price of Liberty: Personality and Politics in Colonial Nigeria* (London: Cambridge University Press, 1973).

Post, K.W.J. and Vickers, M., *Structure and Conflict in Nigeria: 1960–1965* (London: Heinemann, 1973).

Sandbrook, R. and Cohen, R. (eds.), *The Development of an African Working Class* (London: Longman, 1975).

Sano, H., *The Political Economy of Food in Nigeria, 1960–1962* (Uppsala: SIAS, Research Report No. 65, 1983).

Schatil, Ludwig, *Petroleum in Nigeria* (Ibadan: Nigeria Institute for Social and Economic Research, 1969).

Schatz, S.P., *Nigerian Capitalism* (Berkeley: University of California Press, 1977).

Schwarz, F.E.O. (jr), *Nigeria: The Tribes, the Nation or the Race* (Cambridge: Massachusetts Institute of Technology, 1965).

Seibel, H.D. and Trachtman, L., *Industrial Relations in Africa* (London: Macmillan, 1979).

Shaw, T., *Africa's International Affairs: an Analysis and Bibliography* (Halifax: Centre for Foreign Policy Studies, 1983).

Shaw, T. and Aluko, O. (eds.), *Nigerian Foreign Policy: Alternative Perceptions and Projections* (London: Macmillan, 1983).

Simpson, R.L. and I.H. (eds.), *Research in the Sociology of Work: Worker Consciousness* (Greenwich: JAI Press, 1981).

Sklar, R., *Nigerian Political Parties* (Princeton: Princeton University Press, 1963).

Smock, D., *Conflict and Control in an African Trade Union: A Study of the Nigerian Coal Miners Union* (Stanford: Stanford University Press, 1969).

Smyke, R.J. and Storer, D.C., *Nigerian Union of Teachers: An Official History* (Ibadan: OUP, 1974).

Stevenhagen, Rodolfo, *Social Classes in Agrarian Societies* (New York: Anchor Press, 1975).

Stopler, W., *Planning Without Facts* (Cambridge, Mass: Harvard University Press, 1966).

Stremlau, J., *The International Politics of the Nigerian Civil War* (Princeton: Princeton University Press, 1977).

Teriba, O. and Kayode, M.O. (eds.), *Industrial Development in Nigeria: Patterns, Problems and Prospects* (Ibadan: Ibadan University Press, 1977).

Tijani, A. and Williams, D., *Shehu Shagari: My Vision of Nigeria* (London: Frank Cass, 1981).

Toyo, E., *The Working Class and the Nigerian Crisis* (Ibadan: Sketch Publishing Company, 1967).

Tukur, M. and Olagunju, T. (eds.), *Nigeria: In Search of a Viable Polity* (Zaria: ABU Press, 1972).

Ubeki, A.K., *Personnel Management in Nigeria* (Benin: Ethiope Publishing House, 1975).

Usman, Y.B., *For the Liberation of Nigeria* (London: New Beacon, 1979).

—— (ed.), *Political Repression in Nigeria* (Kano: Bala Mohammed Memorial Committee, 1982).

Urieghara, E.E., *Trade Union Law in Nigeria* (Benin City: Ethiope Publishing Co., 1976).

Wallerstein, I. (ed.), *World Inequality* (Montreal: Black Rose Books, 1975).

Warren, B., *Imperialism – Pioneer of Capitalism* (London: New Left Books and Verso, 1981).

Waterman, Peter, *Aristocrats and Plebeians in African Unions? Lagos Port and Dock Workers Organisation and Struggle* (The Hague: Waterman, 1983).

Waugh, A. and Cronje, S., *Biafra: Britain's Shame* (London: Michael Joseph, 1969).

Welch, C.E. (jr.) (ed.), *Soldier and State in Africa* (Evanston: Northwestern University Press, 1970).

Whitaker, C.S. (jr.), *The Politics of Tradition: Continuity and Change in Northern Nigeria* (Princeton: Princeton University Press, 1970).

Widstrand, C. (ed.), *Multinational Firms in Africa* (Uppsala: SIAS, 1975).

Williams, D., *President and Power in Nigeria: The Life of Shehu Shagari* (London: Frank Cass, 1982).

Williams, G., *State and Society in Nigeria* (Idanre: Afrografika Publishers, 1980).

World Bank, *Nigeria: Options for Long-term Development: Report of a Mission Sent to Nigeria* (Baltimore: Johns Hopkins University Press, 1974).

Yansane, A. (ed.), *Decolonization and Dependency – Problems of Develop-*

ment in African Societies (Greenwood Press, 1980).

Zartman, I.W. (ed.), *The Political Economy of Nigeria* (New York: Praeger, 1983).

Zolberg, A.R., *Creating Political Order: Party States of West Africa* (Chicago: Rand McNally, 1966).

Unpublished Works

Adebayo, A.G., 'Petroleum and Nigeria's Foreign Policy, 1970–1979'. M.A. thesis, University of Ife, Nigeria, 1981.

Adekson, J., 'Military Organisation in Multi-Ethnically Segmented Societies: A Theoretical Study with Reference to Three Sub-Saharan African Cases'. Ph.D. Thesis, 1976, Brandeis University, Waltham, USA.

—— 'Towards Explaining Civil-Military Instability in Contemporary Sub-Saharan Africa: A Comparative Political Model', unpublished ms, 1978.

Adeogun, A.A., 'Industrial Relations and the Unions in Nigerian Law'. Paper to the National Seminar on the Unions, the Law and National Development, Kano, September 1975.

Adesanoye, F.I., 'Nigerian Defence Policy'. Lecture to the Second Senior Officers Course, Army Command and Staff College, Jaji, 1977.

Afolabi, Peter (Nigerian High Commissioner to Canada), 'West Africa and the Oil Crisis'. Paper presented at the Norman Paterson School of International Affairs, Carleton University, Ottawa, 1974.

—— 'Nigeria's Development Objectives'. Paper presented at the Department of Geography, Carleton University, Ottawa, 1975.

Aire, J.U., 'Industrial Conflict in Nigeria: Implications for National Labour Policy'. Ph.D thesis, New York University, New York, 1970.

Akinmoladun, Rufus O., 'Oil in Nigeria: A Study in Political Economy of Development'. Ph.D dissertation, Howard University, Washington, D.C., 1976.

Aluko, O., 'Necessity and Freedom in Nigerian Foreign Policy'. Inaugural Lecture, University of Ife, 17 March 1981.

Ameh, S.S., 'Workers' Protection: A Focus on the Labour Decree and the Wages Boards and Industrial Councils Decree'. Paper to the National Seminar on the Unions, the Law and National Development, Kano, September 1975.

Asobie, H.A., 'Domestic Political Structure and Foreign Policy: The Nigerian Experience 1960–1974'. Ph.D Thesis, University of London, 1977.

Awojobi, A., 'Where Our Oil Money Has Gone'. Text of a Lecture delivered at the University of Ife on Tuesday 11 May 1982.

Ayu, I.D., 'Oil, Class Relations and the Distribution of Hunger in Nigeria'. Paper presented at the Annual Conference of the Canadian Association of African Studies, Toronto, May 1982.

Azikiwe, N., Chief, 'Stability in Nigeria after Military Rule: An Analysis of Political Theory'. S.J. Mariere Inaugural Lecture, University of Lagos, 27 October 1972.

Barber, Karin, 'Popular Reactions to the Petronaira'. Paper presented to the Canadian Association of African Studies Conference, Toronto, May 1982.

Dare, L., 'Military Leadership and Political Development in the Western State of Nigeria'. Ph.D thesis, 1972, Carleton University, Canada.

Eboh, C.K., 'The Management of Natural Resources: A Comparative Analysis of Energy Conservation Policy in Developed and a Developing Country'. Ph.D dissertation, University of Houston, 1980.

Ejiofor, S., 'The Changing Features of the Labour Relations Pattern and the Political Economy of Nigeria'. Diploma Paper, Institute of Social Studies, The Hague, 1976.

Emembolu, Gregory E., 'Petroleum and the Development of a Dual Economy: The Nigerian Example'. Ph.D dissertation, University of Colorado at Boulder, 1975.

Enoh, Christian O., 'The Impact of the Petroleum Industry on Socio-Economic Development of Nigeria'. MA Thesis, Mankato State University, Minnesota, 1975.

Esinulu, S.M., 'Nigerian Foreign Policy: Social Roots, Ideological Expression and Political Practice'. MSS Thesis, Institute of Social Studies, The Hague, 1978.

Fajana, F.O., 'Wage Differentials and Economic Development in Nigeria'. Ph.D Thesis, London University, London, 1971.

Falegan, S.B., 'Trends in Nigeria's Balance of Payments and Policy Measures for Self-Reliance'. Paper presented at a NISER workshop on Towards Self-Sufficiency and Self-Reliance in the Nigerian Economy, Ibadan, 1978.

Garba, J.N., 'Foreign Policy and Problems of Economic Development'. An address delivered at the University of Ibadan, 19 February 1977.

Gboyega, E.A., 'Local Government and Political Integration in the Western State 1952–1972'. Ph.D Thesis, University of Ibadan, 1975.

Ihonvbere, J.O., 'Oil Revenues and Rural-Urban Inequity in Nigeria'. Paper to the International Conference Organised by the Institute of International Co-operation and Development, University of Ottawa, October 1981.

———— 'The Political Economy of the Rentier State. Oil and Class Struggles in Nigeria'. Paper to the Annual CAAS Conference, Toronto, May 1982.

Ihonvbere, J.O. and Falola, Toyin, 'The Oil State: Class Struggles, Contradictions and Underdevelopment in Nigeria'.

———— 'The Recycling of Petro-Naira and Nigeria's Integration into World Capitalism'.

———— 'Neo-colonialism, Hegemony and Political Instability in Contemporary Nigeria'.

———— (eds.), *Oil, Economy and the Nigeria Society.*

Ihonvbere, J.O. and Shaw, T.M., 'Nigeria: Oil Production, Class Formation and Social Contradictions in a (Semi?) Peripheral Capitalist Formation'. Paper to the Annual Conference of the Canadian Association of African Studies, Quebec City, May 1983.

———— 'The Political Economy of Nigeria's Foreign Policy Under Military Rule, 1966–1979'.

Ikpah, Azhinto O., 'Oil and Gas Industry and Environmental Pollution: Application of Systems Reliability Analysis for the Evaluation of the States of Environmental Pollution Control in the Nigerian Petroleum Industry'. Ph.D dissertation, University of Texas at Dallas, 1981.

Madujibeya, S.A., 'Economic Enclaves, Technology Transfer and Foreign Investments in Nigeria'. Paper to a Seminar on Urban Culture, School of Oriental and African Studies, University of London, November 1975.

Melson, R., 'Marxists in the Nigerian Labour Movement: A Case Study in the Failure of Ideology'. Ph.D dissertation, Massachusetts Institute of Technology, Massachusetts, 1967.

Odofin, C.D., 'The Impact of the Multinational Oil Corporations on Nigeria's Economic Growth: Theoretical and Empirical Explorations'. Ph.D dissertation, Texas A and M University, 1979.

Ojeli, David, 'The Development of Trade Unionism in Eastern Nigeria'. MSS dissertation, Institute of Social Studies, The Hague, 1975.

Onimode, B. and Osagie, E., 'Economic Interpretation of the Draft Constitution'. Unpublished seminar paper, Dept. of Political Science, University.

Oyemakinde, W., 'A History of Indigenous Labour on the Nigerian Railway, 1895–1945'. Ph.D Thesis, University of Ibadan, Ibadan, 1970.

Oyovbaire, S.E., 'Federalism in Nigeria with Particular Reference to the Midwestern State, 1966–75'. Ph.D Thesis, University of Manchester, 1976.

Pearson, Scott R., 'The Impact of Petroleum on the Nigerian Economy'. Ph.D dissertation, Harvard University, 1968.

Turner, Terisa, 'Class, State and Development of Oil Industry in Nigeria'. Paper presented at the Conference on the Nigerian Government, Institute of Commonwealth Studies, University of London, 1976.

————— 'Oil and Government: The Making and Implementation of Petroleum Policy in Nigeria'. Ph.D dissertation, London School of Economics, 1977.

Udofia, O., 'Trade Unions and Socio-Political Change: A Case Study of Nigeria'. Ph.D Thesis, State University of New York, Buffalo.

Vaniman, D.T., 'The Godani Granodioritic Plutons, Nigerian Petrology and Regional Setting'. Ph.D dissertation, University of California at Santa Cruz, 1976.

Wilson, E.J., 'The Political Economy of Public Corporations in the Energy Sectors of Nigeria and Zaire'. Ph.D dissertation, University of California at Berkeley, 1978.

Wright, Stephen, 'Africa's Emergent Super Power, The Resource Base of Nigerian Foreign Policy'. Paper presented to the British International Studies Association Conference, University of Keele, 1979.

Periodicals and Newspapers

The Daily Times (Lagos)
The Sunday Times (Lagos)
Lagos Weekend (Lagos)
Lagos Eye (Lagos)
Evening Times (Lagos)
National Concord (Lagos)
Sunday Concord (Lagos)
The Guardian (Lagos)
Sunday Sketch (Ibadan)
The Tribune (Ibadan)
Sunday Tribune (Ibadan)
The New Nigerian (Lagos/Kaduna)
The Triumph (Kano)

The Standard (Jos)
The Star (Enugu)
Socialist Forum (Ife)
Labour Champion (NLC, Lagos)
Liberation News (Ibadan/Ife)
Chingaba (Ife — Alliance of Progressive Students)
Forward (Lagos)
Labour Outlook (Lagos)
Caretaker (Lagos)
Newsletter of International Labour Studies (The Hague: ISS)
New Dimension
Daily Punch (Lagos)
Sunday Punch (Lagos)
Financial Punch (Lagos)
The Democrat (Lagos)
The Herald (Ilorin)
The Nigeria Observer (Benin City)
Nigeria Year Book (Lagos: Daily Times/Federal Ministry of Information)
Business Times (Lagos)

Index